WILLIAM
GIBBS
M^cADOO

Kennikat Press
National University Publications
Series in American Studies

General Editor
James P. Shenton
Professor of History, Columbia University

John J. Broesamle

National University Publications
KENNIKAT PRESS ● 1973
Port Washington, N.Y. ● London

WILLIAM GIBBS McADOO

A Passion for Change
1863 – 1917

Acknowledgment is made to these individuals and libraries for permission to quote from correspondence, books, or other materials: William Jennings Bryan, Jr.; Yale University Library; Princeton University Library; Library of Congress; Franklin D. Roosevelt Library; Federal Reserve System; University of Virginia Library; Powell Glass, Jr.; Howard University Library; Duke University Library; Columbia University Library; Hudson and Manhattan Corporation; University of North Carolina Library; University of California, Los Angeles Library; New York Southern Society; Houghton Library Harvard University; Virginia Historical Society.

Library of Congress Catalog Card No. 73-83261
ISBN: 0-8046-9043-x

Manufactured in the United States of America

Published by
Kennikat Press, Inc.
Port Washington, N.Y./London

For Kathy

ACKNOWLEDGMENTS

In the years since work began on this book I have received so much aid from individuals and organizations that I can do little more than hint at it here. Three men helped direct the project almost from the beginning. Eric L. McKitrick provided advice and encouragement which extended over half a decade and went well beyond the bounds of the manuscript itself. I have benefited immensely from William E. Leuchtenburg's remarkable knowledge of the Progressive Era, together with his equally remarkable patience in weighing my comments about it. And the perceptive criticism of Stuart Bruchey has improved every chapter, particularly those dealing with economics and Treasury affairs. I am also greatly indebted to James P. Shenton, Walter P. Metzger, Joseph Dorfman, and Robert H. Connery for their observations, suggestions, and encouragement, and to David W. Budding and Edwin G. Burrows, who read preliminary versions of the manuscript.

I owe a very special debt of gratitude to Francis H. McAdoo and Mrs. Nona McAdoo Park for recounting memories of their father and for opening his papers to me. Francis H. McAdoo proved an outstanding critic, pointing out flaws in my narrative but emphasizing my own freedom of interpretation. And Brice M. Clagett was good enough to share his

Acknowledgements

unique knowledge of the history of the McAdoo family with me and to lend me a number of manuscripts from his personal collection. Without their generous assistance, my effort to sketch the personal side of McAdoo's life would have been next to impossible.

During two pleasant years I spent doing research in Washington, the staff of the Library of Congress was remarkably helpful. I wish to thank Mrs. Carolyn Sung, Richard B. Bickel, Peter M. Jones, Gerald G. Martin, Stefan M. Harrow, and John R. Boroughs, for their unflagging forbearance and good cheer. My principal typist, Mrs. Fayde Macune, managed to make sense of a rough draft so convoluted that I sometimes had trouble following it myself.

Without financial support from the Woodrow Wilson National Fellowship Foundation in 1964-65 and again in 1966-68, this biography could not have been written. Columbia University generously provided a President's Fellowship during 1965-66.

One final note. Anyone who has written a book knows that the process takes a heavy toll of the hours a man would normally spend with his wife and family. A brief sentence does not do justice to the patience of my wife, Kathy, and my children, Carolyn and Robert, who gave me time and a great deal more.

J. J. B.

PREFACE

Few public figures of this century have led careers more varied or more interesting than that of William Gibbs McAdoo. His spectacular rise in politics after 1911 was a subject of frequent contemporary comment, and his role as leader of one wing of the Democratic Party through the 1920's was one of the most important aspects of that tumultuous decade. McAdoo's political career extended from progressivism to the New Deal and embodied many of the paradoxes and conflicts of a nation struggling to adjust to the twentieth century.

This study covers the first fifty-four years of McAdoo's life. It attempts to probe the forces that molded his character and thought; the meaning of his career as a promoter and businessman; the significance of his early participation in politics; and his crucial role as Secretary of the Treasury during the New Freedom era. I have carried the story down to April, 1917, when America plunged into World War I.

McAdoo was a great Secretary of the Treasury. Like the greatest of his predecessors, Alexander Hamilton, he cultivated power adeptly. Yet, in McAdoo's view, power did not exist merely for its own sake; it must be put to good use. He was chiefly interested in building up the Treasury as an independent bastion of strength, with active foreign, farm, and credit policies all its own. Because he succeeded at this, he proved strikingly adept at advancing the public welfare. But, again like Hamilton, he was less successful in fulfilling his own ambitions; he sought the Presidency for a number of years without ever achieving it. Even so, as Secretary of the Treasury from 1913 to 1918, he wielded more influence than have some Chief Executives in American history. Few men have stood near the center of the political stage as long as McAdoo did: he was there for a generation.

Studying McAdoo's early career has involved a number of serious difficulties. Information on the first thirty years of his life is scarce, and I have depended heavily on a series of memoranda which he prepared for the use of his collaborator, W. E. Woodward, in the preparation of McAdoo's autobiography, *Crowded Years.* Large and significant parts of these memoranda were not included in the book, and some segments of them have unfortunately not survived. Insofar as they can be verified by contemporary manuscripts, newspapers, and periodicals, they have proved remarkably accurate.

Certain issues which would best fit an account of McAdoo's career during World War I and the postwar era have not been dealt with here. These include such problems as loans to belligerent nations, the resignation of William Jennings Bryan, the 1916 campaign, and McAdoo's own Presidential aspirations.

CONTENTS

WILLIAM GIBBS McADOO

CHAPTER ONE

POVERTY, FAILURE, AND SUCCESS

I

By the autumn of 1779, the Revolutionary War, as far as Tennessee was concerned, had ended. An eager flood of settlers began to pour westward into the tangled forests of the hinterland. Among them was a North Carolinian named Nicholas Gibbs, who had originally emigrated to America from Germany. In 1782 he settled in Knox County, and the history of that region contains a niche which Gibbs carved for himself during the fading years of the eighteenth century.

Before Gibbs had first set foot on this continent, another hardy pioneer family, sired by a Scotchman named John McAdoo, had begun to branch out through Virginia, North Carolina, and eventually eastern Tennessee. One of McAdoo's grandsons, who shared his ancestor's name, married a granddaughter of Nicholas Gibbs, and in 1820 she bore him a son whom they christened William Gibbs McAdoo.

The child developed into a tall young man of lively intelligence. After a try at schoolteaching, McAdoo decided to enroll at the University of Tennessee (then East Tennessee University) at Knoxville. A day before his graduation in 1845, he was elected as a Whig to the State Legislature. But the country had been drifting toward war with Mexico, and the following year McAdoo, whose family had fought in the young nation's previous struggles, helped organize a company of volunteers. He proved well suited to soldiering; after fighting at Vera Cruz and Cerro Gordo, he was mustered out as a first lieutenant. McAdoo returned to Tennessee, where he joined the bar in 1849. He married, was twice elected attorney general for Knoxville's large judicial circuit, and made a reputation for impartial, vigorous enforcement of the law.

In 1853 McAdoo's wife died, and four years later he married an attractive young widow named Mary Faith McDonald. The new Mrs. McAdoo belonged to the Floyds, a well-known Southern family of landed aristocrats and soldiers. Her grandfather, General John Floyd, had fought in the War of 1812 and in the Creek Indian wars. Later, he served a term in Congress. The career of Floyd's spirited son, Charles, in some ways practically mirrored his father's: he, too, became a general, and built a reputation chasing Indians.

Though his wife had inherited "Bellevue," a plantation near Darien, Georgia, and a large number of slaves, William Gibbs McAdoo considered slavery immoral and wasteful and hoped for a program of gradual compensated emancipation. On the other hand, he became a strong secessionist. After the Civil War broke out, he was rejected for military service because of physical disability. When Knoxville went Unionist, he moved his growing family and their slaves near Marietta, Georgia; and here, on Saturday, October 31, 1863, he made the following entry in his diary:

To-day, about thirty minutes after noon, Mary gave birth to a SON weighing nearly eleven pounds, with long black hair. He bawled lustily, showing a fine pair of lungs, is voracious, and seems to have a vigorous constitution.

They named the child William Gibbs McAdoo, after his father.

Meanwhile, the war had rapidly been transformed from a summer spree into grinding agony. With Confederate ranks steadily thinning, the elder McAdoo was finally admitted into the army as a captain. In the midst of hostilities, his family and slaves moved from "Melora," their home at Marietta, to Midway, a suburb of Milledgeville, Georgia, where, after the war, McAdoo resumed his law practice as district attorney and judge.

Life in the South of the Reconstruction Era bore little resemblance to the prewar years, particularly in towns like Milledgeville, which lay in the wake of Sherman's March. No class lost as much in defeat as the old planter aristocracy. When the McAdoos returned to Bellevue, they found only charred foundations overgrown with weeds; all efforts to rebuild the plantation failed. For two or three years after the war, the elder McAdoo was disfranchised and could not even practice law. Mary, a woman of wide ability, energy, and ambition, sought the literary life—she wrote two novels as well as various sketches, stories, poems, and reviews—yet found her frail constitution taxed by poverty. Her husband shared her poetic temperament but lacked her financial acumen and thought little of money; as a result it was she who managed the family purse.

Their barnlike house in Midway was sparsely furnished and uninviting. The town became particularly cold during the winter. On frigid days, as the wind swept through the uncarpeted floorboards, the entire family huddled together in the sitting room trying to keep warm. Twenty acres of farmland lay behind the house, tilled by a few Negroes. Eventually the family moved into a smaller home in Milledgeville, and William's father took a law office in the former Georgia statehouse nearby.[1]

Despite the bitter poverty, in later life young William would look back wistfully on his childhood. He remembered wandering through pine forests, splitting wood and milking cows, swimming in the mud-red Oconee River, picking wild plums and blackberries, stealing watermelons from neighboring fields, and playing baseball with handmade equipment. And he remembered the pleasure and exaltation of being the leader of a small and combative band of friends.

It cannot be doubted that the child was educationally deprived, in spite of the broad intellectual proclivities of his parents. Throughout the postwar South, schoolchildren suffered from the states' retrenchment policies. In Milledgeville, teachers came and went; and young William, a capable though not a brilliant student, drifted from school to school, spending far more of his days outside the classroom than in it.

Like his wife, the elder McAdoo wrote essays, book reviews, poems, and editorials. His interests were broad, and his taste for the classics led him to insist that young William read them too; but the lad's own literary tastes inclined him toward dime novels instead. At an early age, the boy tried to write one himself, for the royalties it might bring him, but his annoyed mother destroyed the manuscript when only two chapters had been completed. The experiment was never repeated.[2]

If education came irregularly to the McAdoo youngsters, church attendance did not. Though the children wandered through the countryside most of the time, they were faithfully gathered together and bustled off to Sunday school on the Sabbath. The mother was an Episcopalian; a deeply religious Protestant, her husband belonged to no denomination. During the years at Midway and Milledgeville the family attended Presbyterian churches. In 1886, young McAdoo became an Episcopalian.

Writing of his childhood in later years, McAdoo reflected on the role poverty had played in shaping his life:

I believe that character is produced and developed to the highest extent by hardships, suffering and poverty. I have never doubted that whatever of character and capacity I have developed has been, in a large measure, due to the surroundings which General Sherman forced upon the people of my section during that great war, and I feel grateful to him for the favor he has unwittingly bestowed.

The Milledgeville years may have molded McAdoo's character, but in later decades he would also remember the humiliations of privation: going barefoot eight months of the year; the prevalence of disease; the mortification of wearing his father's made-over castoffs; growing up in close proximity to wealthier families; the insecurity of living from month to month on the goodwill and credit of a local merchant; and the almost total isolation of the town. Because of the destitution of the South, young William, who, under conditions prevailing ten years before, would have spent his childhood under the wing of a tutor, now had to think of money. Before he reached the age of twelve, he was working in village stores in an effort to help support his family. Meanwhile he obtained his first experience as a "businessman"—selling Macon and Augusta newspapers to the small number of people in Milledgeville who could afford to buy them.[3]

II

In 1877, when the lad was fourteen, his father was offered an adjunct professorship of history and English at his alma mater, the University of Tennessee. To a backcountry lawyer who frequently received his fees in produce instead of money, it seemed too much to resist. The city had an excellent school system by Southern standards, and when the children were old enough they could attend the university tuition-free. Hence, in the early summer of that year, the family set out for Knoxville.

The elder McAdoo had taught William to read and write before the youth had entered a classroom and had insisted that the boy, who indicated a desire to become a lawyer like his father, take elocution lessons in his office once a week. William had also read the newspapers that he sold. As a result, he was not at a total disadvantage when he entered the Knoxville public schools. His initial difficulties were not scholastic, but social; the children of the city were a tougher lot than the gang William had led in Milledgeville, and he found himself constantly taunted and humiliated by his classmates. Quick-tempered and impetuous, he often got involved in fistfights. It proved a trying experience at first, but before long he began to make new friends.

Young McAdoo progressed so rapidly in school that within two years he was prepared for college. His freshman year at the University of Tennessee began in October, 1879. Somehow he had learned to play a wide variety of instruments (no doubt borrowed), and he joined the school's cadet band. But the greatest honors a Southern university then offered could be won neither on the parade ground nor the gridiron, but in forensics; and before long, McAdoo had taken a larger interest in a debating society than in his studies. By the time he was a sophomore he had become one of the university's readiest extemporaneous debaters. With his cousin, he played an active part in breaking down the hierarchical structure of the club. And both risked unpopularity when, in 1881, they defended Mormonism, which Southerners abhorred, in a public debate. McAdoo's outlook and his entire range of interests expanded in these years. He led an active social life, read newspapers, and discussed public affairs. But because of his father's meager salary, he was never free to devote himself completely to the life of a student. From the time the McAdoos moved to Knoxville, the youth had worked at various odd jobs.

William was sixteen when, in 1880, the Democrats pitted Winfield Scott Hancock against James A. Garfield for the Presidency. By this time, McAdoo later wrote, he had achieved a certain understanding of political issues:

I was an enthusiastic Democrat, on conviction, because I had read a great deal about Jefferson and Hamilton's views of government and I was essentially Jeffersonian in my views and ideals.

But, he hastened to add, "I was not a Democrat by heredity." Although the Knoxville of his youth was predominantly Democratic, the county and the eastern portion of the state were fervently Republican. The elder McAdoo, who had once been a Whig, abhorred Radical Republicanism; but though he took a keen interest in politics, he never attempted to influence the boy's views. And so, young McAdoo appears to have made his political choice in an atmosphere of comparative freedom. The fact that he had not yet attained voting age in 1880 did not deter him from actively supporting Hancock—who, ironically, had been among the ablest Union commanders of the Civil War. A better general than politician, Hancock lost the election.[4]

During the Christmas recess of 1881, in his junior year, McAdoo held a secretarial job in one of the city's district courts. As the vacation neared an end, the clerk of the federal circuit and district courts in the city asked whether he would like to keep the job a few weeks longer, continuing his studies in the evening after work. This offer came at a moment of crisis in McAdoo's educational career: he had always planned to enter law,[5] but realized that on his father's meager salary, attendance at the law school of his choice, the University of Virginia, would be impossible. Hence, he gladly accepted the position. Within a few weeks the deputy clerkship of the circuit court at Chattanooga had been offered him. This was a position of considerable responsibility for a youth of eighteen, and his father concluded that in view of his own slender resources it might afford an unusual opportunity for the boy to study law on his own. So, for the first time in his life, in May, 1882, young McAdoo regretfully left his family and set out for Chattanooga.

The city's legal records had fallen years behind, and bringing them up to date proved a considerable task. Devoting the daytime to his work, McAdoo pored over Blackstone and Kent at night, under the tutorship of the judge of the chancery court in Chattanooga. McAdoo found the city itself distasteful, but he made a large number of friends and cultivated an active social life.

McAdoo's affinity for politics flourished by now, and he took a keen interest in the campaign of 1884. Together with a friend, he went to the Democratic National Convention in Chicago. There, McAdoo had the good fortune to be named an alternate delegate for his Congressional district when the regular appointee failed to arrive. Seated on the floor of the convention, McAdoo got a taste of politics first-hand as Grover Cleveland was nominated in a chorus of cheers. "This convention made a profound impression on my mind and gave a permanent stimulus to my interest in political and public affairs," McAdoo wrote decades afterward. Whenever he was asked why he was studying the legal scholars, he replied: "I am studying for law and statesmanship." In the ensuing campaign, young McAdoo—who reached voting age just before the election—worked "like a Turk" for Cleveland. When his candidate won, "my cup of happiness was certainly full."[6]

III

In January, 1885, McAdoo was admitted to the bar. Though he made the new lawyer's usual blunders in court, he soon built a reputation for competence and diligence. From his first year's practice he managed to make only about $280, but the second year proved more lucrative and opportunities began to appear. Not the least of these was a post as division counsel for the Central Railroad and Banking Company of Georgia, and later, for the Richmond and Danville Railroad—positions of considerable importance for such a young attorney. Presently he began studying the intricate details of the railway business.

Meanwhile, McAdoo had fallen in love with a bright, charming girl from Georgia named Sarah Houstoun Fleming, and in November, 1885, they were married. At the time, he had no financial assets whatever. But by now he was very much a man on the way up, and the responsibilities of marriage seem to have stimulated him toward further achievement. Always a joiner, he entered the Chattanooga Chamber of Commerce and became a city booster, well aware of the fact that this would help nourish his budding career.

It did not take long for his career to flower. But just why, and how, has been obscured by the years. One way or another McAdoo managed to become president of a local coal company. And, with a number of friends, he persuaded an Ohio manufacturer of agricultural implements to locate his firm in Chattanooga. Apparently displacing the original owner of the concern, they renamed it the Chattanooga Hoe and Tool Company, and McAdoo became its president. The achievement was remarkable for a man just embarking on his career. Under McAdoo's guidance, a factory was constructed and machinery installed, and the plant went into operation. Then, because of a lack of time—and perhaps because he wanted something bigger to occupy his energies—he resigned.

By now the focus of McAdoo's attention had changed from law (and probably statesmanship) to business. Many young lawyers entered business during the Gilded Age, for it represented the principal steppingstone to affluence, power, and prestige. And by this time, McAdoo's desire for prestige appears to have become almost compulsive.[7] In part this probably represented compensation for an underprivileged childhood. As a youth, McAdoo seems to have coveted money—something his family could never give him. How deeply he begrudged his father's financial impotence is impossible to determine; but clearly he had no intention of allowing poverty to thwart his ambitions, as it had those of his mother. Doubtless this played a crucial role in his decision to go into business. As time passed, however, money assumed a strictly secondary place in McAdoo's mind. Ambition remained, but it was mitigated by a drive for approval and respect which, in contrast to many entrepreneurs of his day, he eventually sought from the public as a whole rather than merely from his immediate peer group.

McAdoo may have chosen business over politics for other reasons as well. Eastern Tennessee was Republican territory, and the political prospects of a young Democrat sired by secessionists would have been bleak. By 1890, the course of the South's political future had already been charted. The grip of the aristocratic Bourbons had begun to loosen, and a new species of politician—the progenitor of the demagogic Bleases, Bilbos and Longs of the twentieth century—made his appearance. Politics was no longer genteel; and what status remained to it after the Civil War had declined as that of the businessman rose. But the old aristocracy had been a bit sniffish about businessmen, and although McAdoo realized that the day of the planter had passed, a certain disdain for the crassest varieties of money grubbing lingered in his mind. His sense of public service, so typical of the Southern upper crust, also endured.

IV

During the decade of the 1880's, the pace of industrial change in America greatly accelerated. None of the advances made during these years would have more important or far-reaching consequences than the development of methods for harnessing electricity. By 1888 technology matured to the point that electricity could be applied to street railroads, and a number of McAdoo's friends in Chattanooga acquired a line of horse-drawn cars and converted it. "This stimulated my imagination enormously," McAdoo wrote, and he determined to purchase the street lines of Knoxville and electrify them. With the hindsight of his more mature years, he realized that it was "ridiculous" to endeavor to convert the lines of a small city in view of the severe defects in the electrical machinery produced during the Eighties; only a large corporation could have absorbed the waste and inefficiency of continual breakdowns and still come out in the black. But this seemed less obvious at the time, and the young lawyer decided to enter the railroad business.[8]

McAdoo purchased the Knoxville Street Railway Company with characteristic dispatch. He simply approached the leading stockholder, one of the city's wealthiest citizens, and asked his price. After extended negotiations, the cost was set at $200,000—rather more than the line happened to be worth—of which the stockholder demanded $50,000 cash down payment. But where, he wondered, would McAdoo ever get the money?[9]

In 1887, a real estate boom began throughout the South. McAdoo speculated cleverly before it collapsed and got out in time with something less than $25,000 profit, just enough to pay the discount on the Knoxville Street Railway bonds. Still green at high finance despite his recent experience in the tool business, he optimistically assumed that he could get the $50,000 from a local bank (which would serve as trustee) and float a bond issue to raise money for payments and equipment, retaining the common stock after reorganization of the company had been completed. Everything depended upon reliable financial support; and with large numbers of incompetent promoters constantly harassing the country's banking houses in search of loans, such support might prove difficult to obtain.[10]

Despite the business boom of the late 1880's, the bankers of Knoxville and Chattanooga were unprepared to finance long-term investments of the type McAdoo envisioned, and he was compelled to approach the Northeastern money market for the necessary funds. Stopping first in Philadelphia, he determined to deal with the bankers in the most direct fashion possible: he simply marched into the banks, one by one, and asked their officers to hear him out. The sight of such an aggressive young man with a bundle of maps and documents proved thoroughly irritating to some of these men, and none would make the loan.[11]

Unwilling to admit defeat, young McAdoo headed for New York. His luck was no better there, nor did it improve when he went to Boston. But for some reason he decided to try Philadelphia once more, and finally he obtained the support of the Union Trust Company. The president of the organization, a congenial individual with the unlikely name of J. Simpson

Africa, agreed to lend the $50,000 when McAdoo delivered the Knoxville Street Railway bonds as collateral. These bonds would be sold through an investment banking firm in the South. McAdoo would repay the Union's loan, the balance of the purchase price, and the cost of converting the road.[12]

In August, 1889, McAdoo bought the line and became president of the reorganized company, taking a controlling interest himself. A contract was signed for the necessary equipment; then the work of converting the road from mules to machinery began. On May 1, 1890, Knoxville's first electric street railway, and one of the nation's first urban electric transportation systems, was inaugurated. This, McAdoo announced, merely represented the beginning; he intended to make extensions in other directions until Knoxville had a first-rate rapid transit network with the lowest possible fares. The line extended to a park; and McAdoo insisted (with the wise mixture of altruism and business sense that would characterize his career for years to come) that the park be open free to the public for the next decade and a half.[13]

But the job of conversion had only been partially completed when the railroad started to drift toward disaster. The engineers had considerably underestimated the total cost of the process, and by the time the midpoint had been reached the company's reservoir of capital was completely drained. Meanwhile, running the line with both mules and electricity proved inefficient; the electrical machinery itself suffered constant and vastly expensive breakdowns. And the telephone company secured an injunction against the railroad, which delayed progress further yet.

The struggle to keep the line going proved a desperate one. McAdoo had maintained his residence and law practice in Chattanooga; finding himself called away from the city much of the time, he had to enter a partnership to keep his practice afloat. Africa continued to extend loans to him, and by 1891 the railway was indebted some $60,000 to its electric supplier as well. But the company continued to lose money. Apparently it simply could not meet the interest on its bonds, and preparations were made for a receivership. A statement went out to holders of the first mortgage bonds, informing them that the trust company believed this to be the only means of averting default. McAdoo felt convinced that the receivership was unnecessary, for he had already secured aid for his own reorganization scheme. He put up a valiant fight, but in February, 1892, the business lapsed into the hands of a receiver, along with McAdoo's last dollar. Still worse, he had become the accommodation endorser for a large part of the company's paper. A four-year court battle ensued, with McAdoo representing his own company as attorney, since it could not even afford to hire a lawyer. After a number of dramatic legal battles, he secured a reorganization which fulfilled everything he could reasonably expect, including his own release as endorser.[14]

Eventually the struggle was carried onto the streets of Knoxville itself. The original company's property had included a three-mile segment which had been operated with steam engines and which the bondholders had refused to include in the reorganization on equitable terms. McAdoo bid for control of the line, reincorporated it as the Citizens Street Railway Company, and secured a municipal franchise to extend it. The receivers of the Knoxville line suddenly found themselves in competition with one of its old spurs and dragged the matter into court.

On one notable occasion in March, 1897, when McAdoo's company needed to lay three miles of track directly parallel to those of his former road, he smuggled a gang of 200 workmen onto the street at dawn. Knoxville Street Railway officials summoned the police, and a riot ensued in which one of McAdoo's laborers was shot to death and the rest were arrested or dispersed with fire hoses. In the midst of the crisis, McAdoo arrived on the scene, only to be arrested himself and taken off to city hall. By the time he had argued his way free and returned to the street, a crowd of 2,000 excited bystanders had gathered and the mayor was delivering a harangue. Cries of "McAdoo!" "Hurrah for McAdoo!" and "Speech from McAdoo!" went up. With a sympathetic crowd at his heels, McAdoo climbed atop a stone wall opposite the mayor and began to deliver his own speech. The mayor, finding his audience drifting away, stalked off. An injunction was issued, and this matter, too, went into court.[15]

V

The receivership, McAdoo later wrote, was the event which changed the entire course of his career. When the restraining order had been issued, he found himself "very much mortified." He needed more money to pay off his debts than his Chattanooga law practice could provide.

It was obvious to me . . . that I could never overcome the obstacles which the failure of the railroad company had put in my path unless I got upon a very much bigger stage than that which Chattanooga, or any small city in the United States, offered.

Hence, after considerable deliberation, he decided "to move to New York, where, in my opinion, the opportunities were larger than anywhere in the United States."[16]

The move did not turn out to be an easy one. All that remained of McAdoo's assets was his wife's house in Chattanooga, worth about $10,000. Eventually they mortgaged it and set out for the North in June, 1892, with several thousand dollars and "abounding hopes." The giant metropolis, with its miles of brick homes and stores and its bustling ac-

tivity, revived McAdoo's spirits. Even before the family (which now included two children) had packed for its journey, McAdoo had already
picked out a dingy office on Wall Street, where, he understood, the best
opportunities "to build up a lucrative practice existed."[17]

But his chances quickly faded. In May, 1893, the National Cordage
Company suffered a spectacular financial collapse. The stock market went
down with it, and as business after business was sucked into the whirlpool
of bankruptcies, McAdoo's hopes for swift success disappeared.

In the midst of the catastrophe, the loan which he had secured in
Chattanooga ran out. Although he had made a number of acquaintances,
McAdoo had no genuine friends in New York and was generally unknown.
Nor did he succeed in building a law practice, partly because he still had to
make frequent journeys to Knoxville to continue the court battle over the
Street Railway. Under the circumstances, it was not long before the family
fell into desperate financial straits. McAdoo had moved his wife and children into an ancient fifth-floor walk-up apartment on West Eighty-seventh
Street. Rent could not be paid on time, and they lived from month to month
off the credit of a local grocer. Frequently, McAdoo could not even find
ten cents in his pocket for carfare. Meanwhile, the early felicity of his
married life was tragically marred when his wife fell victim to rheumatoid
arthritis. After the birth of their sixth child in 1904, it became apparent
that she would never recover, and a deepening pall fell over the household
as the years passed and she lapsed into chronic invalidism.

"The poverty, the struggle, and the anxiety of this period," McAdoo
later wrote, "are indescribable. My brain and body were put to the supreme
test for several years." He does not seem to have been able to share his
deepest worries with his wife, and the daily battle to fend off starvation began to affect his health: he "suffered terrible depressions" from time to
time, and his weight dropped to 135 pounds, stretched like a bowstring over
a frame more than six feet tall. But perhaps the worst agony he confronted
in these years was self-doubt. "Many times I felt deep down in my soul
that the battle was lost," he remembered afterward:

What troubled me most was the doubt which began to oppress me as to whether
or not I had sufficient brains to win in New York. I was ambitious; I had
dreams of doing big things which taunted me constantly. I felt that it was hor-
ribly unfair for anyone to be created with the irrepressible desire that I had, to
achieve something big in the world, without having been endowed by nature
with the intelligence to do it.

These fears "were a constant source of torture; but I would pull myself
together and re-determine not to give up the fight."[18]

Hence, disastrous as the depression years were to his legal career, he refused to see them wasted. For the first time, he found an opportunity to gratify a lingering desire to read, and particularly, to study history, economics and biography. As he read, he began to reflect on the dilemma of poverty itself, which had interested him from early manhood: "I had a deep feeling . . . that poverty is the most serious indictment of our vaunted civilization." It seemed inexcusable in a country with such vast resources, yet "the inequalities of our social and economic system" apparently did not strike him as "an insuperable obstacle" to the good society, and there is no evidence that he accepted the solutions being proffered by Henry George, Edward Bellamy, and Henry Demarest Lloyd. Rather, he set to work on his own remedies in a book which he entitled the *Abolition of Poverty.*[19]

Only three chapters of the book had been completed when America's sagging economy began to revive, and as opportunity once more beckoned, the manuscript was shelved. Unfortunately, it has not survived; but perhaps the gist of it may be pieced together from McAdoo's later statements on the subject, despite changes of attitude brought on by the years.

McAdoo had never lost faith in Algerism. At the center of the American business system, he visualized the single, aggressive entrepreneur scrambling up the economic ladder. Success was never a matter of pure luck, but always of character and ability. In a remark reminiscent of John D. Rockefeller, McAdoo went so far as to compare the emergence of the captain of industry to the pruning of flowers—"strip the stem of all the buds except one, and concentrate upon the one flower the whole strength and power of the plant." "For the thing that is worth doing, a man must not hesitate to DO AND DARE—DO OR DIE."[20]

McAdoo, then, was an individualist, but an individualist of a new variety. Character was "the fortune of life," and essential to success. But neither success nor character could be measured precisely in dollars:

Material achievement has its value and its satisfactions, but no achievement is comparable to that which contributes something in the way of enduring good to humanity itself.

Energy and enthusiasm could make an ordinary individual into an extraordinary one, but they could also make him grasping and selfish. In his supreme egoism, the predatory business leader all too frequently ignored his debt to the society which had made his achievements possible.

The success of every individual is largely due to the opportunities which the community itself offers for the exercise of his abilities. . . . The best citizen, therefore, is the one who recognizes his debt to the community.[21]

McAdoo reminisced in 1930 that during the late nineteenth century he had believed a country with the youth and resources of the United States could

so re-shape our social and political structure that the development of these resources and their distribution could have been directed along lines that would
have struck down, gradually, the glaring inequalities and major injustices in
social and economic conditions which confronted us.

The chief impediment to this was the greed of the "robber barons," who,
hoarding their wealth at the top of the social pyramid, refused to allow
the "trickle down" theory of prosperity to work and made poverty inevitable. Precisely how McAdoo wanted to restore the open society at the
turn of the century is impossible to determine. One thing is certain, however. In 1900, he felt far more confident that the issue could be settled
within the confines of the contemporary economic system than he would
be as an old man looking back thirty years later.[22]

VI

In Chattanooga, McAdoo had made the acquaintance of Francis R.
Pemberton, the son of a Confederate general. The two men had become
close friends, and after McAdoo saw his opportunities undermined by the
depression they formed a partnership and went into the investment securities business together. It was slow work at first, but eventually commissions began to come in, and they profited from occasional sales of securities (particularly railroad securities) which they obtained from New York
investment houses. Meanwhile, McAdoo's reading had carried him into
the field of corporate finance and law. He diligently began to study reports
dealing with every leading railway in the United States. The wide knowledge he accumulated of railroads, corporations, and corporation law
would prove invaluable in the years ahead.

Nor had McAdoo's interest in politics entirely waned. In the campaign of 1888, he later remarked, "I did all I could, as a private citizen, to
help the Democratic cause." Though he attended party meetings, however,
he demurred from speechmaking. Cleveland lost—"a terrible blow"—but
the election of 1892 saw Cleveland run once more, this time successfully.
Since McAdoo had just arrived in New York and could not vote, it seems
unlikely that he assumed an active political role that year. According to
one account, McAdoo had an inclination to return to Georgia sometime
around 1894 to open a political career by purchasing a Macon newspaper
and using it to attain the Governorship (where he might have got the
money is entirely unclear); but he failed to reach a financial accommoda-
tion with the paper's owner, and the idea was dropped.[23]

By 1896, Grover Cleveland and his Bourbon administration had been
repudiated by his own party, and Democrats from across the depression-

struck nation joined in Chicago to hand the nomination to a young Nebraskan named William Jennings Bryan. This confronted McAdoo, a sound money man, with a difficult choice. He associated Bryan and free silver with "vast numbers of inarticulate people" who plumped enthusiastically for fiscal irresponsibility. The Republican platform contained an alluring plank of gold. But behind the GOP and its candidate, William McKinley, stood Mark Hanna, whom McAdoo loathed. In the end, he opted for the splinter Gold Democrats, but he took no active part in the campaign.[24]

Yet he had always had some inclination toward politics and, apparently, some premonition that one day he would go into politics. Certain Gold Democrats in his district wanted to nominate him for Congress in 1896, and it seems he was strongly tempted to run; but he considered himself too recently arrived to take precedence over more venerable candidates. Apparently he also realized that he would not stand a chance of winning; and it required no special prescience to foresee the eclipse of the Gold Democrats after 1896. McAdoo also came under pressure from leading Democrats and Republicans alike to run for Mayor of Yonkers. (He had moved his family there in 1894.) But he later wrote that "it seemed to me that it would be most unwise to dissipate any part of my energies in politics when I was making a desperate struggle to build up a firm foundation as a lawyer," and once again he demurred.[25]

It has proved impossible to determine which anti-Bryan and Republican organizations wanted McAdoo as a candidate. Perhaps their interest in him stemmed from the fact that at the time he was speaking out in favor of public parks for the poor and regulation of the city's telephone monopoly. But in view of his Southern origin and the fact that he had no reputation in politics, let alone any money, his ability to make such an impression on these men is striking.[26]

By the time William McKinley entered office in 1897, McAdoo had begun painfully to build up a clientele for his practice in New York and for his law firm in Chattanooga. As the country recovered from the depression, so, rather slowly, did McAdoo's fortunes. Before the year was out he and an amiable Irishman, who coincidentally bore the name William McAdoo, formed a law partnership which would last nearly half a decade. The new Mr. McAdoo had served as Congressman from New Jersey and Undersecretary of the Navy during the second Cleveland Administration. Unfortunately, however, he had a curious inability to attract clients.

Not until 1901 did William Gibbs McAdoo transact his first major enterprise as a New York lawyer. With two Pennsylvania businessmen he became interested in the Wilkes-Barre and Hazelton Railroad. The three were entrusted with the task of organizing the concern that owned the line—McAdoo handled the legal end of it—and from this arrangement he eventually pocketed a considerable sum. But this merely presaged things to come: by 1902, the spirit of financial adventure was back in the air, and the opportunities which McAdoo had expected New York to offer ten years before finally began to reappear. Despite changing times, McAdoo's mental map of his future still envisioned staying in law. He would make a moderate amount of money, then put more effort into public affairs. "I had a burning desire to acquit myself with distinction," his autobiography recounts, "and to do something that would prove of genuine benefit to humanity." The chance would not be long in coming.[27]

VII

In 1874, under the direction of a Western railroad builder named DeWitt Clinton Haskin, work had started on a brick-lined railway tunnel under the Hudson River. It was painfully slow work at best, and in 1880 disaster struck when a bulkhead caved in and twenty men got entombed in muck. Two years later, with 2,000 feet of the shaft completed, one of Haskin's principal financial supporters died and operations had to be suspended.

The project was revived by engineers of the English firm of S. Pearson and Son and abundant British capital in 1890, and it seemed that it would be swiftly completed. Haskin's pioneering effort to use compressed air to support the silt which surrounded the shaft until the lining could be installed was again employed. Cast iron rings supplanted masonry. The English company used a circular iron wedge, or "shield," which, driven by hydraulic jacks, plowed slowly through the liquidlike silt beneath the river. The Pearsons had practically doubled the length of Haskin's tunnel when they ran out of funds. The following year, their hopes shriveled, they abandoned the shaft to a group of American bondholders organized as the New York and New Jersey Railway Company.

By the time McAdoo arrived in New York, the tunneling project had been completely shut down. Meanwhile, ferry transportation had become more and more obsolescent: docks were poorly located; boats ran at long intervals and commonly were delayed by fog. Even at the best of times, crossing the river consumed at least twenty minutes. Nor did the price of tickets fall within the means of the mass of commuters who had to cross each day.

McAdoo himself was a frequent passenger on the ferries, and an idea began to loom in his mind. Among his business acquaintances was a well-known corporation lawyer, John R. Dos Passos, who had become involved in the Wilkes-Barre and Hazelton transaction; and one day in 1901, after doing some preliminary investigating on his own, McAdoo mentioned to Dos Passos that he had thought of a scheme for tunneling under the Hudson to supplant the ferry service with a subway line. Dos Passos first told McAdoo of the Haskin failure. The promoter had more than a passing interest in seeing the tunnel finished, for he had a sizable personal investment tied up in it. "Why not take hold of ours and complete it?" he remarked. It was a fantastic break, and McAdoo was simply astonished. He had no money and little experience in big enterprises or engineering. But Dos Passos agreed to get in touch with another lawyer named Frederick B. Jennings, the attorney for the bondholders' committee. As an investor in both the Haskin and Pearson enterprises, Jennings had lost several hundred thousand dollars, and in October he received McAdoo in polite but understandably frigid fashion. Jennings appeared unimpressed with the young lawyer, but reluctantly granted him permission to inspect the tunnel site.[28]

The shaft and machinery had been left in the hands of a firm of engineers headed by Charles M. Jacobs and J. Vipond Davies. Most of the original 3,800-foot tunnel was in good condition, and only 2,000 feet remained to be channeled before it would emerge in New York City. Jacobs assured McAdoo that the shield could be rendered serviceable. The project would only require money.

Meanwhile, McAdoo had already begun to outline in his mind a comprehensive transportation system between New York and New Jersey. The Haskin–Pearson tunnel did not quite fit into it; yet, if the shaft and its equipment could be purchased relatively inexpensively, its very existence might make a good selling point on Wall Street. For the moment, he would simply complete the old tunnel, running it eastwardly under the Hudson and into the city. Connections could be made with the street and elevated networks in Jersey City and Hoboken. Finishing the project would cost an estimated $4,000,000.[29]

After considerable bargaining, McAdoo finally obtained Jennings's confidence and even his friendship, and the price was set at $350,000 for the completed part of the shaft. McAdoo would establish a New York and Jersey Railroad Company with an authorized capital of $6,000,000, which he had to raise in order to buy the tunnel. He planned to issue $5,000,000 in common stock at once and an equal amount in first mortgage, 5 percent bonds. The remaining $1,000,000 of authorized capital would be withheld in preparation for a second tube. It was a sensible and admirably simple scheme, but how could McAdoo raise the necessary funds to resuscitate a tunnel which had failed twice and snuffed out twenty lives? He broached the subject with a friend, Walter Oakman, president of the powerful Guaranty Trust Company. Oakman negotiated an arrangement whereby his company would lend the entire sum necessary to renew the work provided the loan could be underwritten by subscribers of whom his institution approved. Then he added significant impetus to the project by subscribing $100,000 himself. Jennings matched Oakman's contribution, as did an executive of the Brooklyn Rapid Transit Company. Finally, McAdoo approached the leaders of United States Steel, and this, in the end, may have proved decisive. E. C. Converse, a personal friend of McAdoo's, agreed to subscribe $200,000 and gave him a letter of introduction to Judge E. H. Gary, chairman of the board. Gary added $100,000 and, along with his four predecessors on McAdoo's list, agreed to serve as a director of the new tunnel company. "The Judge and I became warm friends," McAdoo later wrote; Gary attended practically every board meeting. [30]

Even with these important initial subscriptions, McAdoo still found himself "regarded by most people as a visionary or a crank," and filling the list of underwriters took time. When it had finally been completed, the question of choosing a president arose. The directors insisted that McAdoo shoulder this burden himself. He realized that the presidency would involve a total commitment, and liquidated his law partnership with William McAdoo and his interest in the investment securities firm. McAdoo's main goal in the tunnel enterprise was income. But while the directors were willing to demand all of his time and attention, he would initially receive only $15,000 a year. "This was hard on me," he later acknowledged, but he became "more interested in the achievement than in the money, so" he "went ahead." [31]

Several things stand out clearly from the scant details that remain of all these transactions. McAdoo had made his hunch materialize by a combination of energy and luck, together with connections which can only be termed remarkable for a lawyer in his position and with his limited resources and experience. After talking with Dos Passos, a business acquaintance, he had spoken with Jennings and Jacobs; then he had recruited his friend, Oakman; he had approached U.S. Steel by way of another connection, E. C. Converse; and finally, via Converse, he had broken through to Gary. After all this, the job of filling the rest of the subscription list had come almost as an anticlimax. Each step was like moving up a stairway, one which McAdoo climbed with extraordinary speed, agility, and (despite some difficulties), ease.

McAdoo's new company decided to hire Jacobs and Davies as engineers for the project and carry on the construction independently. In the summer of 1902, the overhauled Pearson shield once again began to lurch forward. There were mishaps and engineering difficulties, including a rock reef that had to be breached. And the company confronted a number of problems with its labor force. The tremendous air pressure which supported the sides of the tunnel sometimes left men who re-emerged into atmospheric pressure in agony from the bends. Fortunately, this occurred infrequently. McAdoo himself claimed that "no effort or expense is spared by the management to conserve the safety and the health of its employees," and that more precautions had been taken in building this tunnel—among them hiring a staff of resident physicians and maintaining an emergency hospital—than had ever been used under similar circumstances before. McAdoo tried to uphold morale by fre-quently entering the heading himself. [32]

As the shaft moved forward, at a maximum pace of a foot an hour, plans were already being prepared to build a second one, christened the "South Tunnel." This would allow the construction of a single standard gage track in each tube, rather than a double track conveying undersized cars, as the original engineering specifications had called for. Work on this second shaft commenced in 1903, and funds which had been subscribed for the first, or North, tube, were diverted into the new one, on the assumption that the tremendous amount of fresh capital that would be required to drive both projects to completion could be accumulated gradually. For the South Tunnel, Jacobs and Davies used machinery which operated at three times the maximum rate of the old equipment. They installed second, opposing shields in both tubes, and the tunnels began to converge toward the middle of the river. On March 11, 1904, just before noon, the North shaft was "holed through."

VIII

Even before the South Tunnel had been finished, McAdoo sensed that his dream of a broad transportation network was within his grasp. In order for this dream to materialize, however, two additional shafts would have to be driven through downriver and a tube completed be-tween Hoboken and the Pennsylvania Railroad terminal in Jersey City. The Erie and Lackawanna stations, which lay to the north of Jersey City, as well as stations at Newark, must also be woven into the net-work. To avert a sudden jump in real estate values, McAdoo and Oakman secretly purchased a large plot of land west of Church Street in New York early in 1903. Here they planned to construct two office buildings —the largest in the world—and a central terminal for their own company. The entire complex would occupy two city blocks and house some 10,000 tenants.

The next task involved contacting Andrew J. Cassatt, president of the Pennsylvania Railroad, who had thought of constructing his own tunnel network under the river. Work on these tubes had already started by the time McAdoo saw Cassatt in January, 1903. The two men hardly knew each other, and McAdoo realized that the plans he envisioned would destroy the Pennsylvania's lucrative ferry service. But Cassatt agreed to hook up his lines with those of the New York and Jersey. Subsequent agreements carried joint service clear to Newark. A new corporation, the Hudson and Manhattan Railway Company, was organized to build the downtown tunnels, with McAdoo as president.

A number of entrepreneurs on the western side of the Hudson, however, were not as amenable to change as Cassatt. Even before the New York and Jersey had resumed operations in the North Tunnel in 1902, officers of the Delaware, Lackawanna, and Western Railroad—which maintained a terminal at Hoboken and depended on local ferries for its hookup with New York—had suggested that McAdoo's route be altered so as to enter their terminal. If this were done, Lackawanna president W. H. Truesdale assured McAdoo and Jennings, the New York and Jersey would be given right of way under his property and would be afforded yard facilities as well. McAdoo and Jennings agreed to this proposal, and work proceeded on the assumption of Truesdale's good faith.[33]

Late in 1903, Truesdale unexpectedly announced that McAdoo would not be allowed right of way to Hoboken under any circumstances whatever. Then, in the spring of the following year, the Lackawanna suddenly purchased the lucrative Hoboken ferries, and it became obvious that Truesdale had been using the New York and Jersey as a club to force the ferry line to sell out to him. Now he had to forestall competition from the tubes. Truesdale refused to keep his gentleman's agreement with McAdoo, and an extended period of litigation ensued. The two companies argued before the Public Service Commission for a year before the matter was finally dragged into court. When the jury handed down a verdict against him in the fall of 1904, McAdoo appealed to the Court of Errors and Appeals of New Jersey. Meanwhile, the Lackawanna made a show, at least, of intending to tunnel out of Hoboken itself, and the constant delay of the court fight eroded the New York and Jersey's credit. Compared to McAdoo's company, the Lackawanna was a financial giant, but NY and J prestige had risen enormously when the North Tunnel went through in March, 1904. Not until midwinter, 1905, was a final settlement arrived at, out of court. The New York and Jersey dropped its appeal and agreed to pay the Lackawanna $175,000 for a right of way beneath its yards. But the battle had cost more than that: the opening of the tubes had been delayed by more than a year, with an attendant loss of profits, and the court fees had been enormous.[34]

The surface lines in Hudson and Essex counties, which included

Newark and Hoboken, were in the hands of the Public Service Corporation. If implemented, the plans which McAdoo and Cassatt had envisioned could ruin the Corporation's streetcar service to the Pennsylvania ferries, and the financial interests which controlled this service were entirely unwilling to see this happen. The Corporation had an ally in New York, Thomas Fortune Ryan's mammoth Metropolitan Street Railway Company, which had already grown alarmed by the impending threat of the New York and Jersey to break into the shopping districts and usurp the Metropolitan's lucrative business. In May, 1904, the NY and J filed an application to extend a line one and a half miles under Sixth Avenue, and the Metropolitan recoiled. The Metropolitan tried to depress McAdoo's credit; and it established "citizens' associations" to denounce his plans to the authorities. Ryan made frantic efforts to block McAdoo's franchise, and when that failed, to have clauses inserted which could not be met without destroying the New York and Jersey's credit. McAdoo made a personal appearance before the Rapid Transit Commission to plead his case, and Ryan's efforts were temporarily thwarted. But Ryan's prospects for success remained excellent: since he was still involved in litigation over the Lackawanna affair, and had to battle the Public Service Corporation as well, McAdoo found himself engaged on three fronts at once.[35]

The struggle with the Metropolitan lasted through the summer and fall of 1904. The retailers on Sixth Avenue clamored for service, and the Metropolitan planned to thwart McAdoo by pitting these merchants against their competitors on Ninth Avenue; an extension here, it argued, would be better. McAdoo, however, felt sure that he had the public as a whole, and Sixth Avenue in particular, behind him—and he was probably right. In December, at a hearing of the Board of Rapid Transit Commissioners, McAdoo suddenly countered Ryan's strategy by offering to build extensions to both Sixth and Ninth avenues, and the franchise was granted.[36] But the struggle with Ryan had not ended yet.

Before McAdoo attempted to realize his plans of expansion in New Jersey, it seemed desirable that the New York and Jersey and the Hudson and Manhattan be consolidated into a single concern. By January, 1905, the original scheme, involving a total expenditure of $5,000,000, had already been broadened to encompass a $60,000,000 transportation network. Oakman was a good friend of Pliny Fisk, senior partner in the venerable banking house of Harvey Fisk and Sons, and in January, 1905, Fisk agreed to finance the plan. A new construction firm, the Hudson Companies, would be formed to contract with the tunnel companies for completion and equipping of the proposed network of tubes and to accept stocks and bonds in exchange. The Hudson Companies would then sell tunnel company bonds in order to supply capital for further expansion. This proved no small task: the total cost of the Hudson network, including the terminal buildings, eventually mounted to some $72 million.

On January 9, 1905, the new construction company was born, with Oakman as president and McAdoo retaining his old post in the tunnel firms. The following year, the Hudson and Manhattan and New York and Jersey were consolidated into a single organization, the Hudson and Manhattan Railroad Company, with McAdoo as president. Gary, Oakman, Fisk, Jennings, and several other important figures remained on the board of directors.

The Lackawanna struggle ended in February. This left only the Public Service Corporation to be dealt with, and by now McAdoo's companies had grown considerably stronger than they had been the year before. But Ryan still brooded, and on September 20, 1905, amid considerable fanfare, the Metropolitan and the Public Service Corporation suddenly incorporated the so-called Inter-state Tunnel Railway Company, and applied for a charter to build their own tube. On the surface, this appeared to be a logical plan, since together these companies controlled an extensive transit network on both sides of the river. But to McAdoo at least, it appeared to have been designed purely as a bluff, to destroy the confidence of his investors and damage his prospects of raising fresh capital.[37]

McAdoo reacted like a cornered lion. He called a meeting of the board of directors and proposed a counterattack. His strategy involved a two-pronged offensive: first, he would shatter the traction monopoly in Jersey City and Hoboken by constructing his own surface railroad system to compete with the Public Service Corporation. Second, taking advantage of that firm's unpopularity with the citizens it was supposed to serve, he would plunge immediately into the electric light and power field as well! Plans for these offensives were laid in secret.[38]

In October, 1905, with a barrage of bulletins in local newspapers, a Hudson Street Railway Company suddenly appeared on the west bank of the river. By January, the vulnerable Public Service Corporation was prepared to sue for peace and requested a conference. Cassatt felt anxious to liquidate the matter, but McAdoo refused to call off his troops on the basis of another oral agreement. Conferring with McAdoo during a break in the conference, Cassatt remarked with a smile, "McAdoo, you love a fight, don't you?" They returned to the bargaining table and finished hammering out a settlement. The Metropolitan and the Public Service Corporation agreed to scuttle their tunnel scheme, and in return, McAdoo abandoned the street railway. In addition, the Public Service Corporation was induced to grant McAdoo better facilities in its yards at Hoboken. Each side had used robber baron methods and destructive competition to bludgeon the other into submission. Nevertheless, McAdoo had employed a technique in his struggle with the Public Service Corporation which suggested the pattern of things to come: his tactics, if only indirectly, had attempted to make use of public opinion, in which he had developed a great deal of faith.[39]

Fisk now advised McAdoo to see J. P. Morgan about securing further financial support. McAdoo was reluctant, but Fisk insisted; and so, with considerable trepidation, McAdoo went to confront the indomitable financier. He was pleasantly surprised. Morgan displayed none of that ruthlessness for which he had become so infamous. "I formed an admiration for Mr. Morgan from that interview which has persisted ever since," McAdoo later recalled. "Meeting and talking to him changed my entire conception of him." The million dollars which Morgan agreed to subscribe went far toward shoring up the shaky credit structure of the Hudson and Manhattan. But, partly because of the drain from its struggles to expand, the problem of finance was never entirely solved. The company was buffeted violently by the panic of 1907, though it managed to retrench and get through it.[40]

Besides financial troubles, difficulty arose in obtaining concessions from New Jersey politicians. By July, 1907, after remarkable maneuvering by Jersey City officials, McAdoo got an injunction and drove the line into the city, with the support of most of its major newspapers. In February, 1908, Theodore Roosevelt pressed a button at the White House and the first train started rolling through the uptown tunnels toward New Jersey, where a crowd of nearly 20,000 waited expectantly. The tubes were a boon to the state's boosters, for they made large numbers of towns on the west bank of the Hudson mere suburbs of metropolitan New York. The wealthy, in particular, began purchasing more homes in New Jersey once the tunnels had been completed.[41]

By February, 1908, the growing Hudson and Manhattan had become the greatest subaqueous tunnel system in the world. It eventually included four tubes under the river and totalled more than nineteen miles of single track, rivalling the city-built subway in length and exceeding it in cost. Ferry travel across the Hudson had once taken twenty minutes to half an hour; now, the river could be crossed in eight minutes.[42]

CHAPTER TWO

BUSINESSMAN—OF A DIFFERENT SORT

As social Darwinism and Populism declined in the fading years of the nineteenth century, the ascent of progressivism began. It was the start of a movement that would dominate the next decade and a half of American history. Progressivism was born on the state and local level; here the impulse for clean government, electoral reform, trust busting, and social legislation began to grow. After 1902, the injustices which progressives decried gained national exposure in mass-circulation magazines. And in the years that followed the accession of Theodore Roosevelt to the Presidency, a number of executives began to apply some of the precepts of reform to business. Among them was William Gibbs McAdoo.

I

The construction of the Hudson tunnels was an event of vast importance to the subsequent history of New York and New Jersey, but in its way the example set by the policies of the Hudson and Manhattan proved equally significant. Most of these policies emanated from the fertile brain of McAdoo himself. His standard of success, which he once referred to as "practical and wise altruism," envisioned distributing the fruits of capitalism to the public in the form of higher wages and better service. It was not a particularly reflective creed—no deep philosophical or ideological system lay beneath it. At its roots, it was simply a variety of business reform.[1]

McAdoo's aspirations for reform were closely linked to his attitude toward the common man. In 1910 a newspaper correspondent found that McAdoo wanted to talk as much about social welfare as about railroads. McAdoo breakfasted with David Lloyd George in Downing Street one morning that year discussing legislative ideals and care of the poor. "We seem to be more or less in the grip of a certain hide-bound element," he once remarked,

which continues to believe that the great public is incapable of comprehending and intelligently deciding what are conveniently called "complicated problems". This element represents a class of people who do not come into contact with the great mass of the people. They are, therefore, utterly out of sympathy with their views and aspirations, and utterly incapable of interpreting their deeper feelings and irrepressible desire for improvement and betterment of their condition. The mass of whom I speak are those of whom Lincoln always affectionately spoke as "the common people."

. . .

The "common people" possess in some ways a highly developed instinct or common sense, which enables them to decide rightly . . . so-called "complicated" questions. They have, through this instinct or common sense a comprehension second only in its accuracy to mathematics or an exact science.[2]

The widespread hostility which the average corporation had to cope with resulted from decades of indifference "on the part of corporate managers to the interests and just grievances of the public." Among these grievances McAdoo was fond of citing the foibles of his competitors: failure to release truthful information about delays and accidents promptly, resentfulness at complaints and suggestions from commuters, irregular scheduling, and outright hostility toward the public. In New York, traction magnates had traditionally been despised. McAdoo realized that the "old time arbitrary manager is already a back-number and where he still exists, is making a hopeless fight." He rejected out of hand the notion that there was no individual responsibility within the corporation; the soul of each corporation, he argued, was the soul of its dominant individual, and the management reflected it "almost as infallibly as a looking glass reflects an object set before it." "The people have waked up," he mused, "and the moss-backs will have to surrender."[3]

II

McAdoo did not consider respect for the desires and opinions of the masses merely a matter of paternalistic altruism: the public and the corporation were essential to each other. Viewed in this light, public good will was essential to the success of the corporation. Hence, in July,

1909, when the downtown tunnels opened to traffic, McAdoo proclaimed a new policy in the history of rapid transit systems. "We believe," he announced in a phrase which would become famous,

in "the public be *pleased*" policy as opposed to "the public be damned" policy; we believe that that railroad is best which serves the public *best;* that decent treatment of the public evokes decent treatment from the public; that recognition by the corporation of the just rights of the people results in recognition by the people of the just rights of the corporation. A square deal for the people and a square deal for the corporation. The latter is as essential as the former and they are not incompatible.[4]

Emphatically, they were not. When the Hudson Terminal buildings opened, McAdoo ordered 100,000 complaint forms printed—ten for every lessee. The building superintendent was aghast. The company posted signs in its trains inviting suggestions and criticism; letters expressing disapproval always received a response after a prompt investigation had been made. During the year 1910, nearly 50 million passengers went through the tunnels with fewer than fifty complaints.[5]

Employees of the Hudson and Manhattan were noticeably more cordial than those on other lines, and the company made efforts to supervise their behavior and appearance closely. When accidents occurred, newspapers received the entire story immediately. For its passenger service, the H and M used all-steel cars, in contrast to the wooden vehicles purchased by the Metropolitan just a few years before. They were well lighted and equipped with automatic side doors—a remarkable innovation for the time that went far toward ending the chaos which made Ryan's system such an object of opprobrium. McAdoo himself made frequent inspection tours to be sure that everything was kept clean and in working order.

McAdoo would institute virtually any logical scheme which his passengers proposed for improving commuter service. One such plan, engendered by a flood of letters from women complaining of cigar smoke and swearing among male passengers, involved an experiment with cars which carried only ladies. It was publicly announced that separate conveyances would be furnished for three months on a trial basis, and for the first few days the cars were crammed with crinkled chintz and feathers. But within a month, apparently inhibited by the barbs "Hen Car" and "Jane Crowe Car" which the press gleefully showered on them, women had virtually abandoned the new cars altogether. The company continued the experiment for the promised period of time and, when it was discontinued, posted notices explaining why. Despite the Hen Car failure, the effort to please the public went on.

Closely related to McAdoo's position on the question of corporate responsibilities was his attitude toward public utility commissions. He fundamentally agreed with the commission idea, realizing that state and local regulation had come to stay; hence, he welcomed supervision of his own railway system by the Public Service Commission of New York. But such commissions, he argued, must be strictly apolitical in nature, and have their powers closely defined by law. To preserve the rights of private ownership and to ensure the benefits of the profit system, the commissions should be denied "the power to arbitrarily fix rates" or "to undertake the management itself." Regulation by these bodies, as he viewed it, was a consultative process: legislatures should request the consultation and advice of corporate executives in framing public utility bills, and all sides must be heard before these measures passed. McAdoo left no record of his attitude toward the Interstate Commerce Commission. Nor did he discuss the role of the courts, or the issue of federal supervision of corporations' capital structure. Indeed, he seems deliberately to have avoided these and similar major issues of the day.[6]

Fully as difficult to fathom is McAdoo's precise stand on the labor question during these years. He seems to have been somewhat reluctant to discuss this problem, yet it cannot be doubted that he had a fundamentally sympathetic attitude toward labor. McAdoo favored higher wages, without specifying *how much* higher. Rather, his attention appears to have focused on proposals for fringe benefits. He was particularly intrigued by workmen's compensation and company pension programs, and remarked to an audience at Harvard that he confidently envisioned a time

when there will . . . be established *by the corporations, under wise legislation,* benefit funds, as assurance against disability and accidents, so that injured employees may obtain quick and certain relief, in case of accident. There is great force in the argument that certain hazardous risks of the employment should be assumed and borne by the employer, and I believe that enlightened policy will soon dictate this concession to labor.[7]

By 1910, a number of corporations had taken steps to provide pension plans for their workers. This, McAdoo remarked, was "the essence of enlightened management," for it would improve the "character and quality of the employees" and assure "more interested and faithful service." But who would institute the broader social insurance reforms he contemplated? Presumably, he looked forward to a time when such plans would be adopted by business on either a voluntary or compulsory basis; employees who had retired too early to benefit from them would receive state aid. There is no doubt that by this time he had become quite interested in government-administered social insurance programs, particularly those of England and Germany; and, for a brief period, McAdoo corresponded with David Lloyd George about the issue.[8]

McAdoo took considerable precautions in hiring employees for the Hudson and Manhattan, making every effort to choose people who could easily ingratiate themselves with the public. Regulations governing the 2,000 regular employees of the company were stringent. Although McAdoo acknowledged the fact that all of labor's gains had been made through organization, his precise attitude toward the general issue of unionization during this period remains in question. While he would willingly negotiate in person with union officials, he did not feel at all amenable to the idea of accepting union dictation in matters of hiring and firing. Nevertheless, McAdoo had clearly moved ahead of his time on most labor issues, and workers had particularly good reasons to respect him. The Hudson and Manhattan, which hired as many as 8,500 men at once, apparently paid union wages, and required an eight-hour day of its employees at a time when ten or even twelve was considered standard. Special provisions were made for the comfort of every worker, and as a result, the company stayed free of labor problems.⁹

III

All of this raises one final question: to what extent can McAdoo be considered a prototypical "good businessman" of the Progressive Era?¹⁰ Certainly the steps he took to keep his workers happy were not unique. Nor was McAdoo original in his view of the corporation as a kind of social service run in the public interest with open-minded frankness and publicity; a number of other entrepreneurs believed substantially the same thing. The notion of interdependence between the public and the business world had been common in the nineteenth century, and during the first third of the twentieth business became increasingly aware of this interdependence. McAdoo was not even completely alone among executives in remarking that, like individuals, the corporation had a moral side and must make conscious choices between good and evil.

Many businessmen wanted to pacify the work force in order to short-circuit unionization; what seemed to be enlightened labor policy was often little more than a masquerade for paternalistic attempts to buy off the workers. McAdoo did not share the business community's common, deep-seated revulsion toward organized labor; but if he was not a union-hater, his attitude toward unions certainly seems to have been guarded during the early years of the century.

To business, reform often meant protection from unfavorable publicity, government interference, and chaotic competition. Businessmen realized that under certain circumstances, government collaboration could prove useful, and McAdoo's positive attitude toward public utility commissions cannot be considered rare. On the other hand, he did not for a moment envision the role of these commissions to be the mitigation of competition. Unlike large and growing numbers of businessmen, he placed the greatest possible emphasis on maintaining competition, which he viewed as a crucial underpinning of national well-being. And this points up a fundamental philosophical difference between McAdoo and the great majority of men in the business community.

As Robert Wiebe has pointed out, though one of the main thrusts behind progressivism came from business, the typical businessman-reformer tended to view reform differently from other progressives who wished to fulfill social or humanitarian ends. "By 1905," Wiebe writes, "urban progressives were already separating along two paths. While one group used the language of the budget, boosterism, and social control, the other talked of economic justice, human opportunities, and rehabilitated democracy." The businessman distinguished himself by his "tone, patronizing or harsh, toward 'people' who opposed him, an insistence upon business leadership, an obsession with class attacks, . . . plaintive defenses of economic individualism," and, generally, tolerance only for a limited government which would serve business without directly helping anyone else. The men at the top of the progressive movement, however, "combined optimism with a sense of destiny when they talked about the people, its leaders, and limitations on individualism to prevent class strife. The one dogmatized and warned, the other explained and envisioned; the one preserved his ideology regardless of daily contradictions, the other felt his way toward an adjustment of the traditional to the new."[11]

On every count, McAdoo fit not inside, but outside, the broad spectrum of business thought. Practical considerations clearly stood uppermost in the minds of the majority of businessmen and impelled them toward or away from reform; but some had moral motives as well, and clearly this moral strain was of great importance to McAdoo. A public relations pioneer, his altruism did not lack practicality, as he himself acknowledged; but he also emphasized social justice, public service, flexibility, optimism, and humanitarianism without condescension. To say that McAdoo was heavily motivated by humanitarian concerns suggests that his reliance on the dignity and reliability of the common man proved unusual in the business world; that he had weak faith in the ability of business to lead society; that in lodging responsibility for corporate abuses squarely on the shoulders of individual executives he spurned the notion of collective guilt; that he had comparatively little concern with class; that his Public be Pleased policy went beyond ordinary public relations ploys; and that he had an unusual willingness to accept social welfare legislation even at the expense of "individualism." McAdoo was not·absolutely sui generis in these respects; but in the American business community of the early twentieth century, he was certainly quite unusual.

IV

Because of this, by 1909 McAdoo had become a familiar public figure in the Northeast, and was known by reputation, at least in business circles, throughout much of the rest of the country. As for his reputation in the Empire State, the *Boston Herald* was not unduly laudatory when it commented that "the former southerner . . . just now stands out most prominently as the hero of life in New York," in "shining contrast" to other, less scrupulous businessmen. As the months passed, such acclamations appeared with increasing frequency.[12]

During 1909, McAdoo entered his forty-sixth year, though he looked a decade younger. Dressed in black, with a derby hat perched atop a mass of well-plastered black hair, he could often be seen emerging from the Hudson Terminal buildings, wiry and light on his feet, his head and shoulders as erect as a soldier's. His features were sharply-cut—a long nose, a high, narrow forehead, a jutting chin; his deep-set blue eyes were dark, haunting, a bit melancholy. The tightly drawn lips turned up quizzically at the ends. McAdoo's speech was as quick and incisive as a knife cutting through bread, revealing his tremendous forcefulness and vitality.

Yet he had a balanced ease and politeness reminiscent of Southern gentry, and his visage often broke into deep lines and furrows with a smile or a laugh. McAdoo's keen humor was homely and forceful and punctuated with incongruities. An inveterate storyteller and practical joker, he once staged an elaborate mock holdup, complete with masked "bandits," for the benefit of his eldest son while they traveled through Arizona together.

The journalist who left the best early portrait of McAdoo, Burton Hendrick, wrote that McAdoo revealed a "touch of genius:"

He is persuasiveness itself. He has the essential qualities of the successful advocate, a gift of graphic exposition and a simplicity of manner that convinces one of his personal honesty and sincerity. Whatever the subject of conversation,—his tunnels, the subway, politics, general business,—his personality immediately rivets attention. All he has to do is to look one in the face, wheel around in his chair, throw one long leg over the other, and begin, in his quiet Southern drawl, "Look heah, now," and the listener is lost. New light flows in; all doubts disappear; and Mr. McAdoo's point of view becomes the only reasonable and possible one.

McAdoo had little time for fools, however. His aggressiveness with other businessmen occasionally bordered on pugnacity. Beneath his placid exterior lay the quick temper of a man who hated to see mistakes made.[13]

After searching his well-stocked memory of historical characters for a parallel to McAdoo, W. E. Woodward, McAdoo's perceptive collaborator on *Crowded Years,* came up with George Washington. "The resemblance is startling—to me, at least," Woodward wrote. "McAdoo even has Washington's voice, and a good deal of his manner." McAdoo enjoyed women (and they him). He loved to dance, as Washington had. His writing, like Washington's, was "gray, flat, long and stringy, and without sparkle."[14]

But McAdoo was distinctly a product of the late nineteenth and early twentieth centuries, not of the eighteenth. Walter Lippmann called him "a statesman grafted upon a promoter." McAdoo considered "a sense of effort . . . the finest thing in life." He quickly chose his routes and sped down them, never hesitating to brood in the face of adversity or even in the face of prudence. He was an anticipator, a promoter who cared far more about the promotion than the profit. Perhaps this is why his determination always grew so passionate and so unswerving. The usual inhibitions of the financial and political worlds scarcely affected him. He was an outsider who knew how the game was being played inside but did not especially wish to walk in the door and be dealt a hand.[15]

McAdoo could be both blunt and pointed; he did not draw the line at embarrassing other people or even at scandalizing them. But if he showed more candor than many outstanding progressives, he also revealed greater sophistication, greater cleverness. "He has a devilish knowledge of the tender spots," Lippmann remarked, "and a willingness to touch them occasionally." Neither class bias, nor custom, nor propriety, nor any profoundly ingrained set of general principles, could restrain him. Because he loved change, McAdoo rarely shrank from being a herald of new ideas. But he had a keen eye for what the majority of the public wanted, and what it would stand for—in short, for the political possibilities—and he seldom went beyond them.[16]

McAdoo was the very epitome of ideological and political flexibility. His surpassing joys came from solving difficult problems, preferably several at a time; and his constant search for new solutions was characterized more than anything else by a restless sidestepping of ideology. If his social convictions were deeply rooted, they did not run as deep as La Follette's. McAdoo's constitutional convictions were practically nonexistent except when they had to be improvised and thrown up in the path of undesirable ideas. As a result, at one moment he could seem utterly radical; the next, quite conservative. This is not to suggest that McAdoo put on and tore off the mantles of progressivism and conservatism as it suited him; the point is that he never really fastened them on.

The dark side of this freedom from ideological imprisonment lay in the fact that when he embarked beyond the realm of the immediate, the applicable, and the practical, McAdoo had a way of sounding catering and almost banal. As Ray Stannard Baker wrote,

McAdoo has a chain-lightning mind. It not only moves swiftly, but it is not content unless there is quick issue in action. [Woodrow] Wilson loved to talk of principles, to make clear the reason for his convictions. McAdoo instantly reduces everything to action. He seems to dislike talking of anything except action—what he did, where he went, what the other people did, and how the whole matter eventuated.

McAdoo's driving force and chief outlet was constructive action constantly applied to new fields. Incapable of profundity except where his intellect could be used in solving practical problems, he could concentrate only on the concrete, never on the abstract. He was an Edison, not an Einstein. As Woodward observed late in McAdoo's life, "he has no metaphysics—and he does not care to dive down to the bottom of the ocean of life unless he can bring up a pailful of earth to show that he has been there."[17]

Perhaps because he felt comfortable in the world of action but not in the world of ideas, McAdoo operated with almost incredible self-assurance. Seldom after the early years in New York did he moodily plumb the depths of his own character. His doubts, when he had them, were superficial. Rarely did they become strong enough to derail his determination to fulfill some particular goal. His often-quoted aphorisms were unblushing tokens of self-confidence, and, more important, of an underlying faith in the fundamental wholesomeness of his environment. "There is no exception," he remarked, "to the rule that a man can always arrive if [he] does the thing better than anyone else has ever done it." "Given . . . character and the spirit and determination to do, and practicing honesty as an inflexible rule of action, success is certain." These are not the words of a man with deep doubts about the goodness or justness of society; they might, in fact, have come from the mouth of the rankest conservative.[18]

Any limits in McAdoo's vision quickly paled before his uncommon strengths. He was one of the ablest Americans of his time. He had a clear, remarkably receptive mind: explain something to him once and it did not have to be repeated; he would simply pick up the idea and run with it. Tenacity, enthusiasm, drive—with these he more than made up for whatever he lacked in profundity. His warm exuberance often squeezed affection even out of his enemies. The least snobbish of men, McAdoo liked people, no matter what class they came from. Despite keen shrewdness, his sincerity and honesty left little room for guile. It was his unassuming manner, his humanness and humaneness, his optimism and buoyancy of spirit, and perhaps his freedom from intricacy, which gave him his magnetism. "He is as enthusiastic as a boy," one observer wrote in 1913. "He has fine imagination, indomitable courage, and a touch of genius."[19]

An accomplished executive and administrator with very keen business acumen, McAdoo was capable of enormously protracted periods of work. Never idle, he always seemed in a hurry. Yet he had a remarkable capacity for detail. When the Hudson Terminal buildings were erected, for example, he missed not a single particular: he personally purchased the real estate, influenced the architecture, and supervised construction. He organized the Railroad Club, soon to become famous throughout the city, to occupy a top floor, then chose the accouterments to go with it.

But his constitution could not stand the burden he put on it, and each year his health began to deteriorate under the strain. Either alone or with one or two of his children, he made an annual pilgrimage to Europe to recover from physical exhaustion, emaciation, and chronic headaches. He passed weeks at a time at a spa in Kissingen, discussing tunneling and eating five meals a day in an effort to regain the weight which business worries had melted away. He also took occasional trips to Arizona, where, dressed cowboy fashion, he could appease his appetite for the out-of-doors.

Tied to the daily chores of running a corporation, McAdoo found little time for reading. Though he went through a certain amount of history and biography, there is no reason to believe that he was a regular reader of the principal reform periodicals of the day, or that he followed the muckrakers with any degree of consistency. Nor did he come under the sway of the liberal clergy, for he never went to church. In May, 1910, when Edward VII died, McAdoo was aboard the British liner *Oceanic,* and the captain asked him to read Paul's Epistle to the Corinthians in a special memorial service. "Imagine such a thing!" he wrote his wife. "I just said I wouldn't because I couldn't do it properly but no refusal would be accepted so I had to go ahead." Years later, at a White House luncheon, President Wilson said, "Mac, will you ask the blessing?" McAdoo rose. But while seconds ticked embarrassingly away, there was silence. Then he said "Jesus," and sat down abruptly. Next time, after some coaching from his wife, McAdoo read the blessing off the cuff of his shirt.[20]

McAdoo was an utterly fearless individual, and his passion for derring-do found its ultimate gratification in motoring, which eventually became his main source of everyday recreation. His eldest son, who often rode with him, later remembered his father's love of automobiles:

In spite of a slender bank roll and heavy family responsibilities, he purchased a German Mercedes car as early as 1905 and used it to commute from Yonkers to New York. Roads in those days were fairly primitive but this did not prevent my father from speeding along at 45 to 60 miles per hour. To clear the way he blew a horn which sounded like a bugle. Pedestrians, horses and other animals would run for their lives as the big red Mercedes roared past with my father leaning over the wheel in an effort to move even faster.

By 1913, McAdoo had had three close calls with death behind the wheel—

once he was arrested in Germany for racing a locomotive to a grade crossing—and his correspondence was liberally sprinkled with explanations, apologies, and insurance notices.[21]

Immensely popular, McAdoo was one of the comparatively few figures at the beginning of the twentieth century who found themselves frequently requested to address both business organizations and progressive citizens' groups. His speeches were well delivered, invariably reflected the man's progressive way of thinking, and spoke to the fundamental issues of the day. For a number of years, he served as president of the New York Southern Society, an aggregation of influential former Southerners who had, like McAdoo, migrated from Dixie to New York in search of opportunity. Despite his pride in his Southern antecedents (vestiges of his soft Georgia accent never entirely disappeared), he expressed a desire to see persons from all sections of the country admitted to the organization; and, more important, he also made it clear that he harbored no objections whatever to inviting persons to speak on any subject, theory, or ideology. If, during his years in New York, McAdoo continued to identify himself with a single section of the country, he did so mainly out of nostalgia. His home was always filled with visitors from below the Mason-Dixon line, most of them relatives—and most of them "unreconstructed." Convinced that the Northern victory had been a good thing, McAdoo urged them to forget the conflict and adjust to the world as it was. He had never forgotten the greatness of men like Lee and Jackson, but he had little patience with any Southerner who refused to acknowledge the eminence of Abraham Lincoln. Pictures of both Lincoln and Jefferson Davis hung in his New York office. And Southern diehards would have winced had they heard McAdoo deliver an address at the New York City Hall in February, 1911, extolling the "greatness" of Lincoln and Horace Greeley.[22]

V

McAdoo took an interest in foreign affairs which often complemented his role as civic leader. An incident which took place in 1911 well illustrates this facet of his life in New York. For years the Russian government had been casually disregarding a standing commercial treaty it had signed with the United States in 1832, guaranteeing free passage through the country to all American citizens with passports. Russia had tacitly denied entry to—among others—Jews. McAdoo later wrote that he entertained a "deep sympathy . . . with every movement for the benefit of oppressed Jews in every part of the world," and this was almost an understatement. He agreed to lead one group working for abrogation of the treaty. Establishing headquarters for the National Citizens Committee in the Hudson Terminal buildings, McAdoo began to prepare for a mass meeting to call for scrapping the document.[23]

Hundreds of letters went out to Jews and gentiles alike, and on the evening of December 6, under McAdoo's chairmanship, a large crowd gathered in Carnegie Hall to protest the treaty. Among those who spoke that night were McAdoo himself, Speaker of the House Champ Clark, William Randolph Hearst, Senator James O'Gorman of New York, and Governor Woodrow Wilson of New Jersey. "Human rights and the equality of American citizenship are at stake," McAdoo thundered, and he sniped at those (including, impliedly, President William Howard Taft) who "suggest that commercial considerations are paramount to human rights" in international affairs. The meeting broke up after adopting a set of resolutions calling for abrogation of the treaty. A short time later, McAdoo led a delegation to Washington to present these resolutions to the government. Ultimately the treaty was terminated.[24]

McAdoo also became involved in contemporary efforts to usher in an age of international stability. He was associated with the American Peace and Arbitration League and prominently supported the effort to secure a general arbitration treaty with Great Britain. With the advent of the Russo-Japanese War, however, he let his pro-Japanese sentiments be known, and by August, 1905, Theodore Roosevelt, whose own sympathies lay with the Japanese, was cautioning McAdoo that he had become "altogether too partial."[25]

During these years, McAdoo developed a deep interest in the women's rights movement; most of his speeches referred to it. He envisioned millions of women voters who, "owing allegiance to neither political party," could "bring fresh minds to bear upon the problems of the day." This new bloc might compel both parties to attend more closely to the nation's interests, and reinvigorate the two-party system.[26]

McAdoo considered discrimination against women fully as reprehensible in the industrial sphere as in the political. When the question of a differential wage scale for men and women ticket sellers in the Hudson and Manhattan arose, he was adamant. Women, he insisted to his recalcitrant operating superintendent, must be paid "the same salaries you would pay men." "I almost feel more interest in proving that women can be given living wages and that business can prosper on this basis," McAdoo wrote in 1913, "than I do in anything else." When a battle over equal pay erupted beween New York City's women schoolteachers and Governor Charles Evans Hughes, McAdoo wrote a widely quoted letter censuring the Governor's outdated policies.[27]

Though McAdoo belonged to various groups attempting to bring municipal reform to New York, his efforts in these organizations were not of great importance. Despite his other commitments, however, he did find time and money to donate to several beneficent groups. His interest was particularly directed toward the welfare of children, a key theme of humanitarian progressivism.

VI

As McAdoo drifted more and more into the public's vision, and his life became an endless chain of meetings, dinner parties, and speeches, events transpired which would bring him once again into conflict with his old enemy, Thomas Fortune Ryan. The inefficient Interborough subway monopoly—created by a merger of the Metropolitan subway system with August Belmont's Interborough elevated lines in 1906—had treated the public with indifference since its inception, subjecting New York commuters to frequent delays and overcrowded trains. By 1909, general antipathy toward this so-called Traction Trust was mounting to a climax, and it had become clear that some means would have to be found to compel the company to accommodate the city's needs.

The opportunity presented itself when discussion arose over the construction of a badly needed new forty-four mile subway network, designed to encompass Manhattan, Brooklyn, and the Bronx, and christened the Triborough. The Interborough, which had the financial support of J. P. Morgan and Company and reportedly earned a 17 to 18 percent annual profit operating lines which the city had built, insisted that it did not have the estimated $125,000,000 necessary to construct the new system, and that municipal monies would again have to be employed— after which the Interborough would be glad to operate it. Nevertheless, the company had forebodings about the construction of the network, fearing it might be turned over to a competitor and destroy its monopoly, and remained fundamentally opposed to the entire idea.[28]

The stubbornness of the Interborough led large numbers of people to demand a municipally built and operated subway system, and in 1909 a Democratic candidate for mayor who had a strong reform record in Brooklyn, William J. Gaynor, hammered this plank into his platform. Gaynor won the election, but before long many of his supporters became disillusioned. The Mayor, it seemed, was stalling.

In September, 1910, the Public Service Commission finally opened bidding for the new line, and the Interborough predictably declined to use company funds to construct the system. For a time, it appeared that it would not have to; no competitors volunteered.

Then, in November, McAdoo—by now a seasoned veteran of bluffing and battling the Interborough—suddenly submitted a bid of his own: the

Hudson and Manhattan, which, like the Interborough, was backed by the Morgan interests, offered to put up $50,000,000 to equip and operate a slightly modified Triborough network built by the city and to turn it over to municipal control within ten years if service did not prove satisfactory. Meanwhile, the profits would be evenly divided with the city. The proposal, as one newspaper put it, was "stunning"; for, in locking horns with Ryan, McAdoo had removed the one really formidable objection to the Triborough which remained to the Interborough obstructionists, namely, the threat that the city might find a multimillion dollar subway network on its hands with no company to operate it. Invoking the support of the people, McAdoo boasted that nine out of ten of them were behind him—and perhaps he was right. He capitalized on favorable public sentiment by following up his proposition with a quick barrage of attacks on the Interborough. "We have spoken of regulated monopoly," he told an audience at the City Club on December 3. "It is a very fine thing in theory, but it never pans out."[29]

For some reason, however, the Public Service Commission seemed reluctant to take the Hudson and Manhattan offer, and an irritated McAdoo shot off a quick note to that organization, blaming it for the city's lethargy in beginning the new system and setting a deadline of December 15 for acceptance of his bid.[30]

Shortly after McAdoo wrote the commissioners, the Interborough unwrapped its new offer: it would construct a larger route which would cost an estimated $128,000,000, of which $75,000,000 would be supplied out of company funds and $53,000,000 would come from the city treasury. Gaynor almost immediately announced his approval of the bid. McAdoo was expected to submit a fresh proposition, and to those who talked to him, it seemed that he was determined to win. He admitted that the Interborough had caught him off guard but did not consider himself knocked out of the race; beyond this, he seemed reluctant to discuss the subway situation at all. On December 12, as McAdoo's deadline rapidly approached, Gaynor emphatically declared his eagerness to continue the bidding. But McAdoo merely continued to rail against the Interborough's "intolerable monopoly" and its offer to build the Triborough, despite the fact that his competitor's proposition was far more attractive than his own and had been tentatively endorsed by the Mayor. Whether because of personal misgivings, or because of his confidence that he had the support of the people and would not need to make a new bid—for whatever reason, McAdoo was unwilling or unable to act. Meanwhile, the Mayor had come under fire for repudiating his preelection platform and opting for the offer of the "traction monopoly."[31]

On the afternoon of December 13, two days before his bid expired,

McAdoo conferred with the Public Service Commission. Still chained to his dying plea for competition, he reiterated the perils of monopoly to the city's transit system. December 15 came and passed with no explanation from McAdoo or his directors as to why the Hudson and Manhattan offer had been allowed to expire. Rather, McAdoo announced that he intended to withdraw from the rapid transit complex in greater New York altogether, because the municipal authorities had rejected a bid which he considered as liberal as the city could expect, and because making his proposition even more attractive to the city would render it less desirable to his own financial supporters. This was probably the heart of his frustrating dilemma: the finances of the Hudson and Manhattan may well have been stretched to the breaking point in his initial proposal. According to at least one account, McAdoo simply could not enlist sufficient financial support behind it. And, as he later pointed out, such an offer could not be left hanging in the air. When the idea of bidding had arisen, he argued, the question of the rights and wrongs of competition had been subordinated to that of cost. The bids submitted by the two companies were, by their very nature, incomparable. Since the authorities had failed to view the matter this way, he was withdrawing his offer to avoid further delaying construction on a transit network which the public desperately needed.[32]

McAdoo had subordinated ultimate cost to a question of economic theory about which he entertained strong and sincere convictions. At least implicitly, he had also subordinated it to the financial exigencies of his own company. A highly pragmatic businessman, he had nonetheless stipulated that the two bids could not in fact be compared without reference to a higher moral issue. If the public wanted reform, he was saying in effect, then the taxpayers must pay for it, since he had already gone as far as he could.

Meanwhile, public outcry over Gaynor's lethargy (or treachery) continued, and the press revealed that, particularly in the suburbs, dissatisfaction was mounting rapidly. Speaking at Plymouth Church on the evening of January 19, McAdoo joined the chorus and demanded that the city begin building now and worry about the fundamental issue— monopoly or competition—later. He came out for an indeterminate franchise to be granted to whichever company was chosen to operate the line, a suggestion which one newspaper termed "a momentous happening in the history of the relations of American municipalities with public service corporations." But perhaps it also symbolized McAdoo's resignation to the fact that this time the Hudson and Manhattan had been beaten. Although he outlined a fresh plan in the speech, one which called for a modified route designed to cost slightly over $100,000,000, he remarked that he did not intend to submit another bid until the city had definitely rejected that of the Interborough.[33]

The following morning, the press hailed McAdoo's return to the fight. The city controller offered to consider the Plymouth Church plan if it were formally submitted, and several days after the speech McAdoo was asked to attend a meeting of the Public Service Commission. The men closeted themselves for two hours, but when McAdoo emerged he simply repeated that the Hudson and Manhattan would make no new offer until the city guaranteed to turn down the Interborough proposal.

On March 1, apparently ill and suffering from overwork McAdoo suddenly and unexpectedly sailed for Europe. He returned to New York late in April. H and M engineers had been working feverishly in the weeks before his arrival, preparing fresh plans for a Triborough network. McAdoo denied to reporters that he had gone abroad to raise capital and added that he expected no difficulty "whatever" in securing American funds for the venture. But the new proposition never came. Rumors would persist for months that McAdoo intended to make another bid. But gradually, as time passed, the rumors became fainter and fainter, until eventually they disappeared altogether. McAdoo had been checkmated.[34]

VII

Though he had been defeated, McAdoo could at least be solaced by one thing: his offer of November 18 had been the largest factor in forcing liberal concessions from Ryan's Interborough. The very presence of McAdoo's bid had wrung more than $75,000,000 out of a company which, only weeks before, had stubbornly insisted that it could never find the capital to construct its own subway system. Ryan's first franchise had sixty-nine more years to run; by contrast, the offer he submitted in 1911 allowed the city to take the system over after ten years if service proved inefficient. If it had not in fact been implemented, the philosophy of competition as opposed to regulated monopoly had in a single instance at least been vindicated; and it had left a permanent imprint on the subway system of New York.

More significant for present purposes is the impact the incident may have had on McAdoo himself. Precisely how important it was in shaping his future career will never be known; clearly, however, the outcome represented McAdoo's first serious defeat in business in twenty years and came at a time when his career seemed inevitably to be approaching its zenith. Now, the path of opportunity in business had at least temporarily been blocked to him. Construction of the tubes had been one of the great engineering achievements of the time, but now they were finished. Had McAdoo remained in the traction field, he might have been compelled to live out his days as a bureaucrat, and this he was temperamentally ill prepared to do. The obvious alternative was to go into politics.[35]

CHAPTER THREE

FROM TUNNELS TO POLITICS

I

One freezing day in February, 1909, McAdoo received a telegram from Princeton informing him that his eldest son, Francis, had diphtheria. He left at once for New Jersey, and, momentarily stranded on a station platform waiting for a shuttle which connected the main line to the university, he fell into a conversation with one of Princeton's trustees. Woodrow Wilson, the controversial president of the institution, alighted from a New York train and joined them on the platform. The trustee introduced the two men, and by the time Wilson parted from McAdoo at the door of the campus infirmary, one of the fateful friendships of American history had been born.

McAdoo was initially struck by Wilson's bearing, athletic yet dignified, by his courtesy and charm, and by his "great intellectual force and latent power." The two met occasionally thereafter, generally at banquets, until the fall of 1910, when Wilson accepted the gubernatorial nomination of the New Jersey Democracy. McAdoo offered his aid in helping Wilson win, but he harbored self-conscious doubts about the value of the support of a corporation executive who had numerous connections with the so-called moguls of Wall Street. Wilson assured him that his help would be far from unwelcome.[1]

The shift of McAdoo's tremendous energy from the corporate sphere into the political did not occur suddenly. But the interest in politics which had manifested itself so early in his life had never entirely flickered out; it only remained for the right cause—and the right man— to rekindle it at the proper time. McAdoo largely confined his support of Wilson in 1910 to correspondence and conversation. Two years later, after the Triborough struggle had come to a close, his reaction would be far different.

In December, 1911, McAdoo wrote a friend that the world was "going to come to a different view about humanity after a while. If I can play a part before I die in pushing that movement along to an earlier beneficent result, I shall be happy." The obvious pathway was political. "Politics," McAdoo would write in later years, "should be the science of humanity." But ironically, this most vital of sciences lagged far behind the others. "The more I reflect on existing conditions and problems, and the more speeches I hear of the average politician and alleged statesman," he wrote in 1910,

the more I am convinced that there are very few, if any, who have correctly sensed the deep underlying feelings and aspirations of the masses of the people. We are working, undoubtedly, toward a broader and nobler humanitarianism, and some day a real leader, having in his heart that breadth of human sympathy which will make him capable of truly interpreting the tendencies of the day, will crystalize them and give struggling humanity a genuine up-lift.[2]

But who would that leader be?

McAdoo had been contacted by Theodore Roosevelt as early as the spring of 1904, when Roosevelt invited him to a reception at the White House. He had fallen under the Rough Rider's spell. The following October, after the Democrats had unenthusiastically nominated a colorless New Yorker, Alton B. Parker, for the Presidency, McAdoo—still worried about the silverites in his own party—evinced a deep interest in seeing T.R. reelected. When Roosevelt won, McAdoo did not prove averse to the idea of accepting a position on the Panama Canal Commission. He had been "a hearty and earnest supporter" of the President during the Panama controversy of 1903, and a number of friends remarked that he should be given the position. Nevertheless, McAdoo wrote, "I . . . have a horror of being considered an office or favor seeker of any kind." After Roosevelt appointed another man, he and McAdoo still corresponded occasionally.[3]

When T.R. returned from Europe in the summer of 1910, McAdoo served on New York's official greeting committee. But disillusionment soon set in; for within a short time the Colonel seemed a far different kind of reformer from the one McAdoo had supported in 1904. In his

New Nationalism, as it evolved in the months after his return to America, Roosevelt envisioned a fresh approach to reform. At the core of the New Nationalism lay seeds of anti-Jeffersonianism: embracing the idea that the federal government was directly responsible for the welfare of all its citizens, Roosevelt came out for a series of controversial social reforms which included a minimum wage for women, workmen's compensation, prohibition of child labor, and social insurance. In addition, he supported the broad electoral reforms which most progressives desired, announced that he would back a tariff of no more than moderate protection, and echoed older proposals for a graduated inheritance tax and currency reform.

But the New Nationalism bore other ideas as well. One of these was faith in expertise: government, as T.R. and his followers viewed it, must become scientific. Roosevelt also involved himself in a burgeoning feud with the courts. Attacking them as "absolutely reactionary," he announced that he advocated overhauling the judicial system, and came out for the recall of state judicial decisions. Finally, Roosevelt accepted as inevitable the emergence of an entire complex of big businesses and monopolies, but wanted each carefully regulated by the federal government.[4]

It is highly doubtful that McAdoo harbored severe objections to Roosevelt's proposed social legislation, though he may have envisioned a greater role for the states in enforcing it. Doubtless he felt far less embittered toward the judiciary than T.R. did. Yet no record remains of McAdoo ever having addressed himself to any of these specific issues. Nor does he appear to have perceived the subtler implications of the New Nationalism—the potential quashing of individual liberties in the name of the state, for example, or the latent chauvinism and militarism which characterized Roosevelt's speeches.

Rather, McAdoo's unease centered on T.R.'s attitude toward big business. The Southern farm boy who had risen to head an important corporation still considered himself a Jeffersonian and was convinced that government should interfere with business as little

as is compatible with the welfare of all the people but with the multiplication of great corporations intent on enriching themselves, it is necessary for the government to maintain strict control over monopolies and other great businesses which may rób the people if permitted a free rein.

In June, 1911, McAdoo clarified his position on corporations and trusts as coherently as he ever would during these years. He wrote a friend that he had been thinking "a good deal" about the problem and hastily poured out his conclusions:

What amuses me most is the excuse that the Trust makers are trying to beguile the public with, for the formation of the trusts, namely, that modern economic necessity has compelled them. I do not know of a Trust that has been organized for any such reason. Every one of them had their [sic] inception in the greed and ambition of certain men to profit by their organization. Nearly all of them was [sic] born in Wall Street and for the usual Wall Street reason—money. I firmly believe that a governmental policy which will prevent any further combinations of concerns engaged in Interstate commerce will be of real benefit to the country. This having been accomplished, what will result—every concern will meet modern economic necessity by growing in its own proper and legitimate way, as the result of good management and under the stimulus of healthful competition. . . . The plea that labor gets a better wage as a result of it is altogether fallacious. Labor has gotten a better wage, as a rule, because conditions compelled it, and the chief factor in those conditions has been the organization of labor itself, so that it has been in a position to compel recognition.

. . .

Let each of these concerns grow in its own proper and legitimate way. The healthful stimulus of competition will make the management of each concern keener and more alert in the matter of producing better machinery and discovering new and useful inventions, and also in giving the public more reasonable prices than if they were under one administration.

As of 1911, then, McAdoo wanted strict federal regulation of existing monopolies, together with policies that would somehow prevent future combinations *without* stunting the growth of individual corporations. He knew that the ideas of Roosevelt and his New Nationalist colleagues would enthrone trustification rather than destroy it. At this point, T.R. and McAdoo had come to the parting of the ways. "I have always admired him very much," McAdoo wrote the following year, "but, it seems to me that he is making a very grave mistake."[5]

On the other hand, Woodrow Wilson, who was building a brilliant record as reform Governor of New Jersey, appeared to personify the Jeffersonian tradition in American thought (if such a thing actually existed outside the realm of party rhetoric). In 1910, he had ridden into office with the aid of conservatives and the Essex County Democratic machine. But during the campaign he had adopted the vocabulary and much of the substance of progressivism; and by the time he won, conservatives and old-line party stalwarts had reason to wonder why they had ever backed him.

After supporting Wilson in 1910, McAdoo watched the transformation of the "tenderloin state" with increasing interest. Wilson's "amazing power of analysis of our economic and political ills and the high plane upon which his speeches were pitched, and the clean and progressive things he stood for thrilled me," McAdoo wrote in later years. Like McAdoo, Wilson valued the Jeffersonian model of small, competing economic units. He, too, considered high protective tariffs a means of defrauding the public and wished to see them lowered. And,

fully as important, he was a Southerner. Finally, as McAdoo often exclaimed, Wilson seemed a new kind of public figure, free of the taints
of "bossism" and "radicalism" which had done so much to stifle Democratic hopes in the years since 1896. "Wilson," McAdoo wrote, "appeals to the imagination of the American people. He represents something
fresh and vital in public life."[6]

McAdoo was among the first to support Wilson publicly for the
Presidency. In December, 1910, as toastmaster for a Southern Society
banquet in New York, he hailed Lincoln, Cleveland, and Theodore
Roosevelt as three Americans who had "kept faith" with the interests
and aspirations of the people. He added that the political dilemma confronting America now was to maintain the powers of the federal government while at the same time revitalizing those of the states. Then,
introducing Woodrow Wilson, McAdoo asked the audience to "rise and
drink to a future President of the United States." There was a chorus
of cheers, and after the noise had subsided, Wilson, surprised and embarrassed, remarked that he did not feel "as sure as Mr. McAdoo that
I know my destination."[7]

As the year wore on, McAdoo's attention seems momentarily to
have drifted away from politics; but his passion for spectacular motoring
went on unabated. Racing home from a charity meeting with Mrs. J.
Borden Harriman one spring evening, he suddenly reached the crest
of a hill and plunged into a construction zone. The car careened wildly
and rolled over. Mrs. Harriman escaped with bruises, but McAdoo, who
had hurtled twenty feet and landed on his head, found himself hospitalized
with several broken ribs and a fractured arm. As he began to recover,
his spirits revived, and he impatiently wrote a friend that the best cure
for his injuries would be more speeding.[8]

II

Meanwhile, his predictions about Governor Wilson slowly began to
materialize. In the spring of 1911, Wilson made a speaking tour of the
West, and, buoyed by an unexpectedly enthusiastic reception, returned
to New Jersey, as one newspaper put it, "a candidate in the fullest
sense." A number of the Governor's friends, including a young New
York lawyer named William F. McCombs, had been endeavoring to
launch a Wilson boom. McCombs would prove to be the most controversial figure of the campaign. The scion of a Southern family of considerable
means, he had suffered an accident in childhood which had left him
crippled for life. He had studied under Woodrow Wilson at Princeton,
had graduated with the class of 1898, and had eventually established a
lucrative law practice in New York. Contemporaries remarked that his

finely chiseled features betrayed both shrewdness and intelligence. But there was a fatal flaw in McCombs which would manifest itself increasingly as the campaign progressed: he was emotionally unstable.[9]

In response to the clamors of his friends, Wilson agreed to the proposal that a small publicity bureau be established in New York. McCombs managed to accumulate a little money to meet expenses. But Wilson forbade the creation of a large organization, and McCombs and his allies had to rely on an expanding mailing list for publicity.

During these early months of 1911, McAdoo began to drift into the Wilson coterie. He and McCombs had first met in the fall of 1908. They "became warm friends," McAdoo later recalled, and McCombs was soon a familiar weekend visitor in McAdoo's home at Irvington, New York. "At that time," McAdoo wrote, "he betrayed none of the unfortunate characteristics . . . which obsessed him" later; yet McAdoo remembered perceiving "something of a false note" in the young man even in those early years of their friendship. McCombs respected political idealists, but he also belonged to Tammany Hall. He boasted that he had the confidence of Tammany boss Charles Murphy and the friendship of McAdoo's old enemy, Thomas Fortune Ryan; and he laid more emphasis than McAdoo liked on machine politics and the cynical side of political manipulation. When McCombs urged McAdoo to consider a public career, presumably as a member of the machine, McAdoo turned the offer down.[10]

Sometime during the spring of 1911, McCombs visited McAdoo at Irvington and suggested that Governor Wilson should be the next Democratic candidate for the Presidency. McAdoo agreed to cooperate with him, and the two men began to meet once a week or oftener at McAdoo's Railroad Club. Other Wilson boosters sometimes joined them. Wilson himself appears to have taken another major step in drawing McAdoo into the campaign when, in August, he asked editor Walter Hines Page to contact McAdoo and discuss "the general concentration of effort" in the campaign. "I have found him very sagacious and very wide-awake," the Governor added.[11]

In the fall, McAdoo requested an interview with Wilson and was invited to spend a night at the Governor's home. So many objections had been raised in recent years to the close ties between business and politics that McAdoo had hesitated to declare publicly for Wilson. McAdoo asked the Governor if he thought it would do any harm if he came out for him and took part in the campaign. Wilson, who respected McAdoo's knowledge of business techniques, replied that McAdoo's endorsement would be a distinct asset. Few important businessmen, the Governor explained, had joined his political circle, and his opponents claimed he was dangerously hostile to private enterprise. McAdoo's presence in his campaign would help refute these notions.

McAdoo made it clear that he wanted to see Wilson elected because he thought the Governor could lead the nation in the proper direction and rehabilitate the Democratic Party; but that was all McAdoo wanted. "I shall be more than happy to devote all the time I can spare to the movement to nominate you," he commented, "but I beg the privilege of imposing a condition:"

If you should be nominated and elected President, I shall not seek or accept any public office, nor shall I ask any favors at your hands.

"The Governor looked at me almost incredulously for a moment," McAdoo later recalled,

then said: "This is delightfully refreshing. . . . I believe absolutely in your sincerity and disinterestedness and I shall be very happy to have your support on your own terms."

McAdoo also sounded Wilson on McCombs's role in the campaign. "This interview," McAdoo wrote, "established me in the Governor's confidence —a confidence that was never shaken in the years of intimate association that followed."[12]

For his part, the candidate made it clear that the Public be Pleased policy pleased him; it represented precisely the kind of attitude he wanted to see the business community adopt. In fact, McAdoo's meteoric career as a promoter might have served as a model for the kind of individual Wilson admired most: the man on the make. McAdoo's chief characteristic was his remarkable energy. He knew his way through Wall Street, but had not become an insider; financially worldly, he was not of the financial world. This independence, perhaps more than anything else, attracted the Governor to him. McAdoo's view of the corporation as a moral entity closely intertwined with the public welfare paralleled Wilson's; so did his lingering suspicion of big business and its influence on government; his insistence that guilt within the corporation could not be collective but must rest on the shoulders of its leadership; his attitude toward organized labor, guarded without being paranoid; and his faith in the common man.[13]

In other ways, the two men differed, if not in attitude then at least in emphasis. At this point, for example, McAdoo doubtless had more tolerance than Wilson for government collaboration with business. At the same time, perhaps because his membership in the middle class had recently been so tenuous, McAdoo did not share Wilson's fixation with the middle class as the mainspring of American society.

Despite this, they became quite close. During the campaign, the

Governor was much given to fulsome praise of McAdoo's character and ideals. Then too, Wilson appreciated McAdoo's clearheaded manner in everyday political affairs. "There should be a sign on the desk of every reformer," he once exclaimed: "DON'T BE A DAMNED FOOL." Wilson had a remarkable way of accompanying his outspokenness concerning ends with caution as to means and constantly reminded his audiences that the defects of capitalism must be remedied gently. This appears to have delighted McAdoo, and by December, 1911, the two men were carrying on a voluminous correspondence.[14]

McAdoo realized that in Wilson, the Democratic Party had finally found a man around whom progressives, conservatives, and independents might unite. True, the Governor had espoused a number of supposedly "radical" programs in the West; but in future months McAdoo would endeavor to accommodate his conservative friends on Wall Street and in the South to Wilson's new positions. McAdoo was one of only a handful of men in the New York business community who adjudged Wilson safe before the Democratic national convention, and this in itself proved influential.[15]

From the first, McAdoo continued to emphasize that he had entered the campaign "solely . . . to help . . . solve some of the serious political and economic problems that now confront us." He was concerned with tending his tunnels and being "a good citizen," but he had no intention of becoming a "politician." McCombs, on the other hand, was interested precisely in the tactical aspects of the campaign; and in October, Wilson appointed the Tammanyite his campaign manager.[16]

McCombs's political affiliations notwithstanding, the appointment did not seem a bad one at first, though Wilson himself may have had some early misgivings about it. But in the long run, Wilson had made an almost fatal blunder. As a propagandist and manipulator, McCombs could be superb; he had an instinct for politics and a gift for raising funds. But he was weak at the techniques of organization, and as the year progressed, his equanimity began to erode, until, in one harrowing moment, he would almost drag the Wilson campaign down with him.

III

As the last months of 1911 faded away, and the wounds which Theodore Roosevelt had inflicted on the Republican Party failed to heal, other Democratic Presidential aspirants awakened to the fact that 1912 would offer the party its greatest opportunity to elect a President in more than a decade. Among the more prominent of these men were Ohio's conservative Governor, Judson Harmon; Oscar Underwood of Alabama, the House

Majority Leader; and provincial Missouri Congressman Champ Clark.

Of the three, Clark developed into the most formidable rival. An old-school party wheelhorse who had been in the House since the 1890's, Clark had built a progressive voting record and had secured the Speakership in 1911. Though his intelligence and temperament could be questioned, he was both venerable and lovable and had inherited a large portion of the Bryan following. Many old-line, conservative party leaders and moderates also supported him. In later years, as Secretary of the Treasury, McAdoo saw much of Clark and learned to like him. But Clark was not McAdoo's kind of man; McAdoo could never understand what made him popular.

The same month that McCombs received his appointment as manager, he and McAdoo called on a visitor to New York who, by reputation, had considerable political influence in his native Texas. Colonel Edward M. House was a rather unlikely looking political manipulator, spare and with somewhat rodential features. When confronted by McCombs and Mc-Adoo, he seemed noncommittal. But before long he would become a confidant of both Wilson and McAdoo.[17]

Meanwhile, McAdoo had actively entered the campaign. On November 20, he spoke in Chattanooga, and the following day he addressed a group in Knoxville. He felt optimistic; but in January a cloud passed over his confidence as political tensions mounted throughout the South. Of particular concern was Virginia, where the Richmond machine—under the control of Thomas Fortune Ryan, who gave money to both Harmon and Underwood—appeared to be subverting Wilson's chances.

Then too, the financial condition of the Wilson organization left much to be desired: during midwinter, its net bank balance dropped to exactly $55.23. But, thanks to McAdoo's contributions and efforts and those of others, money soon began to accumulate from a number of diverse sources. McCombs, an inveterate fund raiser, decided that it might be possible to tap the reserves of businessman Henry Morgenthau; and he was right. Morgenthau agreed to subscribe $20,000 personally in monthly installments and to solicit more from others. Thereafter, McAdoo, Mc-Combs, and Morgenthau conferred frequently.[18]

Besides finances, perhaps the greatest single problem confronting the Wilson campaign in the winter of 1911-12 was neither Underwood, nor Harmon, nor even Clark, but McCombs. Ambitious, vain, voracious for publicity, thin-skinned and suspicious of other Wilson boosters, McCombs had determined to direct the Wilson movement single-handedly. He had alienated important Democrats and had failed to create a national organization. He had also begun kindling fear and animosities at campaign headquarters. At McAdoo's suggestion he appointed Byron Newton, a former newspaperman and an old friend of McAdoo's, as the new publicity chief after McCombs had forced the former head to resign. About a month later, Newton informed McAdoo that McAdoo, too, had finally aroused McCombs's irrepressible ire. The manager, Newton claimed, had seen McAdoo's name in print in favorable connection with the campaign. McCombs's

face instantly took on the expression of an infuriated animal. He locked the door, seized his cane and beat it into splinters over the desk, cursing and shrieking like a maniac.

McAdoo tried, in effect, to shrug off the manager's idiosyncrasies; but "I found . . . that my efforts were being handicapped considerably by the steadily developing jealousies of McCombs." McAdoo eventually branded the manager a megalomaniac with a split personality.[19]

In January, Wilson began a series of speaking tours which would carry him thousands of miles during the winter and spring of 1912. Meanwhile, realizing that one of the most fragile links in the candidate's chain of support was the South, McAdoo determined to conduct his own foray into this region and the West and attend his daughter's wedding in Albuquerque. McAdoo seized every opportunity to induce Democratic leaders in New Mexico, Arizona, Tennessee, and other states to come out for Wilson. He returned to New York by way of Jackson, Mississippi, where he addressed the State Legislature. By the time McAdoo reached his home at Irvington, he had been absent three weeks. Wilson sentiment seemed to run deep in the states he had visited, and he felt thoroughly encouraged.

Shortly after her husband's return, Sarah McAdoo died suddenly at Irvington. For the moment, McAdoo dropped out of the campaign and disappeared from his office. He turned down all invitations, canceled all speaking engagements. On March 9, he escaped to Bermuda with two of his children. By the 25th McAdoo had returned to his desk, but he remained reluctant to speak in public. Meanwhile, he moved into an apartment on Park Avenue.

One of the worst threats the Wilson campaign faced at this point was an obstinate Wilson-Underwood deadlock in the South. McAdoo felt certain that, although Underwood stock continued to rise in that section, the Alabaman had no chance whatever of being nominated. As the primaries approached and he surveyed the Southern and Western picture, McAdoo seemed most concerned about Mississippi. Though reports from Georgia and Virginia appeared encouraging, the problems that had plagued the Wilson movement from the first—lack of organization and shortage of funds—remained. And time was running out.

The primaries and state conventions began favorably enough late in February, when Wilson carried Oklahoma. Ominous, however, was the result in Kansas, where organizational weakness allowed the state to slip into Clark's column practically by default.

Though he felt more concerned about the problem of organization than any other single issue, McAdoo believed that Wilson might help his cause considerably by making a final Southern tour, and he urged the Governor to take this advice. In mid-April the two men launched a foray into Georgia, and McAdoo, who had originally planned not to make any speeches, separated from the main party and went on a speaking expedition of his own. He returned to New York after five days, convinced that Wilson's trip had probably turned the tide against Underwood.

McAdoo had meanwhile focused his attention on North Carolina, where considerable Wilson sentiment had been drummed up by (among others) a newspaper editor named Josephus Daniels. By the end of April it had begun to appear that in the Tarheel State, at least, Wilson's forces might be well marshaled, though here, as elsewhere, they remained emaciated from lack of funds.

The results of the April primaries were far from encouraging. By now, the Clark drive had shifted into high gear, and on April 9 the Missourian countered Wilson's victory in Wisconsin with a majority in Illinois far more crushing than McAdoo and the other members of the Wilson coterie had envisioned. Suddenly Clark had become the leading contender for the nomination. Two days later he carried New York, and in the following weeks he pocketed the votes of Nebraska and Massachusetts. Few had suspected that Clark's star could rise so rapidly.

If April brought meager rewards, May proved one of the darkest months of Woodrow Wilson's political career. On the first, Georgia fell to Underwood. On May 7, Clark won in Washington; on May 13, Wyoming; May 14, California, New Hampshire, and Nevada; May 16, Iowa and the District of Columbia. Within five weeks, the Missourian had accumulated 324 delegates with strict instructions to vote for him at the convention and had, in addition, probably 150 votes in uninstructed delegations.[20]

By mid-May, Wilson headquarters on Broadway was practically deserted, and many of the Wilsonites of a few weeks before seemed to be disappearing into the swollen ranks of Clark. Only a handful still drifted in and out of the office, McAdoo among them. McCombs's funds had been virtually exhausted, and as the hailstorm of defeats continued, he noticed that Morgenthau had failed to make his usual $4,000 monthly contribution. He asked McAdoo to remind the businessman about the matter; but the moment McAdoo reached him by telephone, Morgenthau replied, "Not another cent! Not another cent!"[21]

Like the rest of the Wilson coterie, McAdoo was surprised and disappointed, particularly about the results in the South. Though he and Colonel House had shared heavy responsibilities for winning that section of the country, neither had corresponded extensively with the other. McAdoo had not campaigned to the fullest in Georgia, nor had he advised Wilson to do so; like the Governor, he had feared the opprobrium attached to outright campaigning, and his political awakening had come too late to salvage the state. On May 21, at the request of Richard E. Byrd, he attended the Virginia nominating convention, but the best compromise the two men and their colleagues could obtain, after endless haggling and a losing skirmish with Thomas Fortune Ryan, was a virtual suspension of the unit rule so that ten delegates out of twenty-four could vote for Wilson.[22]

Yet despite this hailstorm of failures, McAdoo's self-reproach had a tinge of optimism which neither Wilson nor House could share. He did not think Wilson could lose: the public wanted him. Had McAdoo been a particularly reflective person, and had he not been an amateur in politics, he might have abandoned hope. But, as Cassatt had remarked years before, McAdoo loved a fight. As defeat followed bitter defeat, a flood of letters poured from McAdoo's office, admonishing the Governor's friends not to give up. A majority of the delegates, it was true, had been chosen—but they would not vote at Baltimore for another month.

IV

Like McAdoo, most of the Wilson coterie refused to quit merely because they appeared to be tied to a political corpse. Nor were their hopes entirely betrayed. On June 4, North Carolina elected an uninstructed delegation composed largely of Wilson men. In strife-ridden Tennessee, Wilson's supporters managed to accumulate a fourth of the delegates. Meanwhile, Kansas, Maine, New Jersey, and South Carolina had yielded uninstructed delegations among which Wilson supporters could be found; and Texas, Pennsylvania, Oregon, Wisconsin, and Minnesota instructed most or all of their delegates to vote for Wilson. The Governor's chances revived, and even the glum Colonel House began to radiate encouragement. This last-minute success was crowned on May 30, when the chief organ of the Eastern Democracy, the New York *World,* came out for Wilson.

Yet, in order to win, McAdoo felt the Governor must have the support, preferably the outspoken support, of William Jennings Bryan. The efforts to bring the Great Commoner over had been extended and intricate. In April, House persuaded him to state that either Wilson or Clark would be acceptable as a candidate, but beyond this Bryan refused to budge. During the Nebraska primary, with all eyes upon him, he declined to abandon his neutrality. "I am afraid, from what I am told," McAdoo complained, "that he hopes to be a beneficiary of the deadlock which many are now expecting"; the contest might eventually see the Commoner pitted against Wilson. In private, McAdoo began to rail against Bryan for his aloofness.[23]

In mid-June, McAdoo finally determined to see Bryan personally, and confront him as he had confronted Jennings and Gary and Morgan years before. The Republicans were to hold their convention in Chicago and Bryan, he learned, would be there as a newspaper correspondent. Within an hour after McAdoo had made his decision, he was on his way to Chicago.

He found Bryan early in the morning. The crowd that usually surrounded the Commoner churned about in his steaming hotel room; and Bryan ushered McAdoo out into the hall. McAdoo bluntly remarked that he was "anxious to know Bryan's attitude toward Wilson." The interview, as McAdoo later remembered it, progressed this way:

I told Bryan that it was perfectly clear that the allignment [sic] in the Baltimore Convention was between the progressives, on the one hand, and the reactionaries and conservatives, on the other; that I had great respect for Clark, Underwood and Harmon, but that each of them was conservative and that the nomination of neither one of them would satisfy the progressive sentiment of the country, without which no Democrat could be elected. I tried to impress Bryan with the fact that Wilson was the only progressive in the race and that he was thoroughly and dependably so. I adverted to what I believed to be the absolute fact, namely, that it would not be long after the balloting began before the machines and bosses would line up behind Clark as the only way to beat Wilson. I reminded him that I was a member of the New York delegation and had some knowledge of the attitude of Tammany Hall which dominated that delegation and had its ninety delegates bound by the unit rule. I said that I thought that a candidate nominated by Tammany votes in the convention would be damned at the outset—that it would mean defeat for the Democratic Party at the November election.

.   .   .

Bryan agreed with me absolutely that the nomination of a reactionary or conservative by the Democrats and the renomination of President Taft by the reactionary Republicans would mean the election of Roosevelt if he ran as an independent because he would get the progressive strength of the country; that Wilson was the only man who could divide the progressive vote with Roosevelt and win.

Bryan assured McAdoo that he felt "very friendly to Wilson," who was his second choice for the nomination, and remarked:

I am very much impressed by Governor Wilson; I am convinced that he is thoroughly progressive and that he is courageous and dependable. But my state, Nebraska, has instructed its delegation for Clark. I, as a member of the delegation, am bound by my instructions. I must honorably carry them out.

But, after I have discharged this obligation in good faith, I shall feel free to take such course in the convention as my conscience shall dictate. Moreover, if, during the course of the convention, anything should develop to convince me that Clark cannot or ought not to be nominated, I shall support Governor Wilson.

"Colonel," McAdoo replied, "I don't see how you can take any other position. I am sure that Governor Wilson's friends will be entirely satisfied with the course you have indicated."[24]

V

All would depend, then, upon what transpired at Baltimore. After the primaries were over, McCombs and McAdoo had tabulated Wilson's first-ballot strength. It totalled less than one third of the delegates. This came as a bitter disappointment, since both men had expected to go into the convention with a minimum of a third, but McAdoo felt confident that Wilson's full potential would develop after a few ballots had been cast, since a considerable backlog of second-choice strength had been painstakingly built up during the campaign. This secondary support appeared to be more extensive than even the optimistic McAdoo had expected, but it would be impossible to judge how much value could be drawn from it until the balloting actually began. If Wilson somehow got the nomination, he would have clear sailing; the Republicans had split, and Roosevelt had determined to run for President on his own Progressive ticket.[25]

In April, McAdoo had wangled an appointment as a delegate to the Democratic National Convention from the Mayor of Yonkers; hence, McAdoo would be on the floor, in the midst of the crucial Tammany delegation. And, at Wilson's behest, he would be serving as one of the candidate's chief lieutenants during the proceedings. Late in June, McCombs informed McAdoo that the Governor had requested McAdoo's being named Vice-Chairman of the Democratic National Committee if the Wilson forces were successful in the convention. Remarking that the Governor was "the only man living for whom I would accept this post," McAdoo replied "that I will accept and put my soul into the work." But he concluded his response in a rather curious vein: "If I do less well than you expect," he wrote, "only remember that I am not in command and that that necessarily restricts opportunity. I do not offer this as an excuse but as a possible explanation."[26]

McAdoo was referring to McCombs—more specifically, to the internecine strife which the manager's very presence had engendered among the Wilson coterie, and which, by late June, ate at the vitals of the Governor's campaign. Terribly disheartened by the results of the primaries, McCombs became increasingly enveloped in his own phobias and delusions. He had been ill throughout the campaign, and this only increased his lingering, bitter distrust of everyone around him. As the weeks passed, Wilson would find himself spending enormous amounts of time in an effort to convince the manager that the other members of the coterie were not endeavoring to snatch his position away from him, but the Governor's efforts were far from fruitful. McCombs's hatred of his associates, and particularly of McAdoo, never abated. McCombs seems to have listened to at least one person, however, and that was Colonel House. House sympathized with the young man, and early in June he and McCombs repaired to the Colonel's summer home at Beverly, Massachusetts, where House patiently began to teach McCombs the fundamentals of convention strategy.[27]

Despite House's coaching, the Wilson supporters remained essentially a group of amateurs, confronting the best political strategists that the conservative wing of the party could throw against them. Led by a manager who exhibited signs of both paranoia and physical collapse, they had laid no plans for replacing him. They entered the convention with less than a third of the pledged delegates behind them—248 to Clark's 436. It looked, House later wrote, "as if Wilson had a good chance, but nothing more." Yet there were men on the convention floor who were less stoic—and perhaps less realistic—than House. One of them was William Gibbs McAdoo.[28]

CHAPTER FOUR

VICTORY

I

As delegates swarmed from their trains in Baltimore, they stepped into a carnival atmosphere. Brass bands paraded through the city, telephone poles and fences were plastered with candidates' pictures, and clusters of men stood in hotel lobbies, wearing white hatbands labeled "Win with Wilson." McAdoo, McCombs, and a number of other Wilson supporters had arrived early and begun operations at the Emerson Hotel.[1]

Then too, there was Bryan. Arriving directly from Chicago dressed in an alpaca coat, he looked like a caricature of the Boy Orator of '96. After conservatives secured the nomination as temporary chairman for Alton Parker in skirmishing before the convention gathered, the Commoner shot off telegrams to each of the four major Presidential contenders asking them to join him in fighting Parker's selection. McCombs proposed a reply to Bryan's challenge which straddled the issue. Reluctantly, Wilson overruled his manager and sent a response which placed him squarely behind Bryan. Wilson's "greatest asset," the Commoner later wrote, "was the fact that he came out strongly against Parker for temporary chairman"; for Clark's reply bore a striking resemblance to the one by McCombs, and was not to Bryan's liking.[2]

But McCombs felt horrified. McAdoo, unaware of Wilson's telegram, phoned Sea Girt, told Wilson that he was dissatisfied with the manager's proposed response, and urged the Governor to back Bryan. If he did, McAdoo thought the Commoner would eventually come over. Wilson read McAdoo the message he had just sent Bryan, adding that he had forwarded a copy to McCombs. The manager read the telegram, then "threw himself on . . . [a] bed and literally wept hysterically." McAdoo tried to placate him; but McCombs, shackled by the conviction that it would be impossible to secure the nomination without the ninety votes of New York and concerned with the effect the reply would have on the Eastern bosses, believed Wilson had just thrown away his chance for the nomination.[3]

II

The first session of the convention opened on the afternoon of the twenty-fifth, with nearly 10,000 spectators crowding the galleries and eleven hundred delegates on the floor. Bryan fought Parker's nomination as temporary chairman and lost. With Clark's managers "working like beavers for Judge Parker," as the Nebraskan later wrote, the convention went on to give Parker the post. It proved a pyrrhic victory. Bryan was stung by the collusion of the Clark and Tammany delegates in defeating him. And Clark's personal progressivism had become obscured. In the eyes of many delegates, the convention had turned into an internecine party struggle between progressives on one hand and Wall Street on the other, and a flood of telegrams began to pour into Baltimore from people all over the country demanding support for the Commoner. Clark's rather formless brand of progressivism had been publicly compromised in the interest of victory. Wilson's progressivism, almost equally vague at this point, had not. The illusion of a head-on confrontation between progressives and conservatives went far toward undermining Clark's candidacy.[4]

As Parker read—or rather, attempted to read—his keynote address, a chorus of hecklers and the noise people made leaving the hall forced the forensics to be cut short, and the convention adjourned until evening. When the delegates reassembled, Senator Ollie M. James of Kentucky was chosen permanent chairman, and the Wilson forces had every reason to be satisfied.

Even more important than Parker's fiasco was an agreement which was meanwhile being quietly completed behind the scenes. Leading machine politician Roger Sullivan of Illinois, finding himself in deep trouble in the credentials committee because of a competing delegation from Chicago, backed the seating of a Wilson delegation from South Dakota in return for the support of Wilson's man on the committee. This threw ten more votes into the Governor's column, with the prospect of Sullivan's fifty-eight if the boss could be induced to cast them for Wilson.

Because, unlike the fight over Parker, the deal with Sullivan was a quiet affair, Wilson's progressive image remained untarnished.[5]

The next major floor battle arose over the venerable unit rule, which, thanks to the leadership of Wilson's managers, was partially abrogated. Meanwhile, Bryan continued to worry about the presence of "plutocrats" on the floor. On the 27th, he demanded "the withdrawal from this convention of any delegate or delegates constituting or representing the . . . interest" of J. P. Morgan, Thomas Fortune Ryan, or August Belmont— including Ryan and Belmont themselves. An explosion of voices rocked the hall. The resolution, shorn of its key expulsion provision, eventually passed by an overwhelming margin.[6]

Just before the balloting began, McAdoo and a number of others met in McCombs's apartment to plot their strategy. McAdoo was convinced that the Wilson forces could win if his managers acted astutely enough. They must hold back Clark on the early ballots and wait for Wilson's second-choice strength to tell. But as delegates poured into Baltimore McCombs had, according to McAdoo, taken no steps whatever to organize them. Despite House's coaching, it proved difficult to tie the nervous manager down to a definite plan of action. Eventually, however, an outline of basic strategy began to take shape: it was decided that Congressman A. Mitchell Palmer of Pennsylvania should be parliamentary leader and chief Wilson advocate on the floor. Congressman Albert S. Burleson of Texas would command the delegates, with the aid of McAdoo and Thomas P. Gore, the blind Senator from Oklahoma. McAdoo was further responsible for gaining fresh support from Southern delegations. Wilson's managers collected information on each convention delegate, and Wilson men were assigned about five delegates apiece for proselytizing.[7]

Further preparations evolved on a daily, ad hoc basis. Each morning, the Wilson managers convened at the Emerson to plot the day's strategy. Whatever they lacked in numbers, they managed to make up in enthusiasm. Some Wilson men paid frequent visits to neighboring delegations; others circulated large amounts of literature. McAdoo made a point of getting in touch with the leaders of each Wilson contingent on the floor and talked with every friendly delegate he possibly could. He also kept in communication with McCombs, who had a seat on the platform.

At 2:08 on the morning of the twenty-eighth, Judge John W. Wescott stood to nominate Wilson. But before Wescott could open his mouth, gigantic banners unfurled and a parade of Wilson men surged onto the floor. It was an hour and fifteen minutes before Wescott had a chance to give his speech. But despite the uproar, the initial balloting proved disappointing. The Wilson managers tried to secure pledges from Wilson, Harmon, and Underwood supporters never to vote for Clark and had con-

cluded a working agreement with the Underwood men, who held the
balance of power. If the Wilson cause became hopeless, the Governor's
votes would be thrown to Underwood. In return, the Underwood forces
agreed to stay behind their candidate, helping to head off the possibility of
a Clark stampede. Hence, the Clark boom was held in check by the combined forces of Wilson, Underwood, and Harmon, and the first ballot
stood:

Clark 440½
Wilson 324
Harmon 148
Underwood 117½

Nor did the situation change appreciably the following day, as the next
eight ballots were taken.[8]

But a crisis was fast approaching. McAdoo realized that New York's
vote for Harmon was mere bluff and that at the right moment Tammany
chief Charles Murphy would suddenly throw his support to Clark. This
would be the crucial point in the balloting, and a stampede might prove
hard to stop. McAdoo asked a friend in Tammany to inform him the
moment Murphy decided to switch. During the roll call on the ninth
ballot, McAdoo got his warning. He rushed across the floor, telling Wilson
men everywhere that the next ballot would probably signal the stampede.
The Governor's lines could hold, he insisted, and Wilson's secondary
strength could reverse the charge to Clark. The forewarning appeared to
steady the Wilson ranks, perhaps even decisively.[9]

But on the convention floor, pandemonium erupted. The Clark delegates paraded around the hall, singing and yelling, and at the height of
the demonstration Clark's daughter suddenly appeared waving an American flag. Bryan shouldered his way through the seething mass of demon-
strators, shouting, "a progressive candidate must not be besmirched by
New York's vote." But nothing could stop the demonstration, and as the
hands of their watches swept an hour away, McCombs, Palmer, and
Burleson ran back and forth across the floor, imploring the Wilson delegates to stand firm.[10]

When the roll call finally resumed, North Dakota was the first State
to be called. "Ten for Wilson," the delegate shouted, and the Wilsonites
roared. As the balloting progressed, it became obvious that there would
be no stampede. At three minutes past four in the morning, the convention adjourned.[11]

III

Exhausted from lack of sleep and the excitement on the floor, Mc-

Adoo fell into bed as soon as he reached his room. He slept four hours, then rose and went to see McCombs. At about ten, he encountered the manager, "in a hysterical condition . . . . He had simply gone to pieces."

"The jigg's [sic] up," McCombs said. "Clark will be nominated. All my work has been for nothing." After a brief exchange he added:

"Governor Wilson himself has given up."

"What do you mean?" McAdoo shot back.

"I talked to the Governor on the telephone very fully about the situation and told him he could not be nominated and that I thought he ought to release his friends, and the Governor has authorized me to release them. I told the Governor that I would have to have a telegram from him authorizing me to do so as his friends in the convention might not accept my statement."

Whether or not McCombs had actually received the telegram is unclear. But at the moment McAdoo understood McCombs to say he had it and accused the manager of betrayal. Then he rushed to the telephone, called Wilson at Sea Girt, and told him:

"You must not think of accepting McCombs' advice. You are gaining strength all the time. Clark can never get two-thirds of the convention. I am sure that your nomination will be the inevitable outcome if you stay in the race."[12]

McAdoo had called just in time. Wilson was preparing to dictate a message of congratulations to Clark. The Governor told McAdoo that McCombs had said Clark would inevitably be nominated. Wilson had concluded that it would be unfair to bind his supporters any longer. He added that he had told McCombs not to release the delegates without first getting McAdoo's approval. The Governor quickly authorized McAdoo to countermand the instructions he had given McCombs, and the crisis passed.[13]

IV

The convention reassembled in a highly charged atmosphere. Wilson now determined to appeal directly to Bryan, and as the thirteenth ballot was being counted he dictated a message. Insisting that the deadlock was enabling the Tammany delegation "to control the nomination and tie the candidate to itself," he argued that the time had come for each candidate to ensure "his own independence" by refusing to "accept a nomination if it cannot be secured without the aid of that delegation." McCombs was sensible enough not to release this message. If he had, it might seriously have endangered Wilson's standing with a number of boss-controlled delegations.[14]

On the fourteenth ballot, Bryan requested permission to explain his vote. The crowd hushed expectantly. As long as New York backed Clark, the Nebraskan announced, he could not; so he was switching to Wilson. The hall exploded in catcalls and cheering; but the deadlock continued.

On Sunday morning, June 30, McAdoo careened about town in an automobile drumming up support. By now, he had clearly emerged as the most important Wilson supporter in the Tammany ranks. When the New York delegation had caucused before the balloting began, McAdoo had fought for Wilson, but without success. McAdoo sat almost immediately behind Murphy in the convention hall and tried to pry him loose from other candidates; but the boss would not budge. Uneasiness had grown within the delegation, however, fed by Bryan's bottomless bag of insults.[15]

Meanwhile, cause for considerable concern had developed in the Wilson camp. Even when it had seemed Clark would surely win, McAdoo had given out statements predicting that Wilson would inevitably be nominated. But McCombs, ever nervous, had been distressed by Bryan's refusal to back Wilson if the Governor accepted Tammany aid. McCombs had been bargaining like a fishmonger for Tammany support, and now he was caught in a vise. On Sunday, he called Wilson and informed him that it would be impossible to secure the conservative help necessary for the nomination unless he explicitly stated that Bryan would not be named Secretary of State in the event he were elected to the Presidency. Wilson demurred.[16]

But another means could be employed for making the most of whatever support existed for Wilson in the New York delegation without splitting with Bryan, and that was to polarize the delegation itself. McAdoo saw his opportunity and at once went to work. It soon became public knowledge that he intended to challenge the vote. The scheme itself was simple: McAdoo or another Wilson delegate would question Tammany's tally and demand a roll call. McAdoo fully expected that Chairman James would rule that the entire delegation must remain in the Clark column in accordance with the unit rule, which still applied to New York; but this would at least offer a means of demonstrating the Wilson sentiment in Murphy's ranks. As it turned out, McAdoo's plan availed little. When New York was called on the twenty-seventh ballot, one of the Wilsonites rose and called for a poll. But only nine delegates declared for Wilson.[17]

V

By now, however, Clark's base of support had slowly begun to erode. On the twenty-eighth ballot, as the Missourian's backers made frantic efforts to rally, twenty-nine of Indiana's thirty votes went to

Wilson. On the thirtieth ballot, Iowa gave Wilson fourteen of its twenty-six votes, and the Governor passed Clark for the first time. Still, this did not add up to a two-thirds majority, and the Wilson drive might stall at any moment. When Illinois was called on the first ballot of July 2, Sullivan delivered the state into the Wilson column. On the same forty-third ballot, Virginia and West Virginia came over. The Clark ranks were crumbling quickly now.

The forty-fifth ballot spelled crisis. Sullivan's support appeared to be shaky. Then Underwood's managers finally conceded. This knocked the last gasp out of the dying Clark movement. On the forty-sixth ballot, Underwood's name was formally withdrawn and Clark's delegates released. Then New York's turn arrived. "Make your speech as conciliatory as you possibly can," Murphy told his lieutenant, John J. Fitzgerald. The echo of Fitzgerald's staccato "ninety votes for Woodrow Wilson" was greeted with applause, laughter, and jeers. As the votes of the last states disappeared in the din, a reporter caught sight of McAdoo.

He ran around the convention hall almost in a frenzy of ecstasy. After adjournment he hugged several of the Wilson men and danced around with joy. In the excitement he lost his hat, but it mattered not to him.[18]

VI

The cheering at Baltimore died away, and the weary delegates plodded out of the convention hall. But after a week of confetti and balloons, whether he knew it or not, the battle of 1912 had scarcely begun for McAdoo. "When the Baltimore Convention adjourned," he later wrote,

I decided that my brief political career was at an end. My objective had been gained—Wilson had been nominated and, because of the split in the Republican Party . . . I was absolutely convinced that his election was inevitable. Moreover, I had become, in considerable measure, disillusioned, not to say disgusted, by my close contact for this brief period with politics.

He continued to insist that "I am not a candidate for political office or position of any sort." Even so, McAdoo's red Mercedes streaking along the road to Sea Girt became an increasingly familiar sight.[19]

There remained the question of what to do with McCombs. A few days after the convention, McCombs and McAdoo's friend Stuart Gibboney met McAdoo at Bayhead. McCombs had told Gibboney that a plot was being mounted to sidetrack the manager and asked Gibboney to help him muster McAdoo's support for the Chairmanship of the National Committee. After threshing out the matter with the two men McAdoo agreed to back McCombs; though he still believed McCombs had betrayed Wilson at Baltimore, he did not wish to add to the Governor's reputation as an ingrate. This represented the consensus among most of the professional politicians in the Wilson circle, despite the fact that a certain amount of pressure developed to shelve the manager. When the National Committee insisted on McCombs, Wilson reluctantly agreed; he distrusted McCombs and probably wanted McAdoo instead, but he felt grateful to the manager, and in any case could afford no charges of ingratitude. Wilson did intend to have strong men around McCombs as an antidote to his idiosyncrasies, however, and would take him only on the condition that McAdoo should become Vice-Chairman. Technically, McAdoo had already accepted; but "I explained to the Governor," McAdoo wrote,

that I could not very well neglect my duties as president of the Tunnel Company any longer; that I had already devoted the larger part of a year to political work and that my board of directors [most Republicans] was becoming impatient over my long absences and neglect of the . . . company.

Wilson replied that he did not want McAdoo to impair his own interests, but he asked McAdoo to sound his board of directors. The men turned out to be quite generous. McAdoo told Wilson that he feared it would be impossible "to do any effective work in cooperation with" McCombs, "and especially under him," but nevertheless he enlisted for the duration.[20]

McCombs then tried to have McAdoo's appointment blocked, as McAdoo had known he would. When the National Committee elected McCombs Chairman in Chicago on July 15, he neglected to submit McAdoo's name for confirmation. On the twenty-fourth, Wilson sent McCombs a telegram ordering him to notify McAdoo of his nomination. A week later, McAdoo, still jobless, wired the Chairman that he had "decided to reconsider the . . . Vice-Chairmanship." Meanwhile, the campaign had been drifting and McAdoo came under pressure from members of the National Committee to start it moving forward; but he was powerless to act. Eventually McCombs capitulated, though McAdoo's formal appointment did not come until August 3. It had been an ominous beginning.[21]

At the meeting of the National Committee in Chicago, the Wilson men took over control of the party. But the most important work clearly would be done by an elite Campaign Committee, often called the "verandah cabinet." At the core of this cabinet was the old Wilson coterie: McCombs, McAdoo, Robert Hudspeth of New Jersey, Daniels, Gore, Willard Saulsbury of Delaware, Palmer, Joseph E. Davies of Wisconsin, Senator James A. O'Gorman of New York, and Burleson. Above all, these men intended to wage an efficient campaign. After the Bryan clan stepped down at Chicago, business methods were finally introduced to the Democratic Party. At Wilson's direction, his managers made this the first American campaign in which expenditures were controlled under a budget. McAdoo, Morgenthau, and Rolla Wells, all successful business-men, lavished attention on the price of everything from parades to pencils. Under the immediate supervision of an expert Hudson and Manhattan accountant, a system of quasi-scientific management was employed which resembled the one used on McAdoo's own railroad. The contrast with the slipshod, graft-ridden Democratic campaign procedures of the past could not have been greater; and the party emerged from the election in the black. The aim of introducing these methods and then hailing the party's newfound efficiency was not merely to put an end to graft but also to prove that the Democrats could govern—something which still demanded proof.

VII

As campaign tactics began to take shape, so, after a fashion, did Wilson's philosophy. The New Freedom, as he called it, focused on the workings of the market, but it went much farther than that: Wilson be-lieved that the national character and democracy itself stemmed directly from the liberty of petty capitalists, men on the make, to "release their energies" and expand the economy. The emergence of huge trusts seemed to imperil all this by closing whole industries to newcomers. In Wilson's view, certain big businesses and (largely unidentified) political "bosses" had formed an oligarchic alliance; the government as well as the economy had been concentrated in the grip of a handful of men and freedom had begun to slip away.[22]

As a result, in his speeches Wilson conducted a determined, though restrained, assault on what he labelled the "system"—the power and de-cision-making processes of the nation's social and economic leadership. He accused Theodore Roosevelt of wanting to make the alliance between government and business permanent by allowing companies to grow as large as they wished under the guise of federal regulation. Amoral, or immoral, corporate values, Wilson realized, would dominate the society if current trends continued; the organization man, not the man on the make, would reign supreme. Individualism and the national character would die along with small enterprise if this happened, and the ultimate victim would be democracy.[23]

Wilson produced a remarkably broad diagnosis of the nation's social and economic ills in 1912, but—and this is the most crucial point about the New Freedom—he negated much of his critique by offering equally narrow prescriptions for curing them. If certain big businesses involved in unfair practices could be restrained and the petty capitalist set free again, Wilson argued, all would be right once more; he clearly underestimated the tenacity of the "system" he intended to defeat. Just as important, he remained uncertain as to how much of a defeat he wished to inflict; he was ambivalent toward accepting large industry as a permanent fact of American economic life, trapped between Roosevelt's belief, which Wilson shared, that big business (along with big government and other huge private and public institutions) had become inevitable and a longing for the creative individualism of the nineteenth century. Louis D. Brandeis, the progressive lawyer who largely shaped Wilson's antitrust program, succeeded in erasing some of this confusion, but his impact on Wilson was limited. After Baltimore, under Brandeis's tutelage, Wilson shifted his focus from the tariff to the monopoly question, but the two problems were inseparable and the basic issue remained exactly the same: how could opportunity be restored and broadened in the United States?

Wilson presented a three-pronged program for the "redemption" and "emancipation" of the nation: he intended to overhaul the antitrust laws, reform the banking and currency system, and slash tariff rates. Each of these goals would require the enlistment of experts on the side of the government, yet in 1912 Wilson repeatedly denounced reliance on expertise because he felt such dependence would short-circuit public debate and amount to a tacit admission that, as Roosevelt claimed, government experts could control business without any risk of falling under the sway of the industries they were supposed to regulate. In addition, the very necessity for a permanent bureaucracy of experts amounted to another admission that Wilson was not ready to make, an acknowledgment that huge corporations would have to be regulated permanently. Expertise, paternalism, size—to Wilson, each came from exactly the same mold.[24]

Just as he denounced trustification and unfair competition, Wilson attacked paternalistic, "big-brother government" in 1912 and seemed to set his face squarely against special privilege of any kind. He intended to democratize America by bringing classes into common counsel rather than consulting only one and without formally recognizing or specifically supporting any, and to unite all interests in a joint sense of mutual reconciliation. The man on the make was uniquely middle-class man endowed with middle-class mores, and in focusing heavily on the middle class, Wilson predictably tried as much as possible to avoid the subject of labor and social welfare legislation. On the other hand, he left the back door open to such measures by arguing that while no class legislation or special privilege of any sort could be tolerated, no such thing as a working class existed—nearly everyone, after all, was a worker. This could be interpreted to suggest that since labor did not comprise a class, labor legislation was unnecessary; or it could mean that since everyone toiled, no labor measures could be construed as class legislation and hence such bills were entirely tolerable. Wilson drew *both* conclusions, leaving himself perfectly flexible on the subject.[25]

But if any one plan caught his fancy as a cure for America's social and economic difficulties, it was not Roosevelt's welfare statism but the prospect of stimulating prosperity through the cultivation of foreign markets. This called for lower tariffs, increased exports, and expansion of the national merchant marine and banking facilities; and it was the origin of several of the biggest legislative battles of the Wilson era.

The New Freedom did not add up to a coherent philosophy in 1912. Wilson had not arrived at a final, comprehensive series of programs to end the larger difficulties he identified—alienation, class conflict, dehumanization, and the distribution of power. Nor did he fully understand the insufficiency of strictly economic solutions or the existence of a permanent working class which would make the welfare state a necessity. He was unwilling to risk class strife by calling explicitly for class legislation. On the critical issues of government centralization and intervention in the economy, he remained substantially noncommittal. His solutions fell far short of meeting the imperatives implicit in his own analysis. On the other hand, this eloquent but tangled philosophical jungle of ambiguity, irrelevance, and superficiality concealed the crucial quality of flexibility. In the end, the general, tentative nature of the New Freedom would turn out to be one of its strengths.

VIII

Ideology was not McAdoo's forte, and during July and early August, he devoted himself largely to the details of the campaign, particularly to the organization of political clubs. The Democrats enjoyed the support of prominent Republican and independent businessmen who backed Wilson either as an alternative to the "reactionism" of Taft and the widely feared welfare state "radicalism" of T.R., or because they suspected Roosevelt of being a trimmer. Typical of the new organizations into which these men were recruited was the Wilson and Marshall National Business Men's League, which arose from a conference between McAdoo and a number of entrepreneurs in September. With headquarters in New York, the League invited any businessman, whether leading industrialist or corner grocer, to join. McAdoo's most important brainchild, the Contributors' National Wilson and Marshall League, first appeared in the South and West and only later moved into the Northeast. McAdoo himself served as president. Once again, the organization directed its appeal largely toward businessmen.

By the time McAdoo had formally been designated National Committee Vice-Chairman, well-founded and embarrassing rumors had begun to circulate to the effect that there had been a split between him and McCombs which had divided National Headquarters into warring camps. McCombs's jealousy and suspicion of everyone around him had flared again. Wilson personally intervened; then the Chairman's ill health temporarily solved the problem. Around mid-July sickness pulled him part way out of the campaign, and early in August neurasthenia completely felled him. On the thirteenth he wrote Wilson that he felt doubtful whether he could carry out his duties any longer.[26]

With McCombs convalescing in the Adirondacks, the campaign began to drift. But soon McAdoo, who knew nothing about steering a national campaign, had seized the tiller and according to one report "was systematizing his work with the air of a man who expected to have to stay for a fortnight or two." "McAdoo has taken hold here and is working very hard and conscientiously," noted Morgenthau. Two weeks later, McCombs wrote McAdoo in confidence that he wanted everything to continue as if he were there, and that he would resign if that might help. This may have been a threat. In any case, McAdoo advised him not to consider quitting.[27]

The organization McAdoo inherited was in anything but good condition. Nearly a month and a half had passed since Baltimore, yet nothing had been done to start the campaign machine rolling. Office space in New York had not even been leased for National Headquarters; confusion prevailed. Though no one knew whether or not McCombs would return, McAdoo had to proceed as if he would. This meant retaining the Chairman's personal staff, which was less than loyal to McAdoo and became frustrated at the impossibility of bending McAdoo's will to its wishes. Despite Wilson's assurances of support, everyone regarded McAdoo's authority as temporary, and he eventually grew bitter over constant attempts by McCombs and his faction to undermine him.[28]

Nevertheless, once McAdoo took over, the campaign shifted into high gear. "McAdoo kept the campaign going at top speed," one of his friends at headquarters later wrote. "When unduly irritated, the acting Chairman swore like a trooper." Using his genius for organization, McAdoo surrounded himself with men who knew politics. On August 21 the verandah cabinet was split up, with half of its members—among them McAdoo, Morgenthau, Daniels, Saulsbury, Palmer and O'Gorman—remaining behind in New York, and Davies, Burleson, Gore, and others moving to Chicago to direct the Western campaign. The bureaus of the New York headquarters were finally staffed, and the new corps of employees fell into the routine like old campaigners. But the Chicago headquarters was plagued by delays.[29]

Late in August, Wilson and his managers decided that the candidate should not stump the country as Bryan always had but should confine himself to making a few speeches in key areas where he received specific requests to do so. The campaign Wilson originally planned was ironically a throwback to William McKinley. But many political veterans wanted the Governor to speak more. By September, with a good deal of effort, McAdoo had finally convinced Wilson that he should plan more speaking tours, which McAdoo himself arranged; and from then on, except for a brief respite after Roosevelt was shot by a fanatic in Milwaukee, Wilson could rarely be seen on the front porch at Sea Girt.

IX

"The money problem was the first thing that confronted us," McAdoo later wrote. "It was extremely difficult to raise the necessary campaign fund." Before McAdoo became Acting Chairman, Morgenthau, Rolla Wells, and industrialist Charles R. Crane had been fishing for dollars but with indifferent success. As soon as McAdoo took command, the effort stepped up. The key to the problem, however, was not so much the amount the managers would have to work with as who contributed it. The Bryan campaigns had largely been paid for by a handful of magnates. But in 1912, Wilson hinted that Roosevelt's cash came from Wall Street and demanded that his own backers be unsullied. As a result, the party called for subscriptions from the public alone. Morgenthau, chairman of the finance committee, estimated that about a million and a half dollars would be needed for the fight, and that the seven million Democratic voters across the nation could easily supply it. "We will absolutely not accept any contributions from corporations," he declared. An effort was made above all to keep the party free of the taint of questionable money, money which would have to be repaid in favors later on. When Cyrus McCormick made a sizable contribution, it was returned because International Harvester had fallen into an antitrust duel with the Justice Department. Meanwhile, Wilson insisted that all donations be cleared through him for final approval. The party published lists of contributors at frequent intervals throughout the campaign.[30]

The New Freedom, then, was to be financed largely by popular donations from those it would serve. "Poor Men's Money for Wilson Fight," headlined the New York *World,* and across the country the Democratic press echoed the sentiment. Newspapers themselves began raising cash among their subscribers, and the apparent certainty of Wilson's election brought in many bandwagon contributions. Through November 30, 89,854 people sent the party over $1,000,000, but donations of $100 or under amounted to less than a third of the total. More than a third came from forty men, and a similar percentage from New York. Nearly half the campaign fund was mustered during the last two weeks, after McAdoo turned control back over to McCombs. McAdoo would have preferred to close headquarters rather than accept money from a questionable source; but McCombs—whose proficiency at drawing in contributions galled McAdoo—proved less fastidious. Wilson grew suspicious of McCombs's methods, and ironically McAdoo's relative inferiority at fund raising increased Wilson's esteem for him. Since Wilson would win in any case because of the Republican split, the total collection probably counted less toward enhancing his public image than the right intentions, and these the Democrats displayed in abundance.[31]

One of the high points of the Democratic campaign was McAdoo's plan for collecting contributions through the banks. On August 18, he unveiled a scheme whereby donations would be received and forwarded as a "Patriotic Service" from all sections of the country by banks and trust companies. This, he argued, would make good the promise of a "campaign financed by popular subscriptions" and remove "the suspicion of sinister influence" from the Democratic Party and, gratuitously, from the Republicans and Progressives as well. McAdoo had hit upon an exceedingly shrewd idea, and the Democratic press instantly picked it up: anyone who opposed the plan blocked the path of virtue.[32]

Once the scheme had been announced, reporters began interviewing leading bankers in cities throughout the nation. Their response was less than enthusiastic, and banner headlines blazed with indignation. Under the circumstances, the Progressives had to go along with McAdoo. But the Republicans remained aloof, and as late as August 20 not a single bank had sent him a response. "The attitude of Mr. Barnes and of Mr. Vanderlip," two of the bankers who had demurred when the idea was first aired, "is not altogether a surprise to me," McAdoo wryly remarked.[33]

In late August invitations went out to various banks throughout the country to join the enterprise; McAdoo felt gratified at the result. By September 7, nearly 2,000 banks had accepted participation, and Democratic politicians admitted they had never expected the plan to be received so cordially. "The best piece of publicity so far," exulted Josephus Daniels. But as weeks passed, an even better one emerged: Wall Street continued to hold out.[34]

Besides money, the most difficult problem the Campaign Committee had to face in 1912 was overconfidence. On his first trip through the Middle West, McAdoo warned that "our only chance to lose would be through . . . lethargy," and this fear continued to plague him throughout the campaign. The dangers became apparent to all in early September, when the disorganized Democrats in Maine were badly beaten by a united Republican Party.[35]

X

While Wilson's political star rose, so, after a fashion, did McAdoo's. In 1910, according to one source, McAdoo probably could have secured the Democratic nomination for Governor of New York if he had been free enough of other obligations to accept. And McAdoo later remembered Wilson's remarking during the campaign

> that he would be very happy to see me Governor of New York. I told him that I would not, in any circumstances, consider it; that I didn't want political office . . . ; that my first duty was to see that the national campaign was carried to a successful conclusion.

But in the weeks after Baltimore, rumors of a McAdoo candidacy steadily increased. *Collier's* came out in favor of him, and in mid-August a pamphlet was published by a group of his friends entitled, "Does New York Want a Real Governor?"[36]

McAdoo had not taken the boom seriously at first, but he soon saw that it had some substance. The National Committee requested that he turn down the nomination even if it were offered. McAdoo continued publicly to deny his candidacy, but the drive went on until it began to worry old-line politicians in New York. McAdoo had publication of the pamphlet stopped, and in late August and early September he issued several public statements aimed at quashing the boom. "To be even suggested for office," he insisted,

> puts me in an equivocal position and reacts to the disadvantage of the national campaign, particularly in this state, because the inference will be inevitably drawn by some people that I am using the powers of the National Committee to advance my personal interests. This would be an intolerable situation for me, and I could not permit it.

With McAdoo out of the race, one question remained for New York's anti-Murphy Independent Democrats: whom could they recruit to run against Tammany Hall?[37]

Wilson's relationship with Charles Murphy in 1912 was a running sore that refused to heal. The campaign managers feared Tammany might "cut" the national ticket if they antagonized the organization. In midsummer Wilson announced that he would not intervene in the struggle over the gubernatorial nomination in New York or any other state, throwing the Independents, who had received little enough encouragement from Wilson as it was, into confusion. Meanwhile, under the leadership of young Franklin D. Roosevelt, a group of progressives in the legislature had bolted the regular Democratic organization and established the Empire State Democracy, an upstate coalition pledged to support Wilson and oppose the domination of Murphy. The clarion call was sounded for a war on Tammany, but the movement made little headway.

In early September, relations between the Wilson forces and Tammany remained delicately balanced, but the Progressives tipped the scales violently with the surprise nomination of Oscar Straus, an outstanding Jewish progressive, for Governor. Wilson and McAdoo publicly commended the nomination.

Their dilemma grew worse when Wilson, on McAdoo's recommendation, attended a state fair at Syracuse with a view toward nailing down two or three Congressional seats which might otherwise go to the Republicans. What occurred at Syracuse on September 12 resembled an ancient slapstick movie reeled off at high speed. At Wilson's behest, McAdoo had received assurances that the candidate could be insulated from the Tammanyites at the fair; but Wilson and McAdoo spent most of their time trying to dodge Murphy, who wanted to talk, and have his picture taken, with Wilson. The ultimate significance of the charade lay in the fact that Wilson had been warring, rhetorically if not substantively, against the old-line politicians of both parties. He was exceedingly sensitive—and vulnerable—to the constant taunt of T.R. and the Republicans that the Democratic Party was boss-ridden. The New York *World* viewed his attitude toward bossism as his supreme test as a progressive, an apocalyptic view of the question commonly shared by the Independents. In no state was it quite so necessary to preserve ideology as in New York. Yet what if Murphy decided to knife the national ticket?[38]

As convention time approached relations with Tammany grew worse. Upstate Independents clamored for war on Tammany and threatened to bolt to Straus if Wilson demurred. With some success, McAdoo pressed Wilson to repudiate the machine. McAdoo also made it clear that Wilson would not stand for the renomination of Murphy's candidate, Governor John A. Dix. He appealed to Wilson to come out actively against Murphy and Dix, advice Wilson rejected. As a sop to Murphy, Wilson switched from his early stand against Dix to a simple demand for an unbossed convention.[39]

A host of dark horses galloped into the race. Murphy announced that while he favored Dix, he would leave the convention entirely unbossed, and he seemed so sincere that he tricked the Empire State progressives into believing it actually was. After several ballots, Murphy threw the garlands to William Sulzer. Delighted despite Sulzer's Tammany background, the Empire State Democrats withdrew the slate of candidates they had nominated ten days before and pledged their support to the ticket.[40]

XI

"The campaign was an exciting and tremendously interesting experience," McAdoo later recalled.

It is a tremendous inspiration to find yourself a part of a great movement to maintain definite principles of government and to fight for policies which you believe are vital to the nation, and to feel that you are striving with unselfish purpose to achieve something for the common good.

But by September, time had begun to run out for McAdoo as Acting Chairman.[41]

On the fifth, McCombs returned briefly from the Adirondacks to confer with Wilson. The Chairman was still unwell, Wilson observed, but "his mind will not rest easy (which is very important to him) until he has the details in hand." Meanwhile, McCombs's antagonism toward McAdoo still simmered. "No human being within my knowledge," McAdoo later wrote, "could even approximate McCombs in his insane jealousy and envy."

In all my experience, I had never encountered such an extraordinary Jekyl [sic] and Hyde in political life. McCombs certainly had two sides, highly developed, and the evil side was chiefly in the ascendent.

A harsh judgment; but by most accounts, a fair one.[42]

The Chairman's supporters had already cultivated House when McCombs himself came to Boston to confer with the Colonel. McCombs "told a story of perfidy that was hardly believable," House wrote. "McAdoo was the ringleader and he, McCombs, was the victim." The Chairman also tried to make a hundred dollar bet with the Colonel that Wilson would lose! House, who barely knew McAdoo, at first felt sympathetic toward McCombs; but Wilson advised him to suspend judgment until he learned what was going on at National Headquarters. From the Colonel, McAdoo discovered for the first time (or so he later remembered) the existence of the cabal working to undermine him with Wilson and destroy his position in the campaign. The coterie had also been pouring fuel on McCombs's highly flammable jealousies. Though at first a partisan of the Chairman, House wrote that

later I found that it was almost wholly McComb's [sic] fault and that McAdoo was scarcely to blame at all. McCombs was jealous, was dictatorial and egotistical. He was not well enough to attend to the campaign himself, and he could not sit by and allow McAdoo to carry on the work and get a certain amount of newspaper publicity. This latter was particularly galling to McCombs.

But because he already felt vulnerable to charges of ingratitude, Wilson realized that McCombs, who repeatedly threatened to resign, simply was not expendable.[43]

By the sixteenth of October McCombs had again taken command. Within a short time, life at headquarters became almost unbearable for McAdoo. There can be little doubt that Newton was substantially correct when he charged that "immediately upon McCombs' return, he set out to discredit McAdoo and destroy all that he had done." The Chairman cancelled one of his pet campaign projects and tried to thwart any recognition whatever of McAdoo, who became so furious that he wanted to fire the headquarters staff. McCombs feared McAdoo's postelection influence and suggested to House that they move McAdoo permanently across the continent by securing the presidency of a Western railroad for him. An interview between McAdoo and McCombs early in October had failed to smooth things over; meanwhile, Wilson grew anxious about the situation.[44]

Conditions at headquarters got worse and worse. The Chairman was "simply impossible," House commented late in October, "and quite crazy on the subject of McAdoo." Racked by pangs of jealousy, McCombs retreated behind a wall of secretiveness, alcohol, and intrigue; and once again he began to bargain with bosses. If not Wilson's only link with these men, as House claimed, the Chairman was certainly the key link. Meanwhile, McCombs remained in ignorance of the fact that, as House put it, Wilson "thinks of him as a crazy man and desires to quiet him."[45]

Efforts at conciliation having failed, McAdoo agreed to move to the rear of the campaign. "I will eat all of the crow that may be necessary to preserve the peace here and insure your election," he told Wilson, and he even offered to resign. McAdoo did a truly splendid job of retreating from leadership, one which must have put him through sheer torture. On the last day of October, the Colonel observed that McAdoo had "almost effaced himself to secure harmony," much to the gratitude of Wilson. But no matter how admirable his magnanimity and restraint, he was unable to escape the lure of the chase, and Roosevelt and Taft were on the run. With McCombs back, McAdoo was freed from the arduous problem of managing the campaign, and, at first reluctantly, he began accompanying Wilson on his speaking forays. McAdoo also engaged in a daily newspaper debate with George Perkins, his counterpart as beneficent businessman in the Progressive organization, and with Charles Hilles, chairman of the Taft campaign committee, over the great issues of 1912.[46]

By the time McAdoo stepped down as Acting Chairman, the results of the election no longer remained in doubt—if, indeed, they ever had been. On election day, as Wilson joked with friends and strolled with McAdoo and others along the placid lanes of Princeton, he piled up a popular plurality and one of the most lopsided electoral college victories in history. Wilson won 435 votes to Roosevelt's 88 and Taft's 8. Both houses of Congress went Democratic.

"I feel," Oscar Underwood wrote McAdoo two days after the election, "that there is no one man among us all that is entitled to more credit than you are for the proper handling of the political situation." Since

May, McAdoo had ridden the Wilson bandwagon to the forefront of public life. Yet one question remained to be debated by pundits in the weeks to come. Did McAdoo want to stay aboard?[47]

CHAPTER FIVE

SECRETARY OF THE TREASURY

The election of Woodrow Wilson was followed by a torrent of speculation over whom he would bring into office with him. The press had long slated McAdoo for a place in the Cabinet. Yet in the months following the election, on House's advice, McAdoo went back to his railroad and saw almost nothing of the President-elect. Turning down a victory celebration friends planned in his honor, he temporarily cut himself loose from everyday political affairs; but his interest in politics retained its razor edge.

I

McAdoo and House had become warm friends, and they consulted almost daily during the interregnum between the election and the inauguration. Through the Colonel, McAdoo kept au courant with the shaping of the Wilson Cabinet. The two men privately agreed that the circle from which Wilson would have to choose was not overburdened with talent; as House observed, the Democratic Party had been out of power so long that its members were untrained to hold office. "House had a number of times suggested that I ought to be made Secretary of the Treasury," McAdoo wrote.

I talked candidly with House about this. I told him that I could not afford to enter public life; that I had said that I would not accept any office if Mr. Wilson was elected President and that I didn't care to be considered.[1]

For months, it is true, McAdoo had been insisting that he would not take an office under the new Administration. And yet within a short time after the election—and, perhaps, well before—he began to develop a taste for the Cabinet. Possibly it was at first unconscious. But hunger deepens when it goes unfulfilled; and because Wilson was slow in choosing the members, McAdoo's hunger turned into a craving. Even if it had not been there before, and even if it had been suppressed, this craving could not be completely hidden any longer.

If he was to be offered a place, McAdoo wanted only the Secretaryship of Treasury or War.[2] It seems that the President-elect had made up his mind to put McAdoo in the Cabinet by late December, though the specific department remained in question. House thought McAdoo well suited to the Treasury, despite the fact that McAdoo had recently been having financial problems with the Hudson and Manhattan and lived in the Northeast—a suspect locale from which to pick the custodian of the Treasury. The Colonel told McAdoo of his conversations with Wilson, and from then on McAdoo was overcome with nervous anticipation together with alternating cycles of elation and depression. By December 23, House found it harder and harder to calm him down; McAdoo telephoned every few hours. Meanwhile, no doubt bemused, House wrote:

The more I see of McAdoo, the better I like him. He is a splendid fellow, whole-souled, and generous without a tinge of envy, and, with it all, he is honest and progressive.[3]

In a conversation with House on January 8, Wilson speculated whether McAdoo would accept the Governor Generalship of the Philippines. The Colonel responded that McAdoo would only consider a place in the Cabinet, and then they pondered his suitability for Postmaster General. House thought McAdoo would be ideal for this key political post, and at this meeting they almost fitted him into it; only McAdoo's obvious preference for the Treasury kept him out of the position. On February 1, the Treasury was offered. It took little coaxing; McAdoo was ecstatic.[4]

Aside from the appointment of William Jennings Bryan as Secretary of State, no Cabinet nomination stirred as much interest, or controversy, as McAdoo's; and none aroused such fervent last-minute opposition.[5] In part this was because McAdoo did not have a record in public office behind him, and because his political influence in his home state was minimal; yet the opposition focused on his reputation as a promoter and his supposed connections with Wall Street. No one could question the beneficence of McAdoo's Public be Pleased policy; but early in March, William Randolph Hearst's *New York American* began circulating rumors that the Bryan wing of the party had begun pressing the Commoner to block McAdoo's appointment because of McAdoo's alleged ties to the Morgan interests through Harvey Fisk and Sons. Rumor also had it that a Morgan henchman had been working hard to get McAdoo the Treasury portfolio. According to the New York *World,* the battle against McAdoo was conducted by Democrats of all stripes who worried about his alleged association with the "interests."[6]

Though Bryan denied allegations that he would make a major attempt to stop the appointment, he may well have been uneasy about it. The Commoner had a high personal regard for McAdoo, but he also had reservations about McAdoo's connections. Once McAdoo and Bryan were confronting each other regularly across the Cabinet table, however, McAdoo (who had never voted for Bryan and had gone for Taft in 1908) became a champion of the old silver advocate against his detractors. The lurking suspicion which McAdoo felt Bryan harbored toward him as a result of his New York associations rapidly dissipated and the two men became close friends.[7]

McAdoo later believed that Wall Street had greeted his appointment with outright dissatisfaction. Never in and of the New York financial community, he was considered a mere promoter—a term he despised because of its connotation of dishonesty; and he was widely believed to have insufficient familiarity with broad economic problems to be qualified for the post. Then too, he happened to be a Democrat. But the appointment aroused considerably less apprehension in New York than all this would suggest. In May, a prominent financial columnist observed:

If the private and personal opinions of many of those who are identified with banking and financial operations on a great scale could be assembled and published, it would be discovered that, without dissent, Mr. McAdoo is regarded as the strong and wise intellectual force in the Cabinet of President Wilson. Furthermore, he is neither radical nor blindly conservative.

The main question Wall Street financiers had been asking was, who would run the Treasury? The answer clearly left them well pleased.[8]

But if New York felt satisfied, so, in all probability, did the public at large. The press depicted McAdoo as "a man of pronounced executive genius, a financier of broad and intimate knowledge and yet not so intimate as to make him the toady of Wall Street." His knowledge of the methods of the "money power," the argument went, would prove a positive asset in his new post. There was another side to this analysis. Many looked to McAdoo as a ballast of "safe and sane progressivism" against the Commoner's "possible radicalism." The prospect that McAdoo would serve as a counterweight to Bryan doubtless seemed no less attractive to urban progressives than to Wall Street conservatives.[9]

McAdoo's appointment easily went through the Senate on March 5. Congratulations poured in from the financial elite of the nation, content enough with McAdoo because there seemed little reason not to be. He might be an unusual businessman—but at least he was a businessman. Before long, however, some of these men would be far less certain that the President had given them a "safe" Secretary of the Treasury.

II

While the public and press speculated over his probable policies, McAdoo moved his family into a narrow, uncomfortable four-story house in Washington. Two of his daughters still lived at home, and the elder stepped in as head of the household.

McAdoo knew few people in the Capital, but in a short time he would be meeting hundreds. When the Cabinet first convened on March 5, there were several familiar faces at the table besides the President's. Josephus Daniels had been appointed Secretary of the Navy, Burleson had taken over as Postmaster General, and Bryan sat on the President's right as Secretary of State. David F. Houston, a former college administrator and the best-trained economist in the Cabinet, was Secretary of Agriculture; Lindley M. Garrison, capable and uncompromising, Secretary of War; Franklin K. Lane, recently of the Interstate Commerce Commission, Secretary of the Interior; William C. Redfield, former Brooklyn Congressman and a foe of Tammany Hall, Secretary of Commerce; William B. Wilson, once the leading spokesman for workers in the House, Secretary of Labor; and finally James C. McReynolds, cold and proud, Attorney General.

It took McAdoo little time to master the essentials of running his department, and this was fortunate; for the duties of picking subordinates, distributing patronage, and framing legislation had fallen to him even before he took office. McAdoo had a genius for selecting personnel, and he chose his official household very slowly in order to winnow out men of ability.

The most important task involved finding capable Assistant Secretaries. In February McAdoo had sounded Robert Woolley of Virginia, a former antitrust investigator who had played an important role as publicity agent during the campaign. After the inauguration the offer was made, but by now a complication had arisen: McAdoo had decided to appoint John Skelton Williams, like Woolley a Virginian, Assistant Secretary in charge of fiscal affairs. Then something went wrong: some-

one—perhaps McAdoo, possibly the President—decided that only one
Virginian should get an Assistant Secretaryship of the Treasury at a
time. Woolley accepted the Auditorship of the Interior Department instead, and McAdoo later appointed him Director of the Mint. Meanwhile,
word of Woolley's impending Treasury assignment had leaked to the
press. After it had been canceled, Robert La Follette laid siege to the
department editorially. Woolley was thoroughly progressive and an enemy
of the Virginia machine, and La Follette began asking pointedly if the
forces of "privilege" were going to remain in command at the Treasury.[10]

The particular object of La Follette's spleen was McAdoo's appointee, Williams, a man who, in La Follette's eyes, absolutely epitomized
the "interests." In time, it would become clear that Williams had been
ironically misjudged. The scion of an old Virginia family, Williams per-
petually wore a cutaway coat that symbolized his adherence to customs
of an older America. Militant, fearless and impulsive, he would soon
poison his reputation in financial circles because of a determination and
will that brushed aside subtlety and compromise.

Williams's career had run remarkably parallel to McAdoo's. It opened
behind the doors of his father's bank in Richmond; but the focus of
Williams's attention soon switched to railroads, and by the age of thirty-
four he had organized and consolidated the Seaboard Air Line, aggre-
gating some 3,000 miles of track which stretched from New York to
Florida. Then he ran into reverses: after a sharp battle with Thomas
Fortune Ryan in 1904, he lost control of the line and part of the family
fortune as well. Perhaps this experience was what endowed Williams with
an almost pathological distaste for Wall Street.

McAdoo and Williams had been longtime friends and business associates when McAdoo weaned him away from Roosevelt to Wilson in the
spring of 1912. Describing himself as an "independent, sound money
Democrat," Williams, unlike Woolley, had been friendly with the Virginia Democratic machine. He was precisely what McAdoo needed: a
man of keen financial and business acumen. Early in 1914, McAdoo
switched him into the Comptrollership of the Currency. By that time,
Williams's reputation as a conservative had undergone a marked transformation. Convinced that the "interests" had too long held undue sway
over the Treasury—and much given to Populist rhetoric concerning the
"ravenous, cruel, and crazed" confederation of financiers in Wall Street
and "the vicious power of invisible government"—he set out to wipe
away this blight.[11]

McAdoo tendered another Assistant Secretaryship to Charles S. Hamlin, who had held the position during the second Cleveland Administration.
Hamlin first turned McAdoo down, but he offered to reconsider. When

McAdoo telephoned him late in July and asked again, Hamlin agreed to think it over. It was too late, McAdoo replied; the nomination had already been sent to the President! The Senate shortly confirmed Hamlin's appointment as Assistant Secretary in charge of the customs service.[12]

The choice proved excellent. One of the most prominent Democrats in the Republican bastion of New England, Hamlin was progressive, had rendered Wilson important support in 1912, and had the enthusiastic backing of Louis Brandeis and other Massachusetts reformers. Judicious, cautious, and precise, perhaps Hamlin's dominant characteristic was orderliness. He had an almost incredible penchant for detail. More important, Hamlin had earned a reputation as one of the country's leading experts on fiscal, tariff, and customs matters.

During the New Freedom years the top personnel of the Treasury Department underwent a number of changes. When Williams took over the Comptrollership, Hamlin replaced him in the fiscal bureau, and subsequently became Governor of the Federal Reserve Board. Hamlin was followed by William P. Malburn, a Denver lawyer and former banker, who had made a favorable impression on McAdoo during the fight over currency legislation. Malburn took the customs post late in March, 1914, eventually being elevated to the fiscal bureau. In August, 1914, Andrew Peters, a former Massachusetts Congressman who had played an important role in framing the Underwood Tariff, was appointed to the customs division. The final figure who served as Assistant Secretary during these years, Byron Newton, had previously been McAdoo's private secretary and chief lieutenant in the 1912 campaign.

III

Filling these relatively personal appointments was a minor task compared with what followed. In one of his first official acts as President, Wilson authorized a statement that he would refuse to see office seekers unless he solicited the interview himself. Instead, the horde of hungry Democrats, out of national power for sixteen years, would be turned loose on his Cabinet members. Within boundaries set down by the President, the department heads, in consultation with House and Joseph Tumulty, Wilson's private secretary, would make their own appointments. Though only a tenth as much patronage was dispensed by the Treasury as by the Post Office Department, McAdoo controlled far more positions than any Cabinet member but Burleson, and he became a prime target for the onslaught.

As soon as Wilson won, the scent of plums wafted its way to Democratic noses, and from then on McAdoo found himself hounded by

place seekers, a large proportion of them Southerners. With the inauguration, a tide of Democrats swept into Washington. McAdoo's office
became so thronged that when one high outgoing official tried to reach
McAdoo's desk to tender his resignation he could not break through and
finally mailed it in. McAdoo attempted to escape from this siege of place-
hunting dervishes by heading for New York on weekends, but he might
as well have tried to outrun an avalanche. After ten days of this he had
reached the verge of nervous prostration and his office was still jammed;
so he issued a public statement insisting that applications be submitted by
mail.

For the first month, McAdoo wrestled with the patronage problem
almost to the exclusion of any other. Yet he continued to move slowly,
insisting on competence in the appointees even if it meant (as it often
did) antagonizing large numbers of Senators. Meanwhile, in many of his
early appointments, he took counsel with Colonel House. The massive
shakeup some observers had predicted did not materialize. McAdoo
wanted the turnover Democrats demanded, but despite widespread criticism that the Administration was holding its fire against Republican officeholders, he insisted on cleaving to the spirit of the civil service law—
which, in fact, was strengthened materially within the Treasury Department under his tenure. Newton complained that the law had hemmed the
department in so tightly that hardly any jobs could be opened up without
securing an executive order. Then too, under an act Taft had signed the
day before he left office, the customs service had to be reorganized and
a large amount of prime Presidential patronage liquidated. Eventually
Wilsonian legislation would create a number of fresh appointive positions.

In later years, McAdoo criticized Wilson for paying too little attention to party organization. Preoccupied with other matters, McAdoo
wrote, the President failed to realize the power he could amass by working consistently to strengthen the party on a national basis. Progressive
Democratic factions were vying for support throughout the country, and
initially, in keeping with New Freedom ideology, Wilson had intended
to ignore a number of allegedly conservative machine Senators, men who
later lined up solidly behind his legislative program. "The President,"
McAdoo observed,

had fully made up his mind not to recognize these Senators in matters of
patronage, but I saw, after a short time, that it would be a serious mistake
to discriminate against them in this way and that it would be unjust as well.
It was upon my insistence [though others, notably Burleson, were successfully insisting as well] that the President allowed me to treat them, in patronage matters, just as I did other Democratic Senators. Afterward he was very
glad that he had taken this course.

Treasury patronage was Senatorial, and McAdoo made a point of accepting these men's recommendations whenever the candidates measured up to requirements. He viewed bossism as less of a threat to the nation's welfare than the President did, and he had no intention of simply writing off all "regular" or "machine" politicians.[13]

As time passed, Wilson recognized that his legislation would be endangered if the regulars were starved, and his enthusiasm for succoring the progressives, along with his interest in the patronage problem itself, waned. Into the breach, where only the veto power of Wilson and House remained to check them, stepped the regulars, Burleson and Tumulty among them. The result was that the plums went to factions already in power. This sometimes operated to the benefit of the progressives, especially in the Northeast; but often it did not. Despite McAdoo's assurances to the progressives that they would be well treated, he had only limited control; and indeed, he funneled much of his own patronage to the regulars. As a result, many of the tears of disappointed Wilson supporters were showered on McAdoo.[14]

In some states patronage had to be divided between contesting groups of Democrats, and no one was satisfied; elsewhere compromise proved impossible. Such was the case with the Boston Collectorship. After a great deal of factional infighting, McAdoo, House, and Tumulty settled on Edmund Billings, the president of a Boston trust company. Interested in social settlements and prominent in Boston's good government movement, Billings had voted three times for Bryan and had been a strong Wilson supporter. In contrast to the delight of Massachusetts Wilsonians over the appointment, the protests from organization Democrats were deafening. The President grew disturbed over the row, but McAdoo stood firm with Billings. Ultimately Billings got the position, but bitterness over McAdoo's patronage policies in the Bay State rankled for years.[15]

IV

The appointment of Billings involved no concerted, preplanned attempt to smash the Boston Democratic machine. Nor, perhaps, did McAdoo originally harbor such intentions for New York. Publicly, at least, he tried to remain oblivious to party affairs in most states. But whether he wanted to or not, it was almost inevitable that McAdoo would be forced to swim in the rough currents of New York politics.

Most of the positions Tammany wanted from the Administration came from the Treasury, and the organization expected McAdoo and most of the other Cabinet members to be generous. Yet in order to grow, the Independent movement, too, would have to be nourished with federal patronage, especially since the machine controlled the bulk of state offices. McAdoo understood this necessity, advising Burleson that "our

friends in New York are having 'ahelluva' time, and it would be very
opportune if a little recognition could be given to some of those who
fought hardest for the Governor." But as the offices were being doled
out, this advice fell on barren ground. "It distresses me beyond measure,"
McAdoo wrote Tumulty in August, 1913, "that the real friends of the
President are not being appointed to positions in New York State."[16]

Despite his anxiety over this, at first McAdoo resisted the temptation
to intervene directly in New York politics. This did not last long. From
the day he left for Washington, McAdoo was spoken of as ideal timber
for various offices in the Empire State, and now and then small booms
got started. Like McAdoo, House wanted to "cleanse" New York—to use
the Colonel's highly suggestive imagery—and render state and city
government more "efficient." House respected McAdoo's political agility,
and by early March, 1913, the two men had agreed on the principles of
a fundamental strategy for war on the machine. The first offensive would
put an Independent behind the Collector's desk at the Port of New York;
the second would capture the Mayoralty; and the third would place a
"proper man" in the Governor's chair two years hence. The President
supplied a name for the organization his two advisers contemplated:
the New Democracy.[17]

A legend has flourished among historians that McAdoo planned to
use this organization as a steppingstone to the Presidency. Like many
legends, this one is misleading.[18] In 1913, attempting to destroy the power
of Charles Murphy resembled trying to knock down a rock wall with an
automobile. The wall might be breached but it was not likely to tumble,
and the car would suffer mightily in the process. Though identified as an
Independent, McAdoo was not precisely persona non grata with Tammany
at the time he entered the Cabinet, and if he wanted to further his own
political fortunes, he would have done far better to come to terms with
the machine, or at least leave it alone.

Why, then, did Wilson, McAdoo, and House decide to take on
Tammany Hall, with the prospective rewards so slim? The answer, at
least from McAdoo's standpoint, seems to have stemmed from the very
special place Tammany occupied in progressive demonology. Though at
first less opposed to machine Democrats than the President, McAdoo had
no great love for them either. In part this was a matter of sheer principle. But surely he also knew that the maintenance of the Administration's reform credentials required that antibossism be indulged in at
least in the Empire State. Before the Baltimore convention, the city
machines had been among Wilson's most powerful antagonists; Tammany
had been most notorious of all. New York offered at least one opportunity to restructure the party from the grass roots up, in preparation for

future elections. Opposing other Democrats came as nothing new to McAdoo; he had consistently voted against the party's Presidential candidates for more than a decade and a half. Middle-class, good government, antimachine reform campaigns had become common in the Progressive Era; the logic of Wilson's ideological positions and McAdoo's own political background dictated such a contest in New York.

But working with the Independent Democrats involved profound difficulties. Almost incredibly factionalized, they could only be glued together through a series of shifting coalitions. It proved terribly hard to get them to unite even at election time; they seemed to thrive on division. The Independent factions ranged from semisocialists on the left to conservatives and even reactionaries on the right. There was a profusion of titles like Anti-Tammany Jeffersonian Alliance, Anti-Boss Democratic League, and Anti-Murphy Democrats. But beyond aversion to the machine—or at least to present leadership of the machine—methods and goals were kaleidoscopic. Some Independents, like John Purroy Mitchel, were non-Tammany to start with and could fight tenaciously in the interest of a drastic change in party leadership. Others had long been affiliated with Tammany but hated Murphy. In Rochester, Louis Antisdale, editor of a local newspaper and an original Wilson man, actually controlled part of the city's Democratic organization.

Some Independents were capable politicians, but others often acted overtly, even proudly, antipolitical. This attitude toward party is crucial to understanding the New York Independents; for while many of them believed in organization, it proved extremely difficult to draw them all into *one* organization. The root of the problem grew precisely out of their independence, and McAdoo and House soon found that they were trying to fashion coalitions out of sand.

The Independents wanted, as House put it, "some assurance that in the future no Tammany or near Tammany appointment be made." For this kind of patronage dispensation, coordination would be vital, and as his chief lieutenant and personal representative in New York McAdoo chose Stuart Gibboney. A former Virginian now practicing law in New York, Gibboney had been an important Wilson supporter in the recent campaign. Apparently McAdoo gave him something approaching carte blanche over appointments. Meanwhile, McAdoo attempted to obtain a strong political post for Gibboney in New York, and here he stumbled badly. He wanted to make Gibboney District Attorney, but this proved impossible. And when McAdoo tried to secure the Assistant Attorney Generalship at the New York Customs House for his friend, he encountered the icy hostility of McReynolds. Despite the President's intervention in Gibboney's behalf, the Attorney General's opposition

approached the fanatical. Months of pressure from McAdoo merely deteriorated the relations between the two Cabinet members. Late in February, 1914, when it had become apparent that Gibboney's chances were
nil, McAdoo unsuccessfully tried to persuade the Attorney General to
name House's Independent son-in-law, Gordon Auchincloss, to the post.
Meanwhile, thanks to McReynolds, McAdoo's chief patronage dispenser
in New York had no official position.[19]

While this skirmish dragged on, McAdoo fought a far larger battle
over the most important Presidential office in the state, the Collectorship
of the Port. Several days before the inauguration, McAdoo had asked
Franklin Roosevelt if he would like this post or an Assistant Secretaryship of the Treasury. Roosevelt turned both jobs down. After two more
declinations had been received and a third candidate had been dropped,
McAdoo and House finally settled on Independent Frank Polk. On April
11, McAdoo's recommendation went to the President. But Roosevelt,
Antisdale and others found Polk's anti-Tammany credentials wanting
and protested. McAdoo was caught in a crossfire: O'Gorman, whom the
Administration had not consulted as much as it might have regarding its
patronage policies, and who had grown suspicious of McAdoo's motives
in New York, had not been involved in the choice. The Senator submitted his own list of candidates, which did not include Polk. It quickly
became clear that O'Gorman would never consent to Polk, and that a
sharp Senate fight might be in the offing. But McAdoo could be just as
stubborn as O'Gorman; when Wilson suggested naming an anti-Tammany
Democrat from O'Gorman's list, McAdoo and House stood their ground.
Both men urged the President to force confirmation, and as late as April
18 Wilson promised to send Polk's name to the Senate. Then it became
apparent that the President was faltering. McAdoo told House that he
had an inclination to resign if Wilson sustained O'Gorman. For if this
occurred, McAdoo feared, his own influence would be obliterated, and
he might as well leave Washington.[20]

Wilson's fears were reasonable enough: if he antagonized O'Gorman,
he knew, it might imperil the fate of his infant legislative program. On
May 6 and 7 Wilson and McAdoo conferred, and agreed on John Purroy
Mitchel for Collector. O'Gorman went along with this. It was well that
McAdoo and O'Gorman had united on the President's selection of Mitchel, because before he talked with McAdoo on the sixth Wilson had
already decided to seize the initiative and make it. In choosing Mitchel
the President may have intended to deny both McAdoo and Tammany
political sway over the Customs House.[21]

In effect, McAdoo and O'Gorman had both triumphed, and only

Tammany, which considered the appointment a declaration of war, lost. McAdoo had wanted Polk, he said, in order to obtain "an efficient and non-political administration of the Customs House," and because he and Polk were friends and could work together. He could get the same efficiency from Mitchel, however, and on top of this they, too, were friends. But the Independents had learned that in filling the most important positions in the state, their desires would not necessarily be served by the Administration; and McAdoo had learned that if these wishes were not met with precision—in short, if Washington made any gestures toward compromise or conciliation—many of the Independents would bolt.[22]

Mitchel took office in June, and resigned early in October, 1913, to run for Mayor. Wilson, who apparently tried to keep the Administration out of the election, intended to reappoint him Collector in the event he lost. But Mitchel's Fusion ticket attracted the complete support of McAdoo, who lent his name fully to the campaign. When Mitchel won and Tammany lost control of the Assembly, it was a signal for the Independents to take the offensive; Tammany's lifeline of national, city, and county patronage had been partially severed. Dudley Field Malone, who had been serving as Assistant Secretary of State, was chosen to succeed Mitchel as Collector (a move acceptable to O'Gorman, who happened to be Malone's father-in-law). During December, 1913, and January of the following year, the New Democracy—a coalition of upstate Independents, the Mitchel group, and part of the Brooklyn organization—was cemented together.[23]

But if Wilson had ever entertained any enthusiasm for the program, it soon withered. A sine qua non was Mitchel's personal willingness to fashion an anti-Tammany organization in New York City, but he demurred, announcing that he intended to stay out of the New Democracy's contest with the machine. Faced with the prospect of splitting the party in Congress as well as throughout New York, and probably influenced by Mitchel's aloofness, the President sold his stock in the McAdoo-House reform organization during the spring of 1914 and bought paper in another firm of "reformers" created by Tumulty, the new Governor, Martin Glynn—and William F. McCombs. Fearing Democratic defeat in the Congressional and state elections of 1914 if the war on Tammany continued, they presented a prospectus to Wilson that called for Administration recognition of the supremacy of Glynn and McCombs in the New York Democracy in exchange for a purge of Tammany leadership. This plan was a sham—the ensuing reorganization had Murphy's public approval and quite probably his private approval as well; and Murphy retained his grip on the state committee. But the President discovered too late that he had bought watered stock. The change in leadership was minor and merely symbolic. "Acting through McCombs," Arthur Link has pointed out,

Wilson had in effect agreed to call off his war against Tammany in return for promises of good behavior and support of national Democratic policies from Murphy and his allies.[24]

In the meantime, McAdoo and the Independents proceeded as if they had the President's help. They had started late; but at least they were starting. House, who was to act as behind-the-scenes adviser, arranged for McAdoo to function as a one-man clearing house for appointments. Agreeing with the Colonel that all the men they chose should be progressives, McAdoo clearly picked most of the collectors according to this plan. A vast number of threads were involved in weaving an anti-Tammany organization, and McAdoo did far more than his share of the work. "I am having more trouble about these small appointments in . . . New York than in all the rest of the United States," he wrote. Yet the more he applied himself to the task, the more confusion and dissatisfaction seemed to arise:

I have never seen anything like the conflict of views and ideas among the Democrats of New York. Everyone gives me different advice. It seems impossible to satisfy one element, without displeasing another. Where there is such hopeless confusion and diversity of opinion among the members of the party, how can we at Washington be expected to always do the right thing and the wise thing?

"New York situation!" McAdoo wrote House in June, 1914. "What a mess it is!"[25]

While the dispensation of patronage followed its circuitous course, the Independents and regulars also fought over Senatorial and Gubernatorial nominations. William Sulzer had been impeached and ejected from office in the fall of 1913, ostensibly for dishonesty, but in reality, no doubt, for scrapping with Tammany. He was succeeded by Glynn, but in the upcoming primary fight Glynn had to defend his incumbency against John A. Hennessy. Meanwhile, Franklin Roosevelt—with whom McAdoo maintained a consistent political alliance—squared off against James W. Gerard, Ambassador to Germany and organization candidate for the Senate seat. The Hennessy-Roosevelt ticket was fully supported by Mitchel; by most, though not all, of the Independents; and by McAdoo, who had urged Roosevelt to get into the race in the first place and made a strenuous effort to keep Gerard out. The New York Congressional delegation grew bitter over McAdoo's interference. Under pressure from both sides, the President first equivocated, then sided with Glynn and Gerard. Administration spokesmen received instructions to stay neutral.[26]

Hennessy and Roosevelt were badly beaten, and though Hennessy deserted to the Republicans, McAdoo, House, and a number of Independents took up the standard of Glynn and Gerard. Despite the fact that Mitchel and Glynn came to an agreement by which Glynn would have the Mayor's backing, Tammany men ran Glynn's campaign and he showed little inclination to salve the feelings of the Independents. But the President insisted that McAdoo back Glynn and Gerard, and McAdoo's public support of the ticket was outspoken and uncompromising. Privately he remained less than enthusiastic, complaining of the weakness of the ticket and warning Wilson:

Mr. Gibboney and your loyal friends in New York undertook to make the best fight possible to preserve and hold intact the best element of the party in the state, in order that it might have some semblance of organization for use in your behalf in the contest that must come in the future. When that contest comes your only dependable reliance in New York will be this decent and independent element. . . . if they are properly supported in the future, it may enable them to destroy Murphyism and to regenerate the New York democracy.[27]

Despite the defeat of Roosevelt and Hennessy, the Independents had made very heavy gains in the state committee, capturing about a third of it. The outcome of the primaries and the compromise with Glynn did not prove decisive setbacks; nor did massive Democratic losses in the general election (the GOP won the Governorship, the Senatorship, and the Legislature). Indeed, according to one authority, House and Malone managed to move into the vacuum and regain leadership over the Administration's political policies in New York. But in the next two years, the same toxins that had stunted the growth of the Independent movement went on to kill it.[28]

The key to success was patronage, and the correspondence among the Independents alternated between elation and despair as crucial appointments were won or lost. In order to funnel jobs to the Independents in politically meaningful fashion, a consistent patronage *policy* was essential. A Treasury program developed but not an integrated Administration policy, and as a result the Administration probably wound up with fewer friends in the state than if it had allocated all its positions to either one side or the other.

From the beginning it had also been obvious that the tangled threads of patronage would have to be collected in the hands of one man in Washington or in New York itself. No one realized this better than McAdoo; but though he strove for "harmonious action, under decent and intelligent leadership," he apparently did so with growing reluctance. He doubted that the Independents could be guided by anyone; yet they continued to insist on leadership.[29]

At one time or another, Gibboney and Malone were both chosen to coordinate patronage, but according to Antisdale both proved ineffective. Franklin Roosevelt considered McAdoo the only man who could supply proper leadership. McAdoo was not averse to taking the tiller; he wanted the President to turn matters in New York entirely over to him, if possible. But in any event he wanted someone placed in charge so the ship would not continue to drift. If it did, the Independents had made it clear that they would start lowering lifeboats.[30]

From start to finish, however, the assault on Tammany lacked effective support in Washington. Most striking, and damaging, was the behavior of the President himself. The Independents acted, after all, in his name. Yet the problem of pushing his legislative program through Congress was more important to him than a political crusade in New York. Of the bare twenty-seven vote margin the Democrats held in the House in the Sixty-fourth Congress, Tammany Congressmen wielded sixteen; and from the beginning their support of Wilson's reform measures had been as conditional as it was crucial. Rather than hold the wheel himself, the President let McAdoo and Burleson steer in different directions, and this simply alienated both sides.[31]

Besides Wilson, Burleson proved the greatest disappointment to the Independents. The Postmaster General dismissed McAdoo and Malone as "amateurish," and wanted them isolated completely from New York politics. "His idea," House complained when Burleson told him he wanted to build up the regulars, "seems to be that you can make a progressive out of a reactionary by giving him patronage." Another stumbling block was McReynolds. And in the Senate, O'Gorman managed to stall the appointment of Independents even after they had finally been nominated. Between them, these men confirmed the image of Administration indecision and hostility. But not all of the trouble lay in Washington. Mayor Mitchel, who wanted to starve Tammany, did so by giving most of the city patronage to his Republican allies.[32]

This muddling left the Independents suspicious and bitter. The appointments of 1914 were more favorable than those of the preceding year; but in 1915, according to Antisdale, two thirds of the federal officeholders in the state were politically undesirable, and many Independent appointees had not yet been confirmed by the Senate. Meanwhile, Mitchel grew angry at Wilson for turning on him. And other problems developed. Often Republican incumbents remained in office far too long to satisfy the office-hungry Independents. And sometimes McAdoo's collectors were hard to manage, dispensing patronage within their own domains to political undesirables. The Independents' morale dropped, and they felt positively persecuted by Washington. The disposition of an office resembled throwing a bone to a pack of starving hounds; there was not enough to go around, and even the Independents began clawing at one another. What McAdoo wrote of Antisdale could be said of many others: "I have given him everything he has asked for heretofore, but nothing seems to satisfy him except his own way." Old factionalism endured, and new divisions appeared. By the summer of 1915, it looked to House as though McAdoo and Gibboney conducted one concert of Independents in New York, and Malone, Mitchel and Polk another, and each side thought it was leading the entire orchestra. Meanwhile, McAdoo and Malone carried on their own private feud at a time when unity was utterly crucial.[33]

Still another problem was that a number of individuals, some of them highly controversial, claimed to be acting in the name of the Administration. One authorized representative followed another, each undoing much of his predecessor's work. And plenty of resentment, much of it unjustified, smoldered against McAdoo's own representative, Stuart Gibboney. As early as 1913, though popular among some Independents, Gibboney had become a much-persecuted man, and he did not prove outstandingly successful as a political wire-puller. Yet McAdoo stayed with him.

As the election of 1916 approached, a chance still existed to salvage the anti-Tammany movement. But at the Democratic state convention in March, the Independents were weakly represented and went unrecognized by McAdoo or anyone else in the Administration. Washington soon nullified their success in apparently preventing the election of Glynn and Alton Parker as delegates to the upcoming national convention. In May, 1916, the President authorized House to offer Glynn a place on the soon-to-be-appointed Shipping Board. And, in part through the aid of McAdoo and Tumulty, Glynn became temporary chairman of the Democratic national convention. McCombs was nominated for Senator, perhaps, as Frank Polk thought, to jar McAdoo and attract funds from stockbroker Bernard Baruch; for the sake of party harmony, McAdoo lent his support. Meanwhile, at least through the end of July, he publicly kept out of the battle over choosing candidates in New York.[34]

The clouds of disaster parted briefly with the nomination of Samuel Seabury for Governor. He was a man McAdoo could support with enthusiasm, and had been, privately, as early as June. Murphy went along with the Seabury nomination, but Tammany's support was halfhearted. In November, deprived of sufficient votes in New York City, Seabury lost the election.[35]

Meanwhile, in April, the President had offered the Postmastership of New York to one of the most honorable and capable men in Tammany,

State Senator Robert F. Wagner. Wagner turned it down. Having undoubtedly miffed many Independents with the Wagner offer already, Wilson avoided McAdoo's candidate and instead picked Joseph Johnson of Tammany Hall. He told House that he had tapped Johnson explicitly "because it would please Murphy, and Murphy could help him carry out some beneficent legislation and help in other directions where he thought needful."[36]

Perhaps only the selection of Murphy himself could have antagonized more people; certainly no appointment the President had made in New York ever stirred such an outcry. Eventually the uproar led Wilson to drop Johnson and nominate a more palatable regular to the post, but the damage had already occurred. The Johnson affair administered a symbolic coup de grace to the expiring Independent movement. By now, Polk, Malone, and doubtless other Independents were seriously worried about McAdoo's political activity in the state. House's interest had narrowed until it lay "wholly in world politics and [the] international situation." He urged McAdoo to emulate his own Olympian aloofness, pointing out that people claimed McAdoo was trying to organize a machine which would drive him into the Presidency. McAdoo's interest in New York, it appears, had been ebbing, but as far as the Colonel was concerned it did not ebb fast enough. "I have warned him for two years or more that he was pursuing the wrong course in New York," House wrote late in 1916, "and as he has sown so must he reap." The two men the Independents most heavily relied on, then, slowly drifted out of New York politics.[37]

The legacy of a political war waged in idealism was bitterness. McAdoo reflected this in a letter he wrote the President in the autumn of 1914, after the first few battles had been fought and lost:

To those of us in New York who know only too well the meaning and the effect of the activities of the Murphyized New York "machine" and its affiliated selfish interests, and who, before the Convention and since have been your strongest friends and supporters in the face of every kind of difficulty, it has been discouraging that a consistent policy in opposition to the "machine" in New York has not been pursued from the beginning of your administration. My own efforts, my dear Governor, have been constantly back-capped and thwarted. I feel that I ought to tell you this because I have felt keenly the mistakes that were being made in New York. . . . If the administration's policy since March 1913 had been one of consistent opposition to the "machine", unmistakably manifested through its appointments to office, and in other ways, I am sure that the nominees of the party today would be of such a character that Democratic success in the state would not be the least in doubt.[38]

In 1912, Wilson had argued that American democracy had begun to give way to oligarchy, to a cynical alliance between businessmen and political bosses. Yet within two years, the Administration had come to an understanding with virtually every Democratic machine in the country. Throughout the spectrum of New Freedom ideology, nothing died more quickly in practice than antibossism. In part this was because the realities of passing legislation forced Wilson to choose between attacking local political machines or passing bills which might destroy oligarchy, or at least mitigate it, at the national level. It was a distinction Wilson undoubtedly did not want to make; but from the standpoint of his legislative program, at least, he chose correctly. On the other hand, particularly in the case of New York, the internal strain the policy imposed on the Administration turned out to be extreme.

CHAPTER SIX

THE CLASH OVER THE FEDERAL RESERVE, I

Late in 1913, Congress passed the most important piece of financial legislation between the Civil War and the New Deal. From that time until their deaths, several of the principals in the struggle for the Federal Reserve Act argued over which of them deserved the greatest credit for the measure. For the most part, McAdoo gracefully stayed out of the squabbling. But McAdoo himself was among the half dozen key figures in the passage of the act and in the pattern of events that followed.

I

The Wilson Administration, as McAdoo once put it, attempted "to put out the fires of agitation" by dousing them with legislation. In 1913, much of the agitation centered around the state of banking and currency, and it emanated from progressive and conservative circles alike. The national banking system had been largely fashioned during the Civil War and was remarkably uncentralized, uncoordinated, and dysfunctional in time of crisis. Contemporaries criticized the "inelasticity" of the currency supply and argued that the economy suffered when the amount of coin and paper money in circulation failed to expand and contract with the needs of the business community. This criticism, it has since become clear, overlooked the fact that deposits—which by the early twentieth century com-

94

prised a major part of the monetary supply—were elastic. Their expansion and contraction was limited only by the amount of reserves held by the banks. The main problem lay in the rapid depletion of reserves that occurred when business cycles took a downward spin. More than anything else, the country needed a central financial institution that could create reserves, one endowed with the authority to hold the reserves of the commercial banks and increase them through its own power to grant credit. But large numbers of Americans had opposed such an institution since the days of Andrew Jackson.[1]

While contemporaries did not see the fundamental nature of the banking and currency problem with the clarity of hindsight, periodic financial eruptions repeatedly demonstrated that something was wrong. After the panic of 1907, Congress passed the Aldrich-Vreeland Act, a stopgap measure designed to provide $500,000,000 of emergency currency; but the necessity for a major overhaul still remained.

Two fundamental questions were crucial to the money and banking debate. First, who would control any new financial system—the government or the bankers? Second, would the commercial banks or the government fill the nation's currency requirements? These questions were far from new; they went all the way back to Andrew Jackson's time. Debate also focused on a third issue, whether the new reserve system should be centralized or decentralized. In resolving these problems, ideological lines quickly blurred. But the heart of what might be termed the progressive position was a demand for government currency and domination by Washington. Conservatives generally wanted the opposite.

The Aldrich-Vreeland Act had provided for the creation of a National Monetary Commission to investigate the situation. Comprised of members of Congress under the leadership of Senator Nelson Aldrich, the commission spent four years studying the problem. Aldrich also presided over the highly secret and tantalizingly conspiratorial framing of a bill by some of the nation's leading bankers, among them Paul Warburg of Kuhn, Loeb and Company, who claimed paternity of the measure. The bill provided for a weak central bank with little government participation in its operations. Embodied in the report of the National Monetary Commission, the measure went to Congress early in 1912. It attracted a great deal of support from the financial community. But because it was patently a bankers' bill, because the House fell to hostile Democrats, and because of widespread antagonism toward Aldrich himself, the measure was stillborn.[2]

Meantime, a National Citizens' League for the Promotion of a Sound Banking System, organized by businessmen and heavily supported and financed by bankers, had taken root, and its branches spread over most of the nation. As Chairman of its Executive Committee, the group chose Professor J. Laurence Laughlin of the University of Chicago. Early in 1912, the League endorsed the Aldrich bill; but later it steered clear of advocating, at least formally, any particular measure. Instead, it tried to educate the public toward acceptance of certain principles of "sound" banking.

While Wilson had been campaigning, public sentiment for financial reform was stimulated by the revelations of the Pujo "Money Trust" investigation, spearheaded by counsel Samuel Untermyer. Its statistics spoke volumes on the power of Wall Street in the nation's economy. As Wilson entered the Presidency, he fell under a bombardment of advice and demands for banking legislation. Somehow he would have to balance himself on a tightrope between the Bryan wing of the party, which abhorred the Aldrich plan, and the bankers, who abhorred Bryan. It was not going to be easy: by mid-April, 1913, nearly a dozen banking bills had been introduced in Congress.

Meanwhile, a stream of letters begging for financial reform had been pouring into McAdoo's office. He was swamped with so many plans that he found it impossible even to read them all. No one, perhaps, wanted change more than he did. Wilson made it clear that McAdoo would take charge of the executive forces in the battle for legislation, and, under the general direction of the President, cooperate with the managers of the bill in the House and Senate. McAdoo, who had no set plan for reform, also had to educate himself in banking matters. Knowing that he could play only a minor role in framing tariff legislation, which he considered secondary, he spent all his spare time on the banking question, studying the various proposals and making frequent trips to the subtreasury in New York. There, as well as in Washington, he discussed the issue with leading bankers from various sections of the country. But he also made a point of keeping his distance from these men.[3]

Though McAdoo spent much of his time with bankers, he talked with other financial experts as well. Among them was Laughlin and a former student of Laughlin's who, in the long run, would prove more important in the framing of the Federal Reserve bill: H. Parker Willis, former professor of economics at Washington and Lee University and associate editor of the New York *Journal of Commerce*. Willis had been chosen as expert of the legislative subcommittee of the House Committee on Banking and Currency. He had also collaborated with Laughlin in writing a book advocating changes in the nation's financial system. Willis would play an important role in McAdoo's life during the next few years; but somewhere along the line, McAdoo developed a distaste for him which was, to put it mildly, acute.[4]

During this early period, McAdoo also got in touch with Robert Owen of Oklahoma, head of the Senate banking committee. But the most important legislator McAdoo talked with was Carter Glass, a peppery Virginia Congressman who would soon become Chairman of the House Banking and Currency Committee. The two men had never met until McAdoo moved to Washington, but they became good friends.[5]

II

In the campaign of 1912, an effort had been exerted to avoid a confrontation over the banking issue, though whoever won would clearly have to do something about it soon after he became President. Wilson had discussed the question without delving into details. The Bryanesque Democratic platform had merely alluded to the need for reform and declared against the Aldrich bill or any other central banking scheme. "As it stands, it leaves the Democratic party practically free to adopt any plan which may be laid before them," Laughlin grumbled. But this freedom proved almost priceless in the tortuous bargaining that lay ahead.[6]

Willis's appointment as expert had given him considerable leverage in framing banking legislation. He kept in close touch with Laughlin, and in June, 1912, Willis assured his old professor that he had drawn up a draft bill for Glass "along the lines of which you and I spoke." The Congressman appeared to be interested.[7]

Wilson and Glass talked for the first time on December 26. Never totally enthusiastic about the Aldrich scheme, by now the President-elect had a good idea of what he wanted instead. He suggested that the dilemma of controlling a regionally decentralized system, which he preferred, be resolved not by allocating supervision to the Comptroller of the Currency, as Willis and Glass had proposed, but instead by appointing as the "capstone of the edifice" a central governing board. Glass and Willis went to work to incorporate this provision into their measure. On January thirtieth Wilson and Glass conferred at Trenton, where the President-elect tentatively agreed to the new draft bill. It envisioned the creation of a Federal Reserve Board, comprised of six public members and three bankers. They would control a system of at least fifteen regional banks which member institutions were to own. These regional banks would perform various central banking functions, including the issuance of currency, for which they would be liable, against gold and commercial assets.[8]

The Glass bill now had to run three gauntlets at once. One was Robert Owen, irritated at the way Glass and Willis had framed a measure without him. Owen wanted to make reserve notes obligations of the government and to reduce the role bankers would play on the Federal Reserve

Board. He had written his own bill, which had the backing, in principle, of Bryan. But eventually Owen was persuaded to introduce Glass's measure in the Senate.

A second danger was Bryan. Without the Commoner's active support, the Federal Reserve bill might not pass; with his active opposition, it almost certainly would flounder. Practically from the day he took office, Bryan had been asking anxiously about the President's attitude toward the question. For answers, Wilson referred him to McAdoo, who at first had only a general idea of what was transpiring. Embarrassed Treasury officials tried to placate the Secretary of State by assuring him he would find the bill acceptable. When Bryan did finally get a print, he issued a virtual ultimatum calling for government currency—a proposal seconded by a large segment of the Democratic Party and by the AFL; for a purely governmental Federal Reserve Board chosen by the President; and for changes in the sections regarding public deposits so as to insure continuous control over these funds by Washington.[9]

Sometime in mid-May, at Wilson's request, McAdoo conferred with the Commoner in an attempt at least to minimize his differences with the rest of the Administration. McAdoo's performance in office had wiped away Bryan's apparent suspicions of his alleged ties with Wall Street; the two men had become fast friends and even confidants. McAdoo outlined the Federal Reserve bill, and they debated its provisions. After telling Bryan that he agreed with the Commoner's support for government note issues, McAdoo tried to persuade him to endorse asset currency, which Bryan had always opposed. They also discussed the possibility of a circulation tax on Federal Reserve notes, something McAdoo wanted to be left flexible. Bryan seemed mollified, but the precise results and significance of this meeting are impossible to determine. It may have been a turning point in the history of the bill, or it may not.[10]

Whatever the truth of the matter, Bryan did not easily bite the Administration's hook. He insisted on government note issues and a purely governmental Board. Brandeis's ideas also ran in this direction. The only recourse was capitulation, and ultimately, after discussing the matter with Glass, the President notified the Secretary of State that Federal Reserve Treasury notes would be substituted for regional bank notes and that Washington would take entire control of the Board. Bryan finally swung his weight behind the measure, but for the conservatives, the price of winning him over had been high. Willis later observed that for better or worse the changes had transformed the system from "business" to "political" control.[11]

The third source of opposition to the Glass-Owen measure came from bankers, many businessmen, most economists, and most of the press. "The germinal principle of the bill," the *New York Times* complained in June, "appears to be distrust of banks and of bankers." The measure was broadly denounced as "socialistic," but opposition also focused on specifics. Easily the most important issue was the problem of control: bankers and their allies demanded representation on the Federal Reserve Board, if not outright hegemony over it. They considered a minimum number of reserve banks, well below the twelve eventually settled on, imperative; and they wanted to dominate these, too. Bankers thought the bill gave too much power to the Federal Reserve Board, arguing that the authority of the Board over member banks must be limited; that asset currency should be issued, and by the reserve banks themselves, not by the government; and that any scheme for guaranteeing deposits should be rejected.[12]

Yet a remarkable amount of disagreement split conservative ranks along lines of both policy and geography. Though widespread sentiment favored the Aldrich bill, for example, a number of important bankers disliked it. Almost from its inception, a bitter schism rent the National Citizens' League over the question of whether it should promote specifically the Aldrich measure or adopt a more flexible stance (as Laughlin preferred). Wall Street nourished a flourishing animosity toward Laughlin, and he found himself denounced as a deserter among the Aldrich group and persona non grata in the Glass circle as well.[13]

During the first days of the House hearings in January, 1913, the New York *Journal of Commerce* lamented the "deplorable diversity of view upon some important points" among the leading bankers who testified and predicted that it would "greatly impair their influence upon legislation." Actually, the nation could boast little expertise, even among its outstanding bankers, on broad concepts of central banking; and this, combined with their own internecine quarrels and a certain measure of apathy in the financial community, undoubtedly sapped much of their influence in shaping legislation. "The bankers have never been able to agree on anything," Laughlin wrote. Their feuding helps to explain why many bankers threw their support to the Glass-Owen bill; it seemed the only alternative to chaos. And the squabbling left men within the Administration plenty of room for maneuver. If no phalanx of bankers stood rank upon rank against the Administration, the Wilsonians did not have to place a premium on unity either, especially when the Glass bill was in its early, secret stages.[14]

McAdoo, Glass, and Owen glimpsed the importance of keeping moderate businessmen, who were in the majority, friendly; and more than anyone involved in framing banking legislation, McAdoo tried to draw these men into the battle on the side of the Administration. Meanwhile, a number of other Democrats, the President included, unfortunately failed to differentiate between conciliationist businessmen and outright intransigents.[15]

III

May was an eventful month in the history of the Federal Reserve bill, and a controversial one. Fathoming what happened, insofar as that is possible, involves passing through a labyrinth of charge and counter-charge, claim, and counterclaim, of personal antagonism and political machination.

During March, April, and early May, the Glass bill went through another form, termed the third draft. According to Willis, numerous changes were made on a day-to-day basis as he, McAdoo, and Glass threshed the measure out; but eventually the bill returned to a form close to the original—"practically all the changes recommended by the Secretary of the Treasury being found impossible and in most cases being withdrawn by him at his own instance." Meanwhile, Willis and Glass squeezed Laughlin out of the picture.[16]

The provisions of the Glass bill had been kept quite secret in order to prevent special interests from clawing at it. This avoided the necessity of making a myriad of compromises before the measure even went to Congress. Possibly the President himself first divulged the substance of the bill in detail when he gave a digest of it to House in April. The Colonel, in turn, leaked it to Warburg and perhaps to other bankers as well; and Warburg drafted a critique, part of which, at least, favorably impressed McAdoo. According to Willis, McAdoo probably was responsible for the first leak of the bill itself. For a while, McAdoo went along quite amicably with Glass's compulsion for secrecy, but by April he became impatient. Sometime in May he gave a draft to House, remarking later that he believed the measure had matured sufficiently for exposure to a wider audience. By the time McAdoo acknowledged the leak, the Colonel had already sailed for Europe. Paul Warburg turned up on the same ship, and wrote more critiques which were later printed and diffused among a wide circle of bankers. Secrecy had come to an end, and on Wall Street ominous rumblings could be heard.[17]

Then, as Glass later wrote,

something happened that momentarily created consternation. The Secretary of the Treasury, who had seemed to favour the Glass currency bill and who repeatedly had been invited to propose any desirable alterations or additions, appeared to have been taking advice on the subject from some of his New York friends. As a result, he invited me to a conference at a Washington clubhouse,[18] where I was astonished to be told that, unless the currency bill should be greatly revised, the Secretary had reason to believe it would be unacceptable to conservative bankers on one hand and to Mr. Bryan and his radical friends on the other.

McAdoo proposed a number of changes that "did not seem at all vital," and Willis was directed to prepare them for critical examination. Meanwhile, Glass received a letter from an important Chicago banker, George M. Reynolds, warning of "seeing . . . evidences of those in high places to scatter on the currency question" and urging that the Glass bill remain the focus of discussion. The man who had scattered, or at least so it seemed, was McAdoo. Within a short time, he invited Glass to the Treasury and handed him the outline of an entirely new bill.[19]

McAdoo believed the Glass measure would find favor neither with the Bryan group nor with the banking interests; that, as Willis put it, the bill would fall between two stools. Beyond this, McAdoo felt eager, as he later wrote,

to do something which would result, ultimately, in putting the entire banking business of the United States under the supervision and regulation of one sovereignty only—that sovereignty to be the Federal Government.

So McAdoo came up with his own proposal. It never assumed a final, definite form. "The truth is," he wrote, "that no *plan* of this sort ever was matured." Probably the scheme circulated with various changes among different groups of bankers. Yet surviving drafts and fragments of drafts suggest the important points he had in mind.[20]

Briefly, the proposal called for the creation of a highly centralized National Reserve system, to be established as a separate division, or bureau, of the Treasury Department, with headquarters there. The administrative board would be dominated by appointees of the government. The secretaries of the Treasury and Agriculture would be represented, along with five Presidential designees. One draft, making a concession to the financial interests, provided for an unspecified number of bankers on the board, though in others McAdoo personally insisted that no member be affiliated with any banks whatever. The Chairman would be the Secretary of the Treasury, and most of the drafts provided for an officer, selected by the President from the appointive members, to manage the board (or bureau), under the supervision of the Secretary of the Treasury.

The nation's banks would be grouped by the board around local reserve agencies, with which they would carry on business; most of the drafts provided that these agencies should be converted subtreasuries, with the majority of their local officers, or sub-boards, chosen by the central board or by the Secretary of the Treasury. One draft provided somewhat vaguely for only five reserve association banks, with headquarters in as many major cities—clearly a concession to bankers' demands; but several drafts allowed from fifteen up to fifty or more branches

or agencies of the central board, and unquestionably the dominant sentiment favored at least fifteen.

Of vital importance to the plan, as outlined in several drafts, was
the retirement of currently outstanding government notes, national bank
notes, certain bonds, and gold certificates (from which, to the horror of
conservatives, the gold held in trust might be reduced or withdrawn), and
exchange, theoretically without inflation, for a fresh Treasury issue backed
by a gold reserve fund of 50 percent of the value of the notes which were
issued. Provision was made for flexibility by supplementary issues. The
existing national banks would supply the necessary capital for the program. The national banks would be given broader privileges than before,
in order to place them on a more competitive basis with state institutions,
and reserve requirements would be lowered. Finally, arrangements were
made for the admission of state banks and trust companies to the system.[21]

Such a summary does violence to complexity and differences between
drafts, but makes it sufficiently clear that the scheme envisioned, as
McAdoo himself put it later, "in effect, a central bank under government control." The

Treasury bureau was to be . . . owned wholly by the government and financed
largely by the Treasury. The essence of the idea was that the government
itself was to become the rediscount agency for the entire reserve system, including seven or eight thousand banks.

The plan handed a major concession to the progressives by providing for
government supremacy and note issues. On the other hand, it contained
provisions which doubtless pleased the bankers: comparatively simple in
operation, it would unify the currency—a prime goal of the reformers—
as well as reduce reserve requirements for national banks. It envisioned
elimination of at least some federal bonds currently held by the banks,
thus quelling the argument over how to deal with them; and it would
guarantee the banks par value for their bonds. Finally, though varying
from draft to draft, the Treasury scheme, perhaps more than any other,
offered a far easier way of managing government funds than the old
system could provide.[22]

Yet in fact the proposal was bound to satisfy no one. As a compromise
between various schools of thought, it suffered from the very defect Mc-
Adoo had ascribed to the Glass bill: it fell between two stools. When Mc-
Adoo first showed the scheme to Glass, the Congressman asked whether
he was serious. "Hell, yes!" McAdoo replied. He urged Glass to consider
substituting it for his own bill. Yet the question remains an open one just
how seriously McAdoo really did take the proposal. It is impossible to
estimate precisely what percentage of it McAdoo actually wrote, or even
how much of it represented his own views.[23]

Glass, understandably enough, thought McAdoo in earnest. Yet in later years, McAdoo denied that he had been swayed, even momentarily, toward advocating "any plan" against "the Federal Reserve Act," and claimed that Glass had taken the National Reserve scheme too seriously. McAdoo's own account of the matter is this:

This idea [the National Reserve proposal] was under consideration about the middle of May, 1913. It intrigued my imagination, but it did not convince my reason. I felt, however, that it might be used effectively as a part of the Treasury strategy in the Federal Reserve fight. The American Bankers Association and all the big banks in the United States were hell-bent for a privately owned central bank. They were bitterly opposed to the Federal Reserve system. In line with my understanding with the President that I would discuss all plans or ideas for banking reform which were presented to me, I took this idea up with some of the leading bankers in my conferences with them in New York and in Washington, knowing perfectly well that they would condemn it. This they promptly did, with the exception of a few who very guardedly said that such a plan had some merit and that it might be made to work. I saw at once that these few were trying to be polite about it for the reason that they thought it good policy not to express, too openly, antagonism to an idea which the Secretary of the Treasury might favor. I told them that the Democratic party, from the days of Andrew Jackson, had been absolutely opposed to a privately owned central bank; that if the bankers forced the fight for a privately owned central bank, they might force into being a government-controlled central bank. I said that the safest course was for the bankers to get behind the Federal Reserve plan and help the administration get prompt legislation along that line. I saw at once that what I said caused the bankers very great concern, and I wanted it to cause them concern. That was the essential element in my strategy. To set up a back fire of this sort, or to make a flank movement of this kind would, it seemed to me, be very helpful in cooling the opposition to the Federal Reserve plan, even though it did not convert any of the leading bankers to its support. I had explained all of this to President Wilson, and he thoroughly understood it and was in accord with my strategy.[24]

No way exists of proving whether this account, written years after the Federal Reserve Act passed, is completely accurate or not. If Wilson and McAdoo were in league together, it was an extraordinarily well kept secret between the two men; they did not even let Colonel House in on it. As late as July 11, John Skelton Williams still hoped that McAdoo would succeed in substituting the National Reserve proposal for the Glass bill. It also seems curious that if McAdoo wanted to build a backfire he should have clearly implied to men he intended to scare that the National Reserve was simply being considered on a "tentative" basis along with a number of other plans, while at the same time continuing to advocate the scheme enthusiastically to Colonel House. Diminution of the importance of the proposal may, on the other hand, indicate that McAdoo himself did not take it seriously. Years after the event even Glass had to admit the possibility that McAdoo had treated the National Reserve merely as one more plan to be considered.[25]

A second vital question about the National Reserve proposal is who conceived it. In his memoirs, McAdoo merely said that "somebody in the Treasury (I do not remember who it was) brought me a sketchy draft" of the plan. Willis believed the scheme had been written by McAdoo alone "or with the cooperation of members of the Treasury Department, among whom was undoubtedly John Skelton Williams." It was "worked out with" the "personal approval" of the President and displayed "traces of the views expressed by various of the President's political advisors." (The role of McAdoo and Williams in shaping the measure, if not in originating it, can easily be seen in the surviving drafts.) Laughlin thought Untermyer might have been involved as well and on one occasion wrote of an *"Intrigue"* between "Aldrich, Untermeyer [sic], House, [and] Warburg . . . to change [the] Bill." "It seemed clear," he remarked, "that Mr. McAdoo was in touch with those people in New York who were trying to impede the progress of the Glass bill."[26]

But it remained for Glass himself to bring the conspiracy theory into its own, binding up with the National Reserve proposal not only McAdoo, but Untermyer, Owen, and House as well. Glass attributed the paternity of the measure to Untermyer and Owen, "with such help as John Skelton Williams may have rendered." McAdoo then supposedly stamped his approval on it. To be sure, much of the scheme fell in line with Owen's ideas; resentful at the way Glass had personally commandeered the banking issue, perhaps he wanted to spite the Congressman. But after approving the plan, Owen reversed himself when Glass told him he was "almost unalterably opposed to it and believed it would create a political revolution in this country."[27]

The connection of Untermyer with the National Reserve proposal would not be an especially significant question if it merely included his involvement, or noninvolvement, in the framing of the measure. For Untermyer was by no means a reactionary; quite the contrary. But McAdoo and Untermyer were friends, and some suspected that despite his public admonitions not to rely too heavily on bankers' advice in shaping legislation, Untermyer acted in the interests of Wall Street when it came to matters of banking and currency. Glass thought Untermyer had used McAdoo in an attempt to "ditch" the Federal Reserve bill. The Congressman had a deeply ingrained rancor toward Untermyer and entertained a devil theory of his every action, partly because Untermyer—who had helped force the Money Trust investigation on the House in the first place and then proceeded to spearhead it—later tried to seize a major role in writing banking legislation. Untermyer attempted to persuade Laughlin, and apparently Willis as well, to produce a bill for him; and he tried to stick his foot in the door by having the responsibility of drawing up a measure transferred to the Money Trust branch of the Banking and Currency Committee, or, one way or another, by obtaining a degree of control over Glass's own subcommittee. This assault on Glass went so far as to contemplate preventing his succession to the Chairmanship. Untermyer failed, and, understandably enough, the Congressman tried to freeze him out of any subsequent participation in framing the House bill. But Untermyer retained considerable influence over other members of the committee.[28]

Also involved in the National Reserve "conspiracy," according to Carter Glass, was Colonel House, who had written the President in code on May 20 suggesting a clandestine meeting between Wilson and Untermyer to discuss banking reform. "I believe," House confided,

that a sound currency bill can be worked out along the lines suggested by Mr. Untermeyer [sic] and one which Primus [Bryan] and Senator Owen will probably accept.

. . .

. . . I explained it over the 'phone, much more fully, to Pythias [Mc-Adoo] and he also thought that something might be worked out that would be satisfactory.

Untermeyer [sic] tells me that some of the bankers here would approve such a measure.

The difficulty is that Untermeyer [sic] wants too large a share in the making of the measure, but I think this can be overcome by bringing about a general agreement between Primus, Pythias, Owen and Glass, after first getting Untermeyer [sic] committed to it.

. . .

Pythias or Owen could get him to Washington and when he was there you could arrange to see him for an hour in the evening and it is quite possible that no one would know.[29]

According to Glass, the Untermyer scheme referred to by House was specifically "the bureau plan." Yet the Congressman did not feel as positive in his own mind that Untermyer fathered the National Reserve proposal as Glass, his biographers, and a number of subsequent historians have suggested in print. "I have reason to believe, but do not actually know, that Untermyer drafted the scheme," Glass admitted years later. Nor, for that matter, did anyone have concrete proof that Untermyer acted in the interests of Wall Street, though he clearly had a foot planted in both camps.[30]

As a matter of fact, the Untermyer plan, whatever it envisioned, was almost certainly not McAdoo's National Reserve proposal. For one thing, while Untermyer and McAdoo may have conferred after the National Reserve plan had been aired, there is no hard evidence to indicate that they had conversed beforehand. More important, on the very day that House wrote the President suggesting an interview with Untermyer, Mc-Adoo sent the Colonel a hurriedly dictated memorandum which was an

early version of the National Reserve scheme. "Since my talk yesterday
with the Secretary"—meaning Bryan—he wrote,

I am more than ever convinced that we shall have to come to something along
these lines if we are going to succeed, and, for my part, I believe that it is
far preferable to anything that has yet been considered. I am, of course, open
to conviction, as my mind is not so firmly set that it cannot be altered. I
should, however, want good reasons . . . to change my views. We run against
so much of prejudice upon the part of the bankers particularly, to any plan
that does not fit their preconceived and established notions, that we shall, I
think, have to cut away entirely from all the mazes and hazes of previous dis-
cussions and bring out something new and simple and direct.[31]

On the other hand, House and McAdoo had talked over the telephone
about Untermyer's suggestions, and the possibility exists that Untermyer's
thoughts provided the kernel of the memo. As McAdoo later remembered it, House had asked him to prepare "a memorandum about a national reserve in the Treasury Department," expecting to meet a man or
men on board ship (Paul Warburg?) with whom it might be discussed.
If McAdoo did make use of Untermyer's ideas, he must have elaborated
on them considerably. The heart of Untermyer's "plan" was government
currency; but many others, including Bryan, demanded precisely the same
thing. Finally, there is McAdoo's own word on the subject. "Untermyer
never had anything whatever to do with the Treasury plan," he wrote
years after.

I never discussed it with him and he never suggested anything of the sort to
me. . . . Neither had Colonel House anything to do with it.[32]

Whatever its authorship, the National Reserve proposal was a variation on one of the most important themes of McAdoo's tenure in office:
the effort to amass more power in the Treasury. In his New Freedom
rhetoric, Wilson had been decidedly noncommittal on the matter of government centralization. Under pressure from Bryan, decisive changes
had been made in the Glass bill which transformed the measure into a
scheme for a government banking system. Whatever else may be said of
it, McAdoo's National Reserve plan would simply have carried all this one
step farther, strictly centralizing control of the money market under the
Treasury itself. McAdoo had already begun to manipulate the money
market in new and creative ways.[33] He had become a promoter in government, utilizing Treasury funds to support important interests, particularly farmers. In the process, his states' rights notions had for the most
part been set aside. If he had one supreme goal, it was to bring the money
market completely under government management so that all these operations could continue and expand. Since the Treasury (together with the
President) determined economic policy, to McAdoo progressive, governmental control quite simply meant Treasury control.

This is both the most vital and the most frequently overlooked aspect of the entire National Reserve episode. The scheme envisioned creation of a new division in and of the Treasury Department, governed by a board whose chairman would be the Secretary of the Treasury. Generally, drafts of the proposal provided that local reserve agencies would merely be converted subtreasuries, with their officers selected by the board or by the Secretary himself. An administrative officer would manage the system under the supervision of the Secretary of the Treasury. And the Treasury would issue the notes.

Despite the plans McAdoo made for enhancement of Treasury power over the money market, he found himself hampered above all by one person: Woodrow Wilson. The President continued to remain noncommittal on the question of precisely who should wield supreme power within the new reserve system. This indecisiveness would lead to chaos once the provisions of the Glass bill went into operation.

As to the progressivism or conservatism of the National Reserve plan, commentators differed—perhaps because they disagreed over what, exactly, constituted a progressive or conservative banking bill. Then too, knots of ambiguity had purposely been tied into the proposal by its originators. Clearly, however, the scheme contained more to please the left than to solace the right, and because of this it may have made the left more restive.

Glass overheatedly labelled the McAdoo plan a "bastard greenback scheme." Laughlin excoriated it as a "wild fiat-money bill." Together with Willis and Laughlin, Glass began distributing copies among the financial community in an effort to drum up support for his position; and while at one point McAdoo apparently thought he had some backing from the bankers—notably from Reynolds—it quickly became apparent that neither Reynolds nor other leading bankers, economists, or businessmen felt at all enthusiastic. Their fears: big government and cheap money.[34]

Though McAdoo's proposal kindled great uneasiness in banking circles, he continued arguing for it well into June. Meanwhile, the National Reserve had cut Glass adrift, and he feared that unless its opponents' made themselves heard, "we shall go to pieces." "We have simply been brought to a stand-still by the new scheme," the Congressman wrote Willis. He feared the President might back the plan in order to attract the support of Bryan and Owen. "It seemed an end of currency reform for the time," Glass later recalled.[35]

On June 5, Glass conferred with the President at the White House, and proceeded to denounce the measure. "I am surprised, Glass, at your vehemence," Wilson replied. "Mac tells me the scheme has the approval of many practical bankers." The prime figure in question was Reynolds, and when Glass—whose appeals to important bankérs for support against the McAdoo proposal had been successful—made it clear that Reynolds opposed the measure, the President apparently saw that Reynolds had either been afraid to tell McAdoo his real views or else had simply been less than frank. "I fear Mac is deceived," Wilson remarked, "but fortunately the thing has not gone so far it cannot be stopped." The next day McAdoo had a long talk with the President. "I expressed satisfaction with the effect that the suggestion of the Treasury plan had already produced on the bankers," McAdoo later remembered.

The President agreed with me, but was a bit disturbed by the concern Glass had manifested. I told him I thought the object had already been achieved and believed we could abandon any further discussion of the Treasury plan. I said that I would notify Glass to this effect at once, which I did.

       .   .   .
    The President had not given any decision against the scheme. . . . the President and I had decided that the objective had been gained and that the scheme need not be discussed any further.

On June 9 McAdoo informed Glass that, while he still considered the National Reserve proposal economically sound, the Congressman's fears of its political repercussions had been well-founded. Legislation should be based on the Glass bill, he went on; the National Reserve plan would be abandoned.[36]

    There the matter ends, with a question mark. Was the Treasury scheme really a ruse, circulated specifically to scare the bankers? Possibly —but not provably—the answer is No. Perhaps time played tricks with McAdoo's memory; then again, perhaps not. In any case, the President had made his decision against the proposal; and, as Glass later wrote, "McAdoo met the situation like a prince. Not for an instant did he exhibit a sign of resentment or even of disappointment. . . . From that moment, he never wavered." On June 26, the Glass-Owen bill, approved by the President and McAdoo at a White House conference with its sponsors, was introduced into both houses of Congress.[37]

IV

    The months of June and July were largely passed in revising the House bill, unifying the Administration forces, and quelling an uprising of Congressional "radicals" bent, among other things, on inserting provisions for agricultural credit, forbiddance of interlocking bank directorates, strict government control of currency and the banking system, and destruction of the Money Trust. Meanwhile, McAdoo tried to stoke a backfire of public opinion behind the measure and patiently explained the bill to bankers in an attempt to persuade them that it was sound. He "helped amazingly" in overcoming the reluctance of new members of Glass's committee to accept a measure they had played no role in drafting and in smoothing over differences within the committee. "McAdoo is one of the few men in the world who can swear interestingly," Glass mused. "During this period he was positively fascinating."[38]

Meanwhile, another complication arose: the price of United States 2 percent bonds began to drop. At the time, McAdoo felt convinced that "concerted efforts" were being made "to produce a [financial] catastrophe." There was good cause to believe that short selling had gone on in New York at artificially lowered prices—selling which, though allegedly due to fear over the fate of the twos, probably served as a means through which the larger banks could recruit the country banks (which comprised the vast majority of the nation's financial institutions) into their own battalions as they confronted the Federal Reserve bill. No doubt the drop did scare many country bankers, whose profit accounts would be seriously menaced if they had to part with the bonds or if the bonds were marked down to market value. Roughly 95 percent of the twos were held by banks, two thirds of them by country banks, which issued currency against them. And the Secretary of the Treasury had the power to call on the banks for additional bonds to secure outstanding currency whenever the market value of the bonds had fallen to a point where extra security appeared necessary.[39]

McAdoo directed the Comptroller of the Currency to conduct a quiet investigation, and

by this means we discovered . . . enough to justify our belief that there was a well-directed effort to depress the value of the 2% bonds and to intensify the opposition of the country banks.

McAdoo was disturbed, and doubtless angry as well. Wall Street had always seemed unsympathetic to the Administration. So, departing from his usual practice of giving the President advance notice of his major moves—ostensibly because he wanted to keep Wilson clear of responsibility and free to repudiate him—on July 28, as the bonds dropped toward a record low of 95½, McAdoo issued a statement virtually accusing leading New York banks of conspiring to depress their value. The twos were worth par, he insisted; no legislation would be passed which would damage the value of government bonds. He added that if a credit stringency appeared, he would issue emergency currency. And he indicated that he did not intend to call for more security from the national banks as a result of the bond depreciation, since the slump resulted not from a drop in their real value,

but almost wholly to what appears to be a campaign waged with every indication of concerted action on the part of a number of influential New York

City banks to cause apprehension and uneasiness about these bonds, in order to help them in their efforts to defeat the Currency bill.[40]

If the announcement revealed a fresh approach to the financial community in the Treasury Department, it also produced stunned comments from Eastern bankers, newspapers, and politicians. The New York *Sun* labeled the charge "monstrous and unbelievable;" the *New York Tribune* compared McAdoo to Bryan. The statement raised smoke in Congress, where a resolution was unsuccessfully introduced to have *McAdoo* investigated. Republicans tried to force him to prove the existence of a conspiracy, but this failed too. There were Democrats as well as Republicans on the Hill who resented McAdoo's charge, for it put an ace in the hands of their "radical" colleagues; the "radicals" immediately and rejoicingly seized the accusation to back up their demands for another Money Trust inquiry.[41]

McAdoo began investigating the bond sales in New York at once, and so did officers of the New York Stock Exchange. While only one short sale seems to have been uncovered, it tended to confirm the suspicion of a conspiracy. McAdoo also discovered that a surprisingly small amount of bonds had been sold during the much touted plunge. The President— confronted in any case by a fait accompli—supported his maneuver. But the future of the bonds continued to be questioned until the banking bill actually passed, and in September the twos sagged again after reaching a high of 98¾ late in August. Once more, McAdoo had to come to their defense; on October 19 he issued a soothing public letter on the subject. He also tried to see that the Federal Reserve bill was written so as to furnish a continuous market for the bonds, keeping them as near par as practicable. Meanwhile, McAdoo attributed the autumn decline to "deliberate misrepresentations" and fear that large numbers of national banks would refuse to go into the new system and would be compelled to market their bonds.[42]

McAdoo accompanied his public statements on the bond question with a good deal of behind-the-scenes maneuvering, and a large percentage of his energy in helping to frame reserve legislation was taken up with the fate of the twos. After an initial deviation, he stuck very closely to what the banks wanted done with the bonds. At a White House conference between Wilson, McAdoo, Glass, Owen, and a number of bankers late in June, the bankers protested a decision—approved momentarily by the President and McAdoo—to strike the bond-conversion provision of the bill, intended eventually to retire the national bank notes. In Glass's view, at least, the major goal of the Federal Reserve bill was to expunge bond-secured circulation. Doubtless the Congressman got even angrier when he discovered that this feature had been removed at the request of Bryan and with the concurrence of Owen. Sometime after the conference, gradual retirement of the bonds was agreed to as bankers desired, with the twos protected. On July 9, after discussing the matter with Glass and Owen, McAdoo issued a statement reassuring the holders that an amendment would be added to the bill retaining the circulation privilege. After some squabbling, a provision was inserted specifying that the bonds should retain all their privileges for twenty years, in line with McAdoo's suggestions. Further changes went in along the way, and with the passage of the measure the market value of the twos finally revived. "There never had been, for a single second," McAdoo wrote, "any purpose on the part of the administration or the framers of the bill to permit any injury whatever to the banks, and especially to do anything that would impair the value of the 2% bonds." Yet his defection to the conversion heresy, however temporary, had also been symptomatic.[43]

Neither McAdoo, nor Bryan, nor Owen wanted to see the entire custodianship of public funds handed over to the reserve banks. Changes were made in the measure which left the utilization of these banks by the Treasury as fiscal agents and government depositories optional, not compulsory. McAdoo's power grew tremendously through the control he retained over depositing the free funds of the Treasury.[44]

Shortly before the bill passed, the conference committee considered a Senate proposal to eliminate the Comptroller of the Currency, who had supervised the old banking system, from the Federal Reserve Board. Apparently with the President's support, McAdoo strenuously and successfully fought to keep that official on and to vest as much power in him as possible. According to Willis, the Comptroller was retained explicitly to avoid arousing McAdoo's opposition. The Comptroller was also rendered independent of the Board, a development of questionable wisdom from the standpoint of the efficiency of the system as a whole but one which significantly augmented the power of the Treasury vis-à-vis the Board.[45]

How should the Board itself be composed? If a single issue hung in the balance, it was the degree of control Washington would exercise over the new banking system. The first draft of the Glass bill had reflected the Congressman's desire for substantial representation of the banking community; and initially McAdoo, who had no preconceived views on the subject, had not been unfavorable to the idea. The banks, after all, were to own the system and seemed entitled to a share in governing it. He had thought that "the Board might be divided about equally" between agents of the member banks and Presidential appointees; and he had suggested that the representatives of the financial interests be chosen from lists presented by the bankers.[46]

McAdoo probably went through his formal conversion to total federal hegemony within the context of the Glass bill at a meeting at the White House on June 17. By now, with the National Reserve battle behind him, his basic position had been defined; his earlier suspicion of a large federal role in the economy had given way to his new desire to govern the money market. At the White House conference, the President proposed that no banking representatives be appointed to the Board and that it be made a purely governmental body. Glass argued that total exclusion would be unjust to the banks. For a time McAdoo backed him up. But Owen went along with Wilson from the start, and eventually McAdoo came around too, suggesting some form of compromise. The meeting proved decisive; McAdoo began writing that "I am unalterably opposed to allowing the banks or any other class or special interest to choose any part of the Government Board." "The more I have studied this question," he told House,

the more I have become convinced that the right measure is the one which puts the Government in the saddle. I am not the least afraid of a Government bank whose functions are limited to dealings with the banks throughout the country, exercising, at the same time an altruistic control which will prevent the selfish and arbitrary exercise of power now too frequently exerted by certain powerful interests in this country.

On the President's recommendation, an amendment was introduced creating a Federal Advisory Council, staffed entirely by bankers, to make policy recommendations to the Board. This was intended to compensate bankers for their exclusion from the Board itself. And the final act provided that a minimum of two of the five appointees must have a background in banking.[47]

Still another argument, one which clearly pitted conservatives against "radicals," involved insuring the deposits of member banks—a suggestion which made many bankers blanch. The Senate bill provided for such insurance, but the conference committee tossed it out. McAdoo considered this a big mistake.[48]

The Aldrich-Vreeland Act was scheduled to expire in June, 1914. Since the new reserve system could not be put into operation by then, McAdoo suggested that the act be extended until the summer of 1915. This was provided for in the Federal Reserve bill, and changes were made in the procedures of issuing emergency currency which made them more workable. McAdoo also backed compulsory rediscounting between one Federal Reserve bank and another, in order to facilitate mobilization of resources in time of stress. In this and most of the other major disputes over the measure, he generally got substantially what he wanted.

V

Meanwhile the bill had been threading its way through Congress. On

September 9 it was reported to the House, and in little more than a week it passed. In the upper chamber progress was stalled by Democratic insurgents in the banking committee, who prevented a favorable report. Then Frank Vanderlip, president of the National City Bank of New York, came up with a new plan of his own, which bore a curious resemblance to the discarded Treasury scheme, and the ensuing wrangle ate up still more time. Behind the scenes, McAdoo had been hard at work. In September he had considerable success in getting most of the amendments he wanted passed by the conference committee, and sometime after the bill passed the House—probably October 11—he took Robert Owen out on a revenue cutter. Dropping anchor some distance down the Potomac, they reviewed the measure for two days, improving a large number of details but leaving the fundamentals intact. At a council between the President, McAdoo, and Colonel House on October 15, an agreement was reached on strategy for driving the bill through the Senate.[49]

But the Senate persisted in delaying, and fear arose that the bill might be stalled through the end of the year. McAdoo, who had previously hoped a caucus would be unnecessary because he did not want to see banking legislation become a purely partisan question, finally backed this expedient as the only means of driving the measure through. After he consulted a number of important Democrats in the Senate a conference was held, and another followed. Early in December formal debate opened on the bill. "The opposition . . . has been largely shattered," McAdoo wrote Colonel House on the seventh. "It is extraordinary how effectively this has been brought about." On December 19 the bill finally passed the Senate, and the following day the conference committee went into session.[50]

McAdoo, who had been working energetically to swing Senate insurgents behind the measure, kept in constant touch with the Democratic conferees by telephone:

While there were stubborn contests over numerous points, the disposition of the conferees was to go as far as possible to meet the views I expressed because it was assumed that I was reflecting the President's views in the matter.

The conference did not end until the early morning hours of December 22, and when Colonel House arrived at McAdoo's home for breakfast he found McAdoo half asleep in his pajamas.[51]

The President signed the Federal Reserve bill into law the next day.

McAdoo fully understood the weaknesses of the act, but in future years he would also acclaim it:

The strait-jacket in which the business and industry of the United States have been cramped and limited by the old financial laws of the Republican party has been shattered and the country may now grow without restriction to the full limit of healthful and legitimate expansion.

As this suggests, by democratizing credit in order to give a break to the small businessman, the Federal Reserve Act fulfilled a major Wilsonian campaign pledge. The measure was intended to quell money panics and unshackle the nation's energy through a widespread dispersal of banking reserves under government direction. It also demonstrated the ability of the Democratic Party to govern—a matter which had been distinctly subject to dispute.[52]

But the Glass-Owen Act amounted to more than a mere economic or political expedient; it seemed to fulfill a vital moral purpose as well. "It will destroy many abuses and much malevolent power," McAdoo declared. "It overthrew the rule of a small group of men. It places great and weak on an equal footing, with equal opportunities and equal advantages." Mere rhetoric? Not entirely. The measure had been designed for the urban and rural middle class, precisely the class Wilson had focused on in 1912. More specifically, it was tailored for the entrepreneur. To say that it democratized credit is accurate; to say that it had a profound "leveling" effect simply reflects the inherent restrictions in the Wilsonian definition of class.[53]

In the process of legislating for the businessman, the Wilson Administration had taken a long walk down the road of centralization. Ironically, many among the group for whom the bill had been written labeled it "socialistic." McAdoo and others could claim that the measure would be good for businessmen, whether they knew it or not. But more important, in McAdoo's view centralization had become essential in order to liberate the pent-up energy of capitalism itself. He fully understood that no inherent contradiction existed between a strong public sector and the welfare and prosperity of the private sector. During the battle over banking, Wilson had learned that his Secretary of the Treasury had few remaining inhibitions about concentrating power in the federal government and in his own office, particularly if that power could be used to steer the economy and make it function more smoothly. To McAdoo, progressivism meant government intervention, and that meant Treasury intervention. McAdoo had emerged as a man on the make inside the government itself; and the President began to view this with alarm.

VI

In the long struggle over the Federal Reserve Act, the Treasury had managed to hang onto a number of its banking functions; much of the financial history of the next few years would be written around its continuing efforts to enlarge this handhold. The act specified that the Secretary yielded none of his powers; where his prerogatives and the Board's appeared to overlap, they would "be exercised subject to the supervision and control of the Secretary." Theoretically he had surrendered most of his de facto central banking functions to the reserve banks. But the authority of the Treasury melded with that of the Board in a number of places, and though unable to gain statutory hegemony over the Board, the Treasury was still able to put a brake on its independence. The monetary and banking power wielded by McAdoo and Williams, who became Comptroller of the Currency in 1914, greatly enhanced their influence. On the other hand, the nation remained saddled with "forty-nine different banking systems," as McAdoo contemptuously put it, and this complex pattern of decentralization undermined his leverage over banking processes as a whole.[54]

The Board, H. Parker Willis ruefully pointed out later, found itself trapped from the beginning. The goals of the financial interests on the outside had not been significantly altered by passage of the Glass-Owen Act; and the Treasury Department constantly strove from within to slip its own net over the system. The upshot was that self-governing, localistic banking was undermined, and control gravitated toward both the Treasury and the big banks. Unquestionably McAdoo and Williams were mainly responsible, because they tried to bring all the reins together and drive the banks as a team. McAdoo unsuccessfully suggested changes in the original law which would have rendered the Board directly dependent on Congress rather than on the banks for its appropriations. And he backed an amendment which would have allowed the member banks to elect only four of their nine directors, the remaining five to be appointed by the Board. But he failed to swing a majority of the members behind the plan.[55]

Though a number of central banking functions had been shunted from the Treasury to the Board, the Treasury's domination of the money market persisted. Again and again McAdoo and Williams stepped in to shape credit policies, and the intent of the act to pull the Treasury out of the market and to put an end to its activities in behalf of special interests —particularly, in McAdoo's case, cotton producers and other agricultural groups—was thwarted.

Several weeks before the reserve banks opened their doors, McAdoo announced that as soon as they did he would transfer as much of the Treasury's general funds as possible to them. Later, however, he reversed his decision. It was not until November, 1915, perhaps in response to Congressional pressure, that he designated the reserve banks fiscal agents of the government. On January 1 of the following year, roughly $9,000,000 was shifted to these institutions. In order to avoid embarrassing them by suddenly opening the dikes and flooding them with business, McAdoo transferred to each the government funds then on deposit with the national banks in its own city. The delay in taking this step, he explained, stemmed from his desire to have the reserve institutions complete and in smooth running order first. He had also hoped that a satisfactory clearing and collection system might be established beforehand. But despite all this, the majority of pet banks and the bulk of the government funds they held went undisturbed because the inactive deposits stayed where they were, and the Treasury made it clear that this situation would continue.[56]

Since the act did not require that the Treasury surplus be held in reserve banks, and left the Secretary free to allocate money wherever he pleased, McAdoo could maneuver according to his own ideas of banking and credit. Soon after the Federal Reserve went into operation, he began insisting on a set of discount rates keyed to the interest of farmers. And his crop-moving deposits continued almost as if the act had never passed. This generated a great deal of friction within the Federal Reserve Board. Early in 1916 an emerging thrust by several members against the power of the Treasury gained headway when one, Paul Warburg, recommended an amendment which would have prevented McAdoo from making such deposits without consultation with the Board and even from placing funds in the national banks without the Board's consent. It was a declaration of war. McAdoo replied that the President could remove any Secretary of the Treasury who abused his powers, and that there was as much danger that the Board might act erroneously as that the Secretary would. Within a short time, the onslaught had been beaten back.[57]

Still another legacy of an earlier era survived: the subtreasury system was not abandoned until 1921, long after McAdoo had left office. True, the act provided that the reserve banks could hold government funds, which the Secretary would switch from the subtreasuries and national banks which had been serving as depositories. But in response to mounting pressure from the Hill, McAdoo stated that "my earnest conviction [is] that it would be unwise to commit the custody of these trust funds to any private institution or institutions." The subtreasuries, in short, should endure; and they did. Not until nearly a decade after the Glass-Owen Act passed did the reserve banks become the chief fiscal agents of the Treasury.[58]

Yet another function regarded as an aspect of central banking in most countries is the supervision and examination of commercial banks. The act defined the Comptroller's powers in this regard; and while it left his authority dangling precariously between both the Secretary and the Board, the Secretary impliedly had the final word. Williams's independence of the Board and its policies led to considerable friction and an eventual attempt by some of his fellow members to bring him to heel, for he refused to share with either the Board or the reserve banks the findings of the examinations. Within two years, he finally abandoned this stand under pressure. The Comptroller also held that all notes must be issued by and through his own office, though he later yielded somewhat on this point, too. Early in 1916 McAdoo directed Williams to consult the Board on every important step he intended to take.[59]

As far as it had gone toward mitigating the weaknesses of the nation's banking system, then, the Glass-Owen Act ·had not gone far enough. It had finally put a steering wheel on finance but neglected to state exactly who should do the driving. As a result, the Treasury and the Board wound up struggling not only for control of the money market but for control of the reserve system itself.

CHAPTER SEVEN

THE CLASH OVER THE FEDERAL RESERVE, II

With the struggle over the framing of the Glass-Owen bill at an end, the raw flesh of group and sectional antagonism which the fight had laid bare could finally begin to heal. But the dispute over the reserve system would continue unabated within the Federal Reserve Board itself. The battlefield merely shifted from Capitol Hill to the Treasury Building, and the course of the struggle was silently recorded in letters and diaries instead of banner headlines.

I

The first tasks that confronted McAdoo after the measure passed involved mapping out the reserve districts and choosing the central reserve cities. National banks must be admitted to the new system, and reserve banks had to be organized. In order to accomplish this, the act provided for the creation of a Reserve Bank Organization Committee, comprised of the Secretaries of the Treasury and Agriculture and the Comptroller of the Currency. When the committee was established, the Comptrollership still lay vacant; and a Senate struggle delayed Williams's confirmation long enough that the entire project had to be completed largely by McAdoo and Houston acting as a two-man quorum. Late in December, 1913, they plunged into the work.

118

They immediately found themselves in a political riptide. The Federal Reserve Act gave the committee the option of organizing from eight to twelve districts throughout the country, each with its own bank. But every major city wanted a bank, whether it had the resources for one or not. Then too, in the South and West, there was constant fear that the Federal Reserve system would crush local financial institutions, and a cry went up for the establishment of twelve districts to insure maximum decentralization. Frantic conservatives, on the other hand, continued to press for eight.

The problems of organizing the system would be extraordinarily complex, and the onset of war in Europe added a new dimension to the difficulties. Yet there was remarkably little time either for observation or for delving into economic theory. McAdoo and Houston decided to hold hearings in fourteen cities in order to obtain the views of local bankers and businessmen as to how the pie should be cut. They were concerned with the general economic and demographic conditions of each region, with industrial and commercial prospects and requirements and the ability of each to sustain a bank, with financial and mercantile connections, and with sectional patterns of trade. In addition, capital must be fairly divided among the districts that were finally established. Purely local sentiment and political expediency, the two men emphasized, must bow before these considerations.

The hearings opened in New York early in January, 1914. At once a question arose as to how large the New York district should be. Some bankers, including Warburg, called for a large district with a high degree of centralization, to help conserve the massive banking power of the Eastern seaboard. But the Organization Committee quickly decided that notions of creating independent, or self-dependent, districts should be scuttled and that districts along the Atlantic seaboard, where the bulk of the nation's financial resources were located, should be small in comparison with those in the interior. McAdoo made it clear that he found no need for New York to be overly endowed, since the entire system would fall under the sway of the Federal Reserve Board anyway. In the end, he and Houston gave these bankers less than they wanted, though a disproportionately large amount of financial power was predictably concentrated within the New York district.[1]

From Manhattan, the two men traveled to Boston, then across the nation. For five weeks they heard from more than 200 communities in every corner of the country. The rivalry was intense: by the time they returned to Washington, thirty-seven cities had requested banks. Twenty-five failed to get them, and a legacy of bitterness endured for years.[2]

The outlining of districts proved far more difficult than the selection

of cities. The entire process was inevitably somewhat arbitrary. There can
be little doubt that political exigencies dictated the creation of a full com-
plement of twelve districts, even had the committee members personally
favored less; to establish fewer would have split the party over the issue
a second time. But since the winter of 1913, McAdoo had favored twelve
on economic grounds alone. The final decision on number and location
was apparently made at a conference between McAdoo, House, Houston
and Williams on March 25.[3]

II

Still less divorced from politics was the selection of members of the
Federal Reserve Board. The choice clearly would not be easy: many men
qualified for the work did not want to divest themselves of lucrative
financial affiliations and come to work in Washington for $12,000 a year.
Then too, public sentiment, aroused by the Money Trust investigation,
would be incensed if Wall Street were strongly represented on the Board.
McAdoo himself expected the "interests" to exert a mammoth effort to
make the members their puppets.[4]

McAdoo considered it vital to secure a body of men who completely
sympathized with the Federal Reserve Act and would administer it for
the benefit of the nation as a whole. And McAdoo needed men he could
influence so that the promotional role he had cut out for the Treasury
could flourish and expand. As early as December, 1913, House supplied
Wilson with a list of nominees; Tumulty and the Colonel wanted them appointed quickly. But McAdoo, acting remarkably out of character, counseled postponement until the entire field of possible candidates could be
carefully surveyed. "The immediate success of the new system," he wrote
the President, "depends almost wholly upon this Board."[5]

From the outset, however, Wilson and McAdoo differed over the
nature and composition of the Board. The President wanted to appoint
six men who could not be dominated by any single individual, including
McAdoo. But McAdoo considered it

essential that they shall be acceptable to your Secretary of the Treasury.
Team work of the best sort is going to be necessary. My difficulties and
responsibilities are great, and if I should be associated with uncongenial men,
who would not work loyally and unselfishly, my usefulness would be greatly
impaired if not destroyed. We must go carefully and deliberately about these
selections.

"McAdoo," Wilson grumbled, "thinks we are forming a social club."
Realizing that McAdoo had never awakened from his dream of controlling the nation's banking resources, the President practically ignored

his advice. The New Freedom had envisioned a promotional role for government, but Wilson had never planned on an energetic promoter like McAdoo using the Treasury to steer the money market directly from Washington. New Freedom thought had been vague enough that it could be accommodated to this, to be sure; but in 1914 Wilson shrank from it. Ultimately, the key figures in choosing the Board were Wilson and House. The Colonel, who had long disagreed with McAdoo over the issue, wanted a Board acceptable to the banking community. In principle, the President supported House; and House substantially dominated the selection process.[6]

By April 28, they had agreed on their team: former Secretary of State Richard Olney; W. P. G. Harding of Birmingham, president of one of the largest banks in the South; Harry A. Wheeler, Chicago businessman and past president of the United States Chamber of Commerce; Adolph C. Miller, a onetime professor then serving as Undersecretary of the Interior; and Paul Warburg. The choice of Warburg and Wheeler was astute insofar as Warburg's presence helped mollify Wall Street, and Wheeler's the business community. Because these names were on the list and the Bryanites had been shut out, urban bankers greeted the slate with enthusiasm. Shortly after Wilson invited him to join the Board, Olney declined, and Wheeler soon followed. Meanwhile, Warburg, Miller and Harding had accepted. This left two places vacant and gave McAdoo the opening he needed.[7]

Once McAdoo had succeeded in retaining the Comptroller of the Currency on the Board, he lost little time in shifting Williams into the Comptrollership. This gave him one reliable ally. Within three days after House learned of Olney's declination, McAdoo began insisting to the Colonel that Charles Hamlin be appointed. There were several obstacles, the most important of which was that Hamlin's nomination, coming on the heels of Miller's, would subject Wilson to charges that he had tried to pack the Board with members of the Administration. But Hamlin had some important supporters, Brandeis among them. Though eager for the position, Hamlin wisely abstained from lobbying in his own behalf, and at the last moment Wilson, faced with a series of declinations, reluctantly put him on the Board. Apparently on McAdoo's recommendation, and perhaps as a concession, the President also designated Hamlin Governor of the Board for the first year. McAdoo had won his only direct victory in the entire selection process. To fill the other vacancy, Wilson settled on Thomas D. Jones—Chicago businessman, personal friend, and generous contributor to the Democratic Party.[8]

Though the President's final nominees commanded the support of a number of influential progressives, much was being said in the cloakrooms of Congress about the "reactionary" complexion of the Board. The creation of the Federal Reserve system had involved a certain amount of daring; but with the legislation safely on the books, the daring—so far as Wilson was concerned—had come to an end. Partly with a view to choosing men who could not be dominated by McAdoo, the President had decided to run the risk that a majority of his appointees would defer to the big commercial banks instead. This points up once again Wilson's inability to meet the imperatives of his own 1912 critique.[9]

McAdoo certainly did not hate bankers, but he wanted the policies of the Board to be distinctly *his* policies, whether the financial community liked them or not; and he must have taken immediate alarm at the President's nominees, especially Warburg. On the other hand, if McAdoo could gain the support of Miller or any other member in addition to Hamlin and Williams, he would command a majority of the Board and it would make little difference who else sat on it. That being the case, as McAdoo's autobiography put it, "it seemed just and right that a member with the Wall Street point of view should be on the Board, if it was to be well-rounded and representative of all classes of American finance." When a coterie of Senators immediately drew their swords against Jones and Warburg, endorsement of the nominees became a test of loyalty to the Administration; and McAdoo, misgivings and all, ironically emerged in the forefront of the fight for confirmation.[10]

The contest over Jones stirred intense hostility, with Senators O'Gorman, Gilbert M. Hitchcock, and James A. Reed leading the battle against the Administration. Jones was a director of the New Jersey Zinc Company—the so-called Zinc Trust—and of International Harvester, engaged at the time in an antitrust suit with the Justice Department. Despite the best efforts of Wilson and McAdoo, the Senate banking committee voted against confirmation. At the behest of the Administration Jones wrote Wilson that he wished the nomination withdrawn. "Glory Hallelujah," Hitchcock exclaimed. Now he turned his guns on Warburg.[11]

To a number of legislators, Warburg seemed eminently sinister. "Radical" Congressman Joe Eagle unsubtly remarked to Hamlin that the trouble with Warburg was that "he is a Jew, a German, a banker and an alien." True, Warburg did have recent German antecedents: he had not become a citizen of the United States until 1911. Nor did it especially help Warburg's cause when the Senate banking committee found itself inundated with letters in his support from some of the same men who had been denouncing the Administration's antitrust program.[12]

Acting as mediator between the President and Congress, McAdoo requested information from Warburg concerning his allegedly disreputable business dealings. Warburg's reply was apparently unsatisfactory, and on

July 2 the banking committee delayed his confirmation pending further inquiry. When Warburg learned of this situation, which he had feared, he telephoned McAdoo and informed him that he felt offended and that, in order to maintain his dignity, he would refuse to appear before the committee if it called him. Warburg was only waiting to consult his friends, he implied, before withdrawing his acceptance of the nomination altogether. McAdoo tried to placate him, then conferred with a number of Senators. But they felt sensitive about having their prerogative questioned and apparently would not budge. McAdoo made it clear to Warburg that his capitulation would embarrass the President, adding that politics was a militant profession and Warburg should put his armor on. But McAdoo was discovering that Warburg could be as hard to move as the Great Pyramid. Within two hours after McAdoo talked with him on July 3, Warburg had written his withdrawal. Wilson, however, declined to accept it.[13]

Meanwhile, militant progressives asked embarrassing questions about Warburg's financial relations with McAdoo. After Kuhn, Loeb and Company had acted as readjustment managers for the Hudson and Manhattan in 1913, a partner of Warburg had joined the board of directors. McAdoo and Warburg took pains to emphasize that nothing illegitimate or conspiratorial had been involved and that McAdoo had no vested interest in Warburg's confirmation.[14]

During the first week of July, Wilson, McAdoo, and even Hitchcock implored Warburg to appear before the committee, which voted to postpone further action until he did; but Warburg stubbornly refused. Eventually, however, Warburg's resolve began to crack. On July 23, after talking with Senator O'Gorman in West Virginia, he penned a lengthy letter to McAdoo suggesting the basis of an agreement. The sine qua non was that a means be found, in Warburg's words, "to satisfy him that he has the confidence of the Senate to a degree corresponding to that which the President has expressed in appointing him." On the other hand, Warburg did not dispute the Senate's prerogative to question him, and he would appear before the committee.[15]

Several days later, Warburg conferred with Hitchcock on Long Island. The Senator assured him that his colleagues did not intend to affront him, and on July 29, Warburg wrote the President that the conferences with O'Gorman and Hitchcock had been successful and that the cloud of mutual suspicion had blown over. On August 7, after facing the committee, Warburg was confirmed by an overwhelming majority.[16]

That left just one member of the Board to be named. When Jones withdrew, he was replaced at his own suggestion by Frederic A. Delano, a Western railroad president and an uncle of Franklin D. Roosevelt. Far less controversial than Warburg, he had little trouble being confirmed. After weeks of delay, the Administration had finally collected seven men to operate its new banking system. On August 10, with its members already deeply engaged in fighting the domestic effects of the onset of war in Europe, the Federal Reserve Board was sworn in.

III

Anyone browsing in the minutes of the Board for the years that followed might easily conclude that the system meant little to McAdoo. After the first few months, his attendance at meetings dropped off precipitously and he appeared only on the rarest of occasions. While Warburg and Hamlin turned out memoranda by the dozen, McAdoo concentrated on the other duties of his office and committed scarcely any ideas about banking to paper at all. Yet the Board remained near the center of McAdoo's attention throughout his incumbency. At given times, such matters as discount rates and foreign exchange were handled by him and the other members together. But McAdoo's overriding long-range concern lay not so much with these technical questions as with the balance of power in the Board itself. And the key figure in that balance was Paul M. Warburg.

Moderate (by Wall Street standards) in his attitude toward the Glass-Owen bill, Warburg had played a predominant role in the New York branch of the National Citizens' League. He had been a leading supporter of a strong central bank. McAdoo had distrusted him long before the Board had been organized, and years after the passage of the Federal Reserve Act the banker would still be regarded with intense suspicion by most of the framers of the bill. In part this was because of his efforts to change the measure during its long voyage through Congress and because of the dire predictions he had scattered along the way. In November, 1913, having recently talked with McAdoo and a number of Senators, he complained that their prejudices "are only equalled by their ignorance." "I am mortified by the suicidal stubbornness with which sound suggestions have been swept aside so far."[17]

"Sound suggestions" got swept aside to the very end, and by late December Warburg wrote that the only recourse left was to give the Federal Reserve Act a chance, on the assumption that "on the whole" it was "a great step in advance" and that time would soon reveal its defects. The case for "sound" banking must be allowed to rest—"for a while." Yet Warburg himself was of two minds about this. While some of the act's shortcomings could be tolerated for the moment, others must be remedied almost immediately. The fight to write—or, rather, to rewrite—the measure must continue. Warburg's appointment to the Board resolved this ambiguity: by August, 1914, he was flooding McAdoo's office with memoranda for amending the act. The fears of the Congressional "radicals" had proved well-founded.[18]

Warburg believed that the national banks could not long survive if the drive for amendments failed. But within a month after passage, more than five thousand national banks had accepted the provisions of the new measure. By early June, McAdoo predicted that the Federal Reserve would be organized and ready to go into operation within two months; but the battle over confirmations swept away this possibility. The crisis in Europe convinced him that an early opening was absolutely vital; yet, perhaps justifiably, many banking experts were reluctant to launch the system too soon for fear that under the weight of war it might capsize. Some of the Board members believed that if the banks opened now, the strain would force them to shut their doors almost at once.[19]

Opposition to an early opening stemmed mainly from New York, Chicago, and St. Louis. Unpreparedness was the chief rationale—the reserve banks in the latter two cities did not even have governors yet. Executives of the large reserve banks warned McAdoo that it would be physically impossible to open at the early date he wanted. Member banks feared to pay their share of the capital stock and part of their reserve deposits on the assumption that these transfusions would simply weaken them. On October 21, the directors of the reserve banks narrowly voted to override McAdoo's recommendation that opening day be set for November 16 and counseled delay until the thirtieth. But McAdoo had the ultimate power to fix the date, and this test vote did not bind him.

In certain quarters a feeling existed that the reserve system should be regarded as a temporary expedient, to be used only during periods of stress. All that lay between temporary and permanent status was one amendment, and McAdoo feared that if the system did not begin running now the starting gun might never be fired. Then too, many Southern bankers wanted action at once, hoping that the reserve banks would help in marketing cotton and that an early opening might improve business morale. In October McAdoo spoke with the governors and chairmen of most of the reserve banks; practically every one of them counseled long delay. Even so, he reaffirmed the mid-November opening date. When representatives of the Federal Reserve Bank of New York complained that they were unprepared, McAdoo simply insisted that they commence operations whether they had had a chance to complete the desirable preliminaries or not.[20]

Meanwhile, the White House received complaints that the Federal Reserve Board had been deliberately pulling on the reins. The complaints were well-founded. Warburg strongly opposed opening until the act had been "radically amended," and when, on October 10, McAdoo called for speed, Warburg burst out in violent anger. At a meeting on October 15, McAdoo again pressed the issue. The Board postponed its decision, but McAdoo would brook no further delay. On October 24, he simply informed the members that the banks would open on the sixteenth. Delano, Warburg, Harding, and Miller expressed regrets; some of the members, Willis later wrote, considered McAdoo's decision "as a reflection upon themselves and an imprudent or perhaps arrogant assumption of authority." But they had no power to stop him.[21]

Early on November 16, McAdoo's signature on a formal order brought the Federal Reserve system to life. So successful was the transfusion of millions of dollars from old financial arteries to new that the market rate for money, a financial fever chart, scarcely budged. What the *Wall Street Journal* called a "new banking era" had begun.[22]

IV

But from the very beginning, the heart of the new system—the Federal Reserve Board itself—maintained an uneven pulse. The strife within the Board over the opening of the banks merely prologued things to come. As early as October, bitterness and suspicion had begun to hover over each meeting. The underlying reason was a fundamental disagreement over how the system should be run.

In Warburg's view, the original act was sufficiently defective that independent, conservative administration would be essential to avert disaster. He found McAdoo able and personally delightful; but he also knew that McAdoo intended to rule the Board, eventually turning it virtually into a Treasury bureau. And Warburg was bound to object to McAdoo's liberal management of the surplus, the disposition of which Warburg wanted the Board itself to determine.[23]

From the start, Warburg, Miller, and Delano went into opposition like a phalanx against the Administration group of McAdoo, Hamlin, and Williams. Occasionally Harding acted independently of either faction, but he could generally be counted on to side with Warburg. By the fall of 1914 the Warburg group had become so angry at McAdoo's ceaseless pressure that, according to Warburg, each of its members had considered resignation.[24]

Meanwhile, McAdoo had begun to view these men with bitterness and even contempt. No doubt he thought most highly of Harding, though he entertained serious doubts about Harding's basic loyalty to the Federal Reserve system itself. McAdoo dismissed Delano as aloof and bigoted, an unintelligent reactionary. Although Warburg was probably better versed in finance than anyone else in the entire system, Hamlin's characterization of him as a duplicitous "public enemy" reflected the attitude of McAdoo as well.[25]

But the principal target of McAdoo's animosity was Miller. McAdoo had known little of Miller when the nominations had originally been submitted, but apparently he knew enough to oppose Miller's appointment. When Wilson named the Board, many observers wrote it off as another McAdoo fiefdom. No matter what happened, it seemed, he would have the steady support of Williams, Hamlin, *and Miller,* each a Democrat with close ties to the Administration. McAdoo loathed anything that sniffed of personal disloyalty; and Miller went over to the enemy before the shooting even started, abruptly transforming McAdoo's campaign for hegemony over the Board into a desperate defensive struggle against Warburg. Then too, Miller was an ultraconservative, in McAdoo's view, with plenty of sympathy for the banks and none for their customers. As early as November, 1914, House wrote in his diary that McAdoo was intent on getting rid of Miller, and

even goes so far as to desire making an entirely new Board. He thinks it would not be a bad thing if the issue is brought about by the forced resignation of Miller. He believes the present Board is not working for the best interests of the people, but are imbued with the bankers' point of view, and that the Federal Reserve System is now being run as an adjunct to the banks, for the bankers rather than for the people.[26]

The Warburg group had already begun leaning toward the wishes of the commercial bankers and away from the desires of the Treasury Department and the needs (as McAdoo read them) of the entrepreneur.

The relationship of the Board members was complicated by the question of their social status, an issue which nourished far more animosity than its inherent importance would suggest. From the start, the appointive members agonized over where they were to stand in diplomatic reception lines. Several claimed that they would never have accepted their positions had they not been confident they would rank above assistant secretaries. But for months their status remained unsettled—and so, as a result, did they.[27]

Fearing that placing them over assistant secretaries would merely make Warburg and his allies more obstreperous, McAdoo tried to ignore the issue altogether. Eventually, Hamlin observed, it became "perfectly evident" that McAdoo "did not want the B[oar]d to have any high status." When the appointive members were finally put below assistant secretaries along with various boards and commissions, much of the blame fell on McAdoo. After more debating, the Board eventually decided to reject this status, and was left for the moment with no formal social position whatever. Its morale, and the appealing notion of becoming a Supreme Court of Finance, had been bàdly jolted; and, according to Willis, this, in turn, played a part in eroding the Board's sense of independence from political domination.[28]

The status of the Board as a governmental body also fell subject to dispute. Except when McAdoo was away from Washington, Wilson remained almost entirely aloof from the reserve system; and because he relayed his attitudes through McAdoo, members viewed the Secretary of the Treasury as acting in place of, or by authority of, the President, instead of simply on his own. In numerous respects, the Board took on the appearance of a bureau of the Treasury. Once the Warburg faction coalesced, however, it found a vested interest in asserting the Board's independence, and began to do so almost at once.

McAdoo wanted the offices of the Federal Reserve Board to be in the already crowded Treasury Building and had part of one floor cleared for them. After the Board had been ensconced under his roof, he never wished it to move. Much to his annoyance, however, the Warburg group believed this arrangement would give its members the appearance of being mere pawns of the Treasury Department. And the facilities themselves proved unsatisfactory, leading to constant complaint and, from time to time, suggestions for escape. One of the members even proposed that the Board move to Chicago, which would have left McAdoo and Williams neatly isolated a third of a continent away. Only after Harding sided with the McAdoo faction over the issue did it become possible to chain the Board inside the building.[29]

On December 19, 1914, the Attorney General ruled that the Federal Reserve Board was independent of the Treasury. McAdoo still disagreed. He also felt "that for the future of the Board it would be most unfortunate if the belief . . . is allowed to grow, that the Board is the creature of the banks and not independent of them, instead of being a distinctly governmental institution." Sensitivity over these matters endured among both factions and helped to transform disagreements over financial issues, especially whether the Treasury or the Board should govern economic policy, into full-scale personal vendettas.[30]

V

Perhaps the first major altercation arose over the question of what should be done with the staff of the Reserve Bank Organization Committee. McAdoo and Williams wanted it to be taken over permanently by the Board; and, despite the opposition of a number of the members, this is what finally occurred.

A far more important wrangle erupted over foreign trade. The New Freedom aimed at liberating the energy of American capitalism but at the same time directing much of that energy overseas for what Wilson termed a "conquest of the markets of the world." The Wilsonians listed Latin America, in particular, as a primary target for U.S. economic expansion. But American finance had long been reluctant to venture into the region, and McAdoo determined to seize the initiative himself. The Federal Reserve Act, he believed, had given the United States a chance "to become the dominant financial power of the world and to extend our trade to every part of the world."[31]

For in addition to consolidating and organizing credit, the act provided for the creation of branches and agencies of Federal Reserve banks abroad. This seemed to hold out an opportunity to the American exporter by enabling him to compete on relatively equal terms with his European counterpart in obtaining credit. McAdoo assumed that branches of reserve banks could be established in Latin America with little risk. A good deal of the trade of the region could be secured on a dollar basis, and where it could not, other practices could be employed for covering commitments in exchange. These economic incursions, he reasoned, would strengthen the reserve system, ease the inroads of U.S. businessmen and financiers into Latin America, speed up a trend that had already begun among American banks to establish branches there, and lay the groundwork for a widespread expansion of American business and banking at the end of the European war.[32]

In a public letter to the President, McAdoo recommended

that the 12 Federal reserve banks establish promptly joint agencies in the leading cities of all the countries of Central and South America for the purpose of providing enlarged credit facilities.

McAdoo also wanted the statutory powers of these agencies enlarged, though he did not intend to tie up reserve funds in long-term, nonliquid overseas loans. The banks held the initiative; but they needed approval and encouragement from the Board.[33]

During the summer of 1915, the assistant counsel of the Board concluded that the Federal Reserve banks had the right, with certain reservations, to establish joint agencies in foreign countries. Early in October, the President wrote McAdoo a letter endorsing his proposal. McAdoo forwarded the letter to the Board, and two days later he made it public. The Warburg faction responded angrily, viewing publication as an attempt to push it into approving the scheme. Warburg, whom McAdoo himself acknowledged to be the Board's most competent expert on international finance, had already prepared a memorandum on foreign branching at McAdoo's request and had come out against it; and Warburg claimed paternity of the paragraphs of the Federal Reserve Act which dealt with the entire question. Some members opposed involving the system in foreign branching at all, whether it could be safely accomplished or not. The Federal Advisory Council, too, was cool to McAdoo's plan; it had already come out against extending the system into foreign finance or exchange.[34]

The matter was referred to a committee comprised of Warburg, Delano, and Harding. They reported that McAdoo's scheme might endanger the liquidity of the reserve banks and damage confidence in the system. Expansion of American banking abroad must be accomplished by private firms acting singly or jointly and the process should be cautious and gradual. Not only were the economic risks in South America considerable, but the reserve banks had not been endowed with sufficient power to compete effectively outside the United States.[35]

The Warburg group had come out squarely against implementation of one of the most important doctrines of the New Freedom. After trading recriminations, at McAdoo's behest the Board agreed to resubmit McAdoo's plan to the committee so that it might produce a formula for amending the reserve act to allow cooperation among member banks in joint ownership and operation of smaller banks abroad. Meanwhile, the committee slapped Wilson and McAdoo by insisting on publishing its reasons for turning down McAdoo's original suggestion. But McAdoo took all this exceedingly well, eventually capitulating and voting with the majority against his own proposal.[36]

In September, 1916, an amendment finally became law which allowed national banks to take stock up to 10 percent of their capitalization in institutions established to finance foreign trade. These, in turn, would found branches abroad, but could neither receive deposits, make loans, nor compete in other ways with existing banks. Though this put the federal imprint on cooperation between American bankers overseas and reduced the risks of foreign branching, the financial community greeted the amendment with coolness, and there was no rush to make use of it. By the end of 1916 the amendment had clearly fallen short of fulfilling the objectives McAdoo originally had in mind.

The outcome of the branching dispute added a considerable amount of ice to the already frigid relations between McAdoo and the Board. "Although he from time to time considered further the question as to what ought to be done in the direction of developing the foreign service of federal reserve banks," Willis later wrote,

he had not reached any conclusion on the matter when this country entered the war. The problem had been allowed to drop, and a very considerable opposition to any action had developed among the banks of the country. Not only the Federal Advisory Council, but the larger banks interested in the foreign exchange business had begun to express themselves with great positiveness against any kind of intervention.[37]

VI

The smoke from the branching battle had just started to clear when a new struggle arose over redistricting. No other question had aroused so much controversy in the debates over the Glass-Owen bill. The ideological overtones were the same as they had been then, and the issue was taken far more seriously than any of the others which arose within the Board.

By November, 1915, the viability of the reserve districts as they had originally been established was being widely questioned, and numerous appeals pended for readjustments. Baltimore wanted to replace Richmond as a reserve city, and Pittsburgh desired to supplant Cleveland; banks and cities wished to be transferred to different districts; grumbling over the large number of districts never ceased; and the protesters wanted action at once. Behind each complaint and appeal was the pressure of a Senator or Representative demanding justice for his constituents.

The urgency of these demands was mirrored within the Board itself. There had been rumblings over districting from the very start, and by the late spring of 1915 they had grown intense. Warburg continued to insist that the Federal Reserve did not stand a chance of succeeding with as many as twelve districts and that somehow reduction to eight or nine would lift it out of financial purgatory. The failure of the system as a whole to clear a profit during its first year, due to the operating losses of half of the reserve banks, seemed to bear out his prophecy. But McAdoo remained unconverted. While he had no objection to the Board's contemplating a readjustment of the boundaries of various districts, he strenuously opposed slashing their number or switching the locations of the headquarters banks. After all, McAdoo himself had played the most important role in organizing the system; every demand for change cast doubt on his own judgment. And if it were admitted that the number of banks could be reduced, he realized, it would be an important first step down the road to a single central bank—a goal which McAdoo, it seems, clearly thought the Warburg group had in mind.[38]

McAdoo may not have appreciated the impetus behind the drive for readjustment until late September or early October. In mid-October, the question was referred to a committee composed of Warburg, Delano, and Harding. Robert Owen informed these men that when Congress framed the Federal Reserve Act it had, in his opinion, endowed the Board with power to disestablish districts. And up to the time that the committee filed its report on November 13, its members had no reason to suspect that Congress or their colleagues on the Board itself would question either this power or the other prerogatives of reorganization.[39]

Delano forwarded a copy of the report to McAdoo the day it came

out. It was an unabashed plea for redistricting. The boundaries set down
by the Organization Committee, it held, had been based on sheer con-
jecture, and a year's experience had proved them defective. Since half
the reserve banks seemed financially stillborn, the only remedy was
consolidation to "perhaps eight or nine districts." This must be accomplished at once: "So far as any large and comprehensive handling of the
problem is concerned, it is a question of *now or never!*"[40]

When Carter Glass discovered what the committee had in mind, he
sprang like an angry lion. He shot off a letter to Delano declaring that
Congress had vested the Board with no power to expunge reserve districts. On the twentieth, Glass spoke with Warburg. "He said to me that
he was in fullest accord with me as to the desirability of having only
eight banks; that as a matter of fact he never favored more," Warburg
wrote. Glass's objection stemmed from his fear of a Congressional up-
rising and from his conviction that the Board had no legal power of
disestablishment. On the other hand, if the Board would go through
channels—that is, through Congress—he "was willing to fight for us so
as to secure for us the smaller number, as he strongly believed in it."
Meanwhile, Owen reversed himself on the question and supported Glass.[41]

The committee picked Harding to broach the subject of redistricting
with McAdoo. Meanwhile, it delayed filing the report in order to give
McAdoo an opportunity to express his views. Because of an illness in
McAdoo's family, Harding chose not to disturb him. But Williams kept
McAdoo abreast of the committee's maneuvers. On November 12, Harding told Williams frankly that the Warburg group would come out in
favor of redistricting. Unless Wilson personally asked that the report be
withheld, Harding warned, the committee would vote it through. The
Administration, and particularly McAdoo, faced an ultimatum.[42]

The redistricting question came up at a meeting on November 12,
but because of McAdoo's absence discussion was postponed. On November 15, Hamlin passed "one of the most disagreeable days I have ever
experienced" in a prolonged skirmish with the Warburg group over
redistricting. McAdoo had requested that the final decision be delayed
until he could recover from bereavement over the recent death of his
son-in-law and complete his annual report. When Hamlin told the Board
that this would absorb several days, Delano "got very ugly" and moved
for a special meeting the very next day to vote on the issue. Hamlin and
Williams requested a week for contemplation. After a sharp exchange,
they persuaded the Warburg group to withdraw its report and file a
second one. That same day, McAdoo sent a letter to Hamlin endorsing
his request for additional information, declaring against any action on
the report before this information was supplied, recommending a week's

delay in any case, and pointedly discouraging haste. The rear guard skirmish had succeeded.[43]

By the afternoon of Saturday, November 20, the Board found itself confronted by a legal quandary: two of its counsel had arrived at conflicting opinions over the Board's power to redistrict. Late that night, Hamlin telephoned McAdoo, who told him that Attorney General Thomas W. Gregory, McReynolds's successor, had been studying the question at McAdoo's behest for some time. The President, he added, wanted Hamlin formally to request Gregory's opinion. At once, Hamlin sat down to write.[44]

By now, however, the redistricting case had already been decided. Sometime on Saturday, Harding had asked Willis to act as an intermediary with McAdoo. According to Willis's account, Harding wanted a compromise: the committee would lay its report on the table, and McAdoo would yield on a number of other issues. Willis informed McAdoo at once, and McAdoo agreed to talk with Harding the following day. McAdoo had already told Hamlin, however, that he would never agree to a compromise. Then the embattled Treasury group had a windfall. When Harding and McAdoo met, no concessions were requested; instead, Harding told McAdoo that he intended to vote to dismiss the redistricting issue altogether. Harding explained that he realized that any attempt at consolidation would encounter heavy fire from the courts, and that drawn-out litigation would injure the entire reserve system. Whether Warburg knew it or not, his majority had suddenly turned into a minority.[45]

Gregory's opinion reached Hamlin's hands just before the Board convened on Monday. For once, McAdoo attended. The preceding week, he explained, he had asked the Attorney General to examine the question of redistricting; but because McAdoo had been on the Organization Committee, he had preferred not to request a formal opinion himself and had asked Hamlin to do it instead. And Gregory's opinion, Hamlin reported, was that the Federal Reserve Board had no power to abolish any of the reserve districts, or even to transfer reserve banks to different cities. The Board exploded into an uproar, with Warburg claiming that nothing could be more disastrous. But he was powerless to act. Even if the dissidents had had a majority with which to disregard or override Gregory's opinion, which they did not, their attempt to reconstruct the system would doubtless have failed, leaving only a legacy of bitterness. So the issue was shelved by common agreement for a comfortably indefinite period of time. Thanks to McAdoo, the vision of banking consolidation Warburg had glimpsed just over the horizon turned out to be a mirage.[46]

VII

Within a week, Delano had written a memorandum begging for harmony to heal the lacerations which the Board's dignity had suffered in the redistricting battle. But with the election of 1916 coming up it would not be long before trouble began again. Relations among the members had become so stormy that Williams once even contemplated assaulting Delano, and petty squabbles broke out almost daily.[47]

McAdoo's contempt for the Warburg group had become vividly apparent, but his distaste for Miller bordered on sheer hatred. The Board's only professional economist, Miller was competent enough; and at times he could be charming. On other occasions, which came up all too frequently, he suffered from pomposity, verbosity, and a peculiar vacillation which made his opinions change like a kaleidoscope. "He is a far less reasonable and intelligent man" than Warburg, McAdoo informed the President, "and more difficult to deal with." In the summer of 1915 McAdoo wrote House that

to get rid of Miller is imperative. It simply must be done & a man of our kind put in his place or I shall have to quit. My nerves simply will not stand the strain. If I can eliminate this small mischiefmaker, all will go right.[48]

But the Administration group could not reach an agreement over Miller's fate. Williams backed McAdoo; but Hamlin stood like a rock in opposition, largely because he feared the removal of Miller might haunt the Administration politically. If Miller was squeezed out, Delano might even resign. Though McAdoo glimpsed the truth in this argument, he wanted the Warburg group to quit regardless.[49]

Meanwhile, the Board marched toward the brink of politics. "We must be . . . determined and . . . careful to keep the Federal Reserve Banks out of politics," McAdoo urged; and late in 1915 he took a step in this direction by introducing a resolution forbidding political office-holders or committeemen from serving as directors or officers of reserve banks. The Board passed this resolution unanimously. But Warburg and his allies discovered that by launching a political offensive, they might win a major engagement in the long war for hegemony over the nation's banking system. The field of battle now shifted to the organization of the Board itself.[50]

As early as May, 1914, Warburg had swayed House in favor of rotation of the Governorship in two-year cycles, in order to preclude the possibility of a jealous struggle for leadership. It was a good idea, but the Administration failed to act on it, and Hamlin had been appointed to the position for an indefinite period of time. During the summer of 1915 Warburg and Delano put constant pressure on Harding to visit the President and demand rotation. In June of the following year, Delano and Harding called on Wilson without consulting McAdoo in advance, and told the President rotation should be instituted. Half the Board, Hamlin observed, was preparing to go on strike over the issue.[51]

The key antagonist, as usual, was Warburg. Some dissatisfaction existed among the Warburg group over Hamlin's technique of day-to-day management, but more crucial factors were involved than that. Warburg wanted to take the appointive power away from the Administration by making rotation automatic. Then too, McAdoo had seen long before that Warburg was "crazy to have the Governorship rotated so he can be Gov[ernor] some time," and suggested to Hamlin that they hold the position out in front of him like bait in order to silence his opposition. But McAdoo would not allow Warburg actually to take over the post, at least not without a struggle. McAdoo seemed bent on ejecting Delano from the Vice-Governorship and intended to keep him out of the Governorship as well. Miller had never been in the running for either position, and that left just Harding.[52]

As election time drew near, the Warburg group continued to pile rocks on the Administration's chest. Skirting McAdoo, Warburg and Miller spoke with House about rotation, and Delano and Harding broached the subject with Wilson. Delano wrote the President an angry letter threatening that if rotation were not adopted, some of the Board members might inflate the issue even more. Warburg warned House that while he recognized the impropriety of forcing Wilson's hand, "we are determined that it is wasting our time to go on under a 10 year leadership" of Hamlin.

I believe I may say for four of us that we have shown no end of patience and consideration for two long years in order not to embarrass the administration and to keep the system out of acrimonious party debates. But we must now count upon relief, or give up, or fight. Either alternative would be as distasteful to me, as it would be harmful to the system, and I hope therefore that you may be able to put the case clearly before the President.

Both Miller "and Warburg intimate that if Hamlin is reappointed there will be several resignations from the Board," House noted.[53]

As of mid-June, McAdoo favored redesignation of Hamlin as Governor and the substitution of Harding for Delano as Vice-Governor. And as late as July, the President planned to reappoint Hamlin Governor for a year and leave the question of rotation to the future. But the pressure proved too great: Delano and Warburg warned a number of the Administration's friends that they would resign if this were done, and Wilson and McAdoo soon realized that the Warburg group was "determined," in Hamlin's words, "to rule or ruin." Warburg informed House on July 31 that he and his allies awaited the President's decision on the question,

and then we shall have to act, in case his action should be disappointing. I should not at all doubt the outcome if only the President would know the real conditions and the character of the men involved in the question. Meanwhile McA. is dead against "rotation"—claiming that would be tantamount to the abdication of the legal rights of the President. If that were so why could he appoint the first two-year man to act as Governor? He would be doing the same thing over again. McA. claims too that he, as chairman, should have the real "say" in designating the executive. You can readily see what all that means. Are we to be a Treasury Depmt. or an independent board? I know what the country expected and what we expected—and if there should be any doubt, we shall have to ask the country again. But I have no doubt that the President cannot be in accord with Mr. McA. and that he will do the right thing. I have never in my life been in a position which is as humiliating as the present. Here we are like *valets & maids* trying to get a hearing over the head of the butler. I was willing to put up with a lot, but I have reached the limit of what anybody may expect of me in the like of patience and endurance, and my colleagues feel just the same. One way or the other the thing has got to come to an end.

Warburg also enlisted the aid of Glass behind rotation. Then, on August 5, Warburg wrote House that he had had

a direct talk with Mr. McAdoo, even though it embarrassed me to do so for reasons which you can readily understand. On the other hand, I thought that direct methods would be best. We had it hot and heavy and I found him fairly set and stubborn in his views. I am afraid he believed that he was dealing with a bluff game and I am glad to think that I could impress him with the seriousness of the situation.[54]

Four days later, McAdoo sent for Hamlin and told him that the President had reluctantly decided to abandon the struggle and allow the Governorship to rotate on a yearly basis. Wilson fully appreciated the fact that he had been trapped: if Delano and Warburg quit before the election, as McAdoo felt certain they would, it would prove politically costly.[55]

But McAdoo intended to give the Warburg group as little as possible. The President wanted to appoint Delano Governor if he could not save Hamlin, but McAdoo, in House's words, "objected to the point of threatening to resign." Challenged on both flanks, Wilson switched to Harding. If Harding was designated Governor and Warburg supplanted Delano as Vice-Governor, McAdoo reasoned, Delano and probably Warburg would believe Harding had betrayed them. The ensuing wave of personal jealousy might sweep away their maddening unity. Hamlin thought Delano would resign. While McAdoo did not find the prospect unattractive, he saw that Delano had been neatly snared: if Delano quit merely out of pique over not obtaining the Governorship, he would simply make a fool of himself. "Hoist by his own Petard!" Hamlin exulted. "It serves him right."[56]

On August 10, it was publicly announced that the President had designated Harding Governor of the Board and that Warburg would become Vice-Governor. Technically the Warburg faction had won a victory. Yet it had very nearly been a pyrrhic one.[57]

McAdoo's relations with the Warburg group proceeded relatively agreeably during the next few months. He continued to toy with the idea of a purge, and Miller's head, in particular, remained on the block as long as McAdoo ran the Treasury. But the blade never fell. When Mc-Adoo returned to Washington as Senator twenty years later, Adolph Miller would still be sitting on the Federal Reserve Board.

McAdoo's defeat on foreign branching, his victory on redistricting, and the mixed outcome of the rotation struggle—all this spelled dead-lock. Yet in point of fact, the Warburg group simply could not afford a stalemate. While McAdoo had been unable fully to coordinate the reserve system under his own leadership, he had severely curtailed the Board's independence, and the Treasury had continued to dominate the money market. Ultimately, the three-year deadlock between the Administration and Warburg groups was shattered by America's entry into the World War, an event which enabled McAdoo to outflank the Board by dealing, ironically, with Wall Street itself.

CHAPTER EIGHT

THE CABINET AND THE TREASURY

If McAdoo's tenure as Secretary of the Treasury could be characterized in a single word, that word might well be "energetic." He never ceased involving himself in new projects, focusing his attention on each one in turn and pounding away at it until it had been solved. For five years the Treasury resembled a giant battleship, constantly on the move and firing an endless barrage of new ideas and projects into official Washington.

Within government, McAdoo played a role that had become quite familiar to him in private life: the role of promoter. Taking advantage of the ideological flexibility of the New Freedom, he emphasized that he ran the Treasury like a business, adapting to the public sector the best devices of the private. To many in the business community, on the other hand, his ideas often seemed utterly heretical.

I

Ordinarily gregarious, McAdoo became almost a recluse from the day he took office, battling place seekers by day, avoiding speech making, and snatching a few hours, usually at night, to concentrate on legislation. As a widower in mourning he was able to escape many social obligations and, except for vital official appearances, to remain at his desk. The corollary of this was that he rarely got any rest; he simply buried himself in work, overtaxing his strength from the beginning. By the summer of 1913 Wilson's physician began to fear a breakdown if McAdoo kept up the pace; and McAdoo's own doctor eventually threw up his hands, remarking that the Secretary of the Treasury was the only person he knew who had violated all the laws of physical well-being year after year and survived. But McAdoo could not stop; a ten-week bout with appendicitis in the fall of 1915 simply made him work harder to catch up.

On the increasingly rare occasions when he did succeed in tearing free, McAdoo found leisure in streaking through the woods around Washington on horseback. He rode with his close friend Cary Grayson, the President's physician, or with Wilson's daughter Eleanor. McAdoo also played an occasional game of golf or tennis. And he startled Capital society by fox-trotting—the most spectacular (in that era) manifestation of a genial, informal temperament which set him apart from most of his frock-coated predecessors. Fortunately, perhaps, he stopped short of shocking the worst prudes by avoiding the tango.

McAdoo's good nature defused the animosities of many men who violently opposed his policies during these years. "He is so splendidly loyal to his friends," wrote one official, "and where that is consonant also with his conception of his obligation to the public he never fails." When McAdoo did get annoyed, however, the heavens trembled. Public prominence made him vulnerable for the first time to a hostile press, and his nerves were highly sensitive to the journalistic thrashings he inevitably received. Yet McAdoo's relations with his opponents in press and politics normally went along amicably enough; when differences did arise they could usually be smoothed over. McAdoo cultivated reporters and got along well with them. His work drew applause from many quarters; Colonel House was by no means alone in believing that McAdoo ranked among the preeminent secretaries of the Treasury in the nation's history.[1]

II

"Here is the greatest news in the world," McAdoo wrote the Colonel early in March, 1914.

Miss Eleanor and I are engaged! The "Governor" has consented and I am supremely happy. Isn't it wonderful? The days of miracles are not yet over or she never would have accepted me.

Eleanor Wilson, youngest of the President's three daughters, was just half McAdoo's age. He recorded the great attraction she held for him in his autobiography: "she was neither argumentative nor angular, but entirely

womanly—a charming girl, without affectation or pedantry." Warm and
gay, she had also developed an enthusiastic concern about public issues.[2]

McAdoo's engagement to Eleanor put a new face on his public career.
At first he feared it would cause a strain in the Administration. McAdoo
did not want Wilson embarrassed whenever he sided with his Secretary of
the Treasury, partly because it might restrict McAdoo's own freedom of
action. So he offered to resign from the Cabinet. The President demurred.
On the evening of May 7 Eleanor Wilson became Mrs. William G.
McAdoo in the Blue Room of the White House, before a hundred guests.
Originally they had planned a brief honeymoon in Europe; but McAdoo
feared to stray too far from Washington because of ominous conditions in
Mexico. Instead, they honeymooned in New Hampshire.[3]

Though it did not endow him with omnipotence, as many claimed,
McAdoo's marriage brought him closer to the President; at the same
time, McAdoo moved toward independence from Colonel House. Early
in the Administration House had been almost as close to McAdoo as he
was to Wilson; but by October, 1915, the Colonel acknowledged that
"McAdoo had gotten pretty well from under my influence."[4]

Meanwhile, McAdoo had clearly proved himself the most capable,
energetic member of Wilson's official circle, and one of the most
progressive. So far as the President was concerned, the department heads
should rule their own domains, and he delegated a good deal of authority
to them. Not only did McAdoo have the responsibility of running the
Treasury but along with Burleson he also had the function of shepherding
Administration bills through Congress, particularly through the Senate—
no doubt because Wilson considered them the only two men in the Cabinet
with any aptitude for such matters. Privately, the President called McAdoo
and Burleson his legislative "wet nurses."[5]

Wilson held his Cabinet meetings at the most irregular intervals of any
in recent history; and the President, as Richard Fenno has pointed out, ". . .
was not dependent on his Cabinet group in any sense. . . . He wanted to
obtain the sense of the meeting, not as a positive guide or as the answer to a
problem, but as a sounding board against which to project his own ideas."
By design, Wilson avoided making important comments at meetings, and
this, combined with the reluctance of the Cabinet members to raise issues
of their own, tightly circumscribed the range of questions that came up.
As time passed, the President grew more and more tight-lipped at Cabinet
meetings, confining himself to correspondence with each member about
matters concerning his own department and allocating to each "virtually
complete freedom . . . in all routine matters and in the formulation of
many important policies," as long as he found these acceptable.[6]

McAdoo never really had Wilson's ear. The President consulted him on appointments but rarely on policy questions, and never fully confided in him or in the other Cabinet members. McAdoo had a great deal of affection for Wilson; but he concluded that the President had no confidence in the judgment of any of his department heads. Like the rest of them, McAdoo resented Wilson's secretiveness. And McAdoo was irritated at the lack of coordination between the Cabinet and the President. By early 1917 McAdoo had become convinced that Wilson had lost all his "punch" and that things had begun drifting aimlessly. The President allowed his secretaries free rein and paid little attention to what they actually did; he seemed unaware of how well, or how poorly, they performed. As he grew more absorbed in foreign policy, he shrouded himself in reticence and became increasingly secluded. McAdoo found it impossible to arouse in him any interest in political affairs, and the President's grip on Congress began to loosen. By the end of the first term, House considered Wilson a failure as an administrator and credited efficiency among the department heads with much of his success. McAdoo would doubtless have agreed.[7]

"McAdoo remakred [sic] that he and the other Cabinet Members were nothing but clerks," House wrote in the fall of 1918. "This is not true of McAdoo, and that is why the President gets along with him less well. He prefers the . . . type [who are] . . . absolutely subservient to him." McAdoo wanted to make policy and, within his own realm, he did. Nationally recognized as the most successful and forceful member of the Cabinet, he entertained only moderate respect for his fellow secretaries. For one thing, he considered the Cabinet badly constituted from a political standpoint—too many of its members were conservative, unknown, had no political following or experience, and were unable to give Wilson the kind of support he needed in his legislative battles with Congress. For another, they lacked McAdoo's own aggressive combativeness.[8] McAdoo felt, House wrote late in 1916, that the President

should revamp his Cabinet and get rid of the weak members. He also feels that the President is not following the work of the departments as he should. In other words, he feels just as I do. McAdoo said the President had no business head, and what the office needs now is someone with that kind of ability.

Wilson's wife complained to House in 1917 that the President had been growing more and more annoyed at McAdoo because, in the Colonel's words, "McAdoo wishes to advise every Department and the President as well." But at the same time, Wilson's management of the Cabinet (or lack of it) put a premium on the incentive of each secretary; and even more than the others, McAdoo tended to work alone. It was Wilson's practice not to bring up domestic matters for Cabinet review. Instead, the members themselves initiated discussion. When McAdoo failed to raise the vital tariff and currency questions, David Houston observed that these issues

are under the Treasury and . . . McAdoo is a solitaire player. He possesses many of the qualities of leadership. He is self-reliant and has dash, boldness, and courage, but he does not cultivate Cabinet team work and does not invite discussion or suggestion from the Cabinet as a whole.

The germ of the latent conflict between McAdoo and Wilson was that each was "a solitaire player," and in terms of ability both stood far above the men around them. McAdoo wanted power; and from the first, he moved to engross new functions for the Treasury so as to construct, in effect, an independent base of power within the Cabinet itself. McAdoo could be deft about this—as an infighter he proved exceedingly able—and though other department heads did resent his trenching on their prerogatives, his relations with them remained generally genial.[9]

But there was one very notable exception. Early in 1913, McAdoo had ironically and unsuccessfully championed his future rival, A. Mitchell Palmer, for Attorney General over James C. McReynolds. In February, 1914, McAdoo and McReynolds got into a bitter wrangle over the question of whether a commission or the Treasury Department (which normally handled this sort of thing) should construct a new building for the Department of Justice. In this case McAdoo, who wanted his own department to build it, battled to preserve the authority of the Treasury. Burleson moved in as mediator, and in March the dust finally settled. But this incident, combined, perhaps, with differences between McReynolds and McAdoo over patronage and McReynolds's talk of resignation, eventually prompted the President to make what turned out to be one of his most unfortunate appointments when he pushed the Attorney General upstairs to the Supreme Court.[10]

If McAdoo shared at least partial responsibility for putting McReynolds on the Court, he also claimed an important role in seeing that Brandeis arrived there too. When the post fell vacant early in 1916, Wilson asked McAdoo if he had any nominees, adding that he himself had no one in particular in mind but wanted a progressive lawyer. At once McAdoo suggested Brandeis, the President's most trusted adviser on domestic legislation. Could he be confirmed? Wilson wondered. "Yes," was the reply, "but it will be a hell of a fight." The President acceded the following day, asking McAdoo to take charge of any battle that might develop. A vicious and prolonged struggle did ensue because of Brandeis's alleged radicalism and religion. After four months, with a good deal of pressure from the Administration, the nomination was finally confirmed. Brandeis proved a sterling choice, both judicially and politically.[11]

III

During the New Freedom years the powers of the Treasury grew enormously. The passage of the complex income tax law as an amendment to the Underwood-Simmons Tariff Act of 1913 suddenly placed a large burden of responsibility on McAdoo's shoulders. He had only twenty-eight days to make preparations before collection at the source began, and confusion ensued. The unification of the Revenue-Cutter Service and the Life-Saving Service into the United States Coast Guard in 1915, which McAdoo backed with enthusiasm, added efficiency in administration as well as new headaches in organization. Also under McAdoo's jurisdiction was the Public Health Service, whose powers he worked to increase in the interest of the country at large. And a flood of legislation kept him busy organizing and staffing new government boards.

In all of this, McAdoo insisted on efficiency; and the drive for efficiency and for the employment of business methods in government became as much a hallmark of his tenure in the Treasury as it was of the Progressive Era itself. In the progressive context, reforms in administrative procedure were of central importance. In the specifically Democratic context, economy in government harkened back to Jefferson and a legacy of minimal government which in previous years had been elevated to an ideology. "Rigid economy," as McAdoo put it, became an official credo. "I am anxious," he remarked, "to keep the office out of politics. I want to give the country an efficient, straightforward, business administration."[12]

Through reorganization and improved administrative techniques, the Treasury Department functioned smoothly through the New Freedom years and expanded its duties tremendously without increased appropriations. The work force was actually cut; economy squeezed its way into government contracts and customs collection; and the supervision of national banks, and other procedures, improved. The efforts of W. H. Osborn, Commissioner of Internal Revenue, to stop previously tolerated frauds in income and corporation taxes and levies on margarine and whiskey, recovered tens of millions of dollars for the Treasury. Large numbers of Congressmen, Senators, and national committeemen howled, but McAdoo and Osborn continued unswervingly.

Finally, McAdoo conducted a small revolution in public construction procedures. Several thousand building acts, many of them straight out of the pork barrel, were referred to the Treasury each year for construction. Meanwhile, many needy communities went begging. Previous Secretaries of the Treasury had made attempts to cut costs, but without success; legislation passed for the purpose had been ignored. But in 1915, McAdoo formalized a policy he had actually been following for two years with striking savings. It was intended to bring projects into line with local needs at minimum cost and standardize design and construction on a national basis. In 1916 he waged a strenuous fight against further omnibus, pork barrel public building legislation.

Beyond the sheer joy of saving money—a motive which would seem almost quaint in later decades—the battle over buildings had a political function. By cutting costs significantly in public construction and elsewhere, and by the much advertised application of *business* methods to the management of the Treasury, McAdoo was proving that the Democrats had the ability to govern—just as 1912 Democratic campaign procedures and the Federal Reserve Act had shown.

One of the most important steps taken toward greater efficiency under Woodrow Wilson was the appointment of a permanent Tariff Commission. The Underwood Tariff, which the Democrats had passed in 1913, had been supported by McAdoo as a means of "transferring a part of the burdens of taxation from the backs of the masses of the people to the ample shoulders of wealth." But in the framing of the measure he deferred to Underwood and Senate Finance Committee Chairman Furnifold Simmons, who knew considerably more about the subject than he did, and restricted his counsel mainly to the bill's administrative provisions. In the creation of the Tariff Commission, however, McAdoo took a place near the center of the stage.[13]

Under Taft a Tariff Board had been established, but Congress subsequently killed it. Before long, pressure built up for a new one: business sentiment favored it, and the plan had the backing of many protectionists, the United States Chamber of Commerce, the AFL, the Grange, and other farmers' organizations. Even the President, who had originally been hostile to the idea (like many low-tariff Democrats), became a convert by early 1916. New House majority leader Claude Kitchin showed scant enthusiasm, and management of the Tariff Commission bill was turned over to Henry Rainey of Illinois. McAdoo drafted the measure in January, in collaboration with Kitchin (who would at least consult), Houston, and perhaps Daniel Roper of the Post Office Department. Introduced in the House by Rainey on February 1, the bill was strictly an Administration measure and passed the following September as part of revenue legislation.

The bipartisan Commission was comprised of six members appointed to staggered terms. They were assigned to investigate various facets of trade, including the customs laws and their effects, and to serve as an information bank for the President and certain Congressional committees. The Commission received broad power to investigate private records and to summon and examine witnesses under oath. Like the Federal Reserve, the Tariff Commission represented a concession to expertise, a concession which McAdoo would probably never have opposed; and it symbolized the drift of the Administration toward protectionism in certain industries, toward economic nationalism, and toward the notion that the tariff should be employed as an instrument for spurring economic growth.[14]

McAdoo took an extraordinary interest in the personnel of the Tariff Commission, since he expected it to work intimately with his own department. He wanted the commissioners appointed quickly in order to nullify the Republican tariff plank of 1916, but events did not move as fast as he desired. Recommended in March, 1917, the members were: Frank Taussig, Daniel Roper, David Lewis, William Kent, William Culbertson, and Edward Costigan. It was anything but a high tariff phalanx.

IV

"As for myself," McAdoo wrote in 1913,

I am trying to do this job in a way that will help the people of the country. If I can succeed in bringing the average man's pocketbook and his living expenses more on a parity in all cases where the pocketbook is too small, I shall, indeed, be happy.

"The people" was a broad term which turned up repeatedly in progressive rhetoric. It included the business community, minus the nebulous "interests"—that is, it included *most* businessmen—and nothing inconsistent can be found in the solicitude McAdoo manifested toward the welfare of American capitalism from the day he took office. Despite the outcries of many conservatives over Wilsonian legislation, McAdoo and others commonly justified reform as a means of aiding businessmen, particularly those of middling means. This fell perfectly into keeping with the rhetoric of 1912; for the New Freedom aimed precisely at liberating the petty capitalist from the toils of "predatory" trusts and financial interests in the name of a more just and efficient economy.[15]

The Wilson Administration was charitable to the small banker as well as to the small businessman; and if many bankers howled about the Federal Reserve Act, to the Wilsonians this seemed like a child screaming after a dose of castor oil. McAdoo considered his real adversary not the small country bank but Wall Street. In 1916 he confided to an intimate that he would like to write an article about his tenure in the Treasury; the theme would be

the absolute divorce of the Treasury from Wall Street influence or domination by special influences of any character, and its administration wholly and consistently in the interest of the people of the country. That has been the underlying motive in everything I have done.

This aversion to Wall Street went beyond mere rhetoric; it was understandable in personal terms as well. Both McAdoo and John Skelton Williams had been businessmen, and Williams had also been a banker of less than first rank. Each had suffered directly, at one time or another, at the hands of the New York financial community. Most important, the Wilsonian attitude toward Wall Street reflected what might be termed the neo-Jacksonian side of the New Freedom: the suspicion of mammoth aggregations of "illicit" power within a few private institutions. This despite Wilson's own uncertainty about the prospects of limiting huge power clusters in the future. Politically, such suspicion also played a vital symbolic role. In McAdoo's case, Wilsonian ideology, which he shared, simply reinforced personal, nonideological inclinations.[16]

Yet, as McAdoo wrote years later, "I had not then, and have not now, any *unreasonable* prejudices against Wall Street." His relationship with the New York banking community was in fact ambiguous. He had, for example, made big bankers unhappy to the extent that he helped spearhead the creation of a separate economic power center, the Federal Reserve system, without providing any means for direct private control. On the other hand, he patronized some important New York banks.[17]

McAdoo did not go through the ritual of consultation with New York about the moves he intended to make, as his Republican predecessors had; and this aroused great resentment. "When Secretary McAdoo walks in Wall Street," a Western newspaper quipped, "he carries his hat on his head—not in his hand." The remark delighted him. McAdoo repudiated the notion that he ever waged outright war on the moguls of finance, and, in fact, he did not; yet he appears to have taken positive pleasure in needling them. In November, 1913, for example, he remarked to House that Wall Street had begun "to feed out of his hand." The bankers feared that, because of false statements in their returns, they might be sent to prison. Rather than dousing these anxieties, McAdoo stoked them.[18]

This harassment and, more important, almost constant efforts to bring the banking community to heel in minor ways as well as major, aroused considerable hatred of the Administration, and predictions of a "Wilson panic" were legion. McAdoo believed (somewhat exaggeratedly) that big bankers were arrayed in lockstep against the Administration, both for political reasons and because they considered it incompetent to regulate the economic policies of the federal government. Instead of attempting to salve this antagonism, McAdoo exacerbated it even at the expense of his businesslike image. The fight with "privilege" proved real enough, and so did the public image that emerged from it. "The present secretary has aroused the wrath of more big bankers than any other secretary of the treasury in many years," noted the Springfield *Republican.*[19]

Once in office, it did not take McAdoo long to stir the animus of the financial community. When he took over the Treasury, he discovered that while the government had $912,000 earning 2 percent interest in national banks, $48,754,000 on deposit in these institutions netted nothing at all. The reason for the discrepancy was this: the government had been charging 2 percent on its funds in inactive depositories (that is, ones on which the government did not draw checks); but on monies in active depositories, no interest accrued. Then too, it had been Republican practice to keep a far larger sum in the Treasury than was necessary for a working balance—at times as much as $100,000,000—and this yielded no interest either.[20]

For years agitation had been developing, much of it in Congress, for assessment of interest on government deposits, but previous administrations had balked on the ground that the depositories performed a public service. Late in Taft's Administration a House committee recommended an interest levy, and the Democratic platform of 1912 demanded it. On April 30, 1913, McAdoo suddenly announced that starting in June all national banks acting as federal depositories would be charged 2 percent per annum. In addition, he authorized $10,000,000 previously tied up in the Treasury to be placed in the national banks at once, arguing that with interest accruing to the Treasury, larger balances—and hence, increased circulation in the volume of money—were justified. Finally, McAdoo liberalized the character of the securities acceptable for government deposits.[21]

If the banks had been required to pay 2 percent on their average government balances since 1896, the net revenues would have swelled by over $30,000,000—no mean sum during years when the total national debt hovered around a billion dollars. The order brought well over $1,000,000 a year into the Treasury. Yet even so, federal deposits remained attractive, and a flood of appeals poured into the Treasury Department for a share of the $10,000,000 McAdoo intended to release. McAdoo's dispersal of the funds among 607 banks tended to scatter them widely—one of the principal goals of then-impending banking legislation.[22]

Though McAdoo continued to liberalize Treasury policies, and though government deposits remained popular, Wall Street and the banking community greeted the interest order with hostility. Of the 559 active depository banks in May, 1913, nine declined to pay the interest and relinquished their holdings. Despite protests, McAdoo reduced the deposits in a number of others he thought had been allocated excessive amounts by the previous Administration. Of the nine which terminated their status as depositories, several ranked among the largest banks in New York; one of them was the mammoth National City.[23]

V

The shortcomings in the system of public finance that McAdoo had inherited included the fact that government deposits had long been dispensed like patronage. Banks close to the administration in power reaped a harvest of federal funds. The Democratic platform of 1912 had opposed this "pet bank" arrangement and declared in favor of competitive bidding. McAdoo said he opposed allocation of deposits for political reasons, but in power he went along with it. Complaints from various bankers when he took office led him to transfer funds from some national banks to others by suggesting to the Secretary of War that departmental deposits be redistributed. It was "outs" who had protested, and the initial transfers furnished funds to banks whose officers numbered among them men of the Democratic persuasion. It might even be argued that redistribution simply involved democratization of deposits, in the best (or worst) tradition of Andrew Jackson and Roger Taney. In any case, the process continued.[24]

The political nature of government banking, plus McAdoo's suspicion of and austerity toward some large financial institutions, led to a long series of battles between the Treasury and the banks. Hostility toward McAdoo stemmed in part from his rocklike determination to enforce the Federal Reserve Act "fearlessly and with full regard to the spirit and letter of the law," despite persistent pressures to the contrary from the banking community. But the antagonism had begun even before the Federal Reserve Act passed. And to a striking extent it focused in the relationship between the Treasury Department and the largest national bank in the United States, the National City of New York; between William G. McAdoo and Frank A. Vanderlip.[25]

Vanderlip and the President had once known each other well, but their relationship cooled during the 1912 campaign because Wilson refused to let Vanderlip advise him. In March, 1913, after talking with Vanderlip, Colonel House observed that the banker regarded John Skelton Williams as perhaps the worst possible choice for Assistant Secretary; "he thinks Williams a little crazy." Vanderlip pretended, at least, to think highly of McAdoo, with whom he apparently had consulted during the campaign. Their personal relations continued amicably enough, it seems; but on an official level the two men were continually thrown into opposition.[26]

The first incident occurred very shortly after McAdoo took office. For more than eight years, the National City had kept a paid agent behind a desk in the Treasury Department. The agent, McAdoo claimed, had collected advance information after each call of the Comptroller for data regarding the condition of the national banks, a procedure he branded "entirely wrong and indefensible." Late in April, McAdoo publicly directed that the practice should end. He added that Milton Ailes, vice-president of the Riggs National Bank of Washington and Vanderlip's friend and business associate, had acted as employer of the clerk for the National City. "The policy of this Administration," McAdoo remarked tersely, "is 'pitiless publicity.' "[27]

Ailes and the National City both denied any impropriety, and there is evidence that despite the expulsion of their agent Vanderlip and Ailes continued to receive information from other sources in the Treasury. But the incident, together with Vanderlip's bitter response to the 2 percent order, symbolized a rupture in the friendly relations between the Treasury and the New York banking community. McAdoo found himself roundly criticized. It was the first time in a hundred years, complained the officers of the National City, that the institution had been required to defend its honor in public. But it would not be the last. The following year, Williams and the bank engaged in a public duel over whether or not it had made an illegal loan.[28]

The Pujo Committee had labelled the National City Bank one of the worst demons in the so-called Money Trust, and the public hostility of the institution's officers to the Federal Reserve Act was unsurpassed in the financial community. From the time McAdoo evicted its agent and promulgated the 2 percent interest order, the bank conducted repeated attacks on the Treasury Department. The Riggs National Bank happened to be the largest, and one of the oldest and most dignified, financial institutions in the Capital. Both Vanderlip and Ailes had served as assistant secretaries of the Treasury.

In May, Ailes warned Vanderlip that he thought the Administration intended to make a concerted public demonstration of its unfriendliness to big finance by continuing its small-scale harassments, and that the two bankers must be prepared. After the passage of the Federal Reserve Act, John Skelton Williams learned that the National City had allegedly been discouraging state banks from going national. By August, 1914, the president of the Riggs privately referred to Williams as a cur, and when Williams's nomination as Comptroller went before the Senate for confirmation, Ailes testified that he was unqualified for the position.[29]

Bad blood between Williams, Vanderlip, and Ailes came as nothing new. Vanderlip had been involved in purchasing control of the Seaboard Air Line, and had subsequently broken with Williams. The banker had been instrumental in unseating Williams from the directorate of the road; then Ailes had been elected in Williams's stead. Vanderlip claimed that one of Williams's chief goals as Comptroller was vengeance on his two old antagonists.[30]

Perhaps this is true; perhaps not. In any case, both McAdoo and Williams became convinced that the Riggs National Bank had been conducting its business in dangerously irregular and illegal fashion, and that it had received suspiciously preferential treatment under former administrations—specifically, from Ailes and Vanderlip. Early in December, 1913, the *New York Tribune* published articles which alleged that a scandal had taken place in the Treasury and that Williams had been wallowing in it. McAdoo was irate, and on the fourth, at McAdoo's summons, officers of the Riggs National Bank appeared at the Treasury. According to Ailes's account, written several days later, McAdoo told them that he had learned from an unimpeachable source that the story had originated at the bank. McAdoo asked each of the three officers in turn if he was responsible, and each denied it. Then McAdoo accused Ailes, who admitted that he had, in fact, discussed the story with newspapermen and that he believed the *Tribune's* accusations true. But Ailes claimed the story had already broken before the reporters asked his opinion. When Ailes complained that McAdoo had tried to discredit himself and the two banks in evicting their agent, McAdoo (as one version put it)

arose from his chair and advanced menacingly toward . . . Ailes, . . . and in great anger shouted, with a blasphemous oath, "I will order you out of my office."

McAdoo made it clear to the bank's president that he considered Ailes responsible, and that he would hold the institution accountable. "You know," McAdoo warned the president, "what this means to the Riggs National Bank."[31]

McAdoo was intimating, he later told Hamlin, "that if any more attacks emanated from them he might w[ith]draw the Govt deposits from their Bank." Nothing could shake McAdoo's conviction that Ailes had been behind the *Tribune* story, and though McAdoo claimed that the incident did not affect his decision, the following April, when he deposited funds in Washington banks for help in paying the District taxes, McAdoo refused to give the Riggs National a dollar because of its "unjust attacks on himself & Williams." Hamlin warned that there would be a fight. McAdoo "said he did not give a Damn—he would fight them back." Ailes was a "damned scoundrel." Hamlin protested the decision, fearing a scandal and probable Congressional investigation over charges of vengefulness, but McAdoo would not budge. "His action is extraordinary, no matter how unjustly the Riggs Bk attacked W[illiams] & himself," Hamlin wrote.

Williams seems to be his evil genius—he is evidently secretly influencing McAdoo and they are allowing personal vindictiveness to dominate their management of the Treasury finances. If this keeps up I shall resign.

McAdoo made the tax deposit and retained discretion as to where funds should be placed. When they were apportioned early in May, nothing went to the Riggs. In June, McAdoo gave notice that "it is my purpose to withdraw all Government funds from the Riggs National Bank." The institution, he wrote, did a relatively small commercial business, and "in the public interest" the monies could be better placed elsewhere. In July the bank was discontinued as a depository.[32]

On April 12, 1915, the Riggs National filed a suit in equity in the Supreme Court of the District of Columbia in an effort to enjoin McAdoo, Williams, and John Burke, Treasurer of the United States, from unlawfully interfering with it. Among its thirty-seven charges, the bank claimed that McAdoo and Williams had harassed and conspired irreparably to injure it; had grossly exceeded their powers (Williams had demanded detailed information concerning the activities of the institution); and had "prostituted their high office to their personal malice, seeking unlawfully to destroy and unconstitutionally to confiscate the property of the bank." The court issued a temporary restraining order, ruling for a preliminary injunction against the government officials. The order prevented them from paying into the Treasury several thousand dollars in interest on government bonds, held as a penalty against the bank. The injunction restrained Williams from cutting off the institution's authority to function as a depository of reserve bank funds; it also cited the Treasury officials to show cause why the injunction should not be made permanent. In his reply, Williams denied malicious intent and claimed that withdrawals had been made in the face of irregular banking methods; and McAdoo argued that the institution was speculating in stocks and inadequately serving commercial needs. Both men denied the conspiracy charge.[33]

The Riggs case caused McAdoo a great deal of concern, in part, no doubt, because the Republicans and a segment of the press blew it up into a cause célèbre. More important, he construed it as a fight over vindication of impartial enforcement of the banking laws and regarded the suit as a "dastardly attempt to assassinate character and to injure the administration." But the bank tried to make even more of it than that: using the press and sending copies of the bill of complaint to all members of Congress and all national and state banks and trust companies across the country, it claimed to be defending the rights of the entire financial community. The bank had raised the question of how much control the Secretary of the Treasury, and particularly the Comptroller of the Currency, could exercise over the national banks. "The vital point," as McAdoo put it, was the right of the Comptroller to call for the special reports which the bank resisted and his right to assess a fine for its non-compliance with his demand. The issue struck at the very foundation of the Comptroller's authority in the supervision of the National banks, and it was the first time that the question had ever been presented to a court to decide.

The key was not a few thousand dollars, then, but Williams's power. And the issue came up precisely at a time when this power had come under attack both from the Federal Advisory Council, which recommended that his office be abolished and its functions absorbed by the Federal Reserve Board, and from inside the Board itself. The danger to the Comptroller-ship, McAdoo argued, threatened in turn the Administration and even the national banking system. Yet, in reply to its appeals, the Riggs received overwhelming support from its fellow national banks.[34]

Within the Administration circle, meanwhile, the case had caused a serious split. Hamlin—whose misgivings continued to grow—urged compromise. He thought McAdoo was allowing his loyalty to Williams to drag him into a morass. Brandeis believed Williams was in the wrong and wanted the government to remit all penalties, making a trial unnecessary. Like Hamlin he feared that any trial would irreparably injure the reputations of the Secretary of the Treasury and the Administration, no matter who won. The Attorney General and all the lawyers, Brandeis confided to Hamlin, considered the case an ugly one which would probably be lost and should not be allowed to come to trial. But Wilson serenely dismissed the issue as a skirmish between the bank and the Comptroller, assumed it would not involve the Administration, and wanted to see it continue. And McAdoo stuck to his course.[35]

McAdoo considered the bank's record extremely vulnerable to attack. He dismissed the charges of trying to wreck the institution as "preposter-ously false." The President, too, reaffirmed Williams's power, and the Administration called on some of its best legal talent to argue the case: Assistant Attorney General Charles Warren; Louis Brandeis; and (over the apparent opposition of both the President and the Attorney General) Samuel Untermyer.[36]

The case went on and on. Ultimately the court sustained Williams on every point except the comparatively unimportant fine itself, which was lost on a technicality. Conspiracy charges had been dismissed as early as May, 1915, the court upholding Williams's actions. His crucial right to call for the reports and assess the fine were sustained. The Riggs promised Williams that it would operate in compliance with the provisions of the National Bank Act, and in the summer of 1916, he granted a renewal of its charter. A struggle which had reminded many observers of the war between Andrew Jackson and Nicholas Biddle had ended at last.

VI

The Riggs episode became a cause célèbre because it pitted the government directly against the "interests." The role of Saint George came easily to McAdoo, and throughout his tenure he played it with consummate skill. Far less frequently, and with far less fanfare, he assumed a more austere role. This generally occurred when fiscal matters came up: the progressives, like most New Dealers, were decidedly pre-Keynesian. McAdoo believed in balanced budgets.

A low tariff Democrat, McAdoo had long viewed reduced rates and foreign competition as levers against domestic trustification. He also staunchly backed the recently enacted income tax. But the taxation policies of the Wilsonians contrasted sharply and ironically with their tariff program. The levies endorsed by the Administration were, at least up to 1916, strikingly regressive. This hurt the same small businessmen and consumers that lower tariff duties—which had made income taxation necessary to offset lost revenue—had been designed to help. In this instance, the Administration played the political game on both sides.

McAdoo inherited a healthy Treasury from the previous Administration, with abundant resources. In writing a new tariff, the Democrats cut the government's income from customs, the source of roughly two fifths of the general revenues; yet up to the beginning of the World War, which precluded a fair test of the act, the Underwood Tariff considerably exceeded anticipations as a source of money. On the other hand, receipts from the income tax—which had been expected to compensate for the fall in customs revenues, but at low rates—proved disappointing during the first fiscal year of McAdoo's tenure, precipitating talk of a bond issue. Except for permanent investments and national emergencies, McAdoo wrote, "I am and always have been opposed to the issue of bonds to meet current expenditures of the Government. Nothing could be more unsound than to fail to pay as we go."[37]

Charles Hamlin broached the subject in April, advising McAdoo to put out $100,000,000 in Panama bonds to meet the sagging condition of the finances. But McAdoo remained undisturbed. Hamlin persisted; McAdoo, who preferred certificates of indebtedness to bonds, weakened somewhat, but by late May he again believed that it might be possible to avoid an issue—and by mid-July, he was positive.

Then came the war in Europe. On the eve of the conflict, revenues had been increasing and fiscal 1914 produced a balanced budget. But for the month of August, 1914, there was a fall in customs revenue of well

over $10,000,000 compared with the same period the previous year. In
October, the discrepancy grew to nearly $14,000,000. Meanwhile, compli-
cations with Mexico had spawned larger military expenditures, and appropriations for returning Americans from Europe and establishing the War
Risk Insurance Bureau totalled some $8,000,000. McAdoo quickly realized
that the Treasury faced a possible deficit of $100,000,000 for the fiscal year,
and on September 2 he wrote the President suggesting "some form of well
distributed internal revenue taxation" in order "that the revenues of the
Government shall exceed its expenditures." Not only were the questions
of solvency and economic stability involved, but also the redeemability of
greenbacks, since the Treasury largely relied on customs payments for the
gold used in the process.[38]

It would be politically impossible for a Democratic administration
elected on a low tariff platform and with a major downward revision on its
record suddenly to raise schedules once more; such a step would be a con-
fession of failure. Confronted with a choice between taxation or borrowing, the President picked the former (despite the fact that many Democrats
in Congress were up for reelection), and took the responsibility for driving
through legislation designed to raise $100,000,000 in fresh revenue. Mean-
while, experts in the Treasury cast about for items to assess. While such
things as stamps, telephone calls, and bank checks were contemplated, the
discussion seems to have circumvented a levy on wealth. Instead, McAdoo,
Furnifold Simmons, and Oscar Underwood agreed to a draft bill which
would raise the necessary funds entirely through new excise 'duties.[39]

But on September 7, when the Democrats on the House Ways and
Means Committee got down to drawing up a measure, the Southern
agrarians in command wrote a draft discriminating openly against the
North by taking one third from higher income taxes, one third from a
new impost on railroad freight bills, and a final third from levies on wine
and beer. A struggle ensued which lasted until the adjournment of Congress late in October. Arguing that income taxes could be collected only
during the following summer, the President insisted that this provision be
cut out; the revenue must come in at once. The Democrats on the Ways
and Means Committee accomplished this, and the assessment on railroad
freight was practically doubled. The ensuing outcry led to the calling of
a party caucus, but on September 15, before it convened, the President,
McAdoo, Underwood, Simmons and Burleson conferred at the White
House and agreed on a fresh measure which would be acceptable to the
House Democrats. The caucus approved the bill later in the day; after
more discriminatory amendments by Southerners in the House and Senate,
the measure finally passed. The President signed it October 22.[40]

The War Revenue Tax Act raised levies on beer, ales, and wines, tobacco dealers and manufacturers, cosmetics, chewing gum, bankers, brokers, and proprietors of theaters and other places of amusement, and added a schedule of stamp duties. Despite certain differences, the act fundamentally represented a renewal of the revenue legislation passed during the Spanish-American War. It did bite into certain kinds of wealth, but only because Congress insisted. Meanwhile, a number of economy measures were announced.

The war tax law was due to expire at the end of December, 1915. McAdoo had unsuccessfully advised that it be enacted for the duration of the conflict. The same conditions persisted in late 1915 that had led to the passage of the legislation in the first place; customs receipts for the fiscal year ending in June, 1916, were only insignificantly higher than those for the previous year, and revenue from the emergency act proved disappointing. Though many Congressional conservatives wanted to borrow, McAdoo stated emphatically that there would not be a bond issue.

Clearly, something would have to be done: in October, McAdoo presented the largest estimate of federal expenditures ever submitted to Congress in peacetime. Growing outlays were outstripping rising income tax receipts. Roughly three quarters of total federal revenue still came from customs and excise duties, but state attempts to prohibit alcohol and regulate cigarettes cut excise yields. Businessmen had begun grumbling about the emergency act. Finally, pressure had been mounting for preparedness and for shipping legislation, and these would require even more revenue.

McAdoo had firm views on how to finance armaments. "For my part I am strongly in favor of preparedness," he wrote, "and I am strongly in favor of raising by taxation the necessary revenues to pay for it."

I think it the wisest and soundest policy to settle the bills as we go along, as far as it is possible to do so. A nation no more than an individual can go into debt for current expenditures without eventually impairing its credit.

On November 25, McAdoo issued a statement estimating additional revenue needs for 1917 at nearly $113,000,000, assuming the emergency law and customs duty on sugar were retained. Almost $94,000,000 of this was allocated for new defense measures. The sum, nevertheless, could be raised easily "without appreciable burdens upon the American people" and without a bond issue, except, perhaps, for payments on the Panama Canal. He suggested that consideration be given to hiking tax rates on individuals and corporations and reducing the exemption and surtax levels; there should be new levies on gasoline, crude and refined oils, automobile horsepower, internal combustion engines, and other articles. Such taxes, he argued, would be so widely scattered as scarcely to be felt. In December, McAdoo further elaborated on government needs and recommended a drop in the surtax level to incomes of $10,000 or $15,000, rather than the current $20,000. Finally, he wanted postponement of the time when the free sugar provisions of the Underwood Tariff would go into effect until 1919 or 1920.[41]

Two things stood out in McAdoo's revenue program in the fall of 1915. First, a continued aversion to bond issues. Second, a regressive change in the law so that rather than increasing rates exclusively on incomes already being assessed, thousands of people would begin paying for the first time—though McAdoo later came out for a lower rate on incomes at the bottom end of the scale. McAdoo's plan quickly gained the approval of Furnifold Simmons. Just as quickly, Claude Kitchin issued a statement declaring that the Treasury was in dismal condition. Despite the fact that McAdoo and the floor leader were good friends, their economic outlooks often clashed over revenue matters. Kitchin stood to the left of McAdoo on taxation; but perhaps more important to the Congressman's outlook than anything else was his view of preparedness: "the Army and Navy Departments are more crazy this year than last," he wrote late in 1916. On the Hill, Kitchin led the antipreparedness bloc, composed mainly of Southern and Western Democrats. In an argument, he could be hard to budge.[42]

The floor leader would prove stubborn this time for various reasons, and no doubt he aired them vigorously when he and McAdoo conferred in September. Kitchin feared the consequences of bringing hundreds of thousands of people under the income tax for the first time with an election impending. When, by October, it was becoming clear that Wilson and McAdoo had decided to reenact the emergency law and hold onto the sugar duty, Kitchin began to bristle over the apparent executive assault on Congressional prerogatives to frame revenue legislation.

On December 7, the President's annual message recommended measures intended to muster $300,000,000 in additional funds for preparedness along the lines McAdoo had laid out. "Their burdens," Arthur Link has observed, "would have fallen much more heavily on the middle and lower classes than upon the rich who paid, relative to their wealth, scarcely any tax at all." But the message, combined with Wilson's signature in mid-December of a bill extending the emergency act one year, worried politicians and antipreparedness House Democrats and spurred an outcry from the growing numbers of progressives and labor leaders who demanded a tax hike on swollen incomes. Though Wall Street approved of McAdoo's suggestions—or perhaps because it did—a number of Congressional Democrats made it clear that they would not support the proposals even if a party caucus tried to force them into it. "The poor people throughout the country," warned Senator Benjamin Tillman, "are watching us." McAdoo spoke with leaders of Congress and was apparently instrumental in working out an informal agreement which raised sur-taxes, decreased the personal exemptions, kept the sugar duty, and eliminated stamp and special levies recommended by Wilson in his ad-dress. This arrangement momentarily dampened the controversy over revenue. In April, a bill to repeal free sugar slipped through Congress; then legislation came temporarily to a halt. Meanwhile, it seems, the President may have been moving with the tide toward throwing a larger tax burden on the wealthy. Quite possibly McAdoo was changing too, but if the Treasury experts had begun to consider anything "radical," they gave no hint of it.[43]

By May the financial condition of the Treasury had improved sig-nificantly. If fiscal 1915 had produced a slight deficit, fiscal 1916 yielded a surplus. McAdoo predicted that preparedness and other programs, in-cluding rural credits, flood control, and good roads, could be funded easily. On the eighteenth he submitted to Kitchin and Simmons revised estimates indicating that, due to surprisingly large internal revenue and income tax receipts, far less would have to be raised for these expenditures than had been supposed at the beginning of the session. In accordance with a plan approved the preceding week by the President, the $150,000,000 in additional revenue needed for the coming year would be provided by assessments on incomes, inheritances, and munitions.[44]

Vowing to fight the Administration's preparedness program "to the last," Kitchin wrote that if it passed, he wanted to finance it as fully as politically possible through a higher income tax with unlowered exemp-tions and a levy on munitions. If the East demanded preparedness, the East could pay for it. On July 1; he reported a bill which horrified con-servatives. It had been drawn up by the Ways and Means Committee, whose Democratic members entertained ideas along the lines of Kitchin's and could not be controlled by the Administration. Without dropping exemptions, the measure doubled the income tax rate, raised the surtax, levied an impost on estates, repealed the stamp duties embodied in the emergency measure of 1914, and placed an assessment on the gross income of munitions manufacturers. McAdoo had hoped to salvage at least some of the stamp taxes, but complaint against them had been widespread and sentiment was strong in Congress for repealing them, no doubt partly for political reasons. (During the summer, postcards bear-ing pictures of the Boston Tea Party and buttons with the motto "LICK THE DEMOCRATS OR LICK STAMPS" had begun to circulate.) By the time the measure passed, the stamp levy had been cut out. McAdoo fruitlessly endeavored to convince the President that he should try to persuade

Congress to lower exemptions; the final bill was signed without this provision.[45]

The act of September 8, 1916, kept the minimum untaxed income at $3,000; doubled the normal income tax rate; increased the maximum surtax; fixed the normal income rate on corporations at 2 percent, adding fifty cents on each $1,000 of fair valuation of capital stock; and assessed estates (unprecedented at the federal level) and the net profits of munitions manufacturers. It also carried an antidumping amendment. Ironically, under Kitchin the Democratic Party's agrarian left had achieved its clearest victory by successfully battling a Democratic Administration.

VII

Curiously miscast in an austere role, McAdoo played it again when racial friction erupted in the Treasury Department soon after he took office. When Woodrow Wilson ran for President in 1912, he attracted the support of such Negro leaders as W. E. B. Du Bois; Bishop Alexander Walters of the African Methodist Episcopal Zion Church, who headed the National Colored Democratic League; William Monroe Trotter, editor of a black newspaper in Boston; and J. Milton Waldron, leader of the National Independent Political League. Disenchanted with the trimming of Roosevelt and Taft on the race question, and despite serious misgivings about Wilson and his party, these men and others like them closed ranks behind the Democratic banner, or else backed Wilson as independents. In a practically unprecedented Democratic campaign maneuver, the Wilsonites cultivated the black vote.[46]

One of the most influential Wilson boosters was Oswald Garrison Villard, a founder of the NAACP and publisher of *The Nation* and the New York *Evening Post*. In the summer of 1912, Villard and Trotter unsuccessfully pressed Wilson for a public statement on the race issue, including a guarantee that no discrimination would be practiced in doling out the patronage. Though Wilson gave repeated assurances of "absolute fair dealing" and advancement of Negroes' interests, he made no specific guarantees concerning patronage, Wilson wrote, "except that they need not fear *unfair* discrimination." More may have been read into these vague remarks than was really there; in any case, despite Wilson's equivocation, many blacks looked forward optimistically to the beginning of the new administration.[47]

As Governor of New Jersey, Wilson had not been dependent upon Southern votes to put through his legislative program. After March 4, 1913, he was. For years, the Solid South had been saddled with Republican federal officeholders, many of them black. Not enough jobs could be found for all the white Democratic applicants, and Wilson and McAdoo came under pressure from important Southerners, in Congress and out, to segregate and to expel Negroes from office. Senator James K. Vardaman, the outstanding champion of white supremacy on the Hill, announced early in 1914 that he would fight the confirmation of any black to any office in the United States. Meanwhile, a tide of discriminatory legislation flooded Congress. And a number of civil service employees who had worked beside Negroes for years suddenly discovered that, as whites, they were too "good" to be treated this way. A National Democratic Fair Play Association was established to lobby for segregation and a general purge of Republican officeholders.[48]

Despite serious divisions in their own ranks over patronage and persistent rumors in Washington that Negroes would be expelled from the government, black Democrats launched a campaign to hold at least those positions which Negro Republicans had occupied in the past. At the same time, Villard pressed upon Wilson a plan for a National Race Commission. The President seemed entirely convinced that something along these lines was necessary and assured Villard that he was prepared to appoint the commission "if," as the editor later put it, "it became clear that his relations with the Senate and the House would permit it."[49]

Then things began to go wrong. Wilson wanted to wait to grant approval of the project until it became clearer how amicable his position would be with Congress—specifically, with the Southerners in Congress. By October, when he talked with Villard again, it had become clear that this relationship was a conditional one. "I could not grant the Race Commission," he told Villard, "for the reason that it would seem like investigating the South." The President wanted to champion the Negro cause, he protested, and in time he hoped that he could. But he still had to prove himself to the Senate. A number of Senators refused to confirm black appointments, and this was a major impediment. "I will never appoint any colored man to office in the South," he added, "because that would be a social blunder of the worst kind."[50]

By this time, Villard had things far worse than his disappointment over the Race Commission to worry about. Like Wilson, McAdoo had given assurances to Negroes that "I intend to do right by all irrespective of race or color." One of the black leaders remarked that "all my hopes, politically, from this administration are centered in Mr. McAdoo." Wilson and McAdoo had strong precedents to fall back on: Grover Cleveland had held the line against segregationists in his Administration, and under Theodore Roosevelt the number of Negro employees in the federal government had risen dramatically. But for years, segregation had existed to one degree or another in various departments, the Treasury among them.

Never before Wilson took office, however, had anything like a tidal wave of segregation, backed by official orders, swept federal offices in Washington as it did in 1913. The focal points were the Post Office and Treasury departments, the chief employers of Negroes.[51]

Late in May, 1913, orders were issued segregating whites and blacks working in the office of the Recorder of Deeds (previously unsegregated and a focal point of racial tension) in line with demands of the National Democratic Fair Play Association. In July, John Skelton Williams—intensely and self-consciously Southern and rabid on the race question—segregated washrooms in the Treasury Department in his capacity as Acting Secretary of the Treasury. He claimed the facilities provided were equal; so did McAdoo, who wrote that

it is difficult to disregard certain feelings and sentiments of white people in a matter of this sort. The whites constitute the great majority of the employees and are entitled to just consideration, especially when such consideration does not involve the deprivation of the negro of any essential and inherent right.

Robert Woolley, Auditor for the Interior Department, published strict orders segregating similar facilities in his domain, and the Office of the Auditor for the Post Office and the Bureau of Internal Revenue also instituted the policy. But perhaps hardest hit were black employees of the Bureau of Engraving and Printing, where some segregation and discrimination in hiring already existed. Here, again, white complaints began after the inauguration. Williams, who had the bureau under his direct authority, issued a written order for partial segregation, but withdrew it and replaced it with a verbal command similar in effect. As the policy expanded, Williams also ordered that Negroes not be recommended for promotion.[52]

The arrival of Hamlin as Williams's successor in the fiscal division brought a new direction and a fresh approach to race relations in the Treasury Department. Named after the abolitionist Charles Sumner, Hamlin was a friend of Villard, and began working with leaders of the NAACP to stamp out discrimination and move quietly and gradually away from segregation. The issue became acute when, in March, 1914, the Bureau of Engraving and Printing, where segregation lingered longest, moved into a new building designed under the previous Administration and physically ill-suited to segregation. Hamlin saw his chance and pounced. He drafted a letter to the bureau's director which strictly forbade segregation and sent a copy to McAdoo. The letter got no farther, but several days and several conferences later, despite McAdoo's fear that forbiddance of segregation would, in Hamlin's words, arouse "terrible opposition in the South," McAdoo and Hamlin laid down "four general rules" for the bureau:

(1) justice to all; (2) no notices to be posted in toilet rooms; (3) no discrimination in promotions; (4) no partitions in dressing rooms.

McAdoo cleared these principles with Wilson, who wanted them issued verbally. Perhaps out of fear, some Negroes asked for the preservation of at least partial segregation, and a degree of self-segregation endured, at least for a time. But on March 27, Hamlin wrote in his diary that discrimination in promotions, "ordered by Ass[istant] Sec. Williams, has in pursuance of order of CS H[amlin], been entirely done away with and absolute justice in promotions is now being accorded colored employees."[53]

Meanwhile, the toll of black Presidential appointees in the Treasury had been heavy. Despite widespread nonpartisan approval of his performance in office, despite pressure from Villard and Booker T. Washington, and despite McAdoo's exceedingly high opinion of his work, Charles Anderson, Collector of Internal Revenue in New York, was fired as part of a political compromise and replaced by a white Democrat. And the political risks of nominating Negroes to any position remained formidable, as the case of Adam Patterson illustrated.

Since 1897, the post of Register of the Treasury had been held by blacks. Senator Thomas Gore, who badly wanted patronage for Oklahoma, recommended an Indian for the office; but the President and McAdoo, realizing that the position should go to a Negro on grounds of precedent, and probably becoming sensitive to the race question in general, agreed that a black should be appointed. Gore then proposed Patterson, a Negro lawyer. The first black nominated to federal office by the Wilson Administration, Patterson had the support of Walters and Trotter; but Southern senators blew up. Gore requested that Patterson's withdrawal be accepted and the position be given to the Indian; and, accused by many of his supporters of desertion in the face of the enemy, Patterson stepped out of the fight. Sniffish about its minority groups, the Senate confirmed the Indian. Down with Patterson went a plan hatched by McAdoo and the President to turn the Registry into—as McAdoo put it—

a distinctively colored division, with the idea that it would give the negroes an opportunity of national dimensions, to prove their fitness to run, unaided by whites, an important bureau of the Department. We both agreed that it would have a stimulating and beneficial effect upon the progress and development of the negro race.

Villard objected to the plan, but McAdoo held to the argument that segregation did not reflect unfairly upon blacks.[54]

While the battle over Patterson continued, protests over the Treasury's race policies piled up in McAdoo's office. Though south of the Mason-Dixon line the press and politicians lauded federal segregation, even the South produced a certain degree of opposition. In November, 1914, Trotter led a protest delegation to the White House and got into an argument with the President that gained nothing. Wilson claimed segregation had been instituted to quell racial friction.[55]

Trotter's anger was understandable, but Villard had proved more effective in a prolonged series of skirmishes with the President and McAdoo. The nation's foremost white spokesman for black rights, he had a humorless, rigid, and implacable sense of morality. "Like his grandfather, William Lloyd Garrison, whom he worshipped, he insisted on being heard and refused to equivocate." Long an ardent supporter of Woodrow Wilson, Villard had assured Negroes that Wilson would not give a green light to the segregation of federal employees. Now, Villard felt betrayed. Worried above all by the precedents the Administration was setting, he wrote that "if in this cause of human rights I do not win at least a portion of the epithets hurled at my grandfather in his battle, I shall not feel that I am doing effective work." After trying to win over the President and Tumulty (who proved sympathetic) through the summer of 1913, Villard finally decided that " something spectacular must be done to focus attention on this matter and keep it focused." Wilson clung desperately to the argument that segregation actually helped blacks by "exempting them from friction and criticism in the departments." "It is as far as possible from being a movement *against* the negroes," he assured Villard. "I sincerely believe it to be in their interest." The President appeared to want to help the blacks, but he was remarkably vague: "You know my own disposition in the matter," he wrote, "but I find myself absolutely blocked by the sentiment of Senators; not alone Senators from the South, by any means, but Senators from various parts of the country." The situation seemed far more "delicate" than Wilson had imagined before becoming President.[56]

Meanwhile, Villard had also been dueling with McAdoo. In the fall of 1913, the press reported that the Commissioner of Internal Revenue at Atlanta had publicly remarked that "there are no Government positions for Negroes in the South. A Negro's place is in the cornfield." The official later denied the report, but Villard seized the occasion to ask McAdoo for assurance that blacks would not be indiscriminately thrown out of office by Presidentially appointed collectors. When the commissioner actually began removing Negroes—for a time, at least, Treasury officials in the South apparently had sufficient authority to downgrade or fire black civil service employees—Villard's anger flared again. Late in October, he sent McAdoo a copy of a speech he intended to deliver which publicly denigrated the Administration's race policy. McAdoo struck back with a hurriedly composed reply which did not reveal his logic at its best and which generally paralleled the arguments of the President. "I shall not," he said, be a party to the enforced and unwelcome juxtaposition of white and negro employes when it is unnecessary and avoidable without injustice to anybody, and when such enforcement would serve only to engender race animosities detrimental to the welfare of both races and injurious to the public service.[57]

The patronage had been handed out, and throughout the government, the number of Negro officeholders had been sharply cut. Nevertheless, something of a counterrevolution did occur, with McAdoo in the van. He finally assured Villard "that no colored employee of the Treasury Department is going to lose his position, so far as I can control the matter, so long as he faithfully and satisfactorily performs his duties." McAdoo believed in the doctrine of separate but equal; but more than many of his generation, he tended to mean *equal*. He had always gone out of his way to help certain individual blacks in the government service—and he continued to, sometimes aggressively. Fortunately, the President timorously pursued the same tack, though the violent storm that blew in from the South when he nominated a few Negroes to office soon led him to give up altogether.[58]

For decades, McAdoo has been branded as an instigator of federal segregation; and to a degree, he was. If he had simply stood aside and let it happen, he would still have been abetting it. But even at the time, opinions differed over the precise importance of the role McAdoo had played. Wilson acknowledged that several Cabinet members had suggested and initiated the practice, but did not specify which ones.[59]

As in the case of state patronage, the President—himself prejudiced but not an extremist on the subject—appears to have left the segregation question up to his department heads to resolve individually. On April 11, 1913, the issue arose in a Cabinet meeting on the initiative of Burleson. The Postmaster General announced that he eagerly wanted to introduce segregation in his own department and throughout the government. Wilson made it clear that, in the words of Josephus Daniels,

he made no promises in particular to negroes, except to do them justice, and he did not wish to see them have less positions than they now have; but he wished the matter adjusted in a way to make the least friction.

Burleson objected to having white clerks work under any black, including the incumbent Register of the Treasury.

McAdoo doubted whether the Senate would confirm a negro even if the President appointed one for this place, and believed it would be very doubtful. As to the segregation of negro clerks in the Treasury Department under the Registrar, Mr. McAdoo feared it would not work. The difference in salaries, etc., would operate against it.

No final course of action in racial matters was charted, but Burleson said he would begin segregating his own department. No record exists of anyone present having dissented. The President later claimed that segregation had not become a *policy* of his Administration, and he was probably right. The authority had been delegated, either explicitly or, more likely, implicitly—by silence or else by inference.[60]

Nor is it totally clear that McAdoo originally wanted segregation instituted. Williams established the practice; McAdoo did not hear about it until several days later. As McAdoo remarked in a letter to the editor of the antisegregation New York *World*:

The matter came up this way: Last year Asst. Secy. Williams gave directions for separate toilets in The Treasury building. Mr. Wooley [sic], Auditor for the Interior Dept issued a written order to the same effect for the Auditors Office. This order, by the way, concluded with the usual formula "By direction of the Secretary of the Treasury." As a matter of fact I did not know of these orders until some time after they had gone into effect. They relate to details of administration with which it is impossible for the Secretary to keep fully informed. His time is necessarily absorbed in the larger problems which are constantly pressing upon him in this great department. I do not say this to escape responsibility—On the con[trary] I assume it all because after the matter was brought to my attention I felt that the orders should stand. Had I revoked them after the issue had been raised even greater dissatisfaction would have arisen among the whites.[61]

By "whites," McAdoo alluded to white employees; but he might have said white Senators as well. When Wilson and McAdoo both delegated authority over policy, it became almost inevitable that someone, at some level of government, would segregate; and once the process had been instituted, it became politically impossible to reverse it. It had to be defended. So it does not come as a surprise to find Wilson writing a noted white supremacist in July, 1913, that segregation *was* planned Administration policy. Consciences were less troubled because of fragmented opposition; a number of influential Negroes, or so the Administration claimed, had approved the practice.[62]

Today it is taken for granted that segregation is morally indefensible. But since the President so strenuously defended it on explicitly political grounds, the question arises: was it politically "justifiable"? Was it worth trading the black vote for Southerners' votes in Congress—assuming, as Wilson did, that these were on the line?

Villard answered No. As a solution to the dilemma, he suggested recess appointments. Yet these might have antagonized the Southern Senators even more. Villard's own *Evening Post* observed in the fall of 1913 that it was

now admitted . . . that the Senate will not confirm the nomination of any negro, or person known to be however distantly of negro descent, for any position in the Government service in which he will be in command over white persons, particularly over white women. So far as this matter is concerned, the Southerners entirely dominate the position of the Senate; they make no bones of their control, and are well within the truth when they say that they have in it the tacit support of many Northern and Western Senators.

"Water going over the steps will, I believe, finally wear them away," Wilson told Villard.

But I cannot talk to them on the lines of justice; it will have to be on the lines of political expediency and the influence of the Negro vote in the States where they hold the balance of power.

Ultimately, after the 1916 election, Villard recommended that the Administration "eschew politics and compromises" altogether. But Burleson had already made it clear to Wilson that success in putting over his legislative program depended on his skill in managing the party, including the Southerners; and the President had abandoned his plans for succoring white Democratic progressives. Where should he draw the line on the Negro?[63]

In allowing the segregation of bureaus and offices in Washington, Wilson and McAdoo had drifted rather mindlessly into a cross fire. In cashiering black officeholders in the South, on the other hand, they followed a distinct line of political policy. Then they had to defend themselves *and* make concessions, satisfying no one. What must have seemed logical at a time when the Negro's degree of humanity was a common subject of debate in the mass media—expulsion of black Republicans when white Democrats wanted jobs and the segregation of civil service employees—was magnified, perhaps unpredictably, into a major political issue. The time came for a choice, and Wilson, McAdoo, and Burleson decided to trade Senate votes from the party's most important sectional constituency for an incipient black Democratic movement of unknown dimensions. The President opted against the Negro on the assumption that the race issue put his legislative program in jeopardy. In this case, the price of the New Freedom came high.

VIII

On racial matters and the issue of budget balancing, most progressives, including McAdoo, did not diverge profoundly from conservatives. But given McAdoo's pre-Keynesian spending restraints, his role turned out to be remarkably innovative; and this was the substance of his progressivism in government during the New Freedom years.

One of the great ironies of the Wilson era lies in the fact that the President's suspicion of big power clusters led him significantly to enlarge the federal government in order to deal with all the others. McAdoo, who displayed no hesitation whatever in expanding his own department, played a crucial part in this. He envisioned a basically promotional role for the Treasury and the government as a whole, a vast growth in the number of services performed without a drastic hike in expenditures. These two seemingly contradictory ends did not prove incompatible because, during the New Freedom years, the Wilsonians broadened the role of government as a referee and provider of services for the private sector without trying to usher in a full welfare state. McAdoo's efforts to increase the efficiency and economy of his own department, for example, went hand in hand with his drive to expand it. He insisted on keeping Wall Street at a distance at the same time that he mobilized the Treasury behind other capitalists, particularly farmers and entrepreneurs, who often shared his suspicion of big finance.

CHAPTER NINE

COTTON AND CREDIT

One of the major questions raised by McAdoo's accession to power was how he would react to regional and national economic crises. The most recent Democratic precedents stemmed from the Cleveland Administration and were less than encouraging. Within weeks after he took office, events put McAdoo to the test.

I

Late in March, 1913, a mammoth flood swept the Ohio Valley. Hardest hit was Dayton, parts of which lay under twenty feet of water. The city needed help and got aid the day of its request. When his department heads protested that no funds were available, McAdoo shot back "to Hell with appropriations." And when the Superintendent of the Life-Saving Service complained that it would be illegal to transfer every available vessel to Dayton as McAdoo ordered, McAdoo replied, "send the boats immediately to Dayton and I will serve the jail sentence." After the water receded the danger arose of a run on the banks and their officers feared reopening. On April 4 McAdoo sent a national bank examiner to the city, and within a day, following the recommendation of the examiner, he designated every national bank in Dayton a government depository. McAdoo directed that $2,000,000 in federal funds be placed in these

167

institutions, tȯ be secured by state, municipal, or local bonds. On April 17 the examiner reported that the deposits had "relieved the situation immensely"; confidence rose so rapidly that when the banks reopened only $182,800 of the two million was actually requested.[1]

This damn-the-torpedoes determination characterized McAdoo's reaction to credit stringencies as well. His faith in the ability of the Treasury to thwart panics was immense. Repeatedly he tinkered with the nation's economy to keep it from stalling, though such actions were usually neither desired by businessmen nor required by statute.

Most of the demand for intervention arose in the South, and McAdoo's sensitivity to it was as exquisite as that of any Cabinet officer in this century. There were three reasons for this: first, during the New Freedom years the South suffered more than other regions from credit stringencies; second, Southerners occupied a vital place in the Democratic Party and many of the crucial posts in Congress and sent up an annual cry for aid to their section; and third, McAdoo had a Southern bias which probably made him more receptive to these appeals than he might otherwise have been.

Of all the groups in the Democratic Party, the Southern agrarians clamored loudest that the government must step directly into economic affairs in order to benefit depressed interest groups. They had an exceedingly restricted program, aimed almost exclusively at helping the farmer. After 1914, the main objective of these men was federal long-term rural credit legislation, but Wilson stalled things by refusing to accept any scheme for direct government support or subsidies. Such plans, he argued, amounted to a request for special privilege.[2]

When it suited him to use special privilege rhetoric in order to kill what he considered outlandishly "radical" Southern schemes for federal support, McAdoo did so. Populism had not yet receded entirely into dim memory, and he still felt sensitive on this point. Yet after 1913, on a yearly basis, he risked antagonizing the nation's bankers—not just in Wall Street, but often in the South and West as well—in order to mobilize Treasury power to promote an easier supply of credit for farmers. McAdoo apparently had little difficulty choosing between the interests of large and small banks on the one hand and an industry which still absorbed the energies of half the population on the other. The political significance of his policies requires no elaboration. But the ideological importance was perhaps even greater: three years before the President is commonly supposed to have capitulated to class legislation, the Secretary of the Treasury, and thus the Administration itself, had already begun to work directly and specifically in the interest of agriculture at the expense of other groups, special privilege rhetoric to the contrary notwithstanding.

By the end of Wilson's first term, farmers stood to benefit from Administration aid in a number of different realms, among them interstate highway construction, agricultural education, warehousing, and (after the President had reversed himself on the subject) long-term credit.

Since the Civil War, annual Treasury surpluses had been the rule. Because the government took in more than it paid out, it became extremely important to get cash back into circulation somehow. As time went on, successive Secretaries of the Treasury liberalized the interpretation of laws permitting the deposit of Treasury funds in national banks to ease the money market. But none stepped into the market with the boldness of McAdoo. In the first two years of his incumbency, the nation experienced money stringencies of the type which chronically recurred in America during the crop-moving season. One way of thwarting these shortages was government deposits—which, McAdoo made clear, he would make anywhere, anytime assistance was needed.[3]

Early in July, 1913, as the annual apprehension about a stringency began to spread, McAdoo announced that he intended to transfer from $25,000,000 to $50,000,000 into the South and West to anticipate tight money. The general fund had quite enough in it to handle this. Such deposits were not unprecedented, but what followed was. In the past, funds had not been placed entirely in the immediate areas of need, but instead in New York and other monetary centers, to be loaned in turn to country banks. The deposits had been made too late, after panic conditions had already hit; and by the time the money finally got to the farmers, the rate of interest had frequently risen to exorbitant heights.

To the surprise of many New York bankers, McAdoo announced that he planned to make the deposits in the national banks of the two or three principal cities where the crops were actually being harvested. Funds would be loaned to the banks at two percent interest; previously they had been extended without charge. In another break with precedent, McAdoo announced that he would accept prime commercial paper as security for government deposits at 65 percent of face value, as well as the traditional federal, state, and municipal bonds at 75 percent. Commercial paper must first be passed upon by the clearing house committees in the cities where the banks offering it were located; and all commercial paper and bonds would be subject to the final approval of McAdoo himself.

Though some doubts arose as to its legality, this maneuver enabled the banks to obtain funds upon a pledge of paper which they already held, and thus loosened credit. By accepting commercial paper, the Treasury was in effect rediscounting for the national banks—an important goal of the framers of the Federal Reserve Act. Next to this, most attention was aroused in financial circles by McAdoo's announcement that only banks which had at least 40 percent of their authorized circulation out-standing would be eligible for government deposits. This undoubtedly represented an attempt to revive the sagging market for 2 percent federal bonds, which in recent days had hit record lows. McAdoo accepted these bonds at par.

Where should the deposits be made? In order to find out, McAdoo broke with precedent once more by holding three conventions of bankers from the farming regions. Since the Northeast did not require funds, representatives from this area did not receive invitations. On the basis of the bankers' statements, $22,550,000 was allotted to the South and South-west; $19,000,000 to the Middle West and Northwest; and $4,950,000 to the Pacific coast and Rocky Mountain states. The department had been prepared to issue $100,000,000 if necessary; but of the total $46,500,000 allocated for immediate use, only $37,386,000 was needed, almost all of it secured by commercial paper.[4]

The deposits proved a success, and many, if not all, of the bankers in the farming regions were delighted. They ran into just one snag: the funds had been issued on the condition that the money would be dis-tributed to country banks at reasonable rates of interest. But the Treasury Department had no power to fix these rates; it could only admonish. Nor could the Treasury bypass the larger banks in favor of the country institu-tions, since it had no means or time to pass on the quality of the com-mercial paper which would be used as security if the department made deposits in hundreds of small banks in towns throughout the South and West. When these little institutions began to protest that the larger banks would show no mercy if they became the sole depositories, Treasury officials could only shrug their shoulders. The financial centers, they re-plied, had assured the department that its wishes would be fulfilled, and deposits were being made on this condition.[5]

Something more seemed necessary, however. Hence, in mid-August, still another major innovation was initiated when the department an-nounced that any bank which loaned or borrowed funds for speculation would receive no crop-moving deposits whatever. At the same time, the Treasury requested detailed information from every national bank in America in order to help cull the cooperating institutions from the others.[6]

Confidence returned, and the movement of crops proceeded more smoothly than it had for many years. The mere offer of funds eased the situation considerably, and McAdoo believed, perhaps correctly, that it had done a great deal to increase interest in and support for banking legislation, which pended at the time. The crop-moving initiative of 1913 demonstrated what government-managed central banking could accomplish. And certainly it proved one of his most popular acts as Secretary of the Treasury. Congressional "radicals" from the farming states took as much delight in it as did their constituents. And petty capitalists were able to claim McAdoo as their champion against the banks. "I still believe that there is a God in Israel and decent men on earth," wrote an Ohio manufacturer. "What a blow in the solar plexus of the money monopoly!" "Go to it," urged a Denver businessman. "You have these blood suckers on the run."[7]

In New York banking circles, on the other hand, the initiative produced a mixed response. The *Wall Street Journal* vigorously denounced the measure, complaining that "the Treasury scheme is to play politics, under the impression that by extending special countenance to the country bankers it in some way rebukes Wall Street." It is difficult to see why the policy aroused serious opposition. McAdoo had, after all, merely made temporary loans to a number of banks, and the action itself was neither unprecedented nor radical. True, interest rates fell; but the strain on New York banks was also relieved, and a sizable percentage of the crop-moving deposits rapidly flowed into the city. Money rates remained remarkably low at a time when Europe suffered from tight credit, and this may have stimulated the economy as a whole. If men on Wall Street grumbled, they probably did so because they had not been consulted in the first place and had been bypassed when McAdoo distributed the funds. Any benefit New York derived from the deposits was, at most, indirect.[8]

II

Compared with the convulsions of 1914, the money stringency of the previous year had been minor. Yet at first there seemed no cause for alarm. In February McAdoo announced that if the Federal Reserve banks were not open in time to handle crop movement, he would simply manage the situation as he had in 1913.

By July it had become apparent that nearly every agricultural region would produce bumper crops; 21 percent more wheat and nearly 20 percent more cotton were harvested in 1914 than ever before. Replying to McAdoo's request for information, some banks reported no need of government aid; but most wanted help. As a result, late in July McAdoo announced that he intended to deposit roughly $34,000,000—or more, if necessary—for crop moving and other legitimate business needs on conditions similar to those of 1913. He warned that he would refuse to allocate any funds to institutions charging excessive interest, and declined to fill the requests of ten national banks which proved recalcitrant. McAdoo also threatened to withdraw all federal funds from banks refusing accommodations on a "reasonable" basis. As in 1913, most of the deposits were made in the South.[9]

With the onset of the World War in August, the foreign market for cotton temporarily evaporated as the main consuming nations drove at each other's throats. Shipping was demoralized, and grain and especially cotton piled up at the ports. The German and Austrian markets were cut off, and many mills shut down or curtailed buying. The cotton exchanges in Allied countries closed their doors; the exchanges in New York, New Orleans, and other cities quickly followed. Prices tumbled from nearly twelve cents a pound during the last days of July to six cents in September and October. No other industry was so vulnerable, or suffered so much. David Houston questioned whether half the cotton crop could find a market.[10]

The economies of several states depended almost entirely on cotton sales. But exporting farm products was crucial not only to the South but to the nation as a whole. More than any other crop, the fate of cotton hung on its foreign market; and to sustain a favorable balance of trade, the United States had to export the staple. In 1913, more than 60 percent of the crop had been shipped abroad. Unlike the case of wheat, Europe could do without American cotton, at least for a time; and here lay seeds of disaster.

The war started just as the movement of the new cotton crop was about to begin. McAdoo got caught under a withering barrage of demands from all sides to act. In September the National Farmers' Union produced a formula through which the Federal Reserve banks would buy three to four million bales at twelve cents a pound—roughly the price of 1912-13; Congress would tax excess production in 1915. This basic proposal became the orthodox Southern answer to the problem, and valorization schemes began popping up everywhere.

By this time, the greatest pressure on McAdoo came from the Capitol. Texas was perhaps the hardest hit of all the cotton states, and a pesky, powerful Texan, Robert Henry, Chairman of the House Rules Committee, stood in the vanguard of the forces demanding relief. "If I have the power to prevent it," the Congressman announced grandiosely, "we never shall adjourn until we have legislation on the cotton situation." On October 2, Henry wrote McAdoo that he should

announce that within one week he will deposit in the national banks throughout the South several hundred million dollars.

Henry's plan called for a massive issue of bonds and greenbacks; as a precedent, he cited the Dayton flood relief of the year before. After conferences on October 7-8, a Congressional cotton-tobacco bloc was created, and on the ninth Henry introduced the bloc's own bill, which resembled and supplanted his own.[11]

Meanwhile, the President had made it clear that he opposed the

Henry scheme. But the pressure on McAdoo continued to mount. He was against advancing federal funds to producers, believing that such an expedient would compel the government eventually to buy the crop at ten cents a pound, store and insure it, and run the risk of bearing the brunt of a further sag in prices. "Nobody," he warned,

can arbitrarily fix prices. . . . The history of civilization shows that nations have been strewn with wrecks of that character.

. . .

Of course, somebody is going to get hurt. You can not help that. It is our business not to see that nobody shall be hurt, but it is our business to keep in touch with the situation, and, if possible, to prevent anybody from being hurt any more than is absolutely necessary, and that is all you can expect to have accomplished.[12]

On October 9, McAdoo made it clear to Henry that "the Government hasn't got 'several hundred million dollars' in the Treasury" and that under the law he had no right to deposit funds in the South alone:

If we disregard every suffering interest except cotton and make it the sole beneficiary of Governmental favor, what becomes of the Democratic principle "equal rights for all, special privileges to none?" If we enter upon the course you suggest, we must help every distressed industry impartially. . . . It would be a hopeless undertaking, in defiance of every sound principle of finance and economics, with certain disaster at the end.

Plenty of currency was available for the South under existing law, and a good deal of it had already been pumped into the section since the war began, McAdoo continued. But inflation would solve nothing. "It is impossible by legislation to create a market for cotton or to establish a price for it." There were "many things," McAdoo argued,

which the cotton States and the people of the South can do for themselves which the National Government cannot do for them.[13]

McAdoo had flayed the Henry scheme, but in the process he had also laid bare the limits of his own flexibility. True, the only substantial aid that had been rendered the South through early October had come from the Treasury Department. But under pressure, McAdoo drew the line at such things as price supports, a mainstay of the New Deal. Considered an inflationist by many, McAdoo held up the specter of inflation to frighten support away from the valorizers. Frequently denounced for overplaying the role of the federal government, he tried to throw the major burden of relief back onto the states. This heavy and misplaced reliance on the ability of the states was, in fact, an admission that his own program had failed so far and that his bag of tricks was empty.

Henry responded with another letter and more heated rhetoric. "There is a universal cry in the South for help from the National Government," warned South Carolina Senator Benjamin Tillman. In mid-October

McAdoo wrote Josephus Daniels that "I have spent more sleepless nights thinking about cotton than anything else with which I have had to deal since I took charge of the Treasury Department," adding ruefully: "The States of the South can do much but they are apparently doing nothing."[14]

III

McAdoo had called a cotton and tobacco conference for August 24 in Washington. It was an unwieldy affair—more than 200 bankers, producers, and officials attended, among them several Cabinet members and the entire Federal Reserve Board. Other interest groups also sent representatives. Nearly every speaker had his own plan. McAdoo warned that about 4,000,000 bales of the current cotton crop would have to be stored until the following year and warehouse certificates issued for it. The government, he added, was willing to buy a shipping line, and this would win the Latin American market for Southern cotton. Meanwhile, the interim solution should be emergency currency. In return for deposits of federal funds, he agreed to accept from national banks promissory notes secured by warehouse receipts for cotton, tobacco, and naval stores at 75 percent of face value. These receipts, then, would serve as satisfactory banking collateral. This freed bankers to lend farmers up to 75 percent of the face value of their warehouse receipts. The notes, however, could not have more than four months to run. Together with the cooperation of merchants and bankers, McAdoo argued, "these arrangements ought to enable the farmers to pick and market the cotton crop." To conservatives, the scheme seemed inflationary and smacked of "class legislation" and even quasi-valorization; to the more-than-vocal valorizers, it was not enough. Before the gathering adjourned on August 25, McAdoo made it absolutely clear that he would not permanently inflate the currency; nor would he give in to pressure to extend credit through the state banks.[15]

McAdoo appointed a committee of eighteen to consider the cotton dilemma and devise some formula for resolving it. The committee reported a few days later that producers should be aided in holding their cotton until foreign trade revived and that loans should be made by the banks on a basis of eight cents per pound, less whatever margin the lenders set. In addition, the committee recommended that notes with more than five months to run be accepted for rediscount by the Federal Reserve banks—which had not yet opened—and that they be approved by the national currency associations as security for further circulation to the national banks under the Federal Reserve and Aldrich-Vreeland acts. This was fine so far as it went; but it did not go nearly far enough.[16]

Conditions were still desperate; with the market prostrated, an endless stream of cotton poured into Southern warehouses. Prices fell short of production costs. And the clumsy Aldrich-Vreeland Act did not pump out credit fast enough. The emergency currency loans secured by warehouse receipts went only four months before redemption, but cotton could not be moved that quickly. Still worse, state banks, the main source of credit for Southern cotton producers, were ineligible to receive emergency currency directly from the government and often had trouble borrowing it from the national banks which could. Meanwhile, the pressure on McAdoo continued to mount. The cotton insurgents prevented passage of a series of amendments to the Federal Reserve Act by trying to tack on relief provisions. In mid-October Southern senators struggled to get a vote on cotton legislation by coupling it with the Administration's emergency war tax bill and then conducting a filibuster. And Henry was still beating his chest in the House.

On October 21 the Henry bill went down to defeat. If any initiative were to be taken now, it would have to come from the Administration. Sometime in late September or early October, Festus Wade, an important St. Louis banker, had begun to circulate the essentials of a plan for a fund of $150,000,000 to provide loans to Southern cotton producers at six cents a pound, enabling them to hold their crops at least one year. On October 5, this scheme was ratified in St. Louis by a group of bankers from the cotton states. Wade had already broached the subject with McAdoo, who, on October 2, sent a contingent of Southern bankers to St. Louis to develop a plan in collaboration with him. The scheme that gained approval on the fifth had at least the conditional support of McAdoo's delegation, and he thought it had potential.

McAdoo presented the Wade proposal to the Federal Reserve Board, which appointed a committee composed of Hamlin, Warburg, and Harding to confer with Wade and his associates. Several days later McAdoo agreed to support the principle of the scheme but added "that he would *not* endorse this particular plan as he thought interest rates too high." Meanwhile, the Board also decided to back the Wade proposal in principle, but with certain reservations.[17]

On October 13, S. R. Bertron, a prominent New York banker, arranged a dinner for House, Vanderlip, Henry P. Davison of J. P. Morgan and Company, A. Barton Hepburn and Albert H. Wiggin of the Chase National Bank, and other bankers. At the time, House, like McAdoo, opposed the Wade scheme because it contemplated a prohibitive rate of interest, but a tentative understanding was reached by which the bankers present would take $35,000,000 of the $50,000,000 which the plan allotted to New York. Cotton would be bolstered at six cents a pound; interest would run at 6 percent. House phoned McAdoo, who balked at having the Federal Reserve Board take part in the arrangement. The following day, the Colonel pushed the bankers toward a final agreement. Wiggin and Bertron led in closing the deal. Even at this point, McAdoo had still not come into line. "He . . . appeared not to want the Federal Reserve Board to get the credit of putting the plan through," House wrote. "He therefore agreed to throw the weight of his office back of the proposition and to father it." On October 17 McAdoo conferred in New York with House, Warburg, Harding, and several of the bankers; the plan was revised still further, and in a letter to the President on the twenty-ninth McAdoo endorsed the loan fund as "the only practical way to help the cotton situation."[18]

But Wade's plan did not turn out to be the one that finally went through. He had not presented an entirely workable scheme and proved unable to finance it. McAdoo called a conference in New York for October 19, after Wade's proposal had "utterly failed" and the banker turned to McAdoo to breathe new life into it. Among those present were Warburg, Harding, and a number of New York bankers. The outcome was a fresh project; and this Cotton Loan Plan received the unqualified support of McAdoo, Wade, and the Federal Reserve Board. After a day-long conference involving Wade and other financiers on October 24, the revised arrangement, incorporating certain changes, was finally agreed upon. Later more adjustments emerged, some apparently recommended by Wiggin, who had headed a subcommittee of bankers, and the final scheme was adopted November 30. The Federal Reserve Board agreed to administer the undertaking with the aid of various committees. The amount of the fund was scaled down to $135,000,000. New York banks would supply $50,000,000 (by the time the plan was announced they had already done so), provided that banks of the other noncotton-producing states furnished an equal amount. The Southern banks would supply the rest. The six cent pound and 6 percent interest rate were incorporated; loans would run one year with the privilege of renewal for six months. No price fixing was involved; the borrower could sell his collateral anytime and pay off the loan. Meanwhile, the loan would help see him through until a measure of stability returned to Europe.[19]

Despite New York's precommitment to the Cotton Loan Fund, the remaining subscriptions came with difficulty. In part, no doubt, this was because from a banker's standpoint the pool represented a questionable investment, despite vigorous claims to the contrary by McAdoo. Another major snag occurred in Boston, where cotton spinners, who played an important role in managing the banks, pressured these institutions against participating in it. Logically enough, the spinners wanted cotton at a low price, and they wanted local bank credit for themselves. In the end, much to McAdoo's disgust, Boston's subscription was minuscule.[20]

Slow completion of the fund could be extremely dangerous. Cotton poured into Southern warehouses and the producers had to have credit. There was actually a constriction of credit available from New York, possibly because bankers had already committed large amounts to the pool. But a final hurdle had to be surmounted. Many legal experts believed that the fund was illegal, and bankers feared that if they got involved they would run afoul of the Sherman or Clayton antitrust acts. By November 6, four fifths of the pool allocated to the noncotton states had been subscribed, and McAdoo wrote the President that "I am satisfied that I can get the necessary subscriptions to the fund [only] if the Attorney General shall give me an opinion that the plan violates no Federal statute." On November 4, McAdoo and Gregory had discussed the matter; the following day House got in touch with the Attorney General and made sure that he would render a favorable opinion. Gregory gave his sanction, and the stage had been set for completion of the pool.[21]

McAdoo and the fund's other organizers exerted a tremendous amount of pressure on the banking community, but opposition remained powerful. With progress sluggish, newspapers began to predict failure. Then, on November 17, McAdoo and John Skelton Williams lunched with Bernard Baruch, who agreed to subscribe $1,000,000 if necessary. Afterward Warburg reported that Kuhn, Loeb and Company would take $2,000,000. This eased the fund over the hump, and that night McAdoo announced to the press that despite delays caused by "the selfish opposition of certain textile manufacturers and local interests, which have tried to defeat it," the pool had been completed. On November 30, it went into effect.[22]

McAdoo had never worked harder for anything in his life than he did to clear up the cotton dilemma, and by late February, 1915, he believed that the Loan Fund had succeeded in raising prices. But ironically, it did almost nothing to resolve the crisis. At the insistence of the New York bankers, the Central Committee—McAdoo and the other members of the Federal Reserve Board—loaned on the basis of six cent cotton; but a margin was set at 20 percent above the face value of the loan, and the farmer could actually borrow only five cents per pound. The producers could do better by dealing with private banking houses as they had in the past, and by the time the fund had been liquidated on February 1, only $28,000 had been loaned.[23]

While the pool was being completed McAdoo kept an eye on foreign buyers and put pressure on the State Department to make sure that cotton shipped by neutrals could get through to all the belligerents. With foreign demand reviving and prices rising, the necessity for holding cotton began to recede as early as September. Meanwhile, the shipping situation started to ease. And the opening of the Federal Reserve banks in November released a large amount of reserves, enabling more new loans to be made and extensions granted.

In the end, then, the crisis that the Cotton Loan Fund had been so frantically thrown together to meet dissipated without it. But this is not to say that the pool had no effect at all. It probably lured buyers who had been holding out for lower prices into the market, shoring up prices during November and December. More important, it doubtless had a psychological impact on the South. Action, or the appearance of action, can often be as important as the results themselves; so it was with the cotton pool of 1914. Failure to do something about the crisis would have been disastrous to the prestige of the Administration, especially among its vital Southern constituency.

Even so, the South felt bitter—perhaps not as much so as it would have been if nothing had been done, but bitter nonetheless. However much goodwill Northern bankers and the Administration affected, some Southerners suspected that they had really wanted the Cotton Loan Fund to fail all along. Relief had been too meager. And it had been too long in coming.[24]

IV

The key to the cotton situation in 1915, as in 1914, was continued foreign buying, as well as crop diversification and a slash in acreage.[25] Cotton exports and prices rose higher than had seemed likely to most observers during the previous fall; though a large surplus remained from the previous year, decreased use of fertilizer and a slump in labor costs reduced the 1915 cost of production by at least a fifth, and considerable cotton acreage had been converted to cereal crops. From January to May cotton exports were greater than during the same period in the preceding year. Despite some pessimism in the South itself about the coming season—prices began to slide in June and July—W. P. G. Harding wrote McAdoo that there seemed no reason "why there should be any serious problems in connection with the crop marketing this fall." But McAdoo felt far less sanguine, fearing above all that England might declare cotton contraband. "The cotton outlook," he wrote in mid-July, "is dark."[26]

British detention of cotton shipments bound for neutral countries had exacerbated the export situation during the spring and early summer. McAdoo invited representatives of the English Treasury to America to discuss cotton, among other things, and as a result of these conversations and other negotiations, assurance had been received that cotton shipments by neutrals to belligerent nations would be respected. In July and August, while McAdoo was in Maine, Harding had a number of conferences with Sir Richard Crawford, commercial adviser at the British embassy. Crawford and the British Ambassador both warned Harding late in July that their government was on the verge of declaring cotton absolute contraband. They notified and talked with other American officials about this as well. Crawford added assurances that steps had been taken to support the market. Harding worked with Crawford in arranging for compensatory British cotton purchases. Meanwhile, he passed all this on to McAdoo, who had plenty of precise forewarning when the contraband declaration came on August 21.[27]

McAdoo gave out a statement on the twentieth indicating that he would deposit government funds in Federal Reserve banks whenever necessary; and the Federal Reserve Board had arranged preliminary plans for extending the facilities of the new banking system for the fall crop movement. On August 23 McAdoo issued a soothing statement to the effect that if necessary he would deposit $30,000,000 or more in gold in the Federal Reserve banks of Atlanta, Dallas, and Richmond, to enable these three institutions to rediscount loans made on cotton secured by warehouse receipts. For the time being, the government would charge no interest. The banks, in turn, should loan on cotton at 6 percent. This announcement was meant to help avert a panic over possible demoralization of the cotton market and to impress the bankers with the vital necessity of extending abundant credit at reasonable rates. At the time, McAdoo had no idea what measures Crawford would take to stabilize the market, but he believed

that cotton will, upon its merits and without any artificial stimulants, take care of itself once confidence in the situation is thoroughly established.

Only $15,000,000 of the proffered funds had to be deposited, and perhaps McAdoo's statements played some role in relieving the situation. But the limitations in his economic thought had not yet been transcended. The government, he insisted, was doing everything it could; the primary responsibility rested with local banks.[28]

On September 3 McAdoo extended his offer of funds to Federal Reserve banks of the West and Northwest. Wheat farmers had been requesting such assistance, but the offer was turned down, since resources seemed more than sufficient; the other reserve banks outside the South also declined deposits.

Meanwhile, in June, the Federal Reserve Board had appointed a committee to study the cotton situation. The committee concluded that warehouse receipts for nonperishable agricultural staples could serve as a solid basis for bank loans; and on September 3, with McAdoo's blessing—indeed, at his insistence—the Board issued new regulations providing that notes secured by warehouse receipts for these commodities, and with a specified date of maturity, would be rediscounted at a preferential rate of 3 percent by the Federal Reserve banks. But there was one crucial proviso: the member banks could not charge more than 6 percent interest to the borrower to receive the special rate. When several reserve banks stalled in putting this rate into effect, McAdoo—who fought tenaciously for low rediscount rates at Board meetings—advocated the use of compulsion by the Board to push these institutions into line. The new ruling was largely anticipatory and helped shore up Southern morale.[29]

On the same day the regulation was issued, McAdoo announced that he would deposit $5,000,000 in each of the Federal Reserve banks of Richmond, Atlanta, and Dallas, adding that further aid would be extended wherever need arose. This was a small amount for handling a crop which Harding estimated to be worth $800,000,000; and just four days earlier, John Skelton Williams had announced that the banks could manage the crop with no federal help whatever. But McAdoo believed the South would not be content to have mere assurances that he would be standing by. The psychological factor, as the Board itself agreed, remained crucial.[30]

These efforts, linked with the work of the British to sustain the market, and, perhaps, with certain German purchases, dissipated the South's deep anxiety. As the new crop came up for sale, the price steadily rose. The necessity to borrow diminished, and the combined commodity loans by Southern reserve banks up to the first week of November totalled only about $3,500,000. But the offer of federal aid freed other reserve banks to advance credit more liberally than they otherwise would have; thus, the actions of McAdoo and the Board enabled marketing to proceed without the familiar seasonal disturbance in interest rates. The process went on at lower rates than in years past, and millions of dollars were saved for cotton producers that would otherwise have gone to middlemen and speculators.[31]

Late in September, McAdoo ruefully observed that the "selfish interests and fool partisans"—specifically, New Yorkers and New Englanders—had been attacking him for sectional favoritism in his moves to help the cotton producers. Wall Street had vehemently criticized his statement of August 23 and the ensuing deposits as unnecessary interference and, incidentally, as unnecessary competition. And a good deal of discussion arose in high financial circles about the possibility of amending the Federal Reserve Act in a way that would circumscribe the power of the Secretary of the Treasury to deposit and withdraw government funds from the banks.[32]

On the other hand, Southerners were delighted. A telegram even arrived from Robert Henry: "Allow me to congratulate you on your action," he wired late in August. "It is in substance and exact principle what I en[d]eavored to do in Congress last year." But, to the end, Henry remained incorrigible: he still held out for $150,000,000, or $200,000,000, or even $300,000,000, at 4 percent not six.[33]

V

The struggle over crop movements represented one part of a broader problem that confronted McAdoo almost constantly: maintaining an even flow of credit. In the fall of 1914 he wrote Colonel House:

The bank question is the biggest question in my judgment, before the American people today. The country has long suffered from frightful abuses, much worse than from the railroads and from the various forms of industrial trusts. Remedies can be found and will be found beyond a doubt. . . . I am very determined to use every power of my office to make it impossible for the legitimate interests of this country to be penalized by the arbitrary will of men inspired by greed, fear and selfishness which too much characterizes [sic] the usual conduct of the banking business in America.

In February, 1914, he remarked that

we want to reorganize the credit of this country to meet our seasonal demands. We intend to make rediscounting not only respectable but profitable for banks. Our aim is a legitimate expansion of credit.[34]

McAdoo consistently opposed tying up funds in the Treasury unnecessarily; not only did he apportion them for seasonal and emergency relief, but he also retained large deposits in national and Federal Reserve banks across the country on a year-round basis. Meanwhile he conducted a number of spasmodic offensives to free credit in periods when it was tight, offensives which usually caught the banks off guard. The first of these occurred soon after McAdoo took office.

With Europe demanding large quantities of American gold, with seasonal pressures on reserves upcoming, and perhaps also because tariff and currency reform were in the offing when the special session of Congress convened in April, 1913, a large number of banks began to keep an unusually tight rein on credit. Nervous apprehension spread through the business community. The situation seemed to have a sinister side: men in whom McAdoo had considerable confidence informed him that various interests encouraged uncertainty in order to defeat or alter tariff and banking legislation. By early summer, McAdoo felt sure "that there has been a deliberate attempt to frighten the country and to contract credits, and that it has been successful to a considerable degree." By June things looked grim. A "Wilson panic" at the beginning of the Administration might have prevented or at least postponed effective financial legislation. Nor was the European money market in any condition to help—European demands for American gold were one of the important factors behind the uneasiness.[35]

On June 1 McAdoo deposited $10,000,000 in the national banks. It was hoped that this would ease the stringency and demonstrate his willingness to wield the power of the Treasury to unlock credit. But he had not gone far enough. Ten days later McAdoo indicated that he would not hesitate to issue $500,000,000, the full amount of emergency currency allowed under the Aldrich-Vreeland Act. In 1913 this was a staggering sum, more than equal to half the national debt; the total amount of national bank currency in the United States amounted to only $737,065,000. While McAdoo partially explained the statement away by remarking that it bore no relation to the current Wall Street slump, he had made his intentions clear.[36]

There were certain ironies in the offer stemming from serious defects in the Aldrich-Vreeland Act itself. The terms of issue were so onerous that no currency association had ever applied for emergency funds before; nor had McAdoo received any requests from bankers for an issue now. But the announcement scuttled the bankers' excuse that they had been holding funds in reserve for the coming crop movement. At the heart of the statement lay its psychological impact. It was no coincidence that in New York the languishing stock market suddenly rebounded, that the banks released reserves, or that interest rates dropped. Predictably, perhaps, no applications came in for Aldrich-Vreeland notes, evidence that much of the panic talk had been spurious.[37]

In New York banking circles the response was generally hostile, and the *Wall Street Journal* and New York *Journal of Commerce* were sharply critical. The *New York Times* denigrated McAdoo's "theory of Government altruism" as "unsound" and "evil." But outside the money centers, the reaction seems to have been more favorable. McAdoo himself had few doubts about the salutary effect of his announcement. Writing House, he claimed that "a panic in New York" had been "narrowly averted." He had "shown the country that, should a money stringency occur, the banks and not the Government would be responsible for it." But this opening move could not reverse credit contraction for long. Late in November McAdoo issued another statement to the effect that no reason existed for the financial community to be apprehensive about Congress and banking reform and that commercial paper should be accepted as usual.[38]

In the wake of the economic cataclysm brought on by the European war, bankers met all, or nearly all, the legitimate credit needs of business following a brief twinge of hesitation during the first half of August, 1914.

There was no widespread, desperate loan contraction as had occurred in 1907 but, in fact, quite the opposite. And though interest rates climbed steeply from the end of July through much of September, they did not reach the high peaks characteristic of former crises. The situation was met as it should be, by loan expansion; and this played a vital role in staving off a panic.

Many banks, however, chose to refuse credit. This was natural enough: the Federal Reserve system had not yet been activated, and credit restriction and higher interest rates could be expected. But some banks began piling up excess reserves, and interest rates rose to exorbitance— 10 or even 12 percent per annum in the principal cities of the country compared with 2 to 3 percent before the war. Emergency currency was supplied to a number of these cities totalling $210,000,000, and as a result by early November the money situation had improved considerably. But with the stock exchanges shut down no market existed for securities and holders could not sell them in order to pay banks which had jacked up interest rates on their loans. Large sums disappeared from reserve and central reserve cities as interior banks, uneasy over the safety of their deposits in the urban centers and fearful of runs at home, withdrew their funds.[39]

"There is no justification for high interest rates," McAdoo stated flatly in October. He was determined to compel the national banks to conform to state usury laws. Eventually the Federal Reserve system would offer a partial solution, but it would merely set the stage for lower rates. "You must assert your own rights," he warned farmers.[40]

At this point, McAdoo set a new precedent for controlling the money market when he threatened banks with loss of their federal deposits unless they kept interest rates down and loaned to the hilt. In a formal statement on September 21 McAdoo cautioned national banks which had received either Aldrich-Vreeland currency or crop-moving funds to extend credit and keep interest rates low. He had ordered an investigation, he warned, and would not hesitate to pull government deposits out of intractable institutions or cut off their supply of emergency currency. The threat failed; many banks wanted to make loans but could not find borrowers because of the business recession that followed the onset of war. On September 23, again warning that extraordinary and "indefensible" hoarding was going on, McAdoo informed ten Southern banks that for the present he would refuse to deposit the second installment of crop-moving funds with them. McAdoo also announced that in view of the hoarding that he believed threatened the nation's economy he would issue a daily list of institutions holding excessive reserves. He accompanied these moves with a good deal of behind-the-scenes pressure.[41]

On September 25, in another effort to dissolve the clots of reserves, McAdoo published a list of nearly 250 national banks carrying reserves above the legal minimum. Only country banks were named, many of them Southern, and most of them small. Because the situation began to ease, he did not issue any further lists, though he continued to hold out the threat of publicity. But on September 30 he announced that $3,000,000 of government deposits had been recalled from "guilty" banks and transferred to other institutions. And a few days later he resumed his offensive once more, this time attacking banks in the central reserve cities.[42]

Early in November John Skelton Williams, who as Comptroller of the Currency was becoming quite unpopular with the financial community, followed up McAdoo's barrage with telegrams to national banks in New York and other cities asking what their interest rates ran and simultaneously advising that they be cut to 6 percent. Williams also notified New York banks that he intended to publish a list of complying institutions. As a result, nearly all of them did lower their rates. But despite Williams's assault the New York banks were not the chief troublemakers—indeed, they stood to suffer from hoarding by the country banks and up to a certain point, at least, seem to have approved of Treasury policy.[43]

McAdoo and Williams had tried to free credit conservatively, through education and publicity. The general easing of credit which ensued was only partly due to their antihoarding efforts, if at all. Far more important, no doubt, was the restoration of economic equilibrium following the initial crisis in August and the revival of confidence in the business community. But despite the fact that McAdoo had only singled out perhaps 3 percent of the national banks, with roughly 1 percent of the aggregate capital, he and the Comptroller had infuriated large numbers of bankers. On the other hand, the Texas legislature passed a formal resolution of endorsement, and letters flowed in from small businessmen in the South and West. "It is a *Gods* blessing that this country has a *Wilson* and a *McAdoo, hope of the South*," wrote a South Carolina merchant.[44]

McAdoo took another extraordinary measure in 1914 to free credit, one which many observers found ominous. In September, the Funding Board of the State of Tennessee arrived in New York to sell the state's short-term notes in order to finance an obligation maturing October 1. The board needed a loan of $1,400,000, but the banks wanted 8 percent interest. In an attempt to muster the aid of the Treasury Department to secure a lower rate, Luke Lea, United States Senator from Tennessee, conferred with McAdoo on September 24. Fear that the state might default had been mounting, and McAdoo issued a public announcement labeling the situation "preposterous" and warning that if the New York banks refused to take the notes at reasonable interest he would try to find an institution that would.[45]

Lea returned to New York, where he reached an agreement with the president of the National Park Bank: if the Treasury Department would make a deposit of gold with it, the National Park would furnish the loan at 6 percent. McAdoo consummated the arrangement with the bank's president over the telephone; $1,000,000 had already been placed in the institution for crop-moving, and on October 1 McAdoo made a special deposit of $400,000. In Wall Street, where conversation buzzed, McAdoo's move was cited as a precedent, and the Congressional Republicans stirred up a storm.[46]

In 1915, Williams led the crusade against high interest rates, following the general pattern of the year before. Again widespread, shocking complaints of usury arose. And again, the bulk of the offenders were small country banks in the South and West. While only nine were in New York, Texas had 168 and Oklahoma 287.[47]

Williams was far more inclined than his predecessors to wage war on usury. During October circulars went out to the national banks reminding them of a federal statute against violation of state usury laws (which the states themselves had been conspicuously unsuccessful in enforcing). Williams also put indirect pressure on the state banks. Generally these efforts succeeded, and interest rates slumped. But a committee of the American Bankers' Association unanimously passed a resolution objecting to Williams's accusations.[48]

Money rates remained at moderate levels throughout most of 1916. The seasonal strain proved minimal, and with the Federal Reserve system well established, no crop-moving deposits were necessary. But in parts of the South and West, exorbitant interest rates persisted. In January, Williams made it clear that he contemplated initiating proceedings for annulment of the charters of a number of national banks which earned 40 percent interest or above on all their loans—a drastic expedient but, other than publicity, the only one left in his arsenal. Williams called for a Congressional investigation of interest rates, and he wanted the Department of Justice to be endowed with power to bring civil suits against the guilty institutions. His inquiries into the operations of the banks added new names to his rapidly growing list of enemies.[49]

VI

Meanwhile, a major effort had been mounted permanently to solve the credit problems of at least one group harnessed to Southern and Western bank rates. The Federal Farm Loan Act of 1916 represented the first attempt in the nation's history to supply farmers with abundant long-term credit at reasonable interest. It also mollified conservatives to the extent that it kept farm mortgages out of the Federal Reserve system. The legislation bore a certain resemblance to the Glass-Owen measure (which had already furnished short-term agricultural credit through the discounting of agricultural paper by banks in the reserve system). The act provided for the creation of a Federal Farm Loan Bureau in the Treasury Department, administered by a board which included the Secretary of the Treasury and four appointive members. The system embraced twelve Federal Land banks, each in its own district. Cooperative Farm Loan associations handled the borrowing on a first mortgage basis, against the security of land and improvements. Private Joint Stock Land banks were also organized under the supervision of the board.

McAdoo worked closely with the bill's Senate sponsor, Henry F. Hollis. One vital section of the measure provided for the issuance of bonds by the twelve land banks against first mortgage loans; the bonds and the income they produced were to be totally tax-exempt. But how could this exemption be legalized? After threshing out the issue McAdoo and Hollis arrived at a solution: by rendering the farm loan bonds issued under the provisions of the bill instrumentalities of the federal government, they, and the income from them, could become totally tax-free. This provision went into the measure over great opposition from bankers in the farm mortgage business. The President signed the bill in July.

McAdoo prized the new act so highly that he seriously overrated it. Though it did not directly benefit the landless, he predicted that, with proper administration, it would at least "emancipate the farmer from the disadvantages he has so long endured" as "preferred sufferer . . . from a scarcity of money." It would mean security, independence, and self-respect for the agricultural community. And it would put an end to farm tenancy and bring urban families back to the soil.[50]

The measure made the Secretary of the Treasury Chairman ex officio of the Federal Farm Loan Board. His first job involved selecting the other four members. The whole loan system was an organized invitation to political favoritism, and McAdoo fell under pressure reminiscent of the days when he had been putting the Federal Reserve together. One obstacle was Hollis. The Senator did not find most of McAdoo's choices acceptable, and despite Hollis's desire to have allies on the Board McAdoo ignored him completely. Hollis contemplated resigning from Congress; but McAdoo helped soothe his ruffled feelings by appointing one of the Senator's favorites to the Directorship of the Mint.[51]

McAdoo selected the Federal Farm Loan Board subject to Wilson's approval. He wanted to appoint John Skelton Williams Farm Loan

Commissioner, but Williams declined. Instead, McAdoo chose as the system's active executive chief Democrat George W. Norris [52] of Philadelphia, a former lawyer, businessman, and municipal administrator who had experience in banking. A second member, Charles E. Lobdell, was a Republican banker and judge from Kansas. ("The law requires a by-partisan Board, which I think is unfortunate," McAdoo confided to House.) W. S. A. Smith of Iowa, also a Republican, was extremely well known in agricultural circles. And for the final seat on the Board McAdoo picked Herbert Quick of West Virginia, a Democrat who had done good work for the Administration's shipping bill. The Senate quickly confirmed these men.[53]

The first task the Board faced involved dividing the country into twelve federal land bank districts and picking cities for the banks. Hearings began August 21 in Maine. By the time the Board had finished them more than a month later, it had conducted extensive research, traveled 20,000 miles, and held fifty-three hearings in forty-four states. Late in December McAdoo announced the Board's decisions. The next step was to advertise for subscriptions to the capital stock of the twelve banks, appoint their directors and officers, and organize the Farm Loan associations. By late December, thousands of these associations had already been tentatively established. Because the $9,000,000 of initial capital stock was not expected to pay dividends during the first year and would be retired at par as soon as the profits of the system allowed, the public subscriptions proved minuscule. On March 1, following the provisions of the act, the Treasury itself picked up the remaining $8,880,315 of land bank stock at par. The Board established a uniform land bank interest rate of 5 percent on farm mortgages for the entire nation. The Federal Farm Loan system was going into operation—only to be stalled by America's entry into the war.

CHAPTER TEN

THE EUROPEAN WAR AND LATIN AMERICAN MARKETS

I

Between 1907 and 1915, the United States experienced an erratic series of spurts and declines in its economy. During 1912, the warm glow of prosperity enveloped the land; but late in 1913 the clouds of a business depression appeared again. Businessmen, as William Redfield observed, "seem to be doing fairly well now but they are afraid they may not do so well hereafter." As much as anything, they feared the Administration itself. The depression was worldwide and had begun before Wilson took power, but the blame commonly fell on a number of factors involving the alleged "radicalism" of the President and his advisers and their very victory in 1912. The tariff of 1913 had reduced rates and forced many businessmen to readjust their operations, and uncertainty arose over the Glass-Owen bill and the course the Administration's antitrust program would take. All of this was compounded by a gloomy condition among the railroads, the largest purchasers and employers in the country, and a veto of freight rate increases by the ICC.[1]

Some of the reforms of the early Wilson Administration went far toward quelling business hostility, but the depression temporarily undid this. The decline was pinned on the Democrats, and the Administration became the target of capitalists' spleen. Most of all, businessmen wanted an end to new regulatory legislation, an end to unpredictability. In rebuttal, McAdoo simply turned their arguments inside out: legislation had not caused the depression; postponement of new antitrust laws and other measures would simply hinder prosperity.

But with business failures showing a marked rise and unemployment at a dangerous level, Tumulty, Burleson, Garrison, and McReynolds urged the President to go slow with his reform program or abandon it altogether. McAdoo and Bryan were alone in pressing for further legislation. Caught in a cross fire of advice, the President moved to the right and worked to calm the fears of the business community. This shift caused McAdoo a good deal of concern.[2]

The depression was relatively minor, and rather than press for structural reform beyond the scope of the Federal Reserve Act, McAdoo tended to resort to such palliatives as radiating confidence, tinkering with interest rates, and implying that the slump had been caused by a conspiracy of the Administration's enemies. Treasury operations had an inflationary impact during fiscal 1915, which may also have helped. During the first half of 1914, international stability enjoyed a brief restoration following the Balkan conflict. Business activity stayed high; the stock exchange experienced something of a boom; commodity prices remained stable; and credit was easy.

II

McAdoo predicted prosperity, but without knowing that by the end of the summer Europe would be embroiled in total war. By late July, one of the sharpest financial crises of the century was brewing, and the stock exchanges bore the first brunt of it. With prospects for peace dimming, panicky foreign lenders and investors, fearing the United States would suspend gold payments, began to liquidate American securities at a frantic pace. As European stock exchanges closed, the eye of the storm descended on New York and prices suffered their most violent decline since 1907. For the first time in the long history of American panics, European aid was unavailable; the market stood alone.

As late as half an hour before the New York exchange was to open on Friday morning, July 31, the board of governors still intended to begin business as usual at 10:00 o'clock. But the London exchange, last major market for securities still operating in Europe, was on the verge of shutting down. With every foreign exchange closed, New York would become the sole target of frantic dumping of securities; unprecedented selling orders agreeing to any available price arrived at New York banking houses from Europe that very morning. This dumping required immediate gold shipments, and Wall Street would be unable to pay. It was the greatest crisis the exchange had ever confronted.

At about 9:30, J. P. Morgan telephoned McAdoo and explained that the governors of the New York Stock Exchange would soon meet to consider closing. They wanted McAdoo's advice, and Morgan assured him that they would follow it. McAdoo hesitated, questioning whether his opinion would be of any value; but under the circumstances, he added, it seemed wise to shut down. Morgan replied that it would be done, and the same morning, amid cheers, the exchange closed for the second time in its history, not to reopen for months. All other important stock exchanges across the nation quickly followed suit, and so did dealers in unlisted securities. On the same day, McAdoo issued a statement to the effect that he was watching the situation and would help if necessary where he could; $500,000,000 in emergency currency was ready for issue. He also worked with good results to persuade the bankers, whose normal operations had suffered a major blow from the suspension of dealings in securities, to spare brokers and others whose loans, secured by listed stocks and bonds, had been rendered nonliquid by the closing of the exchanges.[3]

In October a new threat crystallized: bankers holding notes for which securities had been put up as collateral might be compelled to demand payment, leading in turn to massive dumping on the Curb and a disastrous price drop. John Skelton Williams thwarted the danger late in the month by ordering national bank examiners to approve every loan secured by listed stocks at their July 30 value. This practically dried up the Curb market and stimulated an immediate revival in prices.[4]

For some time, McAdoo had been certain that an eventual cataclysm in Europe was unavoidable. As relations among the major powers deteriorated, he wrote that "from a humanitarian standpoint the prospect" of a general European war seemed "simply shocking and incomprehensible." But his immediate concern was how well the Treasury could bear such an onslaught; and he found the prospects good. Indeed, "a great European war would eventually greatly inure to our benefit" (McAdoo, the realist, writing).[5]

The outbreak of hostilities in August struck even more fear into Americans marooned in Europe—estimated at the time at more than 100,000—than it did on Wall Street. With sailings cancelled, banks temporarily closed, and foreign exchange and credit conditions in chaos, thousands of tourists were momentarily unable to obtain funds upon traveler's checks and letters of credit. Others were simply penniless. American tourists poured into London and besieged steamship offices in an attempt to get home. On August 5 a ship left Southampton bound for the United States with large numbers of wealthy Americans traveling steerage. McAdoo wrote Bryan urging that "all possible pressure be exerted on the German government to take steps to permit our citizens to be removed from Germany."[6]

Wilson and Bryan determined to authorize the embassies to countersign traveler's checks, letters of credit, and similar documents; and early in August McAdoo and the Secretary of State went before the House and Senate appropriations committees to urge quick allocation of $2,500,000 to be lent against letters of credit and other securities. Meanwhile, $250,000 had already been earmarked to advance funds and transportation for stranded Americans. The President created a relief board which consisted of Bryan, Garrison, and Daniels, with McAdoo as chairman. McAdoo announced that the Treasury and the subtreasuries would receive deposits for Americans in Europe and try to make sure that the money got to the beneficiaries. Roughly $2,260,000 was placed in the Treasury and subtreasuries to accomplish this. On August 6 an American cruiser left for Europe with $1,500,000 in gold, the Assistant Secretary of War, a number of bankers, and two personal representatives of McAdoo on board. Meanwhile $300,000 was cabled ahead to various embassies so that aid could be extended before this ship, and another which soon followed, arrived. On August 21 the relief board decided to make a deposit with the Assistant United States Treasurer at New York to help Americans arriving there from abroad.

In Europe arrangements proceeded smoothly. The ambassadors appointed relief committees. Army officers disbursed funds and even railroad tickets to Americans in order to get them out as quickly as possible. But with British mastery of the Atlantic under challenge, how could Americans return home? The simplest method, one favored by McAdoo, was for the U.S. government to charter German liners stranded in American and Italian ports, running up the Stars and Stripes and operating them under the supervision of United States officials. Germany agreed to the proposition and so did the British, provided the vessels would be manned by American crews under the U.S. flag and returned to neutral ports once the task had been completed; but the proposal was killed by the objections of France. By the time the French finally came around, liners from the Allied nations had gone into operation again and the dilemma had passed.

III

When the armies of Europe began to mobilize, the United States faced financial conditions which might easily have degenerated into a catastrophic panic. The supply of foreign capital had been cut off, and many bankers urged a debt moratorium similar to those declared by the belligerents. Consternation gripped the business community. That the nation withstood the strain far better than it had in 1893 or 1907 was due in large measure to McAdoo, who responded with what one newspaper called a brilliant " 'mobilization of finance,' more rapid and more impressive than the assembling of the best troops in Europe." The steps required to keep the U.S. on an even financial keel were drastic. But, as McAdoo later wrote, "hesitation meant panic and inaction meant national disaster."[7]

Across the country, banks got caught with exceedingly meager surplus lending power at the time the European crisis hit. In New York, bank reserves had been melting for weeks before war was declared because of gold exports and the repatriation of American securities. With the closing of the stock exchange, a fresh problem emerged: banks could not liquidate their investments. All collateral loans, whose liquidation provided the banks with their chief means of increasing free assets, became permanent investments until the exchange could be reopened. At the same time, demand for loans and renewals continued to mount. Under the circumstances, it seemed logical for the banks to resort to clearing house certificates to settle balances among themselves. But danger hid in this expedient too: in the past it had led to restrictions on cash payments. The obvious solution was the Aldrich-Vreeland Act, which the Glass-Owen measure had liberalized and extended. On July 31 McAdoo announced that $500,000,000 of emergency notes were ready for issue. Several days later, he indicated that the Treasury Department was prepared to allocate $100,000,000 to the national banks of New York City if necessary and to other banks across the country as well.

On August 1, McAdoo sent telegrams to the chairmen of the clearing house associations of New York, Chicago and St. Louis requesting them to send committees to confer with him the following Monday. But events began to move slightly ahead of him. By August 2—fortunately a Sunday—the crisis had reached its most dangerous stage. William Woodward, acting Chairman of the New York Clearing House Committee, telephoned McAdoo that day and told him the clearing house wanted McAdoo to parley with major bankers in New York.[8] These men anticipated a run on the banks when they opened next morning. Because they would have to be on hand when the onslaught began, the bankers could not go to Washington. After consulting with the President, McAdoo, with Williams, Hamlin, and Harding in tow, took a train for New York. Bankers met him at the station, and a conference immediately convened at the Vanderbilt. Here McAdoo met more than twenty leaders of the city's financial community. The bankers feared that threatened runs the next morning would lead to a panic; some—perhaps most—of them knew they could not meet their obligations if the country banks began demanding currency. A number wondered whether they should open at all.

After consulting privately with a banker he trusted, McAdoo agreed to help, and the bankers indicated that they wanted as much emergency currency as the law would allow as fast as possible. McAdoo decided to issue to the full[9] on one condition: that the banks pay currency on the demand of either their depositors or of their country correspondents. (Suspension and limitation of such payments and refusals to ship dollars to correspondent banks had caused trouble seven years before.)[10] He also denounced the use of clearing house certificates, which had already begun to appear, fearing they would cause trouble as they had in 1907 and thicken the atmosphere of tension. Though he had no legal authority to halt the process, he warned that he would levy a 10 percent tax on these certificates if they were issued. But he would not object to the employment of clearing houses certificates to settle balances between the New York banks themselves.[11]

By this time it was past midnight. McAdoo informed the bankers that $50,000,000 of emergency currency had already been shipped to New York and would be ready for issue when the banks opened. Frank Vanderlip objected that this would be no help to the National City because it had no outstanding circulation secured by United States bonds, as required under Aldrich-Vreeland. Many other big financial institutions had been caught in the same trap. McAdoo replied that he would back an amendment which would afford relief. He had already arranged for the issuance of $100,000,000 in additional emergency notes to the New York banks in case they were needed. After three hours the conference finally broke up, the bankers pleased with the results. Exuding optimism as usual, McAdoo left for Washington on the morning of the third. Meanwhile, Williams, Hamlin, and Harding stayed in New York, where Assistant Secretary William Malburn later joined them.[12]

McAdoo got back to Washington in the afternoon, in time to help arrange the emergency currency amendment with conferees of the House and Senate. Passed by Congress on August 4, it authorized the Secretary of the Treasury to allow national banks to issue a maximum of circulating notes equivalent to 125 percent of their unimpaired capital and surplus instead of the previous 100 percent; and it eliminated the $500,000,000 maximum of Aldrich-Vreeland currency that could be issued. The amendment extended the benefits of the act to hundreds of previously unprotected banks by providing that the Secretary of the Treasury could, at his own discretion, waive the provision of the measure which prevented additional currency from being furnished to national banks that had not already issued bond-secured notes to the extent of 40 percent of their capital. McAdoo did not hesitate to employ this discretion widely. Again at his own option, McAdoo could now extend emergency currency upon a deposit of adequate collateral to any state bank or trust company that intended to join the Federal Reserve system. In addition, Congress reduced the tax on emergency notes; and, without a specific green light from Congress, Williams lowered the gold reserve requirements for large banks.

On July 30, McAdoo had directed Williams to ship $50,000,000 in emergency currency to New York and smaller amounts to other reserve cities so that funds would be on the scene the moment they were needed. When the New York banks opened Monday morning, August 3, the subtreasury began issuing millions of dollars on the condition that the banks pay currency over their counters at the demand not only of their depositors but of their correspondents across the nation as well. The Administration also worked to forestall the use of clearing house certificates; as a result, they were issued only in a few of the largest cities, and though employed in large amounts, were cancelled within a few months.

As early as Monday morning, after the remedial measures agreed to the previous night had gone into effect, the strain began to ease. Withdrawals of deposits, though larger than usual, did not betoken anything like a major panic. The Aldrich-Vreeland Act was being used for the first time, and by the end of the day the country had more currency in circulation than ever before in its history. The Bureau of Engraving and Printing labored around the clock seven days a week turning out emergency notes. Meanwhile, with McAdoo's help, currency districts were being organized; by October 1 the entire nation had practically been blanketed by them. From August 1 to October 31, after which the volume outstanding began to drop, $141,228,000 of emergency currency was issued to national banks in New York City, over a third of it during the first week alone; $228,330,040 went elsewhere in these three months, and currency associations in forty states eventually received shipments. During the same period, McAdoo deposited $19,446,246 in national banks to move the crops, and $3,400,000 of government funds in New York banks to increase their reserves. Unlike the situation in 1907, the country's banks were able to supply actual currency even under the greatest pressure and to maintain payments over the counter and among themselves without strain. By August 7, New York banks had resumed discounting a large volume of commercial paper at 6 percent. And, thanks to the emergency notes, they managed to safeguard their reserves and even increase them without reducing the volume of their loans. Again, unlike the experiences of 1893 and 1907, practically no banks or stock exchange houses failed, and only a few national banks stopped payments. Hoarding ended; confidence revived. But McAdoo's problems still had not disappeared.[13]

IV

Many of them centered around gold. In the single week ending August 1, the United States lost a stunning $45,000,000 worth. This crisis did not arise overnight. For several years, European bankers had been building up their gold reserves and selling large quantities of American securities in exchange. At the time war erupted American borrowers had large funded and floating debts abroad. According to McAdoo's estimate, roughly $450,000 was owed to London by U.S. businessmen and bankers in obligations maturing on or before January 1, 1915. This was normal enough; the United States suffered a heavily adverse balance of trade during the first half of each year, and then offset it during the fall and winter by exporting agricultural products. But shipping became tied up in August, just as these exports began. British banks, which usually would have carried the debt for a few months until cotton and grain shipments could cancel American obligations, faced a debt moratorium in England and massive financial demands from the military; so London began to insist on prompt settlement, in gold.[14]

At first, McAdoo had been openly sanguine about the situation. But by July 30 his confidence had begun to crack, and a month later he would be considering outright suspension of gold payments. The foreign exchange situation deteriorated alarmingly in July. By the middle of the month, New York suffered from a shortage of sterling exchange and the demand showed no signs of abating.[15]

As soon as war became probable, toward the end of July, the mechanism of foreign exchange began to break down. The price of London exchange rose as high as $7.00 per pound sterling (normal: $4.88-4.89), a prohibitive rate except for extreme necessities. Gold exports alone could replenish the supply of exchange. The United States had to move funds to Europe at once to pay for repatriated American securities; only gold could be used. But this, in turn, posed another dilemma: because of the danger to shipping on the high seas, insurance rates on gold reached prohibitive heights when they were quoted at all, and sailings were cancelled. By late July it had become obvious that Europe might demand vast amounts of gold by flooding the New York market with American securities. These dangers played a major role in closing the exchange, and in bringing on direct government intervention to stave off disaster.

Emergency currency should have helped, for it could be substituted for gold certificates in response to domestic calls for currency, enabling the banks receiving them to husband gold certificates and shore up their reserves against foreign demand. But in practice the banks persisted in their unwillingness to use reserves to meet payments abroad, and foreign rates of exchange remained at adverse levels. On August 6 the situation eased somewhat when it was announced that the French government had deposited roughly $6,000,000 with J. P. Morgan and Company, subject to drafts by the French Ambassador to the United States. Five days later the Bank of England indicated that it was making the Canadian Treasury Department custodian of the gold due the bank in New York. Thus the gold held in North America could be counted as part of the bank's reserve against its note issues and deposit liabilities in England. But these steps proved insufficient; Europe continued to insist on gold shipments to meet maturing obligations. Some way must be found to circumvent tremendous losses from the high price of exchange.

On August 1 bankers in New York slapped an extralegal embargo on gold exports. By the time McAdoo conferred with the clearing house representatives the following day, he had already spoken with brokers; and he, too, decided on an informal embargo. It went into effect, then, by common, tacit agreement. With the stock exchange closed and selling orders going untaken, this temporary expedient conserved bank reserves. But it did not suffice. On August 7 McAdoo announced that the nation must provide sufficient ships to get American crops to Europe and lower the rate on London. He summoned a conference of businessmen, bankers, shipping authorities, and railroad managers to convene at the Treasury on August 14.[16]

When the conference opened, the Cabinet, the Federal Reserve Board, and Congress were liberally represented. Most bankers present probably frowned on the continuance of gold payments, but the bigger banks in New York and elsewhere stood against suspension. Besides mutual assurances of cooperation, a consensus was reached that the key issues included restoration of the market for foreign bills of exchange, the revival of shipping, and establishment by the government of a War Risk Insurance Bureau. The conference called for federal intervention to assist in the negotiation of bills of exchange against exports in order to help throw the balance of trade to America's advantage. It also appealed for changes in the ship registry and navigation laws to help Americans compete with foreign lines. Standing committees were appointed to deal with each of the major issues.[17]

The gold crisis still hovered like a pall on the horizon. One of the major complications was the fact that $82,000,000 in New York City short-term obligations held by France and England would mature at dates between September and January. McAdoo arranged an interview between J. P. Morgan and the Federal Reserve Board for August 20, at which Morgan warned that it might be necessary for the Treasury to step in to salvage the city's credit. McAdoo would make no direct commitments, but, as Morgan understood it,

> would view with favour the steps the New York banks felt it incumbent upon them to take to preserve the credit of New York City. . . . that, if it came to a question of help from the Treasury, if the Treasury was satisfied that any part of the country was in need of help and had done the best it could for itself, the Treasury would give to New York or any part of the country in that condition, such help as it properly could.

A syndicate headed by J. P. Morgan and Company and including all but four of the banks and trust companies in New York was formed in September, and through gold shipments and use of available exchange this met the most burdensome single requirement for means of payment in London.[18]

Yet the crisis in foreign exchange stubbornly persisted. Somehow the supply of sterling exchange would have to be increased, and the demand for it cut. On September 4, a conference of delegates representing all the clearing house banks convened on the invitation of McAdoo and the Federal Reserve Board to discuss the amount of short-term debts owed to Europe by American borrowers and to find a cooperative way of meeting them. James B. Forgan, an important Chicago banker, was selected chairman and authorized to appoint a committee which would devise some plan for freeing exchange. Before the day ended the committee had drawn up a proposal for a gold pool of $150,000,000, to be contributed by the banks; $25,000,000 would be paid immediately to the Bank of England. This report went to the Federal Reserve Board on the eighth. But three days later the Board turned the plan down, contending that the provisions which had been made for managing the New York City debt had rendered drafts of gold from other countries superfluous. The bankers disagreed. The committee conferred with the Board September 18 and 19, and a general plan was finally agreed to. On the nineteenth, the committee submitted a second report, scaling down the proposed fund to $100,000,000 and suggesting arrangements for its administration. Banks outside New York would furnish 55 percent of the gold in proportion to the holdings of the institutions in the reserve cities; success pivoted on whether or not these banks filled their quotas, and the Treasury worked hard and effectively to see that they did. The banks responded well.[19]

By guaranteeing to meet the nation's maturing foreign obligations, the gold pool was designed to relieve the exchange situation and, in the process, to revive confidence, strengthen the country's credit, and give a fillip to exports. To be sure, $100,000,000 fell far short of the total maturing liabilities; nor was any attempt made to provide enough exchange to drive rates back to par. Yet the sum would suffice, bankers reasoned, to convince foreign creditors of American willingness to pay in gold and would lead, in turn, to an extension of obligations and reduced demands for settlement in gold or foreign currencies. This, indeed, is what happened. As *The Nation* observed, it was

a most unusual operation. Except for the recent guarantee of exchange or gold, by New York city's banks, to meet the city government's $82,000,000 maturing foreign obligations, no concerted action, even remotely resembling this, has been witnessed in our financial history.[20]

A committee of bankers in New York administered the pool. Working through the clearing house associations of the central reserve and reserve cities, the Gold Fund Committee had the full sum subscribed in surprisingly short order. Amounts were to be transferred to representatives of the Bank of England as required; and in early October $10,000,000 went to Ottawa under an agreement with the bank. This established corresponding credit in London in favor of the committee, which, in turn, sold exchange against it. The single shipment to Canada was the only one found necessary, and not even all of the exchange created by the $10,000,000 was utilized. A mere $27,000,000 had to be called up. By mid-November the price of sterling exchange had fallen once more to par, and on January 22, 1915, the pool was formally terminated.

Meanwhile, McAdoo took another step to help solve the gold crisis. Through diplomatic channels he informally suggested that the British Chancellor of the Exchequer send representatives to the United States to discuss the intimately related problems of foreign exchange and cotton. London responded by dispatching two men, Sir George Paish, a former editor, and Basil Blackett, who directly represented the British Treasury, to carry on conversations. McAdoo called a meeting for October 23, at which the two Englishmen, a group of the most important American bankers, and the Federal Reserve Board would confer. But already it was becoming clear to many of these men that the impending switch in the balance of trade, together with the stopgap gold fund, would solve the exchange problem even if no further measures emerged. Meanwhile, a cotton pool was in the offing.

Nevertheless, negotiations—extended, intricate, and secret—proceeded on what McAdoo described as a "semi-diplomatic" basis involving the governments and bankers of each country. A number of proposals developed for the extension of acceptance credits in London and for the funding of United States obligations into short-term notes by a bankers' syndicate; and a tentative plan was formulated by a committee of

American bankers under the leadership of Albert H. Wiggin. Transmitted to England, the scheme incubated for several weeks while the problems it had been designed to confront gradually faded away. Toward the end of November Paish returned home, ostensibly to explain the committee's recommendations more fully. By now, McAdoo would have been happy to allow the negotiations to expire altogether.[21]

For by the beginning of November, the crisis had been broken except in the cotton states. In December, thanks to the gold fund, the New York City pool, and the freer movement of commodities to Europe, the tide definitely reversed. The New York Stock Exchange reopened; credit eased; the cotton pool had been formed; sterling exchange was back to normal; and the gold drain, which proved in the final analysis to be relatively light, had been staunched. In early January the British government cabled that there was no longer any need for a formal plan for the adjustment of balances and suggested that the entire subject be thrown back to the bankers. On January 7 McAdoo announced that negotiations had ended. Foreign exchange continued to present problems, but they sprang from a tremendously favorable balance of trade, no longer from an adverse one. In the five years ending in November, 1917, thanks mainly to unprecedented Allied purchases, the portion of the world's gold monetary stock held by the United States swelled from one fifth to more than one third, and America became by far the greatest gold holder in world history.[22]

V

The nation's financial prospects had appeared practically desperate at the time the war began, and the decision to maintain gold payments required courage. By standing almost alone in refusing to suspend, the United States greatly enhanced its economic prestige; this played a major role in quickly making New York the financial capital of the world. Foreign exchange began to move in this country's favor; and as New York became the world's banking depository its position as a lender to foreign nations was increasingly strengthened.

As the year 1914 closed the United States, especially New England and the South, still suffered from a sluggish economy and considerable unemployment. But early in 1915 a transformation occurred. By summer practically the entire nation was rolling forward and prosperity began to spread. Various reasons accounted for this, among them the inauguration of the Federal Reserve system, hikes in railroad freight rates, large crops (though the relative importance of agricultural exports dropped), and a rise in the price of cotton. But one factor overshadowed all of these: a boom in war orders from Europe, which showered contracts on

factories up and down the Eastern seaboard. Meanwhile America underwent another crucial change—it was becoming a creditor nation.

In January, 1916, McAdoo wrote Bernard Baruch that he felt "confident that we are entering upon an era of exceptional development and
stable prosperity superior to any we have heretofore enjoyed." Though
things might eventually go wrong, this prosperity seemed to McAdoo in
the year before America itself went to war remarkably trouble-free.
McAdoo's own role in staving off panic had been brilliant. "In no former
crisis was the aid rendered by the government so immediate and effective," noted a leading economist. Even big bankers and opponents of the
Administration approved. But this intervention had merely conserved
an economic status quo which it took war to change. The conflict had
ushered in prosperity, but McAdoo saw one hitch: "It is because the
United States has not heretofore possessed its full share of the world's
markets that we have had such extremes of prosperity and business depression in the past." Take away the war and add no markets, and the
cycles would simply recur.[23]

At the center of McAdoo's oversimplified view of the American
economy was the Wilsonian belief that

we have reached the point in our economic development where it is essential
to the happiness and welfare of our people that we shall secure our share of
the world's markets because we produce more than we can consume at home,
both in fabricated product and natural resources of the soil.

He quickly saw that Europe at war was turning inward. Its foreign markets lay open, vulnerable, and inviting. With Europe deadlocked, America
might conduct an offensive of its own aimed at capturing a new position
in world commerce. And so, within a few months after it began, McAdoo
set out to put the war to use.[24]

He did not move in a vacuum. His own efforts reflected an emerging
consensus among leaders in business and politics on the subject of expanding the nation's foreign trade and investment. By 1916 this consensus
envisioned a number of preconditions for growth, among them the creation of an international economic system that would enable the United
States to supplant Britain as the linchpin of world commerce and the
establishment of institutional methods for stabilizing international relations. Behind this was a desire to rewrite the rules of foreign commerce
in order to give the American businessman complete trading equality
with his European competitors.[25]

The Paris Economic Conference of 1916 gave an added fillip to
American plans. This meeting laid the groundwork for Entente hegemony
in postwar international trade; specifically, the Allies planned to divide
foreign (and especially Latin American) markets among themselves,

freezing out the United States as far as possible through such policies as tariff preferences and organized discrimination in shipping rates. The Entente governments would play an active role in underwriting all of this.[26]

Wilson's view of the vital relationship between world markets and full employment at home provided a crucial backdrop for the emerging trade consensus in the United States. In 1912 he had spoken of a redistribution of opportunity rather than a redistribution of income among different groups. If the country could increase its foreign commerce and investment, all interests, including labor, would benefit. Despite the fact that each interest's share of the national wealth would remain the same, the economy itself would be larger and everyone would get more.[27] Faced with the fact that cultivating markets abroad would require levels of collaboration between corporations, and between business and government, which Wilson had not foreseen in 1912, the Administration opted for heightened competitiveness against foreign powers at the expense of competition among U.S. exporters.

This went well beyond the foreign trade aspects of early Wilsonian legislation. It signaled the President's desire to reconcile an increase in both trade and economic nationalism—limited protectionism and anti-dumping legislation, for example—and to cushion the impact of the war on American industry. It also represented an attempt to maintain a (blurring) distinction between government and the public interest vis-à-vis business at the same time that Wilson accepted greater cordiality between government and business.

Long before American intervention in the World War in 1917, then, large elements of the business community had joined with the Wilson Administration in agreeing on the key New Freedom plan for guaranteeing national prosperity. Far from being dead and buried, the New Freedom as an approach to foreign trade had scarcely begun to go into full operation by 1914. When it did, it opened up to McAdoo a broad new promotional role in government.

His chief target was the markets of Latin America. On the eve of the war the European colossus stood astride these markets, and Washington had been under pressure from the U.S. business community for more aid in competing there. Powerful European banks, entrenched in the area for over a hundred years, backed the incursions of European merchants, and financed government loans, public services, and businesses. U.S. exporters found themselves as dependent as the Latin Americans on European banking and transportation. But commercial and financial intercourse between the warring nations and Latin America—beginning with the Second Balkan War and then with the outbreak of general hostilities in August, 1914—were sharply curtailed. London exchange, the universal currency of foreign trade, became disrupted; steamship communications declined to intermittence; foreign investment shrank; and European receptivity to Latin American products dropped.

Since Latin American prosperity rested on the money markets of the Old World, the entire continent suffered, many of the countries reaching the brink of financial crisis. By the spring of 1915 conditions had begun to improve, but economic sluggishness persisted. The only avenue of relief was for North Americans to intervene. When they did, the warring powers complained of the United States' selfishly taking advantage of a tragedy—which indeed it was. But with Europe embroiled, Americans pointed out, Latin America found itself endangered too.

U.S. capital had already begun moving into the region, assuming an important role in the mining, rubber, meat packing, and coffee industries, and in fruit and railroads. For years the United States had ranked second among the nations of the world in exports to Latin America, barely yielding first place to Britain; and for two decades the U.S. had been the chief purchaser of the continent's exports. In 1913 the United States took first place in sales to Latin America, widening the gap rapidly in the months that followed; but its balance of trade with the region continued unfavorable. From 1914 to 1917, despite the diversion of American resources to Europe, the value of the U.S. import and export trade with Latin America doubled. With many of their old sources of supply cut off by the war, Latin American buyers resorted increasingly to United States manufactures. Meanwhile, a number of U.S. bankers sought opportunities for expansion in Latin America, and the National City led a slow parade to establish branches there. As U.S. investment increased, within a year after the war began several large Latin American loans had been negotiated in the United States.

The war suddenly afforded the U.S. a chance to supplant the European role in Latin America, and government officials and businessmen quickly saw it. The State Department and Pan American Union went to work to publicize the opportunity and stimulate exports. But the chief burden fell on the Department of Commerce. Secretary Redfield's great ambition had always been to make American businessmen the most important exporters on the planet; as a former foreign representative of an industrial concern and corporation executive, and as ex-president of the American Manufacturers' Export Association, he was well qualified for the work. At the time he took office, however, Congress appropriated far less per year to promote overseas trade than many companies annually spent for advertising—and as a result the Bureau of Foreign and Domestic Commerce was inadequately funded and staffed.[28]

In September, 1914, Redfield and Bryan succeeded in holding a trade conference of diplomatic representatives of Latin American nations and U.S. businessmen. As time passed the State Department moved farther in this direction. Meanwhile, Redfield had reorganized the Bureau of Foreign and Domestic Commerce. Appropriations swelled; business-government cooperation over trade grew close; and plans were laid for a trade offensive around the world. By June, 1915, the Wilson Administration had spent more than the two preceding ones to expand U.S. commerce abroad.[29]

During the prewar period, McAdoo's involvement in foreign affairs, including trade relations, had been minimal. But he had backed Redfield's approach and fully appreciated the export expansion potential of the Underwood Tariff. Despite his early interest in the peace movement, McAdoo inclined toward a "hard line" in foreign relations, at the same time firmly upholding the President's policies. McAdoo's rhetoric, which often sounded much like Wilson's, was tinctured with idealism; but in his mind, idealism and materialism were intertwined. "I have long held the view," he wrote in 1915,

that the territorial and political integrity of all the Nations of the Western Hemisphere must rest ultimately upon a greater degree of cooperation between them and a larger understanding of each other, based upon a greater community of material interests, which, in turn, must produce an enlarged sympathy between all of them in common ideals of liberty, humanity and justice.[30]

McAdoo personified the mixed militance and benevolence, interventionism and anti-imperialism, of the Wilson Administration in foreign affairs. If there was Wilsonian idealism at the core of his thoughts on relations with the Americas, there were also seeds of opportunism: "If we seize the present opportunity for extending our commerce," he wrote in 1916, "we can assure to the country a permanent and stable prosperity, free from the violent fluctuations and uncertainties which have characterized our economic growth in the past." Without these new markets, "we shall have stagnation and depression and idleness and want." Besides its continuity with New Freedom doctrine, the most significant thing about this argument was the assumption that cyclical fluctuations in the economy could be moderated or eliminated—a notion alien to common American economic wisdom in the early twentieth century.[31]

McAdoo's views departed from mere dollar diplomacy masquerading in a cloak of moralistic rhetoric. He believed that together the nations of the Western Hemisphere could police the peace when it finally came; by wielding their collective economic power, they might prevent other countries from going to war. But this provided another variation on a different theme—the idea that new institutional relationships would have to be established in order to keep world markets open. "We can through our mutual interests create with those republics the strongest commercial and political alliance on earth," he argued. It was a vague idea, but it would develop as time passed.[32]

When McAdoo spoke of maintaining the peace, he thought not in political or military but in economic terms. Indeed, his reasoning contained a kernel of isolationism. The Western Hemisphere owed it to itself to take economic measures which would render it independent of future collisions in Europe. At the same time that he spoke of new "world-wide responsibilities" for the United States, he tended to view the Monroe Doctrine as a hemispheric declaration of economic as well as political self-sufficiency and solidarity. Europe would be prostrated for years to come, unable to reassume, for the time being at least, its role as the mainspring of the Latin American economy. Meanwhile, it was "inevitable . . . that North and South America should draw near each other to . . . check the most disastrous effects of the calamity." The U.S. would become the dominant trading nation in Latin America; and the remedy to the embroilment of the Old World, so far as Latin America was concerned, would be "North American capital in abundance." But McAdoo did not intend this to mean North American exploitation in abundance. In the summer of 1915 he confided to the new Secretary of State, Robert Lansing,

that we cannot afford to identify ourselves with any interest, or anything, that works injustice . . . to any of the South and Central American countries. . . . No one feels more strongly than I do about the necessity for our Government protecting every *legitimate* right or interest of our people in foreign countries, but we cannot, of course, afford to become directly, or indirectly, parties to, or defenders of, any exploitation by our people of other countries.[33]

McAdoo began working with Redfield, and quickly supplanted the Secretary of Commerce as the Administration's leading advocate of an expansive commercial policy in Latin America. He intended to divert some of the energy of the small business community, which the New Freedom had promised to liberate, and the large industrial and financial community, which it had pledged to restrain, into foreign channels. One of his greatest gifts to these interests during the New Freedom years was the Pan American Financial Conference of 1915, and men in banking and business, in New York and elsewhere, took a deep interest in it. But it was a gift to be shared, he believed, by Latin America as well. And it had numerous strings attached. If the South and Central Americans accepted capital from the United States, which they seemingly had to have, they must also accept the measure of control (and the risk or reality of exploitation) that had always gone with it. And if the U.S. business community felt tempted by visions of foreign expansion, it would also have to swallow a shipping bill which appalled most conservatives.

VI

With the Pan American Financial Conference, McAdoo embarked on a major venture in the realm of foreign affairs. In late October, 1914, he wrote the President proposing such a gathering. Wilson gave his approval, and McAdoo took up the question with the State Department by asking Bryan to put out feelers to the various governments involved.[34] Meanwhile, the matter was kept quite secret. The response proved favorable, and McAdoo urged that the Latin American nations send delegates competent to deal with the technical problems at issue—ministers of finance and representatives of Central and South American banking houses. In January he asked Congress for an appropriation for the conference; in early March, he got it.

Inter-American conferences dated back to 1889. The gatherings had served as sounding boards but permanent institutional machinery rarely emerged to transform intentions into specific programs. When on occasion it did, the nations involved brooked no limitations upon their sovereignty and shackled progress from the start. Then too, Pan Americanism had been thought of primarily in political, not economic, terms. "The underlying basis for effective political cooperation, namely, commercial interests mutually beneficial to the countries concerned, has been wanting," McAdoo noted. Since, in his estimate, international relations had become more commercial and financial than political in nature, all that would have to change.[35]

McAdoo was not an expert in Pan American affairs and he needed to recruit an experienced lieutenant. In Leo S. Rowe of the University of Pennsylvania, a longtime government consultant, he found an unusually able assistant with a high reputation in South America.

Once the covers had been taken off plans for the gathering, it generated a good deal of public interest. Despite an illness which forced postponement of the conference, and despite the warnings of his physicians to relax for a while and avoid official matters, McAdoo insisted on making the arrangements single-handedly. On May 24 an imposing array of representatives from Latin America and the United States—among them Cabinet members, the Federal Reserve Board, the Federal Trade Commission, foreign ambassadors, bankers and businessmen—filed into the Pan American Union Building in Washington, and the conference opened with McAdoo presiding. It was the largest assembly of dignitaries from the Western Hemisphere since the first Pan American Conference a quarter century before.

The first day and a half were taken up for the most part by speeches of the President, McAdoo, Bryan, and others; but on the afternoon of the twenty-fifth, the delegates settled down to business. The topics submitted for consideration embraced monetary and banking matters, public and private finance, the extension of inter-American markets, postal service, and transportation. In order to deal with these issues on a specific, meaningful basis, McAdoo divided the conferees into group committees, one for each of the eighteen Latin American countries represented, and kept the number of joint sessions at a minimum. The committees held the key to success. Each was placed under the chairmanship of the ranking member of the visiting delegation, so that the initiative would lie with the Latin Americans. To deal with the forty-five official delegates of foreign governments, McAdoo had invited nearly 200 representatives of the financial and commercial interests of the United States, assigning some of the most important to the smaller nations.

The committee plan worked extremely well, and at the request of numerous foreign delegates McAdoo appointed eighteen permanent, unofficial committees to keep in touch with their Latin American counterparts after the conference adjourned. The names of the men he selected read like a Who's Who of business and finance: "I think," a friend of McAdoo's wrote, that people "will be particularly struck by your largeness in appointing men commonly supposed to be antagonistic to you." The group assigned to Argentina, for example, consisted of banker Willard Straight; James A. Farrell, president of U.S. Steel; Frank Vanderlip; Cyrus McCormick; and Henry Ford.[36]

One of the major purposes of the conference involved drawing capital from the United States into the financing of Latin American governments. Far more than U.S. products, the countries of Latin America wanted loans; European credit, virtually the sole source of supply, had suddenly been drained into other channels, and every one of these nations found itself in financial trouble. Then too, if the United States wanted to create a permanent trade relationship with the countries to the south, it must help sustain them. Out of the conference emerged financial arrangements for several Latin American governments. By June, 1915, Argentina and Peru had negotiated loans in the U.S. McAdoo moved to secure credit for other nations, among them Ecuador, Costa Rica, Uruguay, and Brazil. And he issued an order granting preferential tariff treatment to Panama.

The chief problem McAdoo encountered in trying to bring American bankers and Latin American governments together was the fact that U.S. investors, to whom the bankers involved in the loans sold foreign bonds, were reluctant to purchase them for fear that the governments involved—

some of which drew more notoriety from instability than from anything else—might default. McAdoo dismissed these qualms, for the most part, as ill-founded; but the investors wanted assurances that Washington would protect them. McAdoo tried to persuade Wilson and Lansing to guarantee all "reasonable" steps "short of armed intervention." "Unless we can do this," he argued, "we may as well stop, in large measure, our efforts to do anything in South America." But the President, wary of entanglements, feared the reaction this would stir against dollar diplomacy in Latin America. His response to McAdoo's urgent entreaties proved disappointing.[37]

VII

"The most important conference ever held in this country," Edward N. Hurley of the FTC wrote of the Pan American Financial Conference, and the exaggeration was pardonable. It had been a striking success. If few of the visiting delegates had arrived in Washington with specific proposals for luring American capital south, they returned with a good deal of concrete information regarding the views of American financiers.[38]

But McAdoo saw all this as mere spadework. Some kind of permanent or semipermanent organization was required to carry on the efforts the conference had started. The committee on uniformity of laws, which had formulated suggestions for future activities, had submitted a report emphasizing the importance of working out legal tangles in commerce and public finance which tended to snarl trade. To deal with these problems, and to harmonize both procedures and principles of fiscal administration and commercial law, it endorsed a recommendation of McAdoo's for the creation of an International High Commission, composed of sections from each country. The suggestion was adopted unanimously. The nations involved acted quickly, and early in February, 1916, Congress gave the United States section legislative status. McAdoo, who would act as Chairman of the American contingent, urged that the Commission meet as soon as possible at Buenos Aires.

The quasigovernmental International High Commission was established to work out legal problems on an official, technical basis; to facilitate commercial treaties and foreign exchange; to unify trade laws, which varied widely from country to country; and to deal with other issues bound up with the free flow and profitability of commercial relations. Whenever a particular problem required action by all member nations, it was handled either through legislative initiative by individual governments or else through (commonly bypassed) diplomatic channels. Each national branch of the Commission consisted of the minister of finance and several other prominent men. McAdoo's final choices for the United States delegation were strictly blue-ribbon, including, among others, John Bassett Moore of Columbia University; Duncan U. Fletcher, who, besides serving in the Senate, functioned as president of the Southern Commercial Congress; David R. Francis, later Ambassador to Russia; John Fahey of the United States Chamber of Commerce; Elbert Gary; Paul Warburg; George M. Reynolds; Samuel Untermyer; and, as Secretary General, Leo S. Rowe. Meanwhile, McAdoo worked to interest the State Department in his efforts, in order to galvanize another body of men, the ambassadors, to action in working for more intimate trade relations with Latin America. And at the behest of McAdoo, the FTC conducted an inquiry into laws and customs regulations there.

A second measure designed to bring the work of the conference into an institutional framework was McAdoo's appointment of the permanent group committees, which served as information pools for merchants of the nations involved. As a third step, McAdoo proposed that Pan American financial conferences be held annually or biennially in Washington, to be attended by ministers of finance, statesmen, and bankers. Still another expedient, this one proposed by the Uruguayan Minister to the United States and passed unanimously, involved sending delegations of business-men and financiers from the United States to visit South and Central America. McAdoo quickly appointed an unofficial committee under the chairmanship of James A. Farrell to arrange an itinerary and choose the personnel. McAdoo and Farrell completed arrangements for sending seven parties to as many different groups of countries. These committees went south in 1916 and made a highly favorable impression.

McAdoo lost little time in putting men to work examining numerous facets of the trade problem. One difficulty lay in the linguistic barrier, and he devoted considerable attention to urging the compulsory teaching of Spanish in public schools of the United States. Other obstacles included the ignorance of American businessmen of the workings of the metric system; differing postal systems and rates and inefficiency in the mails; the need for direct cable communications and for wireless facilities; and gaps in the Inter-Continental Railway, which connected North and South America via the Isthmus of Panama. Most of the track had already been laid, but nearly 3,000 miles remained and gauges varied from country to country.

All these issues paled before the single, overwhelming problem of shipping. This had been the main theme at the conference, where it had been agreed that improvement was vital. The shortage and increased ex-pense of steamship service for marketing the products of a number of Latin American nations—primarily those farthest from the United States

—had injured their public finances and led to considerable misery among their people.

The delegates had no power to take affirmative action on the shipping question; but some days before the conference had gone into session, McAdoo submitted a memorandum on the subject to the Chilean Ambassador. "It is futile," McAdoo wrote,

to rely upon private capital to engage in a shipping enterprise on the large scale required to meet the situation. The processes of private capital are extremely cautious and slow.

McAdoo suggested that a steamship company—capitalized at $50,000,000 —should be established and incorporated under U.S. law, but with the governments of Latin America, if they chose, subscribing to the capital stock. Washington would subscribe two thirds of the total and the Latin Americans the rest. The United States, as the chief stockholder, would have a controlling interest. No formal action was taken on the proposal, but almost unanimous Latin American support clearly existed for some solution to the shipping dilemma.[39]

On May 25, at the suggestion of the visiting delegates from Argentina, McAdoo appointed a committee of representatives from the various countries with the greatest interest in the problem to consider solutions. Two subcommittees, comprised entirely of Latin Americans, submitted reports; and it was recommended that McAdoo select a permanent committee to deal with shipping. Reversing his former position, McAdoo demurred, contending that the issue must be handled by each nation in its own way—partly because "the shipping question had become something of a political controversy in the United States." The conference adopted no precise program, but McAdoo made a point of keeping the avenue open to suggestions for joint government control of a single shipping corporation.[40]

<h2 style="text-align:center">VIII</h2>

A meeting of the International High Commission was scheduled for April, 1916, at Buenos Aires, and it would be necessary for the United States delegation either to take a naval vessel or travel under a foreign flag; McAdoo chose the former. If the men who accompanied him south had been collaborating on specifically domestic issues instead of foreign ones, it would have been considered an incongruous, if not a conspiratorial, company. For it included not only Duncan Fletcher, and Andrew Peters of the Treasury Department, but Paul Warburg; Samuel Untermyer; Archibald Kains, governor of the Federal Reserve Bank of San Francisco; and John Fahey. Nothing could more clearly have symbolized the new business-government consensus on foreign trade. English and

German hostility to McAdoo's endeavors became unmistakably clear as the vessel steamed toward the Equator, both in the tone of the press and in the attitude of British colonial officials. But generally it was a pleasant voyage. The ship's crew, expecting McAdoo to be an icy potentate, found instead a warm and interesting man who could swear the way they did. McAdoo had become one of the most popular Wilsonians in Latin America, and he got a cordial and enthusiastic reception. It was soon apparent that if nothing else had been achieved, the mission had at least strengthened relations with the countries McAdoo visited.

The conference at Buenos Aires opened April 3 and lasted ten days. All the nations of Latin America except Mexico sent representatives. The meeting continued the progress which had begun at Washington the previous year. On the motion of the United States, the conference elected the Argentine Minister of Finance its president. The delegates agreed upon permanent organization of the International High Commission. A Central Executive Committee of three men was established to coordinate the Commission's work and the relations of its twenty sections, to carry out its recommendations, and to plan future gatherings. Washington became the headquarters of the Committee for the next two years, and thus McAdoo became President, Moore Vice-President, and Rowe Secretary-General. Besides taking up anew the subjects designated for consideration by the financial conference, a host of new topics was added. A hemispheric trade program emerged and dollar exchange was adopted as the basis of Pan American trade. Progress developed on various other issues, among them banking expansion, monetary standardization, uniformity in commercial statistical classification and laws concerning bills of exchange, arbitration of commercial disputes, unification and reduction of travelers' taxes, and communications. In addition, the gathering recommended that Pan American Financial Conferences be held every two years.

But once again, as in 1915, shipping became the overriding issue. Representatives of all the governments with delegations at Buenos Aires made it clear that only the initiative of the United States could remedy the situation because only this nation could muster the necessary resources. Resolutions were adopted unanimously urging the U.S. to solve the problem quickly, for relations between the Americas could never be fully developed without shipping. And, through a series of recommendations, for the first time in any international conference a massive, cooperative policy of government action in communications by sea, as well as by land, was attempted.[41]

Yet, realistically, nothing that could be done at Buenos Aires would possibly go far enough. McAdoo, who had chaired the committee on transportation, remarked that a policy must be found "which will forever free the American States from dependence upon the flags of foreign powers for the protection of their own commerce and the protection of their own physical safety." For it was

certain that conventions of South American financiers and trade conferences and other things will have little effect unless we establish steamship lines, competitive in quality, speed and reliable sailings, and with *reasonable* rates, with those of European countries.[42]

CHAPTER ELEVEN

SHIPS

The paralysis of world trade brought on by the clash of titans in August, 1914, soon eased, but full recovery would be impossible while' the conflict lasted. German and Austrian vessels had been swept from the seas; and as ships of war replaced merchant vessels on the ways of British yards, and German submarines began to take their toll, the English merchant marine slipped into decline. Anxiety over the situation in London was fully justified, for shipbuilding picked up markedly in neutral nations, especially the United States.

With the collapse of credits and the foreign exchange market and a mammoth shipping tie-up when the war hit, American exports plummeted to practically nothing. The index of industrial production sagged 18 percent between August and November, and unemployment rose. But revival came quickly. Never before had the country sent so much abroad as it did in 1915; yet because of the bottleneck in shipping, McAdoo argued that it was not sending nearly enough. The United States annually exported twenty-two times as much as Norway, yet that tiny nation boasted a merchant marine practically twice the size of America's. "We have been a department store without a delivery system," William Redfield remarked, "depending on our rivals for the use of their wagons."[1]

I

In the early summer of 1914, few things appear to have been farther from McAdoo's mind than shipping. The closest he had come to maritime matters involved managing the Panama Tolls repeal measure in the Senate, while Burleson shepherded it through the House. But if it was new to McAdoo, the shipping problem had been around for a long time.

Once second only to Britain's, the United States merchant marine had slipped into decline long before the Civil War. Though it had never caught fire as a political issue, both major parties had paid heed to this situation rather sporadically in their platforms since 1880. Yet neither had done anything effective to strengthen shipping, and when Europe went to war in 1914 the condition of the American merchant marine was, in a word, wretched. The bulk of the tonnage plied coastal waters or the Great Lakes. Foreign shipping concerns had worked out agreements and combinations among themselves to stifle competition on the high seas. Well over half of U.S. imports and exports crossed in British bottoms on the eve of the war, while American vessels accounted for less than 10 percent. With the disappearance of German merchantmen, American exporters found themselves largely at the mercy of England. Yet Britain's grip on the seas might be broken; many English ships and yards had been commandeered by the government; and other vessels had been sunk. Indeed, the fate of Britain herself in August of 1914 seemed uncertain. But even with the supply of available tonnage dwindling, neutrals offered a poor alternative, for they provided only meager war risk insurance. And foreign ship owners had traditionally discriminated against U.S. exporters in favor of their own by shunting business to European firms and charging Americans higher rates. The British, as McAdoo emphasized again and again, were bound to put the interests of their own shippers first.

The war engendered a tremendous resurgence in American shipbuilding: yards which had been abandoned to weeds twenty years before were suddenly rejuvenated, and production rose to capacity. Perhaps never before in the nation's history had a declining industry sprung to action so quickly. But it took months to produce each vessel, and the yards simply could not catch up with demand.

Because of the shortage of tonnage and steadily rising pressure on available shipping, merchant vessels had unprecedented earning potential; and since the government had no statutory power to regulate them, rates soared to unprecedented heights. For the most part, the increase affected cargoes bound for Europe; trade with outlying areas like Africa, the Far East, and Latin America actually shrank. Predictably, speculation was rife. By February, 1915, rates on cotton shipped from New York to Rotterdam had increased 700 percent; from Norfolk to Bremen, 1,100 percent; and from Galveston to Bremen, as much as 1,150 percent. Ocean freight levies continued to rise, rocketing as high as 1,600 percent by the fall. In the lumber, coal, and a few other industries, rates became so inflated that they were literally prohibitive. Shipping capacity could not catch up with demand, and carriers simply took what they wished, leaving the rest sitting on docks and in warehouses, frequently for months. By late 1915, Americans found themselves paying foreign carriers more than $300,000,000 a year *and* getting poor service. "The freight rates which our producers and shippers are forced to bear," McAdoo observed acidly, "are extortionate and outrageous."[2]

The shipping tie-up began at the docks, but it extended far inland. Though some ports were relatively unaffected, the shortage of tonnage at others, including New York, left wharves and grain elevators crammed with material for export. On the Eastern seaboard thousands of loaded railroad cars simply got stored on sidings and in yards, and this, in turn, led to a greater dearth of facilities. Some carriers embargoed material bound for the ports; in New York, early in 1916, there was a general cut off of everything but food and coal. When one line set an embargo, traffic shifted to others, which had to follow suit as the epidemic spread.

The Administration's first effort to stop this chaos came with the Ship Registry bill, drafted by Oscar Underwood and the Commissioner of the Bureau of Navigation. Backed by the business community, the measure went through Congress with little opposition. The act revoked a law providing that in order to be admitted to American registry foreign vessels must be no more than five years old, and it authorized Wilson to suspend a number of regulations dealing with the crews and inspection of ships engaged in foreign trade. The measure met the demands of owners of foreign vessels, most of them under British registry, for permission to hoist the American ensign before the ships got caught in the sights of German submarines. "Personally," McAdoo later wrote,

I have always felt great doubt about the expediency and efficacy of that legislation, but the emergency was so great that I was willing to go every reasonable length to meet it.[3]

McAdoo's questions about the efficacy, if not the expediency, of the measure had justification. In the wake of the bill's passage, between August 18 and December 23, 104 ships did change registry. But McAdoo had no illusions about the permanence of this gain. As long as it remained cheaper to operate these vessels under other flags the owners would transfer them back when hostilities ended. And while a substantial number of ships did hoist the Stars and Stripes, the measure fell far short of satiating the country's hunger for transportation. Wilson, McAdoo, and the framers of the act had expected that American companies would buy the 500,000 tons of German shipping trapped in United States ports, or that the owners would register the vessels under the U.S. flag. But if German-owned ships had gone to sea, they would have been confiscated. And neither the British nor the French would allow Americans to buy German tonnage and then employ it in trade with the entire Continent, though this was far from clear at the time the registry bill passed. In effect, the measure was stillborn, and the vessels remained at anchor. Meanwhile, on September 4, the President signed an executive order which made transfer of foreign-built ships to the American flag easier by suspending certain features of the navigation laws.[4]

The Administration took still another step to protect shipping from the belligerents. At the time war struck, foreign companies wrote more than two thirds of the war risk insurance in the United States. The majority of them were English, and British law prevented them from covering the danger of capture by the Royal Navy. Foreign governments provided coverage for their own merchant fleets, and without it Americans could not compete. The U.S. companies found themselves confronting an onslaught of demand without reinsurance facilities, and had to limit the amount of coverage on any single ship. Sending cargoes to sea with insufficient insurance resembled sending them out in rowboats. With insurance rates skyrocketing, businessmen and their organizations sent up a cry for federal aid. They demanded government-issued coverage at rates fully as favorable as they could obtain if the vessels had been registered under foreign flags.[5]

Just after the armies first clashed in Europe, McAdoo presided over a day-long conference of leading government officials, financiers, and businessmen at the Treasury to arrange policies for meeting the crisis. Among those present were leaders of the shipping industry. It seemed obvious that in order to offset the vast amount of debts maturing by the end of 1914, something must be done to restore shipping conditions to as near normal as possible. The conferees adopted a resolution urging

the United States Government to establish a bureau of war risk insurance, to be administered under the direction of a suitable Government department . . . which shall assume the risks of war on American vessels and American cargoes.

It was an ultimatum by businessmen demanding that the Administration enter the insurance field. But no group needed coverage more than farmers, whose grain and cotton could not move without it. War risk insurance was generally considered unprofitable; why not let Washington take the loss?[6]

McAdoo responded quickly. He contemplated a Treasury bureau which, as long as the war lasted, would issue war risk insurance on ships and cargoes which had been refused reasonable rates by private companies; he assumed at the time that the conflict would be brief. Congress overwhelmingly favored the plan. A bill was drawn up which the President signed on September 2. The War Risk Insurance Bureau went into business the following day, little more than two weeks after the measure had been introduced on the Hill.' It was headed by an old friend of McAdoo's, Wall Street insurance expert William C. De Lanoy.[7]

At the time of the Bureau's creation, rates were practically prohibitive, running as high as 30 percent to cover ships plying the dangerous North Sea; no insurance at all could be secured for voyages to Germany. Once the government went into the business, rates remained steady, mounting no higher than 5 percent. By insuring all shipments to Germany, the Bureau opened the door to cotton exports, and many vessels which would not have obtained coverage in the open market could now sail. Though demand continued to rise, the Bureau functioned with a small amount of capital and had assumed only 10 percent of the war risks by February, 1915. It wrote the bulk of its policies in the first few months after the conflict opened and operated at a good profit; eventually, commercial underwriters were able to compete successfully with government rates.[8]

The War Risk Insurance Bureau represented one of the least troublesome accommodations between government and business in the prewar years. Yet there was a tinge of irony in this. The Wilsonians, who had been trying to push American business into foreign markets, had in turn been pressed by businessmen to jump into competition with private underwriters; and few people seemed dissatisfied. Over other pieces of merchant marine legislation, there would be considerably less agreement.

Late in February, 1915, Congress sent the Seamen's bill to the President, a measure which, in the words of its House sponsor, returned to these men "the ownership of their own bodies" by regulating the conditions of shipboard life. Wilson and Bryan were won over to the bill, but certain doubts arose about the effect the measure would have on the transportation crisis. During recent months, shipping executives had been begging for less stringent regulations over their crews, on the theory that they could keep operating costs down to competitive levels by exploiting their labor. When the President signed the Seamen's bill, leaders of the shipping industry were aghast. The board of directors of the National Association of Manufacturers adopted resolutions calling for the amendment or repeal of the law, while one of McAdoo's businessman advisers labeled it "a measure conceived in ignorance . . . , born in demagogry [sic], cradled in iniquity, and [one] which will end in the destruction of our merchant marine." But labor insisted on strict enforcement and complained when subsequent construction of the act seemed to weaken it. McAdoo apparently had nothing to do with the framing of the Seamen's bill, though he probably favored it. In any case, like it or not, he had to defend the measure.[9]

When the bill passed, the previously prosperous Pacific Mail Steamship Company—which for years had operated vessels from San Francisco to the Orient—suddenly decided to go out of business. There was one reason, the firm announced, for its suicide: the Seamen's Act itself. The real motives may have been different. But panic spread among West coast exporters; for once these vessels disappeared, transpacific service under the U.S. flag would be almost wiped out.[10]

The very threat of the extinction of American steamship service to the Orient was ominous. McAdoo interpreted the termination of the Pacific Mail and its blasts at the Seamen's Act as a direct attack on the Administration, part of "a highly organized campaign" by the "steamship monopolists" aimed at making "the country believe that the Seamen's Bill alone is the cause of our failure to have a merchant marine." The subsequent decision of the company's purchasers to maintain service to the Orient because of high freight rates came as only slight consolation; for they explicitly warned McAdoo that once these rates declined after the war, the Seamen's Act might once again make private shipping under the Stars and Stripes prohibitively expensive. The Pacific Mail episode graphically demonstrated that the number of American steamship lines, too small to begin with, could easily drop still further. But McAdoo was already taking steps to change all this.[11]

II

"The only remaining thing to be done to make our conquest of foreign markets certain," McAdoo argued, "is to restore our merchant marine." "It is the most important question, in my judgment, before the American people to-day,"

the one remaining great problem we must solve, and there is not a shadow of doubt in my mind that the Government of the United States is the only Agency through which it can be solved.

With an adequate merchant marine, the nation would be "firmly establish [ed] . . . in a larger world influence than it has ever possessed. . . . "[12]

Lying in bed around six o'clock on the morning of August 16, 1914, McAdoo mulled over the idea of a shipping corporation, organized under American law, with the government, if necessary, the single stockholder. He scribbled it down on a writing pad next to his bed. "There is a big sentiment," he wrote, for the purchase, by the Government, of a large fleet of ships to supplement our transportation facilities to Europe, and to establish immediately lines to South America and Central America. We have an unusual opportunity for South American trade but without ships we can do nothing. With them we can quickly establish business and political relations that will be of inestimable value to this country—perhaps for all time.

The Ship Registry Bill & the War Risk Insurance measure, will not accomplish much. We shall gain few ships *immediately* because of those laws, and we may gain a large number, if at all, very slowly. Private initiative in the present condition of demoralized and disorganized world finance is almost dead. To raise the capital for a sufficiently effective operation, through private agencies, is practically impossible.

There is a decided objection to government owned & operated merchantmen. Complications of a grave nature might arise with belligerent nations, because of the operations of government merchantmen. Our neutrality could easily be brought into question and a casus belli might easily result.

But there could be no serious questions of this sort if our government was only a stockholder in a company (American) engaged in maratime [sic] pursuits—even though our Government was a majority stockholder in such Company.

Government backing of such a Company has many advantages.

1. Government can always exercise a regulating agency upon rates, upon management, upon policy and upon the trade routes of the ships.

2. Government will participate in the profits of the Company.

3. Government can secure itself for the capital or credit it furnishes, and because of the stability the Company will have by reason of Government backing, the Company can always secure the additional capital required from private sources, on the most advantageous terms.

4. The Government, if a large stockholder, will be justified in encouraging the growth and development of world wide commerce through the operation of the Companys ships, by granting liberal payments for carrying the mails and thereby putting the Company in position to successfully compete with heavily subsidized foreign ships.

5. A splendid naval auxilliary [sic] and naval reserve would be created and made immediately available in time of war.

All of this can be done with the use of a small amount of actual money and the issuance of only 25 to 30 millions of Panama Canal bonds now a part of the assets of the Treasury.

I would suggest that Congress be asked to authorize the expenditure in money or in bonds (preferably bonds) of 25 to 30 million for the purchase of merchant ships.

That authority be given to organize a Corporation under state law, with requisite capital (say $10,000,000) of which the Government shall subscribe $5,100.000 & the remainder be offered to the public; that the government subscribe for any part of the stock which the public fails to take—in addition to the 51% hereinbefore referred to.

That ships purchased by the government be transferred to this Company in consideration of the issue by the Corporation of 4% bonds in an amount equal to the expenditures of the Government, the bonds to be a first lien upon the ships and all property of the Company. Ample provision to be made for sinking fund and depreciation charges.

That the Secretary of the Treasury, the Postmaster General & the Secretary of Commerce be made a Board to vote the Government's stock. . . .

That day McAdoo showed the plan to the President. Wilson knew that
it would infuriate conservatives and provoke a fierce struggle, but he
agreed to go along with it. Probably neither man expected the kind of
storm the measure would eventually arouse.[13]

A number of legitimate questions could be raised about McAdoo's
proposal. For one thing, it seemed "socialistic," and many feared it as the
entering wedge of nationalization. McAdoo himself wrote years later
that he did not

favor . . . the Government going into any sort of business enterprise which
can be handled efficiently by private and individual initiative. . . . My opposition is based on the thought which has come to me through long experience, that politics are sure to get mixed up in the thing, and inefficiency and
waste will be the result.

But he insisted that the country simply could not get decent shipping
facilities without federal intervention; as long as it remained less expensive to operate vessels under foreign flags, particularly because of lower
labor costs, private enterprise would never give the United States a
sufficient merchant fleet of its own. Changes in the ship registry law
alone would not suffice. Those who argued that there was already plenty
of shipping, or that no more vessels could be had, or that the government could not affect the situation with the amount it would willingly
expend, were simply being foolish. "We may as well cry for the moon,"
he remarked, "as to cry for private capital to do this essential job for
the American people."[14]

This implied an end to

sitting stupidly in a corner and following a hoary dogma—the hoary dogma
that the Government must not engage in business when the vital interests of
the country demand that the Government take vigorous hold of this matter.

McAdoo argued explicitly that capitalism must be shelved when private
funds could not be lured into an industry either quickly enough or in
sufficient amounts and when the national interest—liberally construed—
had become involved. "Do we want simply to sit here provincially in the
face of the most magnificent opportunities that have ever been offered
to this country, or to any country in the world?" To McAdoo, the
answer seemed obvious; but he went even further:

I have come to believe that a bill is good if the special interests say it is
socialistic, because I have never found in all my experience that the thing
that was most savagely denounced by the special interests as socialistic did
not turn out to the best interests of the people of this country when it got into
law.[15]

The most striking thing about this conceptual escapade is the ease
with which McAdoo accomplished it. It required little more effort than

would be needed to slip in and out of a new shoe. But it left McAdoo outside the sphere of most progressives; for it implied the potential of almost total flexibility in governmental response to crisis. In the process, it relegated old ideas of laissez-faire to the realm, in McAdoo's evocative phrase, of "mere dogma." His merchant marine plan was a supreme example of federal promotionalism.[16]

This does not mean that the idea was entirely unprecedented, however. As far back as 1791, for example, Congress had authorized the government to subscribe to the capital stock of the First Bank of the United States. More recently, through the Panama Railroad and Steamship Company, Washington had profitably operated a shipping line between New York and the Canal Zone. But for half a century, McAdoo argued, the government had left private firms with a near monopoly of the shipping business, and there was little to show for it: "it is simply fatuous to hope that private capital will provide . . . ships. . . . Our capitalists are not interested in the . . . business."[17]

In the battle over the "socialistic" nature of his plan, McAdoo and other contestants would soon be cutting their way down to first causes. Opponents paraded the virtues commonly associated with free enterprise. At the core of the problem lay the question of efficiency, so important to the progressive generation. "There is a wide difference," McAdoo argued, "between the Government as a government owning and operating ships and the Government becoming a stockholder in a private corporation which is to own and operate the ships." On the other hand, it was vital that Washington be "the chief or sole stockholder." This way it would have the power to establish regular, reliable routes, with vessels and service at least comparable to those of foreign competitors. As far as he was concerned, the corporation could operate steamships apolitically and efficiently; and previous federal experience in business tended to bear him out. But he considered the profit question of minor importance: a profit or loss balance had little significance when the nation's welfare hung in the scales. Neither the Panama Canal nor the Alaskan Railroad, both government projects, had proved lucrative in a conventional sense. What difference did it make?[18]

A number of the most vital shipping lines, McAdoo expected, would run at a loss for some time to come. This would tend to scare private capital away from the corporation, but he did not expect much individual investment in the undertaking anyway. Yet most of the lines might, in fact, prove profitable, enabling the overall operation to come out in the black. In addition, McAdoo was convinced that some type of new, efficient vessel could be designed which American yards would be able to mass produce more cheaply than anything coming off the ways of other nations and that this standardized ship could be run more economically even though manned by high-priced American labor.

Far more serious than the profitability issue was the potential effect of the shipping proposal on U.S. neutrality. If the government held most of the stock in the corporation and a belligerent seized one of its vessels, might it lead to war? Neither Wilson nor McAdoo seems to have pondered this question very deeply, despite the fact that the issue would never be buried during the measure's long passage through Congress. Behind the proposal lay McAdoo's conviction that the only neutral flag commanding the respect of the belligerents was the Stars and Stripes. Yet before the bill had even been drafted, the British and French had established a relatively inflexible position with regard to the acquisition of the German merchant vessels stranded in American ports, and by November Wilson had become greatly concerned over the matter.[19]

If, in the case of shipping, the question of neutrality stimulated any response at all from McAdoo, it was boredom. The point of giving Washington the controlling interest in a company, rather than turning the ships directly over to the government, was to circumscribe the issue altogether. As McAdoo envisioned it, the purchase of foreign vessels would involve total transfer of ownership, and thus neutrality, admittedly vital, would be "punctiliously maintained." But he had difficulty distinguishing between a private American ship and one which the government owned; both would be subject to search, seizure, and trial in a prize court. He insisted that the United States dare not surrender its right as a neutral to buy belligerent vessels for incorporation under its own flag; doing so would, McAdoo later wrote, "have been an act of cowardice. While the Administration didn't intend to buy belligerent ships [sic!], it did not intend to abandon essential American rights." The President clearly agreed. Indeed, McAdoo and Wilson even contemplated the acquisition of British and French ships as well as the interned German ones. But in the unlikely event that outright war threatened because of the purchase of belligerent-owned vessels, they simply would not be bought; the plan would go through without them.[20]

III

The forces which deployed against the shipping measure proved better organized and more formidable, bitter, and relentless than those which had lined up against either the Underwood Tariff or the Federal Reserve bill. How the shipping industry would respond to McAdoo's threat to its gigantic profits had never been in doubt. Though McAdoo seemed surprised at the intensity of the opposition, he made little attempt to conceal the fact that passage of the bill would bite into shipowners' profits.

The maritime interests were in the minority. Why, McAdoo asked, should the nation sacrifice trade already valued at $4,000,000,000 a year for the benefit of $69,000,000 of American capital invested in foreign shipping?[21]

The hostility of the shipowners merely mirrored the animosity of businessmen in general. The onset of war in Europe endowed the words "foreign commerce" with a magical sound in the business community and brought the merchant marine question to the forefront of attention. But the emerging government-business consensus over trade did not embrace an agreement over shipping. Some businessmen worried more about protecting their domestic markets from postwar foreign dumping—an anxiety McAdoo did not fully share—than about overseas expansion.[22]

In May and June, 1915, the United States Chamber of Commerce polled its membership regarding shipping legislation. The results, though crudely compiled, suggest that McAdoo had a sure finger on the pulse of the Democrats' rural constituency. Outside the South, the Atlantic coast states, where the shipping industry was concentrated, turned in a staggering vote against government ownership and operation. On the Pacific coast, where shipping rates had apparently remained somewhat lower, similar sentiment existed. But in the agricultural regions, which depended heavily on crop exports, and in parts of the South and West producing other raw materials for export, opposition was far less pronounced. Throughout the nation, the vote against a government ownership-private lease arrangement was significantly greater than against government ownership and operation. Other indications tend to bear out the hypothesis of sectional disparity which the Chamber's statistics imply.[23]

In their hostility to the McAdoo plan, newspapers and periodicals (other than the reliable Democratic press) ran a close second to businessmen. It seemed almost impossible to obtain favorable journalistic publicity for the bill, particularly in the large Eastern cities. McAdoo complained that on this issue, the Eastern publishers, especially those in New York, were boycotting the Administration. Some newspapers which favored the bill at first had concluded by the following year that the emergency was gone and withdrew their support. Others had been antagonistic from the beginning: an "economic and political monstrosity," howled the New York *Sun;* "a Heresy and a Peril," warned the Philadelphia *Public Ledger;* "preposterous," grumbled the *New York Times;* "crazy," railed the New York *Journal of Commerce.*[24]

These critics joined in denouncing the Administration bill, but they could get together on little else. Though virtually unanimous sentiment favored a large American merchant marine, there seemed to be as many formulas to resolve the shipping dilemma as there were business lobbies. In general, the enemies of McAdoo's plan were able to agree on two things: first, that Washington should intervene in the situation as foreign governments commonly did, by granting subsidies (delicately euphemized as "subventions") to private shipping corporations; and second, that some sort of federal maritime board should be established, but with far fewer teeth than McAdoo wanted to give it. In addition, widespread support existed for certain other "reforms," including abolition of foreign discrimination, government licensing of shipping lines, revision of the navigation laws, and nullification of the Seamen's Act.

Though McAdoo would go along with some changes in the navigation laws, he did not believe they could (or should) be altered against the welfare of the seamen. He rejected ordinary subsidies, the heart of the opposition's proposals, because he believed they merely placed "a premium on inefficiency." Democrats in Congress, he felt, would never support them; the 1912 platform had opposed them; any subvention program would leave the government with no control over the operations, routes, and rates of the firms that funds were allotted to; and one subsidy would open a Pandora's box of demands for others. The biggest lobbies would get the biggest benefits. "The worst possible thing," McAdoo argued, "is to favor any special interests in this country."

The whole iniquity about the subsidy and protective tariff proposition is that it encourages people to look to the government for favor, and when it has once been granted, they come to regard it as a vested right.

Once again, he found himself summoning New Freedom rhetoric to kill unfavorable ideas.[25]

Even with subventions, or anything else that could be applied to speed up the flow of private capital, McAdoo insisted that investment would probably ooze into shipping like molasses, at a time when it should be pouring in like water; the task, at least at the outset, was too large for private capital anyway. Why wait? Not until shipowners and ship builders got a taste of massive world markets would free enterprise come into play; and by then, the United States could be producing vessels more cheaply than any other nation. None of the Administration's proposals, he argued, would interfere with individual investment—the goal was precisely the opposite. But "it is only by the Government dealing with this question in double-fisted fashion that relief can be given."[26]

IV

For whom would the government be doubling its fists? McAdoo's answers were often vague; he directed his appeals at businessmen, workers, and farmers alike. But the frequency with which he mentioned farmers in general, and cotton producers in particular, leads one to the conclusion

that ("special privilege" rhetoric to the contrary notwithstanding) the
bill was written above all to aid the South.

In 1913, 60 percent of the year's cotton crop had been exported.
Then came the crisis in Europe. To secure war risk insurance for shipment
to Germany, cotton had to be carried in American bottoms; this placed a
premium on national tonnage and, in turn, raised transportation charges.
While shipping rates on grain had climbed as high as 900 percent in a
number of ports by the end of January, 1915, they jumped up to 1,100
percent on cotton, at a time when its price had dropped. Especially in
transit to German and Dutch ports, these staples suffered the heaviest
hikes in freight rates of all exports; and this, in turn, cut the income received by producers. As early as December, 1914, German authorities
let it be known that the Central Powers would probably buy a million and
a half bales of cotton during the following year, if vessels could only be
found to carry them. In 1915, perhaps 5,000,000 bales held over from the
previous crop awaited shipment, and McAdoo wrote House that "I would
not be surprised to hear a great howl from the South when the cotton
problem grows acute again this fall."[27]

The so-called "socialistic" nature of the shipping proposal, then,
proved less significant than the fact that it had been designed to benefit
American capitalism as a whole, but particularly Southern agrarian capitalism. It symbolized the continuing effort of the Wilson Administration
to goad and cajole businessmen into expanding overseas at a faster pace
than many of them wanted. More important than any socialism in the
proposal, too, was its inherent nationalism: it comprised a very large part
of an even bigger plan to make the United States the dominant trading
nation on the globe.

If the shipping scheme was biased as to its domestic beneficiary, it
also bore a large element of bias as to its foreign one. Once the war ended,
European demand for American products would inevitably slump; other
purchasers must be found, and found quickly, to take up the slack. When
McAdoo thought of markets, he thought of the Orient and the neutral
nations of the Mediterranean, but Latin America always came first. At
the Pan American Financial Conference, delegates had assured him that
their governments would help cover the cost of establishing shipping facilities between their own countries and the United States in the form of
terminals, docks, and favorable laws; and McAdoo counted on their aid.

V

From the start, McAdoo's closest adviser on maritime matters was
Bernard Baker of Baltimore. Baker had built up his own shipping line
years before, but had subsequently sold out to J. P. Morgan's International

Mercantile Marine and retired from the business. For thirty years, Baker had been clamoring for legislation which would reestablish the American merchant fleet. His aid was so valuable that one important authority (wrongly) called him the real father of the shipping measure that finally passed in 1916. At his own expense Baker published a book supporting the bill, toured the country inspecting port conditions and other matters, and supplied McAdoo with a legion of facts and figures.[28]

The other men McAdoo took into his confidence or consulted at one time or another in framing shipping legislation were for the most part, like Baker, renegade businessmen. One of these, Arthur Farquhar, a Pennsylvania industrialist who depended heavily on the export trade, had been urging government aid to the merchant marine since the 1880's. Another, John Fahey, had been converted to supporting the bill by the trade opportunities he saw in South America. A third, Benjamin Rosenthal of Chicago, served as vice president of a national businessmen's organization and, like Farquhar, had been urging government intervention for years. Rosenthal published a book on the subject and hopped across the country like a traveling salesman endorsing the shipping bill to business groups. McAdoo frequently discussed the measure with William Denman of San Francisco, an admiralty lawyer and old friend. And Seth Low, then president of the New York Chamber of Commerce, tarried briefly in McAdoo's nest of advisers attempting to draw the Administration into a compromise. (McAdoo refused to budge when Low presented his plan, though McAdoo wanted his support to help break the back of Congressional opposition.) It was an auspicious group: Low had been president of Columbia University and Mayor of New York; and Farquhar and Fahey were honorary vice presidents of the United States Chamber of Commerce. Yet it never quite became a brain trust, and in fighting the shipping battle, McAdoo served as his own general.

Finally, there was Redfield. The Secretary of Commerce believed maritime matters should fall within his own domain, and McAdoo agreed. But McAdoo regarded Redfield as "a slow-witted person with very little initiative or energy," and when Redfield came up with no solutions to the problem McAdoo seized the reins himself. Injured and envious, Redfield was somewhat placated by McAdoo's many requests for information, "so that he began to get the idea that he was playing some part in the affair."[29]

VI

Quick action provided the key to the shipping situation. "It is to the strong and courageous and swift that opportunity counts," McAdoo declared.

Shall we sleep while the opportunity to be the dominant financial and industrial power of the world, with all of its great moral potentialities, is trying to force itself into our indifferent grasp, or shall we . . . seize this marvelous opportunity and make America a permanent and vital and irresistible force for the welfare of humanity and the progress of civilization?

The President summoned a conference of several key Congressional committee chairmen and party leaders, who met at the White House August 19. McAdoo attended, as did Underwood, Furnifold Simmons, Joshua Alexander, Chairman of the House Committee on the Merchant Marine and Fisheries, and James P. Clarke, chairman of the Senate commerce committee. Wilson urged the group to approve McAdoo's proposal, which, after an animated discussion, it did. The following day J. P. Morgan appeared at the Treasury Department to denounce any notion of ship purchases by the government. On August 22 McAdoo forwarded a draft of a memorandum which would "be the basis of a bill" to Redfield. The Secretary of Commerce agreed to give the plan his qualified approval; but his doubts about it strongly resembled those which businessmen would be raising in very short order.[30]

The bill McAdoo drew up became a landmark in American economic history. It was an emergency measure, "never . . . contemplated [to] be a permanent operation on the part of the Government." Briefly, it provided for the creation of a private shipping corporation with a capital stock of $10,000,000, to which the government would subscribe 51 percent; the rest would be offered to the public, but Washington would take it if investors proved unreceptive. A Shipping Board would be established, comprised of the Secretary of the Treasury, the Postmaster General, and the Secretary of Commerce. These men would supervise the corporation and have voting power over the government stock. Active management would be entrusted to a board of directors and officers. In addition to the capital stock, $30,000,000 of Panama Canal bonds could be sold and the proceeds utilized to construct or purchase ships, which, in turn, would be handed over to the company. The Panama Railroad vessels, plus suitable and available ships belonging to the departments of War and Navy, would also be transferred to the corporation. The goal was to have a fleet which could be mobilized quickly and launched into service on any routes where American-registered ships were needed. Furthermore, the corporation could charter vessels either for its own service or for charter parties to fill the needs of firms and individuals. The appropriation would be sufficient to construct up to 141 vessels of 5,000 tons deadweight capacity, assuming that half came from British yards; all would be turned out within a year.[31]

Late in August, Alexander and Clarke introduced the Ship Purchase bill into Congress. By now, Washington was alive with hostile lobbyists. On September 8, the Committee on the Merchant Marine reported the measure favorably to the House. Here progress came to a halt. The Democrats in the lower chamber declined to consider the bill, and Clarke's committee would not even report it. The reason for this icy reception was fear that government operation of a fleet comprised for the most part of former German vessels would invite a diplomatic imbroglio with the warring powers. Even more important, the shipping crisis itself had partially lifted. As the Allies fastened their grip in the high seas, for a brief period it seemed the transportation shortage might have ended.[32]

Congress convened again in December, and the Administration renewed its campaign to drive a practically identical bill through. When the Senate Democrats voted to call the measure up for immediate debate early in January, it was like a declaration of war, heralding one of the most tumultuous legislative struggles of the Progressive Era. As the fight continued, the Republicans in the Senate drew closer together, until their ranks were united more solidly than they had been in four years.[33]

During this short session, their main ally turned out to be the calendar. Henry Cabot Lodge cried that "no maritime nation . . . has ever entered the business of owning trading ships" and alleged that a scandal hid behind McAdoo's proposal.[34] The bill was declared the unfinished business of the Senate, and with considerable effort the Democratic caucus agreed to make it binding on party members. The caucus also put certain changes in the measure; but the President seems to have rejected a compromise amendment proffered by Claude Kitchin, which would have terminated the activities of the Shipping Board two years after the war ended—a proposal already agreed to by McAdoo, Burleson, and Duncan U. Fletcher.[35] Nor would Wilson accept an amendment by Lodge which would have forbidden the Shipping Board from purchasing vessels owned by belligerents, though such a compromise at this point might have put the bill over.[36]

The Republicans responded to the Administration's frenzied activity with a determined filibuster. Evoking the specter of socialism, they claimed free enterprise could fill the tonnage gap and that foreign purchasers, not shippers, paid increased rates. If the measure passed, it would shatter American neutrality.

Then, on February 1, the Administration suffered a disaster. Only a handful of Democratic senators felt enthusiastic about the bill, and seven of them suddenly defected. Efforts ensued to refill the ranks with insurgent Republicans, who now held the balance of power. The President even tried to swing one of them over by appointing his brother-in-law to a postmastership in Iowa; but this backfired and probably lost two votes instead of gaining one. The fight in the Senate continued—the upper chamber went through the longest session in Congressional history, and on February 8 the full membership responded to the roll call for the first time since

1893. But the loss of seven votes and the shortness of the session proved decisive. With Wilson's prodding a bill which included the amendment for postwar termination that he had apparently turned down earlier was unenthusiastically pushed through the House by a vote of 215 to 122. But the Senate remained unswayed, and the session ended. McAdoo, who by now had developed a strong taste for party regularity, was in bitter agony.[37]

VII

The American export trade was booming; but it would have been even greater had the Ship Purchase bill passed. While the United States merchant marine grew at an unparalled rate by late 1915, the country, paradoxically, had never been so badly in need of vessels or so heavily dependent on foreign carriers. Large numbers of ships, McAdoo later claimed, could have been bought when the bill first went to Congress at $30 or $40 a ton—as late as December, 1914, plenty could still be had. But by 1916 prices had shot up as high as $300, and hardly any vessels remained for sale.[38]

McAdoo still would not surrender, however. The time had simply arrived to change strategy. The key to the shipping deadlock, he realized, was naval: he must bind commerce so firmly to preparedness that it would be difficult if not impossible to adopt one without accepting the other.

The previous year, Republican Senator John W. Weeks, who later helped filibuster the Ship Purchase bill to death, had submitted a proposal of his own to Congress. It authorized the Secretary of the Navy to create mail lines with naval vessels, which would regularly carry freight, passengers, and mail from the United States to Europe and South America. Presented before hostilities even began, the measure passed the Senate with substantial Republican support. Then it was fused with the Alexander bill and defeated. "Preposterously expensive, unwise, and ineffective," McAdoo called Weeks's proposal.[39]

But Weeks had a point, and in October, 1915, McAdoo sent Wilson a telegram urging him to arrange for the use of army and navy transports on the Pacific in lieu of the Pacific Mail, until a more permanent merchant fleet could be found. Naval vessels were insufficient for the purpose, and McAdoo realized that he had asked the President to stretch his authority to the breaking point. When Wilson passed the suggestion on to Daniels and Garrison, both men replied that nothing could be done without authority from Congress. "I call this stupidity run mad!" McAdoo exclaimed. In December, when Redfield suggested introduction of a joint resolution providing for commercial operation of government transports at the discretion of the President, McAdoo completely supported the idea.[40]

Since, by the summer of 1915, very few privately owned vessels remained to be had, some new source must be found. Why not let the government build its own ships as a preparedness gesture and then use them to carry freight? Republican hawks in Congress would find it difficult to explain why they had voted against a "naval" bill, especially one designed, as McAdoo put it, to

give our Navy a merchant marine auxiliary superior to that possessed by any other nation in the world, thus making our Navy a more effective instrument than . . . any other navy of similar size and power in the world.

It seemed a sound argument. In the Pacific, where seventy-five colliers might be needed at any given moment, the Navy could muster as of March, 1915, exactly nine. Because of the tight market for merchant ships and the backlog of orders, the Navy had no more success in buying them than did private concerns. Under the circumstances, it is not surprising that Josephus Daniels was willing to back a bill for naval auxiliaries; his sympathies had leaned in this direction from the beginning. By late July, the Secretary of the Navy and his staff had been drawn into McAdoo's circle of close advisers. The Captain Commandant of the newly formed Coast Guard, E.P. Bertholf, worked in conjunction with the admirals. In July, McAdoo asked Daniels what auxiliaries he would have to have in the event of war with either Germany or Japan. Daniels estimated the necessary additional gross tonnage at 312,499. On the hustings McAdoo conveniently rounded this off to the nearest half-million.[41]

Once these modern, efficient ships had been built, McAdoo believed, they would fall almost by default into the channels of trade. A naval reserve of officers and men had to be trained, and this could only be done at sea. Why not let the auxiliaries carry freight and earn what he saw as a certain surplus? Even if the ships lost money, it would be a small price to pay for national defense and would be vastly preferable to mothballing them.

By late summer, McAdoo felt confident that public sentiment for a merchant marine had risen markedly since the preceding session of Congress. He was at least partly right. If the first response of the business community to his bill had been outrage, a change in attitude took place through 1915 as hunger for trade sharpened and businessmen's animosity toward the Administration dulled. Another Chamber of Commerce referendum, this one taken in the summer of 1915, revealed that a majority of businessmen wanted the government to own a private Marine Development Company through stock purchase; 80 percent backed federal rate regulation. More and more businessmen demanded ships, and if government intervention was the price, they were willing to pay it.[42]

But to get a new measure through, McAdoo would have to bolster wavering support within the Administration itself. Wilson wanted to go on, partly because of McAdoo's own compulsion; House, however, questioned the expediency of reviving the matter before the 1916 election. He was not the only one raising questions. Even when the first bill had come up for consideration, some of the Cabinet members had been "lukewarm" and privately disapproved of it; this had leaked to Congress and injured chances for passage. With this experience behind him, McAdoo craved Administration unity behind the shipping measure. Instead, he was confronted by a major, if temporary, defection.[43]

McAdoo had seized the months between sessions of Congress as a time to regroup, not sign an armistice, and he did so on the correct assumption that Wilson wanted to stay in the field. But Redfield grew exasperated at McAdoo for proceeding as if the bill had never died and for plunging ahead as if McAdoo himself were President. Along with Houston and House, Redfield wanted the Administration committed to no bill until the Cabinet had a chance to thresh the issue out. While Redfield and Houston both desired a substantial merchant marine, they had become convinced that this was no time to get one. "Candidly," Redfield told McAdoo, "I dread the introduction of such a measure as you propose into the coming Congress. I think it may and probably will disrupt our party. . . . *go slowly.*"[44]

Redfield had been advancing these arguments at least since early July. Apparently he meant them to clear the way for his own plan, which envisioned ships being constructed in Navy yards and then leased out by the government. McAdoo tried to keep this scheme from catching fire until an Administration program could be agreed upon. By early October, he had finally managed to swing Redfield behind his own proposal, though Redfield wanted to make the Shipping Board "a part of the Department of Commerce," with himself as Chairman.[45]

McAdoo had spent an exhausting summer, but he was convinced that if he and the President could keep the rest of the team in harness, they could get a satisfactory shipping measure through Congress. He spent a good part of the summer dictating letters to line up support. In June, he urged an ICC investigation of maritime conditions. At a conference with Kitchin in September, McAdoo "indicated a willingness to modify the bill to some extent" in order to swing wayward Congressional Democrats behind it, and he attempted to ease the passage of the proposal through Congress by working on an agreement with Kitchin. McAdoo felt "confident that public sentiment will favor the measure strongly if we can only get the case before the country," yet so far the shipping question seems to have stirred barely a ripple of public sentiment one way or the other. If the issue were allowed to slip out of the headlines, it might be lost altogether.

So he decided on a transcontinental tour—ostensibly to inspect postal facilities—to keep what sparks of opinion he could find behind shipping legislation well kindled.[46]

VIII

At noon on October 13, 1915, McAdoo and his wife stepped off a train in Indianapolis, where he was scheduled to address the local chamber of commerce that evening. The large crowd that gathered at the platform to meet them could not have guessed that McAdoo carried with him one of the most important speeches of the Wilson era. He had cleared it with the President, with Redfield, and with Daniels; it represented new Administration policy.

"The terrible events of the past year in Europe," McAdoo began,

and the acute situations which have arisen in our foreign relations, have brought forcibly to the front the necessity for greater naval and military preparedness than our people have heretofore believed to be necessary for the national safety. Our "splendid isolation," upon which we have relied so much in the past as our chief protection, has been neutralized in great measure by the developments of modern science.

The shipping measure McAdoo proceeded to outline was more comprehensive than the old one and not mere emergency legislation. It envisioned a permanent government maritime policy. A Shipping Board would be created, comprised of the secretaries of the Navy and Commerce as ex officio members, plus three Presidential appointees. The Board would be authorized to organize one or more corporations and subscribe to all or part of their capital stock, as it saw fit. Actually, McAdoo did not expect investors to take the minority stock; he included the possibility in order to counter the argument that private enterprise should at least have an opportunity to become involved—which McAdoo still regarded as inessential and undesirable. The Board would vote the government stock in electing directors; they, in turn, would choose the corporation's officers and employees. Theoretically, this would eliminate politics from the operation of the concern.

The Shipping Board could lease or charter cargo vessels to firms, individuals, or corporations; but if suitable lessees were unavailable, it would run the ships itself. As the battle fleet grew, so would the fleet of auxiliaries. The vessels had to be approved by the Navy Department and constructed as much as possible in American naval and private shipyards; these, in turn, must be expanded to meet the imperatives of preparedness. The vessels should be manned by American crews.

Congress would appropriate $50,000,000—enough to provide a merchant fleet of from 400,000 to 500,000 gross tons, roughly 25 to 40 percent of the Navy's current needs. This amount of tonnage McAdoo dismissed as too small to "interfere in the slightest degree with private enterprise;" indeed, he claimed, it would serve to stimulate investment. Then too, the vessels could be sold or leased to private interests. And they would set the pace in ship construction and prove the efficiency and profits possible under the American flag, acting as a further spur to the shipyards.

Most facets of the measure McAdoo proposed paled in significance in contrast to his recommendations regarding regulation of carriers on the high seas. In the past, shipping companies had been free of federal supervision, and service had suffered accordingly; McAdoo proposed an end to all that. Shipping, like the railroads, he argued, must be compelled to conform to social and commercial needs. McAdoo wanted all vessels to be declared common carriers while they plied American waters and to be subject to regulation of rates and service by the Shipping Board. He also wanted the Board to be empowered to cooperate with the ICC to ensure that bills of lading and through rates were arranged by U.S. shipping and railroad companies. The Board would be endowed with authority to establish as quickly as possible lines running to both coasts of South America and to the Orient. Cargo vessels could be used in any part of the world and might be concentrated to meet emergencies such as the seasonal demands of cotton producers. The Board could also retaliate against foreign discrimination toward American shippers. And it would reform the navigation laws.[47]

How deeply would this new measure plunge the government into maritime affairs? And for how long? McAdoo's answers left these questions still in doubt. He issued a call for a navy which would free the United States to confront *any* other power on earth, and emphasized that the bill was linked to the preparedness program. His precise goals were perhaps most clearly outlined in a letter he sent Redfield in August. If "the shipping bill was in existence to-day," he wrote,

I would prepare immediately plans and specifications for the most needed types of ships (cargo ships first); get the suggestions of the Navy Department, so as to make the vessels meet, as far as possible, the requirements of naval auxiliaries, and call for bids. I would let contracts to those bidders who could promise the earliest deliveries, favoring always the American ship yards. . . . I would then "scrape the markets of the world" for available tonnage, buying such as is suitable. . . . I would then charter, if necessary, every available vessel to meet the pressing needs of the moment. I would in addition to all of this have our navy yards (if Congress would grant the authority) build certain types of merchant vessels, suitable for naval auxiliaries, and, to that extent, supplement the ship building facilities of the country. In less than two years we could create a very respectable fleet, and we could, during that time, enormously influence the ocean rate situation in the most important parts of the world; if not throughout the world, forcing reductions in many of the present exorbitant rates and saving large sums to American producers.

With the Government behind the enterprise, every one would have confidence in its ability to sustain itself against all comers, and, therefore, could rely upon a sustained service and reasonable rates.[48]

Again and again McAdoo outlined his proposals as he made his way across the country. He emphasized the naval features over the commercial, hoping this would fire the public imagination; and he was delighted with the response, especially in agricultural regions. Even Congress seemed more receptive. From November through January McAdoo threshed out working drafts in consultation with his colleagues and advisers. Despite the involvement of the Navy Department, the measure retained its commercial character. By January 10 a formal bill was ready for Congress, and the President gave it his blessing. In the meantime, so had the American Federation of Labor and the International Seamen's Union of America. McAdoo pressed Wilson hurriedly to secure an agreement between Alexander and Clarke, who had played a crucial role in killing the previous bill in the Senate. This accomplished, the legislation was introduced in the House.

During the process of revision in the lower chamber, important changes went into the bill. As an effort to muster the maximum number of votes, the measure was altered by Alexander's committee to provide for the termination of the activities of the Shipping Board within five years after the war ended. On May 20 the bill passed the House by a fifty-vote margin. Repeated Republican attempts to weaken it still further had failed, but McAdoo took nothing for granted in the Senate, where the Democrats were perhaps more apathetic than divided. By mid-June the Democrats in the upper chamber had been lined up behind the measure, and McAdoo wrote: "Let the Republicans vote against it if they want to; so much the better for us." But the intraparty schism in the Senate had been smoothed over at a price: the revised bill prevented the government from buying any ship flying a belligerent ensign or any vessel already engaged in American trade unless it was on the verge of being withdrawn; no ship could be purchased which fell below 75 percent of its original efficiency; and the measure forbade the government operation of merchant vessels until all efforts to arrange leases or sell ships to private firms on Washington's terms had failed.[49]

On August 30, despite considerable indifference in the Senate and the delaying tactics of the opposition, the bill finally passed the upper chamber by a strict party vote. The House agreed to the Senate amendments, and the President signed the measure on September 7. It allocated $50,000,000 to the Shipping Board for the purchase and construction of merchant vessels; these could be sold or leased to private citizens, but the government might repossess them whenever necessary. American carriers received protection against cutthroat foreign competition. And though the act required the Board to arrange for bidding so that private interests would have a chance to operate government ships, at least the Board was empowered to establish lines to Latin America and other parts of the world.

The legislation was far less than McAdoo had hoped for. As he wrote the President in September, it had

been tremendously emasculated. The shipping interests, foreign and domestic, devoted all their energies to this emasculation, because they hoped that a weakening of the bill would greatly increase the administrative difficulties, which is, of course, true.

McAdoo had wanted a Board with Cabinet members on it and with the wide powers of the British Board of Trade; he failed to get it. The measure was mainly regulatory—the Board's power to augment the merchant marine itself was diminutive. Nor did Congress intend the government to operate the vessels, except as a last resort. McAdoo made it clear that he viewed the act merely as a beginning, despite the five-year limit written into it by the House. Yet, shortcomings aside, he labeled the measure the most useful stimulus to foreign trade and the nation's welfare since the Federal Reserve Act, and he expected that the powers with which the Board had been endowed would eventually lead to the development of a permanent maritime policy.[50]

The key to the future lay with the men on the Shipping Board. "It is," McAdoo warned Wilson,

of the utmost importance that we should proceed with the greatest care in selecting the personnel of this Board. A mistake here will set us back irretrievably. I am not "talking through my hat" when I say this, because I know whereof I speak. I would earnestly suggest, therefore, that you go slow about appointing this Board and give me ample time to investigate all the men who are worth consideration.

McAdoo had given the President the same advice about the Federal Reserve Board, and it had been ignored. This time Wilson decided to listen, and McAdoo made all of the final selections. Among the men he picked were Baker and Denman, his two first choices. McAdoo also considered it essential to choose a Southerner; the nod went to Theodore Brent, a New Orleans Republican. Another appointee, John A. Donald of New York, had, like Baker, built a shipping company early in the century. And from the Middle West McAdoo selected J. B. White, a lumberman with a knowledge of exporting.[51]

The Shipping Board would have a stormy career, and the trouble began almost at once. McAdoo suggested to Baker that it would be well for the group to consider appointing a representative of the Pacific Coast to the Chairmanship. This meant Denman, and Wilson backed the plan. Baker, who had important policy differences with Denman, resented the Administration's interference in the internal workings of the Board and sent in his resignation the following day. Obviously irate, the President accepted it at once. Baker was replaced at McAdoo's suggestion by Raymond Stevens, of New Hampshire, a former Congressman and counsel for the Federal Trade Commission.[52]

IX

Despite the squabbling, at least the Shipping Board had finally gone into operation. A few ideas jotted down on a scratch pad had culminated in one of the most important measures of the Wilson era.

The span between the coming of World War I in 1914 and the passage of the Shipping Act on the eve of American entry represented a period of new departures by the Wilson Administration. For McAdoo specifically, two aspects of Wilsonian ideology had proved especially important during these years: its emphasis on foreign markets and its implicit flexibility. Without the flexibility, McAdoo's role as a promoter in government would have been impossible; without the focus on markets, his constant innovations might have come to an end.

The antiprivilege rhetoric and sentiment of 1912 had also carried over into the following years. McAdoo made a point of holding Wall Street at a distance while he worked directly in the interest of farmers and other businessmen. And while McAdoo did not embrace total welfare statism, he did offer special privileges to agriculture, which had previously gotten very few. All the while, in good New Freedom fashion, he continued to damn "class legislation."

In order to continue his accustomed role as promoter after he entered government, McAdoo had found it necessary to amass increasing power in the Treasury. But his quest for control of the money market had taken him far enough ahead of the President that it generated considerable friction between the two men by 1914. McAdoo bent ideology to fit his energetic, personal promotionalism faster than Wilson—a centralizer himself as it turned out—was willing to adjust.

Ultimately, in the case of foreign markets, the President and the Secretary of the Treasury rejoined one another on common ground. This was not without irony. Practically from the start, McAdoo had realized that a massive public sector could work for and increase the welfare of the private sector; that in the case of the Federal Reserve Act, for example, centralization was vital in order to unshackle capitalism and realize Wilson's goals. As early as 1913, the President's suspicion of huge aggregations of private power had already led him to begin expanding federal power in order to try to free the small businessman. McAdoo had played a vital role in this, and he shortly began to demonstrate a willingness to go even farther by partially shelving capitalism in the shipping industry if this seemed necessary for the benefit of capitalism as a whole. The Shipping Act stunningly exemplified the flexibility of the Treasury and the Administration and a willingness to walk away from what had been widely interpreted as the gist of Wilsonian ideology. At this point, the Administration caused alarm in the business community. But the quest for foreign markets also led the Wilsonians to opt for cooperation over competition in order to guarantee general domestic prosperity and tranquility. Rather than symbolizing the death of the New Freedom, this represented no more than a shift in focus. The Shipping Act marked the end of one phase of McAdoo's tenure in the Treasury and the beginning of another. Within a short time, the department would be transformed into a great weapon of financial warfare.

NOTES

CHAPTER ONE

1. William had two brothers and four sisters; a half sister also lived with the family.
2. "Mr. McAdoo's First Attempt at Being an Author." McAdoo MSS.
3. "William Gibbs McAdoo"; "Recollections of Milledgeville," June 3, 1930; "Milledgeville," June 14, 1930. McAdoo MSS.
4. "Some Early Political Experiences," June 27, 1930. McAdoo MSS.
5. There seems to have been only one period in which this was not the case. Probably around the end of 1878, young McAdoo aspired to a career in the Navy. His father asked a local Republican Congressman who owed him a favor about an appointment for William to the Naval Academy. The Representative agreed to the idea, provided the youth could pass the entrance exam. William studied months in preparation and passed the test, but for some reason the Congressman refused to make the appointment and declined even to support him as an alternate. ("Naval Academy," April 9, 1930; MS of autobiography. McAdoo MSS.)
6. "Some Early Political Experiences," June 27, 1930. McAdoo MSS.
7. For his understanding of this aspect of McAdoo's character, the author is indebted to his eldest son, Francis H. McAdoo, who discussed it at length in an interview on March 14, 1965. An extremely useful analysis of the power-oriented personality, upon which the author has relied heavily, may be found in Lasswell, *Power and Personality,* pp. 39ff. (S.S.).
8. "Chattanooga," June 26, 1930. McAdoo MSS.
9. "W.G.M.'s Early Years," March 5, 1930. McAdoo MSS.
10. "Re: Financing of Knoxville Street Railroad," July 2, 1930. McAdoo MSS; McAdoo, *Crowded Years,* p. 45 (P.S.).
11. "Re: Financing of Knoxville Street Railroad," July 2, 1930. McAdoo MSS.
12. *Ibid.*
13. *Knoxville Daily Tribune,* May 2, 1890; Price, "Secretary McAdoo: A Cabinet Officer Who Does Things," 247.

14. Stokes to McAdoo, October 11, 1890; contract between the Knoxville Electric Railway Company and the Thomson-Houston Electric Company, November 6, 1891; statement of McAdoo to the bondholders, January 14, 1892; "Chattanooga," June 26, 1930. McAdoo MSS.
15. *Knoxville Journal*, March 3, 1897; "Chattanooga," June 26, 1930. McAdoo MSS.
16. "Chattanooga," June 26, 1930; "New York—1892," July 2, 1930. McAdoo MSS.
17. "New York—1892," July 2, 1930. McAdoo MSS.
18. Memorandum on New York, July 14, 1930. McAdoo MSS.
19. *Ibid.*
20. Loeb interview, August 10, 1911. McAdoo MSS.
21. *Ibid.*
22. Memorandum on New York, July 14, 1930. McAdoo MSS.
23. *New York Herald*, July 3, 1904; memorandum, June 27, 1930. McAdoo MSS.
24. New York *World*, February 15, 1908; notes for autobiography; memorandum on New York, July 14, 1930. McAdoo MSS.
25. *New York Press*, October 14, 1896; memorandum on New York, July 14, 1930; MS of autobiography. McAdoo MSS.
26. *Yonkers Herald*, February 18, 1896.
27. McAdoo, *Crowded Years*, p. 64 (P.S.).
28. Memorandum on New York, July 14, 1930. McAdoo MSS; McAdoo, *Crowded Years*, pp. 67, 70 (P.S.).
29. Memorandum on New York, July 14, 1930. McAdoo MSS.
30. *Ibid.;* McAdoo, *Crowded Years*, p. 74 (P.S.). In 1905, another major figure on Wall Street, Cornelius Vanderbilt, was elected to the board of directors.
31. Memorandum on New York, July 14, 1930. McAdoo MSS.
32. Jacobs to McAdoo, January 16, 1906. Hudson and Manhattan MSS; minutes, no. 626, November 20, 1902; memorandum on New York, July 14, 1930. McAdoo MSS.
33. "Memorandum for Counsel." Hudson and Manhattan MSS; "Lackawanna Railroad Fight." McAdoo MSS.
34. Jersey City *Jersey Journal*, May 28, 1904; "Memorandum for Counsel." Hudson and Manhattan MSS; "Lackawanna Railroad Fight"; MS of autobiography. McAdoo MSS; *New York Commercial*, October 25, 1904.
35. Hendrick, "McAdoo," 630; Hendrick, "McAdoo and the Subway," 493; "Public Service Corporation Declares War"; "The Metropolitan Street Railway Company Also Declares War." McAdoo MSS.
36. The Ninth Avenue extension was not constructed, however.
37. *New York Times*, September 21, 1905; "The Picture—January 1, 1905." McAdoo MSS. The name of the Metropolitan had meanwhile been changed to the New York City Railway Company. It continued to be known in public parlance as the Metropolitan, however, and will be so designated here to avoid confusion.
38. "The Picture—January 1, 1905." McAdoo MSS.
39. *Ibid.;* agreement between the Public Service Corporation of New Jersey *et al.* and the Hudson and Manhattan Railroad Company *et al.* regarding the Hoboken Terminal, April 23, 1906. Hudson and Manhattan MSS.
40. *Wall Street Journal*, May 1, 1913; "Mr. Morgan Takes an Interest," July 14, 1930. McAdoo MSS.
41. Jersey City *Jersey Journal*, May 24, July 9, 1907; *Hoboken Hudson Observer*, May 27, 1907; *Newark Evening News*, June 11, 1907.
42. "Hudson and Manhattan Railroad Company. Hudson Tunnel System," February, 1908. Hudson and Manhattan MSS; "Hudson and Manhattan Railroad Company," March 2, 1910. McAdoo MSS.

CHAPTER TWO

1. William G. McAdoo, "The Relations Between Public Service Corporations and

the Public." Lecture delivered to the Graduate School of Business Administration, Harvard University, April 6, 1910. McAdoo MSS.

2. "Speech of W. G. McAdoo at the Press Club, January 21, 1911." McAdoo MSS.

3. McAdoo, "The Relations Between Public Service Corporations and the Public" (not to be confused with McAdoo's Harvard speech; see the bibliography [O.S.] for the full citation); McAdoo, "Decent Treatment of the Public by Corporations and Regulation of Monopolies" (O.S.).

4. "Speech Delivered by William G. McAdoo, President of Hudson and Manhattan Railroad Company, at City Hall Park, Jersey City, N. J., July 19th, 1909, upon the Opening of the Hudson River Tunnels Between the Hudson Terminal, New York, and Jersey City, N. J." McAdoo MSS. In effect, this policy had actually been initiated in February, 1908, when the uptown tunnels were opened.

5. *Brooklyn Daily Eagle,* December 4, 1910; McAdoo, "Decent Treatment of the Public by Corporations and Regulation of Monopolies" (O.S.).

6. William G. McAdoo, "The Relations Between Public Service Corporations and the Public." Lecture delivered to the Graduate School of Business Administration, Harvard University, April 6, 1910. McAdoo MSS; McAdoo, "The Relations Between Public Service Corporations and the Public" (O.S.).

7. William G. McAdoo, "The Relations Between Public Service Corporations and the Public." Lecture delivered to the Graduate School of Business Administration, Harvard University, April 6, 1910. McAdoo MSS. (Italics added.)

8. *Ibid.;* Graff to McAdoo, May 23, 1911. McAdoo MSS.

9. Minutes, April 20, 1903. McAdoo MSS; memorandum of a conference between the Associated Building Trades of New York and William G. McAdoo, April 25,1905. Hudson and Manhattan MSS.

10. The following analysis of business thought is drawn in part from: Heald, *The Social Responsibilities of Business;* Wiebe, *Businessmen and Reform;* Hays, *The Response to Industrialism;* Wiebe, *The Search for Order* (the foregoing all S.S.); and Hays, "The Politics of Reform in Municipal Government," each *passim.*

11. Wiebe, *The Search for Order,* p. 176 (S.S.); Wiebe, *Businessmen and Reform,* pp. 204-05 (S.S.).

12. July 21, 1909. By 1911, McAdoo was being referred to by journalist Burton Hendrick as "probably the most popular citizen of New York." Commuters rarely alluded to the Hudson and Manhattan by its proper name; rather, they personified it as "the McAdoo Tunnels." McAdoo was widely compared to Lincoln, Gladstone and Clay. (Hendrick, "McAdoo and the Subway," 495; New York *World,* December 9, 1910; *Brooklyn Daily Eagle,* December 4, 1910; New York *Morning Telegraph,* November 20, 1910; "McAdoo, the Man Who Went Hunting for Trouble and Found It," 287-88.)

13. Hendrick, "McAdoo and the Subway," 491.

14. "Note About W. G. McAdoo," March 12, 1930. McAdoo MSS.

15. Lippmann, *Men of Destiny,* p. 113 (S.S.); McAdoo, *Crowded Years,* p. 528 (P.S.).

16. Lippmann, *Men of Destiny,* p. 116 (S.S.).

17. "Interview with William Gibbs McAdoo," n.d. Baker MSS; "Note About W. G. McAdoo," March 12, 1930. McAdoo MSS.

18. Loeb interview, August 10, 1911. McAdoo MSS.

19. House Diary, II, 272.

20. Author's interview with Francis H. McAdoo and Nona McAdoo Park, March 14, 1965; McAdoo to his wife, May 19, 1910. McAdoo MSS; Hatch, *Edith Bolling Wilson,* pp. 71-72 (S.S.).

21. Francis H. McAdoo to the author, April 4, 1965.

22. New York *World,* February 15, 1908; Francis H. McAdoo to the author, April 4, 1965; McAdoo to Gwathmey, n.d.; "Speech of William G. McAdoo at City Hall, New York, on the Centenary of the Birth of Horace Greeley, February

3, 1911." McAdoo MSS.
23. McAdoo to Green, September 29, 1913. McAdoo MSS.
24. *Russia and the American Passport: Report of the Proceeding of the Mass Meeting Held at Carnegie Hall, New York City; Wednesday Evening, Dec. 6, 1911, under the auspices of The National Citizens Committee,* pp. 5, 7-9. McAdoo MSS.
25. (Illegible) to McAdoo, April 26, 1905; Roosevelt to McAdoo, August 31, 1905. McAdoo MSS.
26. "Woman's Coming Power in Politics." McAdoo MSS.
27. McAdoo to Miller, May 8, 1913; "William Gibbs McAdoo." McAdoo MSS.
28. Hendrick, "McAdoo and the Subway," 499; *Pittsburgh Dispatch,* December 11, 1910.
29. *Brooklyn Daily Eagle,* November 27, 1910; New York *Evening Mail,* November 19, 1910; Hendrick, "McAdoo and the Subway," 500; Fitzherbert, "The Public Be Pleased," 7-8; New York *World,* December 4, 1910.
30. New York *American,* December 5, 1910. Later, this bid was rejected.
31. New York *World,* December 13, 1910.
32. *Brooklyn Daily Eagle,* December 15, 1910; *New York Press,* February 18, 1913; New York *World,* December 15, 1910.
33. New York *American,* January 20, 1911.
34. New York *Financial America,* April 28, 1911; *Brooklyn Daily Eagle,* April 28, 1911.
35. *New York Evening Journal,* December 8, 1910; *Brooklyn Citizen,* January 20, 1911.

CHAPTER THREE

1. "I Meet Woodrow Wilson," September 23, 1930. McAdoo MSS.
2. McAdoo to Brisbane, February 15, 1910; McAdoo to Riordan, December 22, 1911; "McAdoo Says." McAdoo MSS.
3. William McAdoo to Roosevelt, November 18, 1904; William Gibbs McAdoo to Roosevelt, November 26, 1904. McAdoo MSS.
4. Roosevelt to Johnson, October 27, 1911. Roosevelt, *Letters,* VII, 418-22, 512 (P.S.).
5. "Notes on Atlanta Speech," n.d.; McAdoo to Newton, June 7, 1911; McAdoo to Williams, January 13, 1912. McAdoo MSS.
6. "I Meet McCombs," September 23, 1930; McAdoo to Gonzales, January 19, 1912. McAdoo MSS.
7. New York *Sun,* December 13, 1910; New York *World,* December 15, 1910.
8. McAdoo to O'Neale, June 3, 1911. McAdoo MSS.
9. Springfield (Massachusetts) *Republican,* May 28, 1911, quoted in Link, *Wilson: The Road to the White House,* pp. 326-27 (S.S.).
10. "I Meet McCombs," September 23, 1930. McAdoo MSS.
11. Wilson to Page, August 21, 1911, quoted in Baker, *Wilson,* III, 234 (S.S.).
12. This account is based upon several sources, including notes for autobiography; memorandum by McAdoo, March 7, 1930. McAdoo MSS; "Interview with William Gibbs McAdoo," n.d. Baker MSS; McAdoo and Gaffey, *The Woodrow Wilsons,* pp. 133-34 (P.S.); and Baker, *Wilson,* III, 443 (S.S.). There is at least one hint that McAdoo was eager to get into politics for good as early as the autumn of 1911. See House Diary, II, 284.
13. "Memorandum of a Conversation with Mr. and Mrs. McAdoo and Miss Margaret Wilson at the Plaza Hotel, May 9, 1928"; "Interview with William Gibbs Mc-Adoo," n.d. Baker MSS.
14. McAdoo and Gaffey, *The Woodrow Wilsons,* p. 122 (P.S.).
15. Lawrence, *The True Story of Woodrow Wilson,* p. 72 (P.S.).
16. McAdoo to Crozier, November 22, 1911; McAdoo to Fendig, May 4, 1912. McAdoo MSS.

17. Notes for autobiography. McAdoo MSS; House, "Reminiscences: 1858-1912," 50-51.
18. Lyons, *McCombs*, p. 25 (P.S.; Maurice Lyons was McCombs's secretary); "I Meet McCombs," September 23, 1930. McAdoo MSS; Morgenthau, *All In a Life-Time*, p. 137 (P.S.). McAdoo proved an adept fund raiser; during the pre-convention period he mustered well over $6,000, more than half of which he pulled from his own pocket.
19. Byron R. Newton, "The Wilson Campaign"; notes for autobiography. McAdoo MSS; Lyons, *McCombs*, p. 19 (P.S.); McAdoo, *Crowded Years*, pp. 115-17(P.S.).
20. McAdoo, *Crowded Years*, pp. 129-30 (P.S.). Meanwhile, McAdoo had helped persuade Wilson to veto as unfair to the railroads an important bill aimed at abolishing dangerous railway grade crossings in New Jersey.
21. "I Meet McCombs," September 23, 1930. McAdoo MSS. Morgenthau's support resumed after Wilson had won the nomination.
22. McAdoo to Seely, December 21, 1911; McAdoo to Gray, May 4, 1912; McAdoo to Peabody, May 27, 1912; McAdoo to Graham, May 28, 1912; notes for auto-biography; "Autobiography." McAdoo MSS.
23. House, "Reminiscences: 1858-1912," 55; McAdoo to Peabody, May 27, June 3, 1912. McAdoo MSS.
24. This account is based on McAdoo's own notes for his autobiography. McAdoo MSS; and on "Interview with William Gibbs McAdoo," n.d. Baker MSS.
25. "Autobiography," June 30, 1930. McAdoo MSS.
26. Notes for autobiography. McAdoo MSS; McAdoo to Wilson, June 25, 1912. Wilson MSS.
27. McCombs to House, August 28, 1911, May 19, 1912. House MSS; Tumulty, *Woodrow Wilson As I Know Him*, p. 129 (P.S.).
28. House, "Reminiscences: 1858-1912," 56.

CHAPTER FOUR

1. No attempt will be made here to do more than trace McAdoo's course through the Baltimore convention. For a more detailed account, see Coletta, *Bryan*, II, 51-85 (S.S.).
2. Wilson to Bryan, June 22, 1912. Wilson MSS; Tumulty, *Woodrow Wilson As I Know Him*, pp. 110-11; Bryan, *A Tale of Two Conventions*, pp. 198-99; Bryan and Bryan, *Memoirs*, pp. 336-37 (the foregoing all P.S.).
3. Notes for autobiography. McAdoo MSS.
4. Jersey City *Jersey Journal*, June 26, 1912; Bryan, *A Tale of Two Conventions*, p. 192 (P.S.); Baker, *Wilson*, III, 341 (S.S.); Daniels, *The Life of Woodrow Wilson*, p. 110 (P.S.).
5. Link, *Wilson: The Road to the White House*, pp. 440-41 (S.S.); Mullen, *Western Democrat*, pp. 170-71 (P.S.).
6. Woodson, *Proceedings of the . . . Convention*, pp. 76-78, 129 (P.S.).
7. "Autobiography." McAdoo MSS.
8. Woodson, *Proceedings of the . . . Convention*, p. 196 (P.S.); Link, *Wilson: The Road to the White House*, p. 450 (S.S.); Richardson, *House*, p. 293 (S.S.).
9. "Autobiography." McAdoo MSS; McAdoo to Baker, October 15, 1928. Baker MSS.
10. Baker, *Wilson*, III, 349 (S.S.).
11. Link, *Wilson: The Road to the White House*, p. 449 (S.S.).
12. Notes for autobiography. McAdoo MSS.
13. Tumulty, *Woodrow Wilson As I Know Him*, p. 121 (P.S.); McAdoo to Tumulty, September 24, 1930. Baker MSS. The memoirs and letters of the men involved are liberally laced with conflicting accounts of this incident.
14. Memorandum, June 29, 1912. Wilson MSS.
15. New York *Evening Post*, June 27, 1912.

16. New York *World*, June 30, 1912; Tumulty, *Woodrow Wilson As I Know Him*, p. 118 (P.S.); Daniels, *The Life of Woodrow Wilson*, p. 62 (P.S.); Daniels, "Wilson and Bryan," 50.
17. Woodson, *Proceedings of the . . . Convention*, pp. 283-85 (P.S.). From this time on the Wilson men in the New York delegation continued to call for polls simply to maintain the image of a divided delegation.
18. *New York Tribune*, July 3, 1912; New York *Evening Post*, July 3, 1912. McAdoo became one of the claimants to the credit (or lack of it) for the nomination of Thomas R. Marshall of Indiana for Vice-President.
19. *New York Herald*, July 7, 1912; notes for autobiography. McAdoo MSS.
20. Gibboney to McAdoo, September 9, 1930; "W. F. McCombs," March 7, 1930; notes for autobiography. McAdoo MSS; Walworth, *Woodrow Wilson*, Bk. I, 236 (S.S.); Daniels, *The Wilson Era*, p. 68 (P.S.).
21. McAdoo to McCombs, July 30, 1912; Lyons to McAdoo, October 29, 1914, and enclosure. McAdoo MSS.
22. Wilson, *Crossroads of Freedom*, pp. 156, 314 (P.S.). The following discussion is largely based upon an analysis of Wilson's 1912 speeches, as compiled in this work. Only quotations will be cited specifically by page.
23. *Ibid.*, p. 399.
24. *Ibid.*, pp. 351, 354.
25. *Ibid.*, p. 491.
26. Wilson MSS.
27. New York *Evening Post*, August 14, 1912; Morgenthau to Peabody, August 16, 1912. Peabody MSS; McCombs to McAdoo, August 30, 1912. McAdoo MSS. Inevitably McAdoo was criticized for having taken over so quickly after McCombs left, but as Vice-Chairman he had very little choice. Wilson himself refused to deal with the minutiae of organizing the campaign.
28. Byron R. Newton, "The Wilson Campaign"; notes for autobiography. McAdoo MSS.
29. Unpublished memoirs of Robert Woolley. Woolley MSS; notes for autobiography. McAdoo MSS. Wilson appointed Davies Vice-Chairman in charge of the Chicago headquarters, with McAdoo in command at New York.
30. New York *Sun*, August 13, September 8, 1912; notes for autobiography. McAdoo MSS; statement of William Jennings Bryan, October 16, 1912; Dodge to McCormick, October 22, 1912. Bryan MSS; *New York Times*, August 13, 1912.
31. New York *World*, August 13, 1912; Wells, *Report of the Treasurer, passim* (P.S.); House Diary, I, 6, 49-50; Walworth, *Woodrow Wilson*, Bk. I, 236 (S.S.).
32. *New York Times*, August 19, 1912.
33. *Ibid.*, August 20, 1912.
34. *Brooklyn Daily Eagle*, September 15, 1912; New York *Sun*, September 2, 1912. Toward the end of the campaign, McAdoo published an article arguing that "if the people of this country are going to permanently purify their government," the federal government must pay the cost of running for office. ("M'Adoo Reviews Campaign," New York *Evening Post*, November 2, 1912.)
35. *Cleveland News*, August 23, 1912.
36. Shaw, "President Wilson's Cabinet," 440; notes for autobiography. McAdoo MSS; New York *World*, August 12, 1912; *Knoxville Sentinel*, September 6, 1912; House Diary, I, 2. McCombs tried to undercut the possibility of a McAdoo campaign.
37. New York *Sun*, September 12, 1912; *New York Commercial*, September 13, 1912; McAdoo, *Crowded Years*, p. 169 (P.S.).
38. New York *World*, September 23, 1912. For different accounts of what transpired at Syracuse, see "Charles F. Murphy and Woodrow Wilson"; notes for autobiography. McAdoo MSS; and Link, *Wilson: The Road to the White House*, pp. 495-96 (S.S.).

39. *New York Times,* September 23, 1912; New York *World,* September 24, 1912; House Diary, I, 2.
40. Freidel, *The Apprenticeship,* p. 145 (S.S.).
41. Notes for autobiography. McAdoo MSS.
42. Wilson to Dodge, September 11, 1912. Baker MSS; marginal note by McAdoo on MS of Byron R. Newton, "The Wilson Campaign"; notes for autobiography. McAdoo MSS.
43. House, "Reminiscences . . . 1858-1912," 58; notes for autobiography. McAdoo MSS; Wilson to House, September 11, 1912. Baker MSS.
44. Byron R. Newton, "The Wilson Campaign." McAdoo MSS; House Diary, I, 1-4, 8, 10, 12.
45. Unpublished memoirs of Robert Woolley. Woolley MSS; House Diary, I, 2, 4, 12-13.
46. House Diary, I, 12-15; Baker, *Wilson,* III, 397 (S.S.); unpublished memoirs of Robert Woolley. Woolley MSS.
47. Underwood to McAdoo, November 7, 1912. McAdoo MSS.

CHAPTER FIVE

1. House Diary, I, 52; notes for autobiography. McAdoo MSS.
2. House Diary, I, 9, 21, 77. David F. Houston, who became Secretary of Agriculture, later claimed that sometime in December, 1912, House sounded him on the Treasury; but Houston demurred. In January, Wilson temporarily slated industrialist Charles R. Crane for the post. (Houston, *Eight Years With Wilson's Cabinet,* I, 9 [P.S.]; House Diary, I, 55, 83.)
   Exactly how much effort McAdoo exerted to become a Cabinet member is unclear. Oswald Garrison Villard, whose autobiography was generally hostile to McAdoo, claimed that McAdoo had approached him, James Kerney, and others who had worked to nominate Wilson, seeking their "aid in persuading Mr. Wilson that he should become Secretary of the Treasury." Kerney reinforced the notion that McAdoo had waged an active campaign for the position and claimed that because of attacks on McAdoo by McCombs and Morgenthau, the President-elect was reluctant to appoint him. Only pressure from McAdoo, House and Tumulty, Kerney wrote, led Wilson to capitulate. According to House's son-in-law and confidant, Gordon Auchincloss, Wilson's reluctance stemmed from the fact that for a time McAdoo had been his political manager. (Kerney, *The Political Education of Woodrow Wilson,* pp. 253, 299-300 [P.S.]; Auchincloss Diary, December 13, 1914; Villard, *Fighting Years,* p. 223 [P.S.].)
3. House Diary, I, 35-39, 42; Baker, *Wilson,* III, 443 (S.S.). On the state of the Hudson and Manhattan see Broesamle, "Businessman in Politics," pp. 161-62 (O.S.).
4. House Diary, I, 55, 83, 92; notes for autobiography. McAdoo MSS. He urged House to take the Treasury portfolio, however, and allow him to take War. So strongly did McAdoo press him, House wrote, that the Colonel finally had to acknowledge that both positions had already been offered. (*Ibid.,* 92.)
5. Much of this opposition was generated by McCombs and Morgenthau, who wanted the post themselves. McCombs ultimately wound up with no position; Morgenthau took the Turkish Ambassadorship. See Tumulty, *Woodrow Wilson As I Know Him,* p. 137 (P.S.); and Kerney, *The Political Education of Woodrow Wilson,* p. 299 (P.S.).
6. *Washington Post,* March 2, 1913; *Denver Daily News,* March 3, 1913; New York *World,* March 4, 1913.
7. Gonzales to Wilson, January 29, 1913; notes for autobiography. McAdoo MSS; New York *Evening Post,* March 3, 1913.
8. Notes for autobiography; "Various Observations by Mr. McAdoo." McAdoo MSS; "Holland's Letter," *Wall Street Journal,* May 1, 1913; *Wall Street Journal,*

244   WILLIAM GIBBS McADOO

February 17, March 4, 1913.

9. *Boston Post,* March 5, 1913; New York *Morning Telegraph,* March 3, 1913; Jersey City *Jersey Journal,* March 4, 1913.

10. La Follette, "The System at Work," 1.

11. "John Skelton Williams," 400; Washington *Evening Star,* March 13, 1913; New York *Sun,* March 14, 1913; Hendrick, "A New Federal Tribunal," 566; notes for autobiography. McAdoo MSS.

12. Hamlin Diary, II, 2-6, 8-9.

13. Notes for autobiography. McAdoo MSS.

14. Link, *Wilson: The New Freedom,* pp. 157-63 (S.S.); "Interview with Albert Sidney Burleson," n.d. Baker MSS.

15. O'Neil to McAdoo, September 15, 1916. McAdoo MSS. For the broader implications of Administration patronage allocation in Massachusetts, see Abrams, *Conservatism in a Progressive Era* (S.S.), especially pp. 286-87.

16. New York *World,* March 6, 1913; McAdoo to Burleson, April 30, 1913; McAdoo to Tumulty, August 1, 1913. McAdoo MSS.

17. House Diary, I, 130; IV, 14.

18. The assumption that McAdoo was trying to build his own Presidential machine in New York seems to be based partly on contemporary innuendos (for example, Kerney, *The Political Education of Woodrow Wilson,* p. 308 [P.S.]; and Auchincloss to House, June 26, [1914]. House MSS). More specifically, it grows out of a rumor circulated by Stuart Gibboney—a highly questionable witness—and recorded by House in the summer of 1914. According to the Colonel, Gibboney had been spreading the word that McAdoo planned to run for President when Wilson retired, and (though House's meaning blurs somewhat here), that therefore only McAdoo men would be appointed in New York. Nowhere is there any evidence that Gibboney got this revelation from McAdoo; House's account implies that Gibboney based his remarks on rumor. Hence, one is left with evidence whose original source remains unknown, which had been relayed two and possibly three times, and which was written down quite unclearly. There is, quite simply, no solid evidence for the Presidential rumor. (House Diary, V, 125-26.)

19. House to McAdoo, March 4, 1914. House MSS; Hamlin Diary, II, 67-68, 71; House Diary, III, 362; McAdoo to McReynolds, February 24, 1914. McAdoo MSS.

20. Freidel, *The Apprenticeship,* p. 155 (S.S.); New York *World,* April 18, 22, 1913; Peabody to McAdoo, April 14, 18, 1913; Gibboney to McAdoo, April 20, 1913. McAdoo MSS; *New York Times,* April 18, 1913; Link, *Wilson: The New Freedom,* p. 166 (S.S.); House Diary, II, 191, 204, 206, 211.

21. House Diary, II, 204-05, 211-12; Kerney, *The Political Education of Woodrow Wilson,* p. 320 (P.S.).

22. McAdoo to Polk, May 9, 1913. Polk MSS.

23. House Diary, II, 208, 267-68; III, 319.

24. Lewinson, *John Purroy Mitchel,* pp. 208-09 (S.S.); Link, *Wilson: The New Freedom,* pp. 168-69 (S.S.); Malone to House, March 7, 1914; Antisdale to Hare, February 13, [1914]. House MSS. Edwin R. Lewinson (p. 208) gives a somewhat different account of this agreement.

25. McAdoo to Peabody, February 17, 1915; McAdoo to Eastmond, July 6, 1915. McAdoo MSS; McAdoo to House, June 28, 1914. House MSS.

26. Daniels, *Years of Peace,* p. 131 (P.S.); undated memorandum by McAdoo; McAdoo to Gerard, September 19, 1914; Mitchel to Hennessy, September 14, 1914. McAdoo MSS; Kerney, *The Political Education of Woodrow Wilson,* p. 324 (P.S.); Link, *Wilson: The New Freedom,* pp. 170-71 (S.S.); Lewinson, *John Purroy Mitchel,* p. 210 (S.S.). Gibboney played an important role in helping to finance the Roosevelt-Hennessy campaign. Even the President joined in at first by trying, like McAdoo, to keep Gerard out of the race. (Freidel,

The Apprenticeship, p. 183 [S.S.]; Daniels, Years of Peace, pp. 131-32 [P.S.]; House Diary, V, 160-61.)

27. House Diary, V, 188, 192; Gibboney to McAdoo, October 27, 1914. McAdoo MSS; Blum, Tumulty, pp. 79-80 (S.S.); McAdoo to Wilson, October 29, 1914. Wilson MSS.
28. Blum, Tumulty, p. 117 (S.S.).
29. McAdoo to Redfield, July 14, 1915. McAdoo MSS; McAdoo to House, February 22, 1914. House MSS.
30. McAdoo to House, February 22, 1914. House MSS.
31. New York Sun, March 3, 1915.
32. House Diary, V, 216.
33. Antisdale to House, November 13, 1914; Auchincloss to House, December 19, [no year]. House MSS; Peabody to McAdoo, February 10, 1915; McAdoo to Gibboney, July 28, 1916. McAdoo MSS; House Diary, V, 221; VII, 173.
34. Platt to McAdoo, May 27, November 11, 1916; McAdoo to House, September 23, 1916. McAdoo MSS; Polk to House, August 18, 1916. House MSS; McAdoo to Baruch, September 21, [1916]. Baruch MSS.
35. In fact, the nomination of Seabury represented a major defeat for the Independents. It grew out of a compromise in which Franklin Roosevelt played an important part. McAdoo and Wilson, who insisted on Seabury, got him; in exchange, Tammany was left to exercise its own whims in organizing New York City. See Freidel, The Apprenticeship, pp. 190-91 (S.S.).
36. House Diary, VIII, 120.
37. House Diary, V, 186, 256-57; VII, 120, 268, 327; IX, 219, 224-25, 244.
38. October 29, 1914. Wilson MSS.

CHAPTER SIX

1. San Francisco Bulletin, February 3, 1914.
2. House Diary, II, 163; Vanderlip and Sparkes, From Farm Boy to Financier, pp. 213-18 (P.S.).
3. Notes for autobiography. McAdoo MSS. Before his appointment had even been announced, McAdoo had begun to take soundings among the banking fraternity. He and the President agreed that each interest concerned should at least be consulted, and all plans presented by responsible parties considered, if only to satisfy them that they had been afforded a fair opportunity to present their views before the final bill passed. The bankers were, he later recalled, virtually unanimous in advocating a centralized banking system. (Ibid.; House Diary, I, 40, 80.)
4. Willis to Laughlin, July 18, 1912. Laughlin MSS; Willis, The Federal Reserve System, p. 109 (P.S.); Laughlin, Banking Reform (P.S.); "Notes About People." McAdoo MSS. Willis's only connection with the National Citizens' League was through Laughlin, and Willis considered himself "under no obligation" to the organization. (Willis to Laughlin, August 26, 1912. Laughlin MSS.)
5. The fact that McAdoo and Glass had not known each other brought a temporary halt to the progress of the bill which Willis and the Congressman had been drafting. McAdoo's appointment to the Treasury did not become public until early March, and Glass had to postpone any communication with the new Secretary until then. Sometime around the middle of the month, McAdoo telephoned Glass and said he wanted to discuss the measure. McAdoo added that, despite reports to the contrary (from Willis, among others), he was neither intimate nor allied with Wall Street. This call started the bill forward once more. (Willis, The Federal Reserve System, pp. 168-69 [P.S.]; Willis to Glass, March 13, 1913. Willis MSS.)
6. "Report of the Chairman of the Executive Committee on the Work of the National Citizens' League," October 1, 1912. Laughlin MSS.

7. Willis to Laughlin, June 17, 1912. Laughlin MSS. The interrelationship between bills prepared by Aldrich and his bankers, and those drawn up by Laughlin and Willis, presents a maze which no scholar has yet been able fully to traverse; nor is such an effort within the province of this biography.

8. "Memorandum of a Conversation with Senator Carter Glass at Mrs. Wilson's Home on December 17, 1925." Baker MSS; Glass, *Adventure*, pp. 91-92 (P.S.); Willis, *The Federal Reserve System*, pp. 1,531-53 (P.S.); Link, *Wilson: The New Freedom*, p. 205 (S.S.).

9. Morrison to McAdoo, June 17, 1913. McAdoo MSS; Willis, *The Federal Reserve System*, pp. 245, 247 (P.S.).

10. Notes for autobiography. McAdoo MSS. For a more detailed discussion of this incident, see Broesamle, "Businessman in Politics," pp. 217ff. (O.S.).

11. Memorandum by Bryan, July 6, 1913. Bryan MSS; Willis, *The Federal Reserve System*, p. 256 (P.S.).

12. *New York Times*, June 20, 1913.

13. Willis to Laughlin, August 22, 26, October 3, 1912. Laughlin MSS; Laughlin, *The Federal Reserve Act*, pp. 62-72 (P.S.).

14. Clipping from New York *Journal of Commerce*, January 9 (?), 1913, Hamlin MSS; Willis, *The Federal Reserve System*, p. 405 (P.S.); Laughlin, *The Federal Reserve Act*. p. 59 (P.S.); Laughlin to Simmons, January 15, 1914. Laughlin MSS.

15. Wiebe, *Businessmen and Reform*, p. 134 (S.S.).

16. Undated fragment. Laughlin MSS; Willis, *The Federal Reserve System*, p. 148 (P.S.).

17. Willis, *The Federal Reserve System*, pp. 177-79, 191-94 (P.S.); Glass, *Adventure*, pp. 94-96 (P.S.); Willis to Glass, May 2, 1913. Willis MSS; Baker, *Wilson*, IV, 150 (S.S.). According to Warburg (who claimed to have met House aboard ship unexpectedly), the plan the Colonel showed him was McAdoo's National Reserve scheme. (Warburg, *The Federal Reserve System*, I, 97 and *passim* [P.S.].)

18. This conference took place late in May, with Williams and Willis also present. For details, see Willis, *The Federal Reserve System*, p. 195 (P.S.); and Glass to Baker, February 2, 1927. Baker MSS. It cannot be determined precisely what changes McAdoo recommended. Prior to the conference, those he suggested appear to have been mostly minor.

19. Glass, *Adventure*, pp. 99-100 (P.S.).

20. Willis, *The Federal Reserve System*, p. 194 (P.S.); McAdoo to House, May 20, 1913; notes for autobiography. McAdoo MSS.

21. This brief review is based on drafts and fragments in the McAdoo MSS and on another printed in Willis, *The Federal Reserve System*, pp. 196-201 (P.S.). Also of use, though somewhat misleading, is Willis's discussion of the plan in *ibid.*, pp. 194ff. See also McAdoo's own review in notes for his autobiography. McAdoo MSS.

22. Willis to McAdoo, June 5, 1913. Willis MSS; notes for autobiography. McAdoo MSS; McAdoo, *Crowded Years*, p. 242 (P.S.).

23. Glass, *Adventure*, p. 101 (P.S.).

24. McAdoo to Glass, January 31, 1927. Glass MSS; notes for autobiography. McAdoo MSS.

25. Notes for autobiography; Williams to McAdoo, July 11, 1913; McAdoo to Reynolds, June 16, 1913. McAdoo MSS; McAdoo to House, June 20, 1913. House MSS; Glass to McAdoo, February 5, 1927. Glass MSS.

26. Undated fragments. Laughlin MSS; McAdoo, *Crowded Years*, p. 242 (P.S.); Willis, *The Federal Reserve System*, pp. 195-96, 207 (P.S.).

27. Glass to Baker, February 3, 1927. Baker MSS; Glass to McAdoo, February 5, 1927. Glass MSS; Glass, *Adventure*, p. 101 (P.S.); unpublished reply of Glass to Untermyer, n.d. McAdoo MSS.

28. Glass, *Adventure*, p. 106 (P.S.); Willis, *The Federal Reserve System*, pp. 108, 135-37 (P.S.); unpublished reply of Glass to Untermyer, n.d. McAdoo MSS; Laughlin to Glass, February 5, 1927; Laughlin to Willis, November 21, 1912; Glass to Laughlin, February 2, 1927. Laughlin MSS; Glass to Baker, July 5, 1927. Baker MSS; House Diary, II, 228.
29. Smith and Beasley, *Carter Glass*, pp. 107-08 (S.S.). There is no evidence that such a meeting took place.
30. Glass, *Adventure*, p. 106 (P.S.); Glass to Baker, February 3, 1927. Baker MSS.
31. McAdoo to House, May 20, 1913. McAdoo MSS.
32. Notes for autobiography. McAdoo MSS; House Diary, II, 228. Warburg's response was negative. House apparently did not even read the Treasury proposal until July 28! (House to McAdoo, July 29, 1913. House MSS.)
33. See especially Ch. IX.
34. Glass to Baker, August 2, 11, 1926. Baker MSS; Laughlin, *The Federal Reserve Act*, pp. 158, 187 (P.S.); undated fragment. Laughlin MSS; Willis, *The Federal Reserve System*, pp. 195, 208-09, 240-41 (P.S.); Glass, *Adventure*, pp. 101-04 (P.S.); notes for autobiography. McAdoo MSS.
35. Glass to Willis, June 6, 1913. Willis MSS; Glass, *Adventure*, pp. 101-02 (P.S.).
36. Glass, *Adventure*, pp. 102-04, 107-09 (P.S.); notes for autobiography. McAdoo MSS; Glass to Willis, June 9, 1913. Willis MSS. Willis glumly concluded that the whole episode had threatened party harmony and "probably delayed progress by several weeks at a time when haste was imperative if there was to be any action." Glass, too, complained of a "narrow escape . . . from wrecking currency reform and precipitating another government bank upheaval!" "This," McAdoo wrote, "is really quite amusing. . . . At no time was currency reform endangered in the faintest degree by what I was doing. On the contrary, it was being helped." (Willis, *The Federal Reserve System*, p. 207 [P.S.]; Glass, *Adventure*, p. III [P.S.]; notes for autobiography. McAdoo MSS.)
37. Glass, *Adventure*, p. 110 (P.S.).
38. *Ibid.*, pp. 110, 127.
39. McAdoo to Plummer, July 2, 1913; notes for autobiography. McAdoo MSS; *New York Times*, July 29, 1913; Willis, *The Federal Reserve System*, pp. 412-13 (P.S.); *Boston Herald*, October 10, 1913; Hepburn, *Currency*, p. 416 (S.S.).
40. McAdoo to Williams, July 14, 1913; notes for autobiography. McAdoo MSS; *St. Louis Globe-Democrat*, July 29, 1913; *New York Times*, July 29, 1913.
41. New York *Sun*, July 30, 31, 1913; *New York Tribune*, New York *World*, *New York Times*, all July 30, 1913.
42. McAdoo to Duncan, October 18, 1913; McAdoo to Francis, October 13, 1913; notes for autobiography. McAdoo MSS; *New York Times*, July 30, 1913; Willis to Glass, July 11, 1913. Willis MSS.
43. Glass, *Adventure*, pp. 116-18 (P.S.); *New York Times*, July 10, 1913; *Washington Post*, July 15-17, 1913; notes for autobiography. McAdoo MSS.
44. Willis, *The Federal Reserve System*, p. 260 (P.S.); Warburg, *The Federal Reserve System*, I, 129 (P.S.). The original Glass bill provided that federal funds must be deposited with the reserve banks. Apparently McAdoo was instrumental in changing this in the Senate.
45. Willis, *The Federal Reserve System*, p. 795 (P.S.).
46. *Ibid.*, pp. 439-40, 795; notes for autobiography. McAdoo MSS; Glass, *Adventure*, p. 114 (P.S.); McAdoo, *Crowded Years*, p. 222 (P.S.).
47. Willis, *The Federal Reserve System*, p. 251 (P.S.); Glass, *Adventure*, p. 113 (P.S.); McAdoo to O'Neil, July 25, 1913. McAdoo MSS; McAdoo to House, June 18, 1913. House MSS.
48. Undated fragment. McAdoo MSS; Willis to Glass, April 16, 1913. Willis MSS.
49. McAdoo to House, October 11, 1913. House MSS; notes for autobiography.

McAdoo MSS.
50. McAdoo to House, December 7, 1913. House MSS. Among other things, McAdoo was apparently using the threat of a grand jury investigation of banking irregularities to club opponents of the bill in New York into submission. (House Diary, III, 327.)
51. Notes for autobiography. McAdoo MSS.
52. U.S. Secretary of the Treasury (McAdoo), *Prosperity and the Future*, pp. 3-4 (P.D.).
53. McAdoo to Xavier, January 13, 1914; article from *Houston Chronicle*, n.d. McAdoo MSS.
54. U.S. Board of Governors of the Federal Reserve System, *Federal Reserve Act*, p. 31 (P.D.); notes for autobiography. McAdoo MSS.
55. Willis, *The Theory and Practice of Central Banking*, pp. 101-03 (P.S.).
56. McAdoo to the Federal Reserve Board, November 23, 1915. McAdoo MSS; Willis, *The Federal Reserve System*, p. 1,113 (P.S.). For further details, see Chapter VIII.
57. Hamlin Diary, III, 69, 177, 181-83.
58. U.S. Secretary of the Treasury (McAdoo), *Subtreasuries and their Relation to the Federal Reserve Banks, passim* (P.D.). Early in 1918, McAdoo, who had apparently undergone a change of heart, convinced Congress that the subtreasury system must be liquidated.
59. Warburg Diary, October 5, 19, 1915; Hamlin Diary, III, 57-58, 63, 70, 177, 183-84, 241.

CHAPTER SEVEN

1. Warburg to McAdoo, January 9, 1913. McAdoo MSS; New York *Journal of Commerce*, January 8, 9, 1914; Washington *Evening Star*, January 6, 1914; Houston, *Eight Years With Wilson's Cabinet*, I, 109 (P.S.).
2. New York *Journal of Commerce*, April 11, 1914.
3. McAdoo to House, February 22, 1914. House MSS; House Diary, IV, 36.
4. Hamlin Diary, II, 147.
5. House Diary, II, 398, 400, 402; McAdoo to Wilson, December 20, 1913. Wilson MSS.
6. House Diary, III, 402; IV, 62, 83; McAdoo to Wilson, December 20, 1913. Wilson MSS; Link, *Wilson: The New Freedom*, p. 451 (S.S.). "The President wishes to take these appointments away from politics as far as possible," House wrote, "and he does not think it would be proper to have McAdoo, Williams and Hamlin from the same Department on the Board. Of course, he is right." Wilson later reversed his view and by December, 1914, agreed with McAdoo. But by then it was too late. (House Diary, III, 402; IV, 62; V, 239.)
7. *Ibid.*, V, 62; Wiebe, *Businessmen and Reform*, p. 137 (S.S.).
8. House Diary, IV, 69. Gordon Auchincloss later wrote that McAdoo had asked House as a personal favor to cease advising the President after the Colonel had placed Olney, Miller, Harding, and Warburg on the Board. Then, McAdoo slipped in Hamlin, "who has proved what E.M.H. knew him to be, a rubber stamp for McAdoo." (Auchincloss Diary, December 27, 1914.)
9. *Boston Daily Advertiser*, May 6, 1914; New York *Sun*, July 3, 1914.
10. McAdoo, *Crowded Years*, p. 280 (P.S.).
11. Jones to Wilson, July 20, 1914, printed in *Boston Evening Transcript*, July 24, 1914; Washington *Evening Star*, July 24, 1914; House Diary, V, 140.
12. Hamlin Diary, III, 272; Washington *Evening Star*, July 12, 1914. Hamlin was paraphrasing Eagle.
13. Undated statement by Warburg. Warburg MSS.
14. *New York Herald*, July 9, 1914; *New York Times*, June 25, July 11, 1914.

15. Warburg to McAdoo, July 23, 1914, and attached memorandum. McAdoo MSS.
16. Washington *Evening Star,* July 29, 1914; Warburg to Wilson, July 29, 1914. Wilson MSS.
17. Warburg to Cassel, November 7, 1913. Warburg MSS; Warburg to House, July 7, September 26, 1913. House MSS. On the framers' suspicions of Warburg, see, for example, Glass to Willis, July 30, 1926; Willis to Glass, July 31, 1926. Willis MSS; and Hamlin Diary, II, 148.
18. Warburg to Wexler, December 26, 1913. Warburg MSS; Warburg to Laughlin, February 2, 1914; Warburg to Marshall, [February, 1914]. Laughlin MSS.
19. McAdoo to Hamlin, August 12, 1915. McAdoo MSS; *New York Tribune,* June 5, 1914; Willis, *The Federal Reserve System,* p. 643 (P.S.). At least two other members of the Board, Miller and Harding, shared Warburg's assumptions about amendments and the survival of the system. (McAdoo to Hamlin, August 12, 1915. McAdoo MSS; Hamlin Diary, II, 170.)
20. McAdoo, *Crowded Years,* pp. 288-89 (P.S.).
21. Hamlin Diary, II, 159, 168, 170; Hamlin to Warburg, November 29, 1915; Warburg to McAdoo, August 27, 1914. McAdoo MSS; Minutes of the Federal Reserve Board, I, 238, 265-266; Willis, *The Federal Reserve System,* p. 645 (P.S.). Willis had been appointed Secretary of the Board.
22. November 16, 1914.
23. Warburg to Wade, December 12, 1913. Warburg MSS; Hamlin Diary, III, 193; House Diary, V, 234.
24. House Diary, VII, 332.
25. Notes for autobiography. McAdoo MSS; Hamlin Diary, III, 63-64, 240, 270-71; VI, 12.
26. Hamlin Diary, II, 148; III, 63, 141; VII, 204; notes for autobiography. McAdoo MSS.
27. With the exception of Harding. "Note About the Federal Reserve Board," March 8, 1930. McAdoo MSS; Hamlin Diary, II, 193.
28. Hamlin Diary, II, 193; Willis, *The Federal Reserve System,* pp. 674-75 (P.S.).
29. Willis, *The Federal Reserve System,* p. 674 (P.S.); notes for autobiography. McAdoo MSS.
30. *Boston Evening Record,* December 21, 1914; McAdoo to Hamlin, August 22, 1915. McAdoo MSS. McAdoo himself requested Attorney General Thomas W. Gregory's opinion. Gregory informed Hamlin that the issue had not been difficult to decide but implied that McAdoo had "held [it] up" for quite some time. (Hamlin Diary, II, 195-96.)
31. Wilson, *Crossroads of Freedom,* p. 47 (P.S.); McAdoo to Norris, August 27, 1915. McAdoo MSS.
32. Undated press release. McAdoo MSS; Willis, *The Federal Reserve System,* pp. 1,239-40 (P.S.).
33. McAdoo to Wilson, September 6, 1915, printed in U.S. Secretary of the Treasury (McAdoo), *Annual Report . . . for the Fiscal Year Ended June 30, 1915,* pp. 87-97 (P.D.).
34. Wilson to McAdoo, October 5, 1915. Wilson MSS; Hamlin Diary, III, 72; Warburg Diary, October 8, 1915; House Diary, II, 163; "Note About the Federal Reserve Board," March 8, 1930; Paul Warburg, "Foreign Agencies; Federal Reserve Banks—National Banks. Report to the Federal Reserve Board," *passim.* McAdoo MSS.
35. Hamlin Diary III, 75; "Report of the Committee on Foreign Branching," October 12, 1915. McAdoo MSS.
36. Hamlin Diary, III, 75; Paul Warburg, untitled draft of committee report on foreign branching, December 6, [1915]. McAdoo MSS; Warburg Diary, October 12, 1915; Washington *Evening Star,* October 13, 1915.

250   WILLIAM GIBBS MCADOO

37. Willis, *The Federal Reserve System,* pp. 1,229, 1,244-45 (P.S.).
38. Minutes of the Federal Reserve Board, II, 1,019; Hamlin Diary, III, 126, 241; Willis, *The Federal Reserve System,* p. 733 (P.S.).
39. Delano *et al.* to the Federal Reserve Board, December 2, 1915. McAdoo MSS.
40. Delano *et al.* to the Federal Reserve Board, November 13, 1915. McAdoo MSS. Whether the committee intended to lavish even greater financial power on New York and reduce the number of districts below eight is debatable.
41. Glass to Delano, November 13, 1915; Owen to the Federal Reserve Board, November 20, 1915. McAdoo MSS; memorandum by Warburg, November 22, 1915. Warburg MSS.
42. Hamlin, "Review." Baker MSS.
43. *Ibid.*; Hamlin Diary, III, 100; McAdoo to Hamlin, November 15, 1915. McAdoo MSS. The second report was essentially a shrunken version of the original.
44. Hamlin, "Review." Baker MSS; McAdoo to Gregory, November 17, 1915. McAdoo MSS; Hamlin Diary, III, 116. At this point Wilson had grown so exasperated at what he considered usurpation of power by the Warburg faction that he apparently contemplated reorganization of the Board. (Glass, *Adventure,* pp. 270-71 [P.S.].)
45. Hamlin, "Review." Baker MSS.
46. Minutes of the Federal Reserve Board, II, 1,009-10, 1,014, 1,025; Hamlin Diary, III, 116-20; Willis, *The Federal Reserve System,* pp. 735-36 (P.S.); Delano *et al.* to the Federal Reserve Board, December 2, 1915. McAdoo MSS.
47. Hamlin Diary, III, 187.
48. August 13, 1915. House MSS; McAdoo to Wilson, August 21, 1915. Wilson MSS. McAdoo wrote House again on August 15 that "the President has absolute power of removal for cause. All he has to say is 'unfit' or 'incompetent' [or] 'unsatisfactory' unless resignation is forthcoming. I can't stand M.'s & Warburg's mischief making much longer, although a substitute for M. would settle everything. If Houston could be made Gov. (?) & M. pleased, it would be ideal. It can be done if the Boss & H. are willing." (House MSS.)
49. Hamlin Diary, III, 60-63, 66-67, 141, 235.
50. McAdoo to Peabody, December 27, 1915. McAdoo MSS.
51. House Diary, IV, 81; Hamlin Diary, III, 233, 235, 240; IV, 24; Hamlin to his wife, June 19, 1916. Hamlin MSS.
52. Hamlin Diary, III, 161, 231-32, 235, 240, 243, 269-70.
53. Warburg to House, June 20, 1916; Warburg to House, n.d. House MSS; House Diary, IX, 206; Delano to Wilson, June 13, July 25, 1916. Wilson MSS; Hamlin Diary, III, 193.
54. House Diary, IX, 232; Wilson to House, July 2, 1916. Baker MSS; Hamlin Diary, III, 269, 283; Warburg to House, July 31, August 5, 1916. House MSS.
55. Hamlin Diary, III, 269.
56. *Ibid.,* 240, 269-72; House Diary, IX, 223.
57. Hamlin Diary, III, 280-83.

CHAPTER EIGHT

1. Davies to House, March 10, 1915. House MSS; House Diary, V, 186.
2. McAdoo to House, March 3, [1914]. House MSS; McAdoo, *Crowded Years,* p. 273 (P.S.).
3. Notes for autobiography. McAdoo MSS. McAdoo later thought his place in the President's family did embarrass Wilson at times with both the public and the Cabinet. Wilson continually had to choose between opposite positions held by his department heads. The suspicion remained, however latent it might be, that their familial relationship played some part in these decisions. (House Diary, XI, 235.)
   According to Wilson's second wife, the President had opposed the engagement because of McAdoo's age. (Walworth, *Woodrow Wilson,* Bk. I ,393 [S.S.].)
4. House Diary, VII, 274.

5. *Ibid.,* V, 150-51, 215; McAdoo and Gaffey, *The Woodrow Wilsons,* pp. 282-83 (P.S.).
6. Fenno, *The President's Cabinet,* pp. 92, 119-20, 124 (S.S.); Link, *Wilson: The New Freedom,* pp. 75-77 (S.S.); House Diary, III, 341.
7. House Diary, II, 266; IV, 50; V, 205; IX, 223, 313; X, 10, 18-19, 139; XI, 234-35; McAdoo to House, February 22, 1914. House MSS.
8. House Diary, II, 254; XIV, 227, 241; notes for autobiography. McAdoo MSS.
9. House Diary, IX, 315; X, 89; Houston, *Eight Years With Wilson's Cabinet,* I, 68 (P.S.).
10. House Diary, I, 50; Kerney, *The Political Education of Woodrow Wilson,* pp. 296-97 (P.S.).
11. "Various Observations by Mr. McAdoo"; "Louis D. Brandeis for the United States Supreme Court," June 8, 1931. McAdoo MSS. Attorney General Gregory, it should be added, also deserved credit for the appointment.
12. McAdoo to Newton *et al.,* October 2, 1914; McAdoo to Peabody, April 16, 1913. McAdoo MSS.
13. U.S. Secretary of the Treasury (McAdoo), *Prosperity and the Future,* p. 5 (P.D.).
14. Link, *Wilson: Confusions and Crises, 1915-1916,* pp. 344-45 (S.S.).
15. McAdoo to Nicholson, December 1, 1913. McAdoo MSS.
16. McAdoo to Cooksey, September 5, 1916. McAdoo MSS.
17. Notes for autobiography. McAdoo MSS. (Italics added.)
18. Springfield (Massachusetts) *Republican,* May 7, 1914; notes for autobiography. McAdoo MSS; House Diary, III, 340.
19. House Diary, VII, 204; Hendrick, "McAdoo," 632; notes for autobiography. McAdoo MSS; Springfield (Massachusetts) *Republican,* January 30, 1917.
20. "What the New Secretary of the Treasury Is Doing." McAdoo MSS; *New York Times,* May 1, 1913.
21. *Washington Post,* May 1, 1913.
22. *New York Times,* May 2, 1913; U.S. Secretary of the Treasury (McAdoo), *Annual Report . . . for the Fiscal Year Ended June 30, 1914,* p. 25 (P.D.); *Washington Post,* May 2, June 2, 1913.
23. Also known in common parlance as the City Bank. New York *Journal of Commerce,* May 2, 3, 1913; *New York Times,* May 2, 1913; *Washington Post,* June 2, 1913; U.S. Secretary of the Treasury (McAdoo), *Annual Report . . . for the Fiscal Year Ended June 30, 1913,* p. 5 (P.D.); notes for autobiography. McAdoo MSS.
24. McAdoo to Garrison, October 17, 1913. McAdoo MSS.
25. McAdoo to Ingle, November 5, 1915. McAdoo MSS.
26. House Diary, I, 132-33; "Statement for Counsel," n.d. McAdoo MSS; Vanderlip and Sparkes, *From Farm Boy to Financier,* pp. 225-26 (P.S.).
27. New York *World,* April 24, 1913, April 13, 1915; *New York Times,* April 24, 1913; McAdoo to Dodge, May 28, 1913. McAdoo MSS.
28. Ailes to Vanderlip, July 7, 1913, May 2, 1914; Vass to Vanderlip, September 30, 1913. Vanderlip MSS; Hendrick, "McAdoo," 631; New York *World,* April 13, 1915.
29. Ailes to Vanderlip, May 3, 1913; Glover to Vanderlip, August 27, 1914. Vanderlip MSS; Williams to McAdoo, May 29, 1914. McAdoo MSS; New York *Sun,* April 13, 1915; *Washington Post,* January 16, 1914. According to the New York *World,* Thomas Fortune Ryan turned up in the forefront of the campaign against confirmation. (January 14, 1914.)
30. Vanderlip and Sparkes, *From Farm Boy to Financier,* p. 238 (P.S.).
31. New York *Sun,* April 13, 1915; "Statement for Counsel," n.d. McAdoo MSS; McAdoo to Daniels, April 30, 1916. Daniels MSS; Williams to McLean, July 29, 1919. Williams MSS; Hamlin Diary, II, 72; Washington *Evening Star,* April 13, 1915; Ailes to Vanderlip, December 8, 1913. Vanderlip MSS.
32. Hamlin Diary II, 72-73, 123-26, 130; "Statement for Counsel," n.d. McAdoo

MSS; McAdoo to Glover, June 11, 1914. Vanderlip MSS.

33. Washington *Evening Star,* April 12-13, May 12-13, 16, 1915; New York *Sun,* April 13, 1915.

34. McAdoo to Cooksey, September 8, 1916; McAdoo to McKellar, May 26, 1915; McAdoo to Stone, June 30, 1916; McAdoo to Brandeis, July 4, 1915. McAdoo MSS; Washington *Evening Star,* April 24, 1915.

35. Hamlin Diary, III, 9-18.

36. McAdoo to Harris, May 20, 1915; McAdoo to [Martin], June 8, 1915. McAdoo MSS; *New York Times,* April 28, 1915.

37. *New York Times,* January 1, 1917; McAdoo to Simmons, January 2, 1917. McAdoo MSS.

38. McAdoo to Wilson, September 2, 3, 1914. McAdoo MSS.

39. Link, *Wilson: The Struggle for Neutrality, 1914-1915,* p. 102 (S.S.).

40. *Ibid.,* pp. 103-04.

41. McAdoo to Shaw, January 2, 1917; McAdoo to Riordan, July 10, 1916. McAdoo MSS; *Washington Post,* November 26, 1915; McAdoo, "Can We Afford Preparedness?" 513.

42. Washington *Evening Star,* November 26, 1915; Kitchin to Dodd, December 16, 1916. Kitchin MSS.

43. Link, *Wilson: Campaigns for Progressivism and Peace, 1916-1917,* pp. 60-63; Walworth, *Woodrow Wilson,* Bk. II, 50; Paul, *Taxation in the United States,* p. 106 (the foregoing all S.S.); Kitchin to Bryan, December 13, 1915. Kitchin MSS; Tillman to McAdoo, June 23, 1916. McAdoo MSS.

44. New York *Journal of Commerce,* May 19, 1916.

45. Kitchin to Dunn, February 3, 1916; to Haynes, February 9, 1916; to House, February 11, 1916; to McDowell, March 8, 1916; and to Travis, August 11, 1916. Kitchin MSS.

46. Link, "The Negro as a Factor in the Campaign of 1912," 84-86.

47. Villard to Wilson, August 14, 28, 1912; Wilson to Villard, August 23, 1912 (italics added). Villard MSS; Trotter to Wilson, July 18, 1912, February 12, 1913. Wilson MSS; *The New Republic,* I (November 21, 1914), 5; Link, "The Negro as a Factor in the Campaign of 1912," 92; Washington *Evening Star,* March 1, 1913. McAdoo and Villard worked together during the campaign to plot strategy. McAdoo had accepted an invitation from Villard in 1910 to be a sponsor of the NAACP Summer celebration; and in 1911, McAdoo had served as a Vice-President of the one hundredth anniversary celebration of the birth of Charles Sumner. According to Villard, McAdoo expressed anxiety on one occasion that Wilson would be too friendly toward Negroes, though whether McAdoo feared a crack in the walls of white supremacy or, more likely, political repercussions in the South, cannot be determined. (Kellogg, *NAACP,* p. 157 [S.S.].)

Leading blacks, including Waldron, Du Bois, Walters, and Trotter, worked diligently in Wilson's behalf, but to what effect is a question historians have not yet satisfactorily answered. What is important for the purposes of this biography— how the Wilsonians assessed the voting pattern—also remains unclear. Suffice it to say that the evidence seemed so mixed that one could pluck from it whatever matched his prejudices, or lack of them. Quite probably the Democrats won more Negro votes in 1912 than ever before, as has often been claimed; but to accomplish this would not have required a shift in voting behavior of any great magnitude, and party leaders doubtless knew it.

48. Washington *Evening Star,* April 30, May 26, 1913, January 21, 1914; "Friction," 269.

49. Villard to Leavell, May 15, 1913. Villard MSS; Villard, *Fighting Years,* p. 237 (P.S.).

50. Villard, *Fighting Years,* p. 237 (P.S.); Villard to Wilson, August 18, 1913. Villard MSS; excised material from Villard's autobiography, enclosed in White to Wilkins, October 4, 1938. NAACP MSS.

51. Walters to McAdoo, December 17, 1914. McAdoo MSS.
52. *Washington Post,* May 28, 1913; Hendrick, "A New Federal Tribunal," 567; Hamlin Diary, II, 94-95, 100, 104-07, 110-13; Williams to McAdoo, July 25, 1913; McAdoo to Cobb, November 26, 1914; Woolley to his staff, n.d. McAdoo MSS; Boston *Guardian,* November 1, 1913.
53. Hamlin to Ralph, March 9, 1914. Hamlin MSS; Hamlin to McAdoo, November 21, 1914. McAdoo MSS; Hamlin Diary, II, 101, 115-17. The fourth rule was left flexible enough to allow some discretion to the director of the bureau, in order that he could mediate cases of individual dissatisfaction; a fifth rule, mentioned only in Hamlin's diary, and specifying no discrimination in the work rooms, carried the same proviso. The director was given all five instructions; how much latitude he used cannot be determined. (Hamlin Diary, II, 108.)
54. Wilson to McAdoo, June 27, 1913. Wilson MSS; McAdoo to Gore, October 10, 1913; McAdoo to Villard, October 27, 1913. McAdoo MSS.
55. "Opinion: Mr. Trotter and Mr. Wilson," 120; Washington *Evening Star,* November 12, 1914.
56. Wreszin, *Villard,* pp. 4, 6 (S.S.); Humes, *Villard,* p. 81 (S.S.); Villard to Washington, August 5, 1912. Washington MSS; Villard, "The President and the Segregation at Washington," 804; Villard to Hemphill, November 6, 1913. Hemphill Family MSS; Tumulty to Villard, September 7, 1915; Wilson to Villard, July 23, August 21, 29, 1913. Wilson MSS; Villard to Grimké, November 5, 1913. Grimké MSS.
57. *Boston Evening Transcript,* October 24 (?), 1913, clipping in Hamlin MSS; McAdoo to Villard, October 27, 1913. McAdoo MSS; Kellogg, *NAACP,* p. 171 (S.S.).
58. McAdoo to Villard, October 22, 1913. McAdoo MSS; Burton to Lynch, April 10, 1914. Terrell MSS; Link, *Wilson: The New Freedom,* p. 249 (S.S.).
59. Wilson to Villard, July 23, 1913. Villard MSS; Washington *Evening Star,* November 6, 1913.
60. Daniels, *Cabinet Diaries,* pp. 32-33 (P.S.); Washington *Evening Star,* November 6, 1913.
61. This is not to imply that McAdoo and Williams might not have already reached a preliminary agreement to segregate the department. But if they did, no evidence of it survives.
62. Williams to McAdoo, July 25, 1913; McAdoo to Cobb, November 26, 1914. McAdoo MSS; Baker, *Wilson,* IV, 221-22 (S.S.); Wilson to Villard, July 23, August 29, 1913. Villard MSS; Daniels, *Cabinet Diaries,* pp. 32-33 (P.S.).
63. New York *Evening Post,* October 21, 1913; excised material from Villard's autobiography, enclosed in White to Wilkins, October 4, 1938. NAACP MSS; Villard to Tumulty, November 10, 1916. Wilson MSS.

CHAPTER NINE

1. Byron R. Newton, "Inauguration of Wilson and Early Days at Treasury—Pressure of Patronage—First Appointments, Etc."; "James M. Cox"; Goodheart to the Comptroller of the Currency, April 17, 1913; memorandum from Williams to McAdoo, November 22, 1913. McAdoo MSS. Another reason for this was probably the fact that the banks did not really want to take advantage of McAdoo's offer, since he insisted that they put up security. (Daniels, *Cabinet Diaries,* p. 29 [P.S.].)
2. Link, "The South and the 'New Freedom,' " 277, 281-82.
3. New York *World,* July 13, 1914. In 1912 United States deposits with the national banks hit the lowest point in a cycle which had set in during 1908; then they began to climb again, and after McAdoo's accession to power the trend sped up markedly, thanks, in part at least, to crop-moving deposits. The pattern of these deposits continued a consistent Treasury policy of keeping the amount held by

New York banks at a low level. In 1899, the percentage of government deposits in New York national banks varied between 34 and 42 percent; in 1913, between 3 and 7 percent. (Patterson, "Government Deposits in the National Banks," 80-81.)

4. Washington *Evening Star*, August 8, 1913; U.S. Secretary of the Treasury (McAdoo), *Annual Report . . . for the Fiscal Year Ended June 30, 1915*, pp. 12-13 (P.D.); New York *World*, July 13, 1914.
5. Washington *Evening Star*, August 3, 13, 1913.
6. *New York Tribune*, August 13, 1913.
7. *New York Times*, August 2, 1913; Philadelphia *Public Ledger*, November 24, 1913; Robinson to McAdoo, August 11, 1913. McAdoo MSS.
8. *New York Times*, August 2, 1913; *Wall Street Journal*, August 15, October 23, 1913; *New York Commercial*, June 18, 1914.
9. Washington *Evening Star*, September 24, 1914.
10. Sprague, "The Crisis of 1914 in the United States," 515; Houston to McAdoo, October 16, 1914. McAdoo MSS.
11. Henry, *For the Relief of the Cotton Growers*, p. 4 (P.D.); Henry to McAdoo, October 2, 1914. McAdoo MSS.
12. U.S. *Congressional Record*, 63rd Cong., 2d Sess., 1914, LI, Part 17, Appendix, 954 (P.D.); *Washington Post*, October 8, 1914.
13. McAdoo MSS.
14. October 14, 1914; Tillman to McAdoo, October 13, 1914. McAdoo MSS.
15. New York *Journal of Commerce*, August 25, 1914; McAdoo to Henry, October 9, 1914. McAdoo MSS; U.S. *Congressional Record*, 63rd Cong., 2d Sess., 1914, LI, Part 17, Appendix, 955 (P.D.); *New York Commercial*, August 26, 1914; *Washington Post*, August 26, 1914. One objection to McAdoo's plan was that there were not enough warehouses to hold the cotton which would be put up as collateral for loans. McAdoo defined his way out of this corner by making it clear that adequate warehousing meant anything that protected the cotton. This could mean an unbonded shed or even a barbed wire fence.
    Such serious complaints arose that banks were lending emergency currency in insufficient quantities, and that hoarding and usury were going on, that McAdoo announced that he would withhold the second installment of Aldrich-Vreeland notes until the situation could be investigated.
16. Nor did a "buy-a-bale of cotton" crusade or an effort to cut crop acreage through legislation. And the Administration's Smith-Lever bill for federal licensing and inspection of warehouses—which could have made borrowing against warehouse receipts easier—was bottled up in the House.
17. Hamlin Diary, II, 168.
18. McAdoo MSS; House Diary, V, 192-97.
19. Harding to McAdoo, February 26, 1915; McAdoo to Harding, February 23, 1915. McAdoo MSS; Minutes of the Federal Reserve Board, I, 258-63, 266, 283, 390; New York *Journal of Commerce*, October 26, 1914.
20. Higginson to McAdoo, November 14, 1914. McAdoo MSS; Hamlin Diary, II, 184.
21. McAdoo to Wilson, November 4, 6, 1914. McAdoo MSS; Hamlin Diary, II, 180; House Diary, V, 213.
22. John Skelton Williams to his father, November 18, 1914. Williams MSS; *Washington Post*, November 18, 1914.
23. McAdoo to the Class "A" subscribers to the Cotton Loan Fund, April 4, 1916. Hamlin MSS; Link, *Wilson: The Struggle for Neutrality, 1914-1915*, p. 101 (S.S.). In addition to the Central Committee, the fund was administered by a Cotton Loan Committee composed of Harding, Warburg, Wiggin, and other prominent bankers. These men were directly responsible for management, while the Central Committee performed supervisory functions. As in the case of the gold pool, discussed in the following chapter, the arrangements for operation proved somewhat clumsy.

24. Link, *Wilson: The Struggle for Neutrality, 1914-1915*, pp. 101-02 (S.S.).
25. On this point see McAdoo's statement of November 18, quoted in the New York *Sun*, November 19, 1914. Here McAdoo urged that the bankers "influence the character of crops by imposing proper conditions on the advances they may make to the farmers."
26. Harding, *Formative Period*, p. 42 (P.S.); Harding to McAdoo, July 19, 1915. McAdoo MSS; McAdoo to House, July 13, 1915. House MSS.
27. McAdoo to Wilson, October 29, 1914; Harding to McAdoo, July 31, August 18, 1915. McAdoo MSS; Harding, *Formative Period*, p. 42 (P.S.).
28. *Washington Post*, August 24, 1915; McAdoo to Harding, August 26, 1915. McAdoo MSS. See also Link, *Wilson: The Struggle for Neutrality, 1914-1915*, pp. 606-15 (S.S.). McAdoo wrote on August 24 that he was trying to arrange for a mandatory 6 percent rate on loans backed by his deposits, and he wanted the Board to put the three banks in a position to rediscount on commodity paper at a very low rate—not more than 2 percent—to achieve this. It was an unusual suggestion, he admitted, but one fully justified by unusual circumstances. The reserve system clearly had sufficient resources to handle crop movement, but the current rate between reserve banks ranged between 3½ and 4 percent; the three depositories would have been forced to borrow from other reserve banks at these rates, and a 6 percent loan to the producers would have been impossible. McAdoo determined to charge no interest on the deposits in order to keep rates at the lowest possible level.

The announcement raised a commotion within the (unconsulted) Federal Reserve Board; its members generally agreed that the reserve banks could handle the demand and that McAdoo's deposits would merely weaken the financial condition of some of these institutions. Early in September, Harding told the members that McAdoo wanted the Board, in framing a regulation for lower rates on commodity paper, to provide that banks should be able to obtain these rates only when they did not charge their customers more than twice the rate of rediscount. Warburg suggested a compromise, which McAdoo finally accepted.

By 1917, a majority of the Board regarded preferential rates on commodity paper unfavorably. Such rates proved of virtually no aid to the producers; for the banks generally remained unwilling to loan at 6 percent except in the larger centers of the South. (McAdoo to Kitchin, August 24, 1915; McAdoo to Harding, August 26, 1915. McAdoo MSS; U.S. Secretary of the Treasury [McAdoo], *Annual Report . . . for the Fiscal Year Ended June 30, 1915*, pp. 6-7 [P.D.]; Hamlin Diary, III, 54-55; Harding, *Formative Period*, p. 46 [P.S.].)
29. Hamlin Diary, III, 3-6, 61.
30. *Ibid.*, 180-81; New York *Journal of Commerce*, September 15, 1915.
31. New York *Journal of Commerce*, September 15, 1915; U.S. Secretary of the Treasury (McAdoo), *Annual Report . . . for the Fiscal Year Ended June 30, 1915*, pp. 5-6, 8 (P.D.); W.P.G. Harding, "Federal Reserve Act and the Farmer." McAdoo MSS.
32. McAdoo to Long, September 22, 1915; McAdoo to Ingle, October 6, 1915. McAdoo MSS; *Boston Evening Transcript*, August 25, 1915; New York *Journal of Commerce*, August 25, September 15, 1915; Chicago *Daily Tribune*, August 5, 1915.
33. Henry to McAdoo, August 24, September 9, 1915. McAdoo MSS.
34. McAdoo to House, October 12, 1914. McAdoo MSS; *San Francisco Bulletin*, February 3, 1914.
35. Notes for autobiography; McAdoo to Gonzales, June 17, 1913. McAdoo MSS.
36. *Washington Post*, June 12, 1913; notes for autobiography. McAdoo MSS; *New York Times*, June 13, 1913.
37. *Newark Evening News*, June 14, 1913; *Baltimore Sun*, June 13, 1913; New York *World*, June 14, 1913; *New York Commercial*, June 14, 1913; *Boston Evening Transcript*, June 18, 1913; notes for autobiography. McAdoo MSS.

38. *Wall Street Journal,* June 17, 1913; New York *Journal of Commerce,* June 17, 1913; *New York Times,* December 4, 1913; McAdoo to House, June 18, 1913. House MSS.
39. U.S. Secretary of the Treasury (McAdoo), *Annual Report . . . for the Fiscal Year Ended June 30, 1914,* p. 20 (P.D.); U.S. Comptroller of the Currency (Williams), *Annual Report . . . to the First Session of the Sixty-Fourth Congress,* p. 21 (P.D.).
40. New York *World,* October 7, 1914; *St. Louis Republic,* October 16, 1915.
41. *Washington Post,* September 22, 1914; New York *World,* September 24, 1914.
42. *Washington Post,* September 26, 1914; Clifford, *Independence,* p. 53 (S.S.); *Wall Street Journal,* October 8, 1914.
43. Williams to the national banks of New York City, November 2, 1914; Williams to McAdoo, and attachments, November 18, 1914. McAdoo MSS; House Diary, IX, 233; U.S. Comptroller of the Currency (Williams), *Annual Report . . . to the First Session of the Sixty-Fourth Congress,* pp. 21-22 (P.D.).
44. U.S. Secretary of the Treasury (McAdoo), *Annual Report . . . for the Fiscal Year Ended June 30, 1914,* p. 20 (P.D.); "Business and Trade Conditions," 1; Chicago *Daily Tribune,* September 28, 1914; Drennan to McAdoo, n.d. McAdoo MSS.
45. Notes for autobiography. McAdoo MSS; clipping from *New York Times,* October 4(?), 1914. Hamlin MSS.
46. Delafield to McAdoo, September 25, 1914; McAdoo to Underwood, October 12, 1914. McAdoo MSS; *Nashville Tennessean and The Nashville American,* September 26, 1914.
47. U.S. Comptroller of the Currency (Williams), *Annual Report . . . to the First Session of the Sixty-Fourth Congress,* pp. 28-29 (P.D.).
48. Washington *Evening Star,* February 12, 1915; U.S. Comptroller of the Currency (Williams), *Annual Report . . . to the First Session of the Sixty-Fourth Congress,* p. 25 (P.D.).
49. New York *Sun,* January 22, 1916; Washington *Evening Star,* January 21, 1916.
50. McAdoo to House, July 17, 1916; statement by McAdoo, August 7, 1916; article from *Houston Chronicle,* n.d. McAdoo MSS. How enthusiastic McAdoo was about the bill before it passed is questionable. See Willis, *The Federal Reserve System,* pp. 837, 1,466 (P.S.).
51. McAdoo to Hollis, July 27, 28, 1916. McAdoo MSS.
52. Not to be confused with the famous Nebraska Senator of the same name.
53. McAdoo to House, July 17, 1916. McAdoo MSS.

CHAPTER TEN

1. Redfield to McAdoo, December 13, 1913. McAdoo MSS.
2. Link, *Wilson: The New Freedom,* pp. 443, 446-49 (S.S.); House Diary, V, 207.
3. Notes for autobiography. McAdoo MSS; Noble, *New York Stock Exchange,* p. 3 (S.S.).
4. *New York Times,* October 27, 1914.
5. McAdoo to Fisk (date illegible). McAdoo MSS.
6. August 10, 1914. McAdoo MSS.
7. *Washington Post,* August 4, 1914; McAdoo to Glynn, February 24, 1916. McAdoo MSS.
8. McAdoo had already conferred with Woodward and another banker in Washington on August 1. They had assured McAdoo that no clearing house certificates would be issued; but when they returned to New York, they discovered that it had been decided in the meantime to use these certificates. At this point, the decision was taken to ask McAdoo to come. (Vanderlip and Sparkes, *From Farm Boy to Financier,* p. 240 [P.S.].)
9. By giving this assurance, McAdoo committed the Treasury to redeeming several

hundred million dollars of emergency currency in gold; but the Treasury had neither at present nor in prospect a sufficient amount of the metal for this purpose. The banks were required by law to deposit in gold only 5 percent of the amount of currency issued them for redemption. And though it was unlikely that the Treasury would be compelled to redeem these funds at par in gold, he still ran a serious risk. McAdoo was "acutely aware that I might have to sell government bonds to buy gold to redeem this emergency currency if, for any reason, the banks failed to provide it. But hesitation or delay would have been fatal." (Notes for autobiography. McAdoo MSS.)

10. In an interview with Ray Stannard Baker years later, McAdoo said he had laid down different conditions. Thus, precisely how hard and fast any of these conditions were remains open to question. ("Interview with William Gibbs Mc-Adoo," n.d. Baker MSS.)
11. Memorandum, July 1, 1930. McAdoo MSS; Synon, *McAdoo*, p. 136 (S.S.).
12. Memorandum, July 1, 1930. McAdoo MSS; New York *World*, August 3, 1914. These men were to oversee the currency distribution and approve a scheme for employing cash instead of certificates at clearing houses across the nation in settling daily balances.
13. *Washington Post*, August 4, 8, 1914; U.S. Secretary of the Treasury (McAdoo), *Annual Report . . . for the Fiscal Year Ended June 30, 1914*, p. 3 (P.D.); U.S. Comptroller of the Currency (Williams), *Annual Report . . . to the Third Session of the Sixty-Third Congress*, pp. 13, 15 (P.D.); Conant, "American Finance in the War Tempest," 327; Sprague, "The Crisis of 1914," 519; Noyes, *War Period*, p. 74 (S.S.).
14. *Washington Post*, August 1, 1914; U.S. Secretary of the Treasury (McAdoo), *Annual Report . . . for the Fiscal Year Ended June 30, 1914*, p. 17 (P.D.); *New York Times*, January 8, 1915.
15. McAdoo to Redfield, July 30, 1914. McAdoo MSS; Hamlin Diary, II, 160.
16. Brown, "The Government and the Money Market," 201; New York *World*, August 8, 1914.
17. Noyes, *War Period*, p. 83 (S.S.); statement of August 14, 1914. McAdoo MSS.
18. Morgan to McAdoo, August 21, 1914. McAdoo MSS.
19. Forgan *et al.* to McAdoo, September 4, 1914. McAdoo MSS; Brown, "The Government and the Money Market," 205; *New York Times*, September 13, 1914; Forgan *et al.* to McAdoo and the Federal Reserve Board, September 19, 1914, printed in U.S. Secretary of the Treasury (McAdoo), *Annual Report . . . for the Fiscal Year Ended June 30, 1914*, pp. 73-74 (P.D.); Sprague, "The Crisis of 1914," 530.
20. "Finance: The '$100,000,000 Gold Pool,' " 417.
21. New York *Journal of Commerce*, November 21, 1914.
22. U.S. Secretary of the Treasury (McAdoo), *Annual Report . . . for the Fiscal Year Ended June 30, 1917*, p. 24 (P.D.); Washington *Evening Star*, April 3, 1917.
23. McAdoo to Baruch, January 5, 1916. Baruch MSS; Sprague, "The Crisis of 1914," 533; Wiebe, *Businessmen and Reform*, pp. 149-50 (S.S.); "The Report of the Treasury," 706; Washington *Evening Star*, November 3, 1915.
24. McAdoo to Gompers, June 29, 1915. McAdoo MSS.
25. Parrini, *Heir to Empire*, pp. 1, 10 (S.S.).
26. *Ibid.*, pp. 15-16, 20.
27. On this point, see *ibid.*, p. 2.
28. Hendrick, "A Commercial Traveler in the Cabinet," 566, 569; Redfield, "Our Growing Foreign Commerce," 552.
29. "Your Government of the United States," 146.
30. McAdoo to Pérez Triana, June 25, 1915. McAdoo MSS.
31. McAdoo to Henry, February 16, 1916. McAdoo MSS; Madison (Wisconsin) *State Journal*, October 31, 1915.

32. William G. McAdoo, address of April 18, 1916; article from *Houston Chronicle,* n.d. McAdoo MSS.

33. U.S. Secretary of the Treasury (McAdoo), *Prosperity and the Future,* p. 8 (P.D.); Raleigh *News and Observer,* June 4, 1916; *Washington Post,* June 3, 1915; U.S. Secretary of the Treasury (McAdoo), *An Address . . . at Buenos Aires,* p. 7 (P.D.); McAdoo to Lansing, July 8, 1915. McAdoo MSS.

34. Eighteen Latin American nations were eventually represented at the conference. Haiti and Mexico did not receive invitations.

35. McAdoo, "The Pan American Financial Conference," 394.

36. Clarkson to McAdoo, June 23, 1915. McAdoo MSS.

37. McAdoo to Wilson, August 23, 1915; McAdoo to Lansing, August 23, 1915. McAdoo MSS; Wilson to McAdoo, August 26, 1915. Wilson MSS; Tulchin, *Aftermath of War,* pp. 7-9 (S.S.).

38. Hurley to McAdoo, May 25, 1915. McAdoo MSS.

39. Memorandum, May 17, 1915. McAdoo MSS.

40. U.S. Secretary of the Treasury (McAdoo), *Annual Report . . . for the Fiscal Year Ended June 30, 1915,* pp. 90-91 (P.D.); *New York Times,* June 14, 1915.

41. Press release, May 8, 1916. Hamlin MSS; Baltimore *Sun,* May 11, 1916; New York *Journal of Commerce,* April 14, 1916; U.S. Secretary of the Treasury (McAdoo), *Annual Report . . . for the Fiscal Year Ended June 30, 1916,* p. 12 (P.D.).

42. *Appendix to the Report of the United States Section of the International High Commission . . . 1916,* p. 54 (P.D.); McAdoo to Wilson, November 28, 1914. Wilson MSS. McAdoo completed the trip by conferring with the presidents of Chile, Argentina, and Brazil concerning a suggestion of Woodrow Wilson that the South and Central American nations and the United States enter into a joint agreement to respect each other's territorial integrity. The proposal came to nothing.

CHAPTER ELEVEN

1. *San Francisco Examiner,* November 5, 1915; William C. Redfield "The American Merchant Marine." Address before the Civic Club, Brooklyn, December 15, 1915. McAdoo MSS.

2. U.S. Secretary of the Treasury (McAdoo, and Redfield), *Increased Ocean Transportation Rates,* II, 15 (P.D.); memorandum by McCoy, n.d.; McAdoo to Cooper, June 3, 1916. McAdoo MSS; U.S. Secretary of the Treasury (McAdoo), *A Naval Auxiliary Merchant Marine,* pp. 8, 20 (P.D.); New York *Evening Post,* January 24, 1915; McAdoo, *Crowded Years,* p. 304 (P.S.).

3. McAdoo to Smith, November 10, 1915. McAdoo MSS.

4. U.S. Secretary of the Treasury (McAdoo, and Redfield), *Increased Ocean Transportation Rates,* I, 17-19 (P.D.). On the question of German shipping, see Link, *Wilson: The Struggle for Neutrality, 1914-1915,* p. 84 (S.S.).

5. Low et al. to McAdoo, August 22, 1914. McAdoo MSS.

6. U.S. Secretary of the Treasury (McAdoo), *The Shipping Bill: Address . . . on January 9, 1915,* p. 15 (P.D.).

7. The Bureau was managed by a Director, assisted by an advisory board of three experts. The measure allocated $5,000,000 to cover payment of losses.

8. De Lanoy to McAdoo, February 9, 1915; Parker to McAdoo, February 9, 1915; report enclosed in Patchin to McAdoo, July 27, 1916. McAdoo MSS. The very fact that the Bureau ran at a comfortable profit indicates that it competed with private companies without driving rates down to ruinous levels. That it was willing to assume risk at low rates lured commercial firms into doing the same.

9. Furuseth to Wilson, March 6, 1915. Wilson MSS; "Opinions of Ship Owners on the Law," 7; *New York Tribune,* July 20, 1915; *New York Herald,* July 20, 1915; New York *Journal of Commerce,* October 23, 1915; Farquhar to McAdoo, October 28, 1915. Woolley MSS.

10. Campbell to Scidmore, August 16, 1915; Manson to Owens, June 19, 1915. McAdoo MSS.
11. McAdoo to Norris, August 27, 1915; Straight to McAdoo, February 23, 1916. McAdoo MSS.
12. U.S. Secretary of the Treasury (McAdoo), *The Shipping Bill: Address . . . on January 9, 1915,* p. 10 (P.D.); McAdoo to Woodruff, July 7, 1915; McAdoo to McGuire, August 7, 1915; McAdoo to Fontaine, January 20, 1915. McAdoo MSS.
13. Undated fragment; "Note on the Shipping Bill," April 8, 1930; notes for autobiography. McAdoo MSS. The first page of McAdoo's proposal is missing from the McAdoo MSS, but is quoted in Synon, *McAdoo,* p. 179 (S.S.).
14. "Notes on President Wilson;" McAdoo to Pence, August 12, 1915. McAdoo MSS.
15. *New York Times,* January 10, 1915; U.S. House of Representatives, Committee on the Merchant Marine and Fisheries, *Creating a Shipping Board,* p. 330 (P.D.); "Address of Hon. W. G. McAdoo, Secretary of the Treasury, at Helena, Montana, October 28, 1915;" McAdoo to Kunz, February 24, 1915. McAdoo MSS.
16. U.S. Secretary of the Treasury (McAdoo), *The Shipping Bill: Address . . . on January 9, 1915,* p. 18 (P.D.).
17. McAdoo to Gold, August 1, 1915. McAdoo MSS.
18. McAdoo to Fahey, May 17, 1915; McAdoo to Norris, August 27, 1915. McAdoo MSS.
19. McAdoo to Parker, July 6, 1915. McAdoo MSS; Wilson to McAdoo, November 8, 1914. Wilson MSS. For further details, see Link, *Wilson: The Struggle for Neutrality, 1914-1915,* pp. 88-90 (S.S.). The British, Link points out, were willing to accede to American operation of the German ships, but only on the condition that the vessels never be used, even indirectly, in trade with Germany. The President seems neither to have understood nor agreed to this proviso.
20. Undated memorandum; McAdoo to Matthews, September 4, 1914; McAdoo to Norris, February 24, 1915; notes for autobiography; McAdoo to Baker, November 21, 1914; McAdoo to Alexander, January 26, 1915. McAdoo MSS; Link, *Wilson: The Struggle for Neutrality, 1914-1915,* p. 150 (S.S.); *New York Times,* February 11, 1915.
21. McAdoo to Pyle, February 24, 1915. McAdoo MSS.
22. Though McAdoo dismissed this anxiety, he predicted the keenest kind of competition over foreign markets after the war and considered an American merchant marine essential to hold and strengthen the country's position in international trade. Nor did he expect, as some did, a depression in the United States when peace was restored. He felt confident that economic incursions in Latin America and continued demand from Europe would more than offset the disappearance of war orders. McAdoo favored "reasonable" antidumping legislation which would prevent "unfair competition," but he feared that "we can't adopt anti-dumping clauses against the rest of the world and expect them to let us dump freely in their markets." The result would be an international trade war. Moderate legislation, though not essential, would serve "simply as a precaution and as an assurance to the timid and hesitating." (McAdoo, "The Pan American Financial Conference; Its Meaning," 3; U.S. Secretary of the Treasury [McAdoo], *Prosperity and the Future,* pp. 6-7 [P.D.]; McAdoo to Ross, June 26, 1916; McAdoo to Wilson, January 3, 1917. McAdoo MSS.)
23. Chamber of Commerce of the United States of America, *Referendum Number Nine, passim* (O.S.). See also Link, *Wilson: The Struggle for Neutrality, 1914-1915,* p. 156 (S.S.).
24. August 5, 1915; September 3, 1914; October 7, 1915; and October 14 (?), 1915, respectively, the last in Hamlin MSS; McAdoo to Shaw, January 25, 1915; McAdoo to Collins, August 4, 1916. McAdoo MSS.

25. U.S. House of Representatives, Committee on the Merchant Marine and Fisheries, *Creating a Shipping Board,* p. 303 (P.D.); "Address of Hon. W. G. McAdoo, Secretary of the Treasury, at Helena, Montana, October 28, 1915;" McAdoo to Wexler, June 29, 1915. McAdoo MSS.

26. Typed transcript of McAdoo's testimony before the House Committee on the Merchant Marine and Fisheries, September 1, 1914. Privately held.

27. July 8, 1915; Simmons to McAdoo, December 19, 1914. McAdoo MSS; U.S. Secretary of the Treasury (McAdoo, and Redfield), *Increased Ocean Transportation Rates,* II, 17 (P.D.).

28. Hurley, *The New Merchant Marine,* p. 22 (P.S.).

29. "Note on the Shipping Bill," April 8, 1930. McAdoo MSS.

30. U.S. Secretary of the Treasury (McAdoo), *A Naval Auxiliary Merchant Marine,* p. 24 (P.D.); notes for autobiography; McAdoo to Redfield, August 22, 1914; Redfield to McAdoo, August 24, 1914. McAdoo MSS; *New York Times,* August 20, 21, 1914.

31. Typed transcript of McAdoo's testimony before the House Committee on the Merchant Marine and Fisheries, September 1, 1914. Privately held; McAdoo to Smith, February 9, 1915; undated memorandum. McAdoo MSS; U.S. Secretary of the Treasury (McAdoo), *The Shipping Bill: Address . . . on January 9, 1915,* p. 13 (P.D.).

32. Link, *Wilson: The Struggle for Neutrality, 1914-1915,* pp. 88-91 (S.S.).

33. *Washington Post,* January 22, 31, 1915.

34. Lodge, for one, alleged that McAdoo, Paul Warburg, and others around the President were involved in a corrupt arrangement to buy interned German vessels. After some very brief Senate hearings and an investigation of the role private maritime interests had played in trying to kill the Ship Purchase bill, both McAdoo and the "Shipping Trust" were exonerated.

35. This is the conclusion of Jeffrey J. Safford, who is conducting an exhaustive investigation of American shipping policy during the period.

36. *Washington Post,* January 5, 1915; Link, *Wilson: The Struggle for Neutrality, 1914-1915,* pp. 149-51 (S.S.).

37. Link, *Wilson: The Struggle for Neutrality, 1914-1915,* pp. 145, 155-58 (S.S.); *Mobile Register,* June 5, 1915; *Washington Post,* February 9, 17, 19, 1915; McAdoo, *Crowded Years,* p. 309 (P.S.).

38. Notes for autobiography. McAdoo MSS; *Appendix to the Report of the United States Section of the International High Commission . . . 1916,* p. 55 (P.D.).

39. U.S. Secretary of the Treasury (McAdoo), *A Naval Auxiliary Merchant Marine,* p. 18 (P.D.).

40. McAdoo to Wilson, October 26, 1915; Wilson to McAdoo, November 9, 1915. Wilson MSS; McAdoo to Schiff, November 26, 1915. McAdoo MSS.

41. McAdoo to Smith, November 10, 1915; McAdoo to Daniels, July 20, 1915; Daniels to McAdoo, September 17, 1915. McAdoo MSS; Cowie, *Logistics,* pp. 21-22, 39 (P.S.); *Denver Post,* October 17, 1915.

42. Wiebe, *Businessmen and Reform,* pp. 145-47 (S.S.).

43. House Diary, VII, 218, 277; McAdoo to Redfield, August 20, 1915. McAdoo MSS.

44. Redfield to McAdoo, September 13, 1915 (italics added). McAdoo MSS; House Diary, VII, 217-18.

45. Redfield to McAdoo, September 13, 1915; fragment of letter from Cooksey to McAdoo, n.d.; McAdoo to Redfield, August 20, 1915; McAdoo to Wilson, October 9, 1915; Redfield to McAdoo, October 8, 1915. McAdoo MSS.

46. Kitchin to Allen, September 20, 1915. Kitchin MSS; McAdoo to Kitchin, September 18, 1915; McAdoo to Untermyer, October 22, 1915. McAdoo MSS.

47. The preceding paragraphs were taken largely from U.S. Secretary of the Treasury (McAdoo), *A Naval Auxiliary Merchant Marine, passim* (P.D.).

48. August 20, 1915. McAdoo MSS; *St. Louis Republic,* October 16, 1915.

49. McAdoo to Rosenthal, June 17, 1916. McAdoo MSS; *Washington Post*, July 9, 1916.
50. McAdoo to Wilson, September 4, 1916. Wilson MSS; *New York Times*, September 8, 1916; Hurley, *The New Merchant Marine*, p. 22 (P.S.); McAdoo to Shearn, February 29, 1916; McAdoo to Krell, May 29, 1916. McAdoo MSS.
51. McAdoo to Wilson, September 4, 1916. Wilson MSS.
52. *Atlanta Journal*, January 27, 1917; Baker to McAdoo, January 25, February 27, 1917. McAdoo MSS; Wilson to McAdoo, January 25, 1917. Baker MSS; *New York Times*, January 28, 1917.

SELECT BIBLIOGRAPHY

Where needed for clarity, abbreviations are used in the Notes to indicate to which part of the Bibliography reference is made, as follows: P.S.=Books and Pamphlets, Primary Sources; S.S.=Books, Secondary Sources; P.D.= Public Documents; O.S.=Other Sources. Unless otherwise specified, a title in quotation marks refers to the section of the Bibliography headed Articles. The terms—capitalized but not in quotation marks—Diary, Minutes, Notes, Papers, Reminiscences, and Scrapbooks refer to items in the alphabetical list of Manuscript Collections.

MANUSCRIPT COLLECTIONS

The Diary and Papers of Gordon Auchincloss, Yale University Library.

The Papers of Newton D. Baker, Library of Congress.

The Papers of Ray Stannard Baker, Library of Congress (cited in notes as Baker MSS).

The Papers of Bernard Baruch, Princeton University Library.

The Papers of Albert J. Beveridge, Library of Congress.

The Notes of John M. Blum on the Papers of Joseph P. Tumulty, Yale University Library.

The Papers of William Jennings Bryan, Library of Congress.

The Papers of Albert S. Burleson, Library of Congress.

The Papers of Josephus Daniels, Library of Congress.

262

The Papers of Joseph E. Davies, Library of Congress.

The Papers of Frederic A. Delano, Franklin D. Roosevelt Library.

The Papers of the Federal Farm Loan Board, National Archives.

The Minutes of the Federal Reserve Board, Federal Reserve Building, Washington, D.C.

The Papers of Carter Glass, University of Virginia Library.

The Papers of Thomas W. Gregory, Library of Congress.

The Papers of Archibald H. Grimké, Howard University Library.

The Diary, Papers, and Scrapbooks of Charles S. Hamlin, Library of Congress.

The Papers of Florence Jaffray Harriman, Library of Congress.

The Hemphill Family Papers, Duke University Library.

The Papers of A. Barton Hepburn, Columbia University Library.

The Papers of Gilbert M. Hitchcock, Library of Congress.

The Reminiscences, Diary, and Papers of Edward M. House, Yale University Library.

The Papers of David F. Houston, Harvard University Library.

The Papers of the Hudson and Manhattan Corporation, New York.

The Diary of Charles M. Jacobs, Columbia University Library.

The Papers of William Kent, Yale University Library.

The Papers of Claude Kitchin, University of North Carolina Library.

The Papers of Franklin K. Lane, Library of the University of California, Berkeley.

The Papers of Robert Lansing, Library of Congress.

The Papers of J. Laurence Laughlin, Library of Congress.

The Papers of Maurice Lyons, Library of Congress.

The Diary of Mary Faith Floyd McAdoo, privately held.

The Diary of William G. McAdoo, Sr., privately held.

The Papers of William G. McAdoo, Library of Congress (cited in notes as McAdoo MSS).

The Papers of William G. McAdoo, privately held.

The Papers of William G. McAdoo, Library of the University of California, Los Angeles.

The Papers of George McAneny, Columbia University Library.

The Papers of Adolph C. Miller, Federal Reserve Building, Washington, D.C.

The Papers of George Fort Milton, Library of Congress.

The Papers of John Purroy Mitchel, Library of Congress.

The Papers of John Bassett Moore, Library of Congress.

The Papers of Henry Morgenthau, Library of Congress.

The Papers of the National Association for the Advancement of Colored People, Library of Congress.

The Papers of the New York Southern Society, New York.

The Papers of Robert L. Owen, Library of Congress.

The Papers of Walter Hines Page, Harvard University Library.

The Papers of George Foster Peabody, Library of Congress.

The Papers of the Pennsylvania Railroad, Philadelphia.

The Papers of James D. Phelan, Library of the University of California, Berkeley.

The Diary and Papers of Frank Polk, Yale University Library.

The Papers of Henry T. Rainey, Library of Congress.

The Papers of William C. Redfield, Library of Congress.

The Papers of Franklin D. Roosevelt, Franklin D. Roosevelt Library.

The Papers of Furnifold M. Simmons, Duke University Library.

The Papers of Joel E. Spingarn, Howard University Library.

The Papers of James Stillman, Columbia University Library.

The Papers of William Sulzer, New York Public Library.

The Papers of Robert H. Terrell, Library of Congress.

The Papers of the Department of the Treasury, National Archives.

The Papers of Joseph P. Tumulty, Library of Congress.

The Papers of Samuel Untermyer, American Jewish Archives.

The Papers of Frank A. Vanderlip, Columbia University Library.

The Papers of Oswald Garrison Villard, Harvard University Library.

The Diary and Papers of Paul M. Warburg, Yale University Library.

The Papers of Booker T. Washington, Library of Congress.

The Papers of John Skelton Williams, Virginia Historical Society.

The Papers of H. Parker Willis, Columbia University Library.

The Papers of Edith Bolling Wilson, Library of Congress.

The Papers of Woodrow Wilson, Library of Congress (cited in notes as Wilson MSS).

The Papers of Carter G. Woodson, Library of Congress.

The Papers of Robert W. Woolley, Library of Congress.

NEWSPAPERS

Albany *Daily Press and Knickerbocker*. 1912.
Albany *Times-Union*. 1913.
Allentown (Pennsylvania) *Morning Call*. 1913.
Atlanta *Constitution*. 1914.
Atlanta Journal. 1913, 1915, 1917.
Baltimore American. 1913.
Baltimore News. 1912.
Baltimore *Sun*. 1912-13, 1915-16.
Birmingham (Alabama) *Age-Herald*. 1913.
Boston Daily Advertiser. 1914.
Boston Evening Record. 1914.
Boston Evening Transcript. 1912-15.
Boston *Guardian*. 1913.
Boston Herald. 1913.
Boston Post. 1913.
Brooklyn Citizen. 1910-12.
Brooklyn Daily Eagle. 1910-13.
Brooklyn Daily Times. 1911.
Brooklyn *Standard-Union*. 1911-12.
Buffalo Times. 1913.
Chattanooga *Daily Times*. 1911, 1913.
Chicago *Daily Tribune*. 1913-15.
Chicago Defender. 1913.
Chicago Evening Post. 1913.
Chicago Examiner. 1915.
Chicago Record-Herald. 1912.
Christian Science Monitor. 1915-16.
Cincinnati Enquirer. 1913.
Cleveland News. 1912.
Columbia (South Carolina) *Record*. 1913.
Columbia (South Carolina) *State*. 1913.
The Commercial and Financial Chronicle. 1914.
The Commoner. 1911.
Cumberland (Maryland) *Evening Times*. 1912.
Denver Daily News. 1913.
Denver Post. 1915.
Detroit Free Press. 1912.
Elizabeth (New Jersey) *Evening Times*. 1912.
Fort Worth Record. 1913.
Hartford (Connecticut) *Times*. 1913.
Hoboken Hudson Observer. 1907.

Houston Chronicle. 1913.
Houston Post. 1913.
Huntsville (Alabama) *Evening Banner*. 1913.
Jacksonville *Florida Times-Union*. 1914.
Jamestown (New York) *Post*. 1913.
The Jeffersonian. 1914.
Jersey City *Jersey Journal*. 1904, 1907, 1912-13.
Kansas City Star. 1913-14.
Knoxville Daily Tribune. 1890.
Knoxville Journal. 1897, 1913.
Knoxville Sentinel. 1912.
Lexington (Kentucky) *Herald*. 1913.
Lincoln (Nebraska) *Daily News*. 1913.
London Daily Mail. 1910.
London *Times Weekly Edition*. 1915.
Louisville *Courier-Journal*. 1914-15.
Madison (Wisconsin) *State Journal*. 1915.
Manchester (New Hampshire) *Union*. 1913.
Milwaukee Journal. 1913.
Minneapolis Journal. 1913, 1915.
Mobile Item. 1910.
Mobile Register. 1915.
Montgomery Advertiser. 1912-13.
Nashville Banner. 1912.
Nashville Tennessean and The Nashville American. 1913-14.
Newark Evening News. 1907, 1912-13.
Newark Star. 1913.
New Haven *Daily Morning Courier*. 1913.
New York American. 1910-12.
New York Commercial. 1904, 1911-14.
New York Evening Journal. 1910, 1912.
New York *Evening Mail*. 1910.
New York *Evening Post*. 1912-13, 1915.
New York *Evening Telegram*. 1912.
New York *Financial America*. 1911.
New York *Globe and Commercial Advertiser*. 1911-13.

New York Herald. 1904, 1906, 1909-16.

New York *Industrial News.* 1911.

New York *Journal of Commerce and Commercial Bulletin.* 1911-16.

New York *Morning Telegraph.* 1910, 1913.

New York Press. 1896, 1910, 1913.

New York *Sun.* 1903, 1910-16.

New York Times. 1904-05, 1910, 1912-17.

New York Tribune. 1910, 1912-15.

New York *World.* 1907-16.

Norristown (Pennsylvania) *Daily Register.* 1912.

Philadelphia Enquirer. 1913.

Philadelphia *Evening Bulletin.* 1913.

Philadelphia *Evening Telegraph.* 1912.

Philadelphia *Public Ledger.* 1913-14.

Philadelphia Record. 1912.

Pittsburgh Dispatch. 1910.

Pittsburgh *Sun.* 1912.

Pittsburgh Times. 1913.

Portland *Oregonian.* 1915.

Raleigh *News and Observer.* 1916.

Richmond *Times-Dispatch.* 1913.

Rochester (New York) *Daily Chronicle.* 1912.

Rochester (New York) *Herald.* 1912, 1914-15.

St. Louis Globe-Democrat. 1912-13.

St. Louis Post-Dispatch. 1913.

St. Louis Republic. 1913-15.

St. Louis Star. 1915.

San Francisco Bulletin. 1914.

San Francisco Examiner. 1915.

South Bend (Indiana) *Daily Tribune.* 1913.

Springfield (Massachusetts) *Republican.* 1911-12, 1914, 1916-17.

Syracuse Herald. 1913.

Syracuse *Post-Standard.* 1913.

Wall Street Journal. 1912-14, 1916.

Washington *Evening Star.* 1905, 1913-17.

Washington Herald. 1913, 1915.

Washington Post. 1912-17.

Waterloo (Iowa) *Times-Tribune.* 1913.

Winston-Salem Journal. 1915.

Yonkers Herald. 1896.

ARTICLES

"Along the Color Line: Political," *The Crisis,* IV (September, 1912), 215-17.

"Arbitration and Pan American Trade; A Definite Result of the Conference, a Practical Movement to Settle Trade Disputes," *The Nation's Business,* III, Pt. II, 10-11.

Baker, Bernard N. "The Importance of an American Merchant Marine," *America's Interests As Affected by The European War.* Vol. LX of the *Annals of the American Academy of Political and Social Science* (July, 1915), 52-57.

Barrett, John. "All America in Conference," *The Outlook,* CX (May 26, 1915), 171-72.

————. "The Pan-American Financial Conference," *The Independent,* LXXXII (May 24, 1915), 332-33.

"Books and Things," *The New Republic,* V (January 29, 1916), 337.

Broesamle, John J. "The Struggle for Control of the Federal Reserve System, 1914-1917," *Mid-America,* LII (October, 1970), 280-97.

Brown, William Adams. "The Government and the Money Market," Benjamin Haggott Beckhart, James G. Smith, and William Adams Brown, *External and Internal Relations.* Vol. IV of *The New York Money Market.* Edited by Benjamin Haggott Beckhart. New York: Columbia University Press, 1932.

"Business and Trade Conditions," *The Price Current-Grain Reporter,* LXXII (September 30, 1914), 1-2.

"The Case Against Mr. Jones," *The Nation,* IC (July 23, 1914), 92-93.

"Champ Clark," *Collier's Weekly,* XLIX (June 1, 1912), 8.

Coletta, Paolo E. "William Jennings Bryan and Currency and Banking Reform," *Nebraska History,* XLV (March, 1964), 31-57.

Conant, Charles A. "American Finance in the War Tempest," *Review of Reviews,* L (September, 1914), 325-28.

Corrington, Murray. "The Clearing House as a Basis for Currency Issues. The Owen-Glass Bill," *Banking Law Journal* (August, 1913). Reprint.

Creel, George. "The O'Gorman Bunk," *Harper's Weekly,* LIX (August 22, 1914), 172-74.

"The Crookedness of the Hudson Tunnel," *Scientific American,* XCVIII (March 14, 1908), 178.

Daniels, Josephus. "Wilson and Bryan," *The Saturday Evening Post,* CXCVIII (September 5, 1925), 6-7, 48, 50, 52, 54.

Dunn, Arthur Wallace, "Pan-American Financial Conference," *Review of Reviews,* LI (June, 1915), 728-33.

"Editorial: Politics," *The Crisis,* IV (August, 1912), 180-81.

Fahey, John H. "The Southern States and Foreign Trade," *The World's Work,* XXIX (December, 1914), 189-90.

————. "What We Can Do," *Everybody's Magazine,* XXXIII (November, 1915), 590-92.

Farrell, James A. "Central and South American Trade as Affected by the European War," *America's Interests As Affected by The European War.* Vol. LX of the *Annals of the American Academy of Political and Social Science* (July, 1915), 60-68.

"Finance: The '$100,000,000 Gold Pool,' " *The Nation,* IC (October 1, 1914), 417.

"Finance: Two Ways of Doing It," *The Nation,* XCVII (August 7, 1913), 131.

Fitzherbert, Anthony. "The Public Be Pleased: William G. McAdoo and the Hudson Tubes," *Headlights* (Electric Railroader's Association, New York; June, 1964).

"Friction," *The Independent,* LXXX (November 23, 1914), 269.

Gras, N. S. B. "Shifts in Public Relations," *Bulletin of the Business Historical Society,* XIX (October, 1945), 97-148.

Griffin, Henry Farrand. "What's Ahead for Business? A Series of Interviews with Leaders in the Business World," I: "Our Banking and Currency Experiment," *The Independent,* LXXVIII (April 20, 1914), 126-28.

Hamlin, Charles Sumner. "What We Are Trying to Do To Encourage Trade Between South America and the United States," *The World's Work,* XXIX (December, 1914), 151-52.

Harvey, George. "The President's Vision, Is It True or Illusive?" *New York Times Magazine* (December 28, 1913), 4.

Hays, Samuel P. "The Politics of Reform in Municipal Government in the Progressive Era," *Pacific Northwest Quarterly,* LV (October, 1964), 157-69.

Henderson, Gerard. "The Ship Purchase Bill," *The New Republic,* IV (October 23, 1915), 302-04.

Hendrick, Burton J. "A Commercial Traveler in the Cabinet; Fourth Article of Who Govern the United States; Secretary William C. Redfield, of the Department of Commerce," *The World's Work,* XXVI (September, 1913), 564-72.

————. "A New Federal Tribunal," *The World's Work,* XXVIII (October, 1914), 563-75.

————. "An American Marine," *The World's Work,* XXIX (December, 1914), 153-59.

————. "McAdoo," *The World's Work,* XXVI (October, 1913), 626-37.

————. "McAdoo and the Subway," *McClure's Magazine,* XXXVI (March, 1911), 484-500.

"How McAdoo Won Cassatt Over," *Literary Digest,* XLVI (March 22, 1913), 682.

"The Hudson River Tunnel," *Scientific American,* LXXXIX (August 22, 1903), 132-33.

"The Hudson River Tunnel," *Scientific American,* XC (March 26, 1904), 253-54.

Inglis, William. "Celebrities at Home: William Gibbs McAdoo," *Harper's Weekly,* LIII (October 16, 1909), 10-12, 32.

"In the Public Eye: A Business Man in Politics," *The Outlook,* CII (September 28, 1912), 227-28.

"In the Public Eye: Oscar S. Straus," *The Outlook,* CII (September 28, 1912), 228-29.

"Investments and Finance: Mr. Vanderlip on the Currency Bill," *The Literary Digest,* XLVII (October 25, 1913), 785-87.

"John Skelton Williams: The Center of the Latest Cyclone Gathering in Washington," *Current Opinion,* LVIII (June, 1915), 399-400.

Johnson, Evans C. "The Underwood Forces and the Democratic Nomination of 1912," *The Historian,* XXXI (February, 1969), 173-93.

Kaufman, Burton I. "United States Trade and Latin America: The Wilson Years," *The Journal of American History,* LVIII (September, 1971), 342-63.

Kellock, Harold. "Warburg, the Revolutionist," *The Century Magazine*, XC (May, 1915), 79-86.

Kelly, Fred C. "Discovering McAdoo," *Harper's Weekly*, LX (January 2, 1915), 14.

Keys, C. M. "The New Democracy of Business," *The World's Work*, XXV (February, 1913), 400-20.

La Follette, Robert M. "The System at Work," *La Follette's Weekly*, V (April 12, 1913), 1.

Lanier, Henry Wysham. "Mr. McAdoo—On Some Vital Problems," *Review of Reviews*, LXI (May, 1920), 486-91.

Link, Arthur S. "The Negro as a Factor in the Campaign of 1912," *The Journal of Negro History*, XXXII (January, 1947), 81-99.

_____. "The South and the 'New Freedom': An Interpretation,", *American History: Recent Interpretations*. Book II: *Since 1865*. Edited by Abraham S. Eisenstadt. New York: Thomas Y. Crowell Co., c. 1969.

"Little Stories About Big Men," *Transportation*, XI (February, 1933), 19-21.

Lodge, Henry Cabot. "The Shipping Bill and March Fourth," *The Outlook*, CIX (February 24, 1915), 430-33.

McAdoo, William Gibbs. "Can We Afford Preparedness?" *The Independent*, LXXXIV (December 27, 1915), 513.

_____. "The International High Commission and Pan American Cooperation," *The American Journal of International Law*, II (October, 1917), 772-89.

_____. "The Kind of Man Woodrow Wilson Is," *The Century Magazine*, LXXXV (March, 1913), 744-53.

_____. "A Naval Auxiliary and its Value," *National Monthly*, VII (November, 1915), 147, 158.

_____. "The Pan American Financial Conference," *The World's Work*, XXX (August, 1915), 393-96.

_____. "The Pan American Financial Conference; Its Meaning and the Hopes It Holds Out," *The Nation's Business*, III, Pt. II (June 15, 1915), 3-5.

_____. "Secretary McAdoo on Prosperity," *National Monthly* (July, 1916), 19-20.

_____. "The Soul of a Corporation," *The World's Work*, XXIII (March, 1912), 579-92.

_____. "Wanted: American Ships," *The Outlook*, CXIII (June 7, 1916), 326-30.

"McAdoo, the Man Who Went Hunting for Trouble and Found It," *Current Opinion*, LIV (April, 1913), 286-88.

McGregor. "Around the Capitol: Segregation in the Departments," *Harper's Weekly*, LIX (December 26, 1914), 620-21.

————. "The Secretary of the Treasury," *Harper's Weekly*, LIX (October 24, 1914), 399-401.

MacGregor, Donald. "Why Not Pay Yourself an Income Tax?" *American Magazine*, LXXXII (August, 1916), 51-52.

Malone, Dudley Field. "John Purroy Mitchel," *The World's Work*, XXVII (February, 1914), 391-97.

"The Meaning of the Pan American Conference," *The Nation's Business*, III, Pt. I (June 15, 1915), 4.

"Mr. McAdoo's $1,000,000 Order," *The Literary Digest*, XLVI (May 17, 1913), 1,114.

"Mr. Mitchel's Personality and Qualifications," *The Outlook*, CIV (August 9, 1913), 779-80.

"National Association for the Advancement of Colored People: Segregation in Government Departments," *The Crisis*, VI (November, 1913), 343-44.

"The New Collector of the Port of New York," *The Outlook*, CIV (May 17, 1913), 86.

The New Republic, I (November 21, 1914), 5.

"Notable Southern Families: The McAdoos," *The Lookout* (January 8, 1916).

"Notes from the Capital: Governor of the Federal Reserve Board," *The Nation*, CI (October 14, 1915), 4.

"Notes from the Capital: Senator Vardaman," *The Nation*, CIV (April 12, 1917), 438-39.

"The Opening of the First Hudson River Tunnel," *Engineering News*, LIX (February 27, 1908), 230-34.

"Opinion: Federal Segregation," *The Crisis*, VI (November, 1913), 331-34.

"Opinion: Mr. Trotter and Mr. Wilson," *The Crisis*, IX (January, 1915), 119-27.

"Opinions of Ship Owners on the Law," *The Nation's Business*, III (July 15, 1915), 7.

Osborn, George C. "The Problem of the Negro in Government, 1913," *The Historian*, XXIII (May, 1961), 330-47.

Owen, Robert L. "The Origin, Plan, and Purpose of the Currency Bill," *The North American Review*, CXCVIII (October, 1913), 556-69.

"Pan-American Finance," *The New Republic*, III (May 22, 1915), 58-59.

"The Pan American Financial Conference," *Bulletin of the Pan American Union*. House Doc. No. 1400, Pt. 10. 63rd Cong., 3rd Sess., XL (April, 1915), 438-40.

"The Pan American Financial Conference," *Bulletin of the Pan American Union*. House Doc. No. 1400, Pt. 11. 63rd Cong., 3rd Sess., XL (May, 1915), 569-600.

"Pan American Financial Conference: Its Results," *Bulletin of the Pan American Union*. House Doc. No. 1400, Pt. 12. 63rd Cong., 3rd Sess. (June, 1915), 750-54.

Patterson, E. M. "Government Deposits in the National Banks," *Journal of Political Economy*, XXII (January, 1914), 79-82.

"The Pennsylvania Tunnel at New York City," *Scientific American*, XC (January 16, 1904), 42.

"Personal Glimpses: 'Pitchfork Ben' Tillman Dies Like a Soldier at his Post," *The Literary Digest*, LVIII (July 27, 1918), 32, 36.

Peters, Andrew J. "The Underwood Tariff as a Producer of Revenue," *Readjustments in Taxation*. Vol. LVIII of the *Annals of the American Academy of Political and Social Science* (March, 1915), 12-14.

————. "The War Risk Insurance Bureau," *The Nation's Business*, II (December 15, 1914).

P. L., "Books and Things," *The New Republic*, V (January 29, 1916), 337.

"The President and the Negro," *The Nation*, CXIV (August 7, 1913), 114.

"President Wilson: His Inauguration, Cabinet, and Problems," *The Outlook*, CIII (March 15, 1913), 553-67.

"President Wilson's Cabinet," *Review of Reviews*, XLVII (April, 1913), 440.

"The President's Indorsement of Negro Segregation," *The Literary Digest*, IL (November 28, 1914), 1,052-54.

"The President's Sop to Tammany," *The Nation*, CII (April 27, 1916), 450-51.

Price, Theodore H. "Secretary McAdoo: A Cabinet Officer who Does Things," *The Outlook*, CXVII (October 17, 1917), 246-48.

"Progress of the Great Railway Tunnels Under the Hudson River Between New York and Jersey City," *Scientific American*, LXIII (November 1, 1890), 279-80.

"Progress of the New Jersey Tunnels and Subways," *Scientific American*, XCIII (December 6, 1905), 459-61.

"The Progress of the World," *Review of Reviews*, XLVI (September, 1912), 259-87.

Quick, Herbert. "Shall We Give Up the Ship? How the Administration Proposes to Build Up a Merchant Marine," *The Saturday Evening Post*, CLXXXVIII (February 5, 1916), 6-8, 32-33.

"Race Discrimination at Washington," *The Independent*, LXXVI (November 20, 1913), 330.

"Race Segregation at Washington," *The Independent*, LXXX (November 23, 1914), 275.

Redfield, William C. "How the War Will Affect Commerce," *Harper's Weekly*, LX (June 26, 1915), 615-16.

————. "Our Growing Foreign Commerce," *The Independent*, LXXVIII (June 29, 1914), 552-53.

————. "The Present Merchant-Marine Problem," *Atlantic Monthly*, CXV (February, 1915), 271-81.

————. "What One Department Has Done," *Harper's Weekly*, LXII (March 18, 1916), 273-74.

"The Report of the Treasury," *The Nation*, IC (December 17, 1914), 706-07.

"Reports of General Committees; Practical Suggestions and Findings of the Larger Committees," *The Nation's Business*, III, Pt. II (June 15, 1915), 9-10.

"Republican Progressives for Wilson," *National Monthly*, IV (November, 1912), 138.

"Reserve Bank Appointments—And Disappointments," *The Literary Digest*, XLVIII (April 18, 1914), 885-88.

"The Reserve Board at Work," *The Literary Digest*, XLIX (August 22, 1914), 295-96.

"The Reserve Board Nominations," *The Independent*, LXXIX (July 20, 1914), 84-85.

"Results of Meeting of International High Commission in Buenos Aires," *Bulletin of the Pan American Union*, XLIII (July, 1916), 1-4.

"The Riggs Bank Case," *The Outlook*, CIX (April 28, 1915), 953-54.

"The Riggs Bank Row," *The Literary Digest*, L (April 24, 1915), 939-40.

Roosevelt, Theodore. "Platform Insincerity," *The Outlook*, CI (July 27, 1912), 659-63.

Shaw, Albert. "President Wilson's Cabinet," *Review of Reviews*, XLVII (April, 1913), 423-40.

Sklar, Martin J. "Woodrow Wilson and the Political Economy of Modern United States Liberalism," *For a New America: Essays in History and Politics from Studies on the Left, 1959-1967*. Edited by James Weinstein and David W. Eakins. New York: Random House, c. 1970.

Sprague, O. M. W. "The Crisis of 1914 in the United States," *The American Economic Review*, V (September, 1915), 499-533.

————. "The War and the Financial Situation in the United States," *Quarterly Journal of Economics*, XXIX (November, 1914), 181-86.

"The Story of the Conference; What Brought it About, What Happened at the Meetings, and the Permanent Results Achieved," *The Nation's Business*, III, Pt. II (June 15, 1915), 6-8.

"The Treasury Deposit Experiment," *The Bache Review*, XXI (October 4, 1913), 5-6.

"The United States Chamber of Commerce and the Shipping Bill," *The Outlook*, CIX (March 3, 1915), 494-95.

Untermyer, Samuel. "Why the Currency Bill Should Pass," *The North American Review*, CXCVIII (October, 1913), 498-526.

Vanderlip, Frank A. "How to Amend the Currency Bill," *The North American Review*, CXCVIII (November 4, 1913), 698-707.

Van Norman, Louis E. "The Achievement of the Hudson Tunnels," *Review of Reviews*, XXXVII (April, 1908), 425-32.

'Vieillard,' "Notes from the Capital: The Secretary of the Treasury," *The Nation*, C (April 29, 1915), 466-67.

Villard, Oswald Garrison. "The Mystery of Woodrow Wilson," *The North American Review*, CCIV (September, 1916), 362-72.

_____. "The President and the Segregation at Washington," *The North American Review*, CXCVIII (December, 1913), 800-07.

_____. "The Shifting Administration," *The Nation*, CII (February 17, 1916), 189-91.

"Washington Notes," *Journal of Political Economy*, XXII (November, 1914), 901-09.

"Washington Notes: The Federal Reserve Board As A Government Body," *The Journal of Political Economy*, XXIII (January, 1915), 73-75.

Watchorn, Robert. "The Builder of the Hudson Tunnels," *The Outlook*, XC (December 6, 1908), 909-14.

Weiss, Nancy J. "The Negro and the New Freedom: Fighting Wilsonian Segregation," *Political Science Quarterly*, LXXXIV (March, 1969), 61-79.

Welliver, Judson C. "The New Cabinet," *Munsey's Magazine*, XLIX (May, 1913), 165-77.

Wolgemuth, Kathleen L. "Woodrow Wilson and Federal Segregation," *Journal of Negro History*, XLIV (April, 1959), 158-73.

_____. "Woodrow Wilson's Appointment Policy and the Negro," *Journal of Southern History*, XXIV (November, 1958), 457-71.

Woolley, Robert Wickliffe. "The Race for Federal Jobs," *The World's Work*, XXV (March, 1913), 552-59.

"Work of the International High Commission at Buenos Aires," *Bulletin of the Pan American Union*. House Doc. No. 39, Pt. 10. 64th Cong., 1st Sess., XLII (April, 1916), 453-56.

"The Work of the Pan American Financial Conference," *Bulletin of the Pan American Union*, XIV (August, 1917), 165-71.

"Your Government of the United States; The Newest Part of the Government," *World's Work*, XXX (June, 1915), 145-47.

BOOKS AND PAMPHLETS: PRIMARY SOURCES

Baker, Bernard Nadal, and Essary, J. Frederick. *Ships*. Baltimore: John Murphy Co., c. 1916.

Baruch, Bernard M. *Baruch: The Public Years*. New York: Holt, Rinehart and Winston, c. 1960.

Bowers, Claude. *My Life: The Memoirs of Claude Bowers*. New York: Simon and Schuster, 1962.

Bryan, William Jennings. *A Tale of Two Conventions; Being an Account of the Republican and Democratic National Conventions of June, 1912, With an Outline of the Progressive National Convention of August in the Same Year*. New York: Funk and Wagnalls, 1912.

_____, and Bryan, Mary Baird. *The Memoirs of William Jennings Bryan*.

Philadelphia: The John C. Winston Co., c. 1925.

Clark, Champ. *My Quarter Century of American Politics.* 2 vols. New York: Harper and Brothers, 1920.

The Cotton Growing States Today from the Merchandise Credit Grantor's Standpoint. New York: National Association of Credit Men, n.d.

Cowie, T. J. *Logistics.* Newport, Rhode Island: U.S. Naval War College, March 5, 1915.

Creel, George. *Rebel At Large: Recollections of Fifty Crowded Years.* New York: G. P. Putnam's Sons, c. 1947.

Croly, Herbert. *The Promise of American Life.* New York: Capricorn Books, 1964.

Daniels, Josephus. *The Cabinet Diaries of Josephus Daniels, 1913-1921.* Edited by E. David Cronon. Lincoln: University of Nebraska Press, c. 1963.

————. *The Life of Woodrow Wilson, 1856-1924.* Philadelphia: The John C. Winston Co., c. 1924.

————. *The Wilson Era: Years of Peace—1910-1917.* Chapel Hill: University of North Carolina Press, 1946.

Du Bois, W. E. Burghardt. *Dusk of Dawn: An Essay Toward an Autobiography of a Race Concept.* New York: Harcourt, Brace and Co., c. 1940.

Farquhar, A. B., and Crowther, Samuel. *The First Million the Hardest; An Autobiography.* Garden City, New York: Doubleday, Page and Co., 1922.

————, and Farquhar, Henry. *Economic and Industrial Delusions: A Discussion of the Case for Protection.* New York: G. P. Putnam's Sons, 1891.

Farrell, James A., and Patchin, Robert H. *The War and South American Trade.* National Foreign Trade Council, Information Bulletin No. 1. September 8, 1914.

Forgan, James B. *Review of Proposed Banking and Currency Bill.* Privately printed, n.d.

Gerard, James W. *My First Eighty-Three Years in America; The Memoirs of James W. Gerard.* Garden City, New York: Doubleday and Co., 1951.

Glass, Carter. *An Adventure in Constructive Finance.* Garden City, New York: Doubleday, Page and Co., 1927.

Harding, W. P. G. *The Formative Period of the Federal Reserve System (During the World Crisis).* Boston: Houghton Mifflin Co., 1925.

Harriman, Mrs. J. Borden. *From Pinafores to Politics.* London: George Allen and Unwin, n.d.

House, Edward M. *The Intimate Papers of Colonel House.* 4 vols. Edited by Charles Seymour. Boston: Houghton Mifflin Co., 1926.

Houston, David F. *Eight Years With Wilson's Cabinet, 1913 to 1920; With a Personal Estimate of the President.* 2 vols. Garden City, New York: Doubleday, Page and Co., 1926.

Hull, Cordell. *The Memoirs of Cordell Hull.* 2 vols. New York: The Macmillan Co., 1948.

Hurley, Edward N. *The New Merchant Marine*. New York: The Century Co., 1920.

Kent, Elizabeth T. *William Kent, Independent: A Biography*. Privately printed, n.d.

Kerney, James. *The Political Education of Woodrow Wilson*. New York: The Century Co., c. 1926.

Lane, Franklin K. *The Letters of Franklin K. Lane; Personal and Political*. Edited By Anne Wintermute Lane and Louise Herrick Wall. Boston: Houghton Mifflin Co., c. 1922.

Laughlin, J. Laurence. *Banking Progress*. New York: Charles Scribner's Sons, 1920.

_____ (ed.). *Banking Reform*. Chicago: The National Citizens' League for the Promotion of a Sound Banking System, 1912.

_____. *The Federal Reserve Act: Its Origin and Problems*. New York: The Macmillan Co., 1933.

Lawrence, David. *The True Story of Woodrow Wilson*. New York: George H. Doran, 1924.

Lippmann, Walter. *Drift and Mastery: An Attempt to Diagnose the Current Unrest*. Englewood Cliffs, New Jersey: Prentice-Hall, c. 1961.

Lyons, Maurice F. *William F. McCombs the President Maker*. Cincinnati: The Bancroft Co., c. 1922.

McAdoo, Eleanor Wilson, and Gaffey, Margaret Y. *The Woodrow Wilsons*. New York: The Macmillan Co., 1937.

McAdoo, William G. *Crowded Years: The Reminiscences of William G. McAdoo*. Boston: Houghton Mifflin Co., 1931. Reprinted by Kennikat Press, Port Washington, New York, 1971.

McCombs, William F. *Making Woodrow Wilson President*. New York: Fairview Publishing Co., 1921.

Malburn, William P. *What Happened to Our Banks*. Indianapolis: The Bobbs-Merrill Co., c. 1934.

Morgenthau, Henry. *All In a Life-Time*. Garden City, New York: Doubleday, Page and Co., 1922.

Mullen, Arthur F. *Western Democrat*. New York: Wilfred Funk, 1940.

Ocean Shipping: The Basic Principles of Marine Transportation with Particular Reference to the Foreign Trade of the United States. National Foreign Trade Council, November, 1915.

Owen, Robert L. *The Federal Reserve Act*. New York: The Century Co., 1919.

Pease, Otis (ed.). *The Progressive Years: The Spirit and Achievement of American Reform*. New York: George Braziller, 1962.

Pending Banking Legislation; Letters by Officers of The National City Bank of New York to the Banking and Currency Committees of the Congress of the United States. New York: The National City Bank, 1913.

Pérez Triana, Santiago. *The Pan-American Financial Conference of 1915.* London: William Heinemann, 1915.

Redfield, William C. *With Congress and Cabinet.* Garden City, New York: Doubleday, Page and Co., 1924.

Reynolds, George M. *The Administration Currency Bill.* Privately printed, 1913.

Roosevelt, Theodore. *The Letters of Theodore Roosevelt.* Vol. VII: *The Days of Armageddon: 1909-1914.* Edited by Elting E. Morison. Cambridge, Massachusetts: Harvard University Press, 1954.

————. *The New Nationalism.* Englewood Cliffs, New Jersey: Prentice-Hall, c. 1961.

————. *The Works of Theodore Roosevelt.* Vol. XV: *State Papers as Governor and President, 1899-1909.* National ed. New York: Charles Scribner's Sons, 1926.

Roper, Daniel C., and Lovette, Frank H. *Fifty Years of Public Life.* Durham, North Carolina: Duke University Press, 1941.

Rosenthal, Benjamin J. *The Need of the Hour: An American Merchant Marine.* Chicago: Privately printed, 1915.

Ship Purchase Bill: Opposite Views Expressed by Hon. William G. McAdoo, Secretary of the Treasury, and Hon. Theodore E. Burton, Senator from Ohio, at the Third Annual Meeting of the Chamber of Commerce of the United States. Privately printed (1915).

Tumulty, Joseph P. *Woodrow Wilson As I Know Him.* Garden City, New York: Garden City Publishing Co., 1925.

Underwood, Oscar W. *Drifting Sands of Party Politics.* New York: The Century Co., c. 1931.

Untermyer, Samuel. *Who Is Entitled to the Credit for the Federal Reserve Act? An Answer to Senator Carter Glass.* Privately printed, n.d.

Vanderlip, Frank A., and Sparkes, Boyden. *From Farm Boy to Financier.* New York: D. Appleton-Century Co., 1935.

Villard, Oswald Garrison. *Fighting Years: Memoirs of a Liberal Editor.* New York: Harcourt, Brace and Co., c. 1939.

Walters, Alexander. *My Life and Work.* New York: Fleming H. Revell Co., c. 1917.

Warburg, Paul M. *The Federal Reserve System: Its Origin and Growth.* 2 vols. New York: The Macmillan Co., 1930.

————. *Should there be Four or Eight Federal Reserve Banks? A Suggestion for a Compromise.* Privately printed, n.d.

Wells, Rolla. *Report of the Treasurer, Democratic National Committee; Presidential Campaign, 1912.* St. Louis: Democratic National Committee, 1913.

Weyl, Walter E. *The New Democracy: An Essay on Certain Political and Economic Tendencies in the United States.* New York: Harper Torchbooks, 1964.

Willis, Henry Parker. *The Federal Reserve System: Legislation, Organization and Operation.* New York: The Ronald Press Co., 1923.

————. *The Theory and Practice of Central Banking; With Special Reference to American Experience, 1913-1935.* New York: Harper and Bros., 1936.

————, and Steiner, William H. *Federal Reserve Banking Practice.* New York: D. Appleton and Co., 1926.

Wilson, Woodrow. *A Crossroads of Freedom; the 1912 Campaign Speeches of Woodrow Wilson.* Edited by John Wells Davidson. New Haven: Yale University Press, 1956.

————. *The New Freedom: A Call for the Emancipation of the Generous Energies of a People.* Englewood Cliffs, New Jersey: Prentice-Hall, c. 1961.

Woodson, Urey (ed.). *Official Report of the Proceedings of the Democratic National Convention Held in Baltimore, Maryland, June 25, 26, 27, 28, 29 and July 1 and 2, 1912, Resulting in the Nomination of Hon. Woodrow Wilson (of New Jersey) for President and Hon. Thomas Riley Marshall (of Indiana) for Vice-President.* Chicago: Peterson Linotyping Co., 1912.

BOOKS: SECONDARY SOURCES

Abrams, Richard M. *Conservatism in a Progressive Era: Massachusetts Politics, 1900-1912.* Cambridge, Massachusetts: Harvard University Press, 1964.

Adler, Cyrus. *Jacob H. Schiff: His Life and Letters.* 2 vols. Garden City, New York: Doubleday, Doran and Co., 1928.

Annin, Robert. *Woodrow Wilson: A Character Study.* New York: Dodd, Mead and Co., 1924.

Baker, Ray Stannard. *Woodrow Wilson: Life and Letters.* 8 vols. Garden City, New York: Doubleday, Doran and Co., 1927-39.

Bell, H. C. F. *Woodrow Wilson and the People.* Garden City, New York: Doubleday, Doran and Co., 1945.

Billington, Monroe Lee. *Thomas P. Gore: The Blind Senator from Oklahoma.* Lawrence: The University of Kansas Press, 1967.

Blum, John M. *Joe Tumulty and the Wilson Era.* Boston: Houghton Mifflin Co., c. 1951.

————. *Woodrow Wilson and the Politics of Morality.* In *The Library of American Biography.* Edited by Oscar Handlin. Boston: Little, Brown and Co., c. 1956.

Bremner, Robert H. *From the Depths: The Discovery of Poverty in the United States.* New York: New York University Press, 1964.

Chamberlain, Rudolph W. *There Is No Truce: A Life of Thomas Mott Osborne.* New York: The Macmillan Co., 1935.

Chambers, William Nisbet. *The Democrats, 1789-1964: A Short History of a Popular Party.* Princeton, New Jersey: D. Van Nostrand Co., c. 1964.

Chandler, Lester V. *Benjamin Strong, Central Banker.* Washington: The Brookings Institution, 1958.

Clifford, A. Jerome. *The Independence of the Federal Reserve System.* Philadelphia: University of Pennsylvania Press, c. 1965.

Coben, Stanley. *A. Mitchell Palmer: Politician.* New York: Columbia University Press, 1963.

Cohen, Naomi W. *A Dual Heritage: The Public Career of Oscar S. Straus.* Philadelphia: The Jewish Publication Society of America, 1969.

Coit, Margaret. *Mr. Baruch.* Boston: Houghton Mifflin Co., 1957.

Coletta, Paolo E. *William Jennings Bryan.* Vol II: *Progressive Politician and Moral Statesman, 1909-1915.* Lincoln: University of Nebraska Press, c. 1969.

Diamond, Sigmund. *The Reputation of the American Businessman.* Cambridge, Massachusetts: Harvard University Press, 1955.

Faulkner, Harold U. *The Decline of Laissez Faire, 1897-1917.* Vol. VII of *The Economic History of the United States.* Edited by Henry David *et al.* New York: Holt, Rinehart and Winston, 1962.

Fenno, Richard F., Jr. *The President's Cabinet: An Analysis in the Period From Wilson to Eisenhower.* New York: Vintage Books, c. 1959.

Field, Carter. *Bernard Baruch: Park Bench Statesman.* New York: Whittlesey House (McGraw-Hill Book Co.), c. 1944.

Fine, Sidney. *Laissez Faire and the General-Welfare State: A Study of Conflict in American Thought, 1865-1901.* Ann Arbor, Michigan: Ann Arbor Paperbacks, 1964.

Forcey, Charles. *The Crossroads of Liberalism: Croly, Weyl, Lippmann, and the Progressive Era, 1900-1925.* New York: Oxford University Press, 1961.

Fox, Stephen R. *The Guardian of Boston: William Monroe Trotter.* New York: Atheneum, 1970.

Franklin, John Hope. *From Slavery to Freedom: A History of Negro Americans.* 3rd ed. New York: Alfred A. Knopf, 1967.

Freidel, Frank. *Franklin D. Roosevelt: The Apprenticeship.* Boston: Little, Brown and Co., c. 1952.

Friedman, Jacob Alexis. *The Impeachment of Governor William Sulzer.* ("Studies in History, Economics and Public Law," Columbia University, No. 447.) New York: Columbia University Press, 1939.

Gaines, Tilford C. *Techniques of Treasury Debt Management.* Glencoe, Illinois: The Free Press, c. 1962.

George, Alexander L., and Juliette L. *Woodrow Wilson and Colonel House: A Personality Study.* New York: Dover Publications, 1964.

Gilbert, Charles. *American Financing of World War I.* Westport, Connecticut: Greenwood Publishing Corp., c. 1970.

Glad, Paul W. *The Trumpet Soundeth: William Jennings Bryan and His Democracy, 1896-1912.* University of Nebraska Press, 1960.

Goldman, Eric F. *Rendezvous With Destiny: A History of Modern American Reform.* New York: Alfred A. Knopf, 1958.

Gossett, Thomas F. *Race: The History of an Idea in America.* Dallas: Southern Methodist University Press, 1963.

Harbaugh, William Henry. *Power and Responsibility: The Life and Times of Theodore Roosevelt.* New York: Farrar, Straus and Cudahy, 1961.

Hatch, Alden. *Edith Bolling Wilson: First Lady Extraordinary.* New York: Dodd, Mead and Co., 1961.

Hayes, Laurence J. W. *The Negro Federal Government Worker: A Study of his Classification Status in the District of Columbia, 1883-1938.* ("The Howard University Studies in the Social Sciences," Vol. III, No. 1.) Washington: The Graduate School, Howard University, 1941.

Hays, Samuel P. *The Response to Industrialism: 1885-1914.* In *The Chicago History of American Civilization* series. Edited by Daniel J. Boorstin. Chicago: University of Chicago Press, 1964.

Heald, Morrell. *The Social Responsibilities of Business; Company and Community, 1900-1960.* Cleveland: Case Western Reserve University Press, 1970.

Hepburn, A. Barton. *A History of Currency in the United States.* Revised ed. New York: The Macmillan Co., 1924.

Hofstadter, Richard. *The Age of Reform: From Bryan to F. D. R.* New York: Vintage Books, c. 1955.

_____. *Social Darwinism in American Thought.* Revised ed. Boston: The Beacon Press, 1962.

Hollingsworth, J. Rogers. *The Whirligig of Politics: The Democracy of Cleveland and Bryan.* Chicago: University of Chicago Press, c. 1963.

Holmes, William F. *The White Chief: James Kimble Vardaman.* Baton Rouge: Louisiana State University Press, c. 1970.

Howe, M. A. De Wolfe. *Portrait of an Independent: Moorfield Storey, 1845-1929.* Boston: Houghton Mifflin Co., 1932.

Hugh-Jones, E. M. *Woodrow Wilson and American Liberalism.* London: Hodder and Stoughton, 1947.

Humes, D. Joy. *Oswald Garrison Villard, Liberal of the 1920's.* Syracuse: Syracuse University Press, 1960.

Hutchins, John G. B. *The American Maritime Industries and Public Policy, 1789-1914; An Economic History.* ("Harvard Economic Studies," Vol. LXXI.) Cambridge, Massachusetts: Harvard University Press, 1941.

Kellogg, Charles Flint. *NAACP: A History of the National Association for the Advancement of Colored People.* Vol. I: *1909-1920.* Baltimore: The Johns Hopkins Press, c. 1967.

Kelly, Frank K. *The Fight for the White House: The Story of 1912.* New York: Thomas Y. Crowell Co., c. 1961.

Keso, Edward Elmer. *The Senatorial Career of Robert Latham Owen*. Gardenvale, Canada: Privately printed, c. 1938.

Key, V. O., Jr. *Politics, Parties, & Pressure Groups*. 5th ed. New York: Thomas Y. Crowell Co., c. 1964.

Kirkland, Edward C. *Industry Comes of Age: Business, Labor and Public Policy, 1860-1897*. Vol. VI of *The Economic History of the United States*. Edited by Henry David *et al.* New York: Holt, Rinehart and Winston, 1962.

Kolko, Gabriel. *The Triumph of Conservatism: A Reinterpretation of American History, 1900-1916*. Glencoe, Illinois: The Free Press, c. 1963.

Krislov, Samuel. *The Negro in Federal Employment: The Quest for Equal Opportunity*. Minneapolis: University of Minnesota Press, c. 1967.

Lasch, Christopher. *The New Radicalism in America: 1889-1963; The Intellectual as a Social Type*. New York: Alfred A. Knopf, 1965.

Lasswell, Harold. *Power and Personality*. New York: W. W. Norton and Co., c. 1948.

Latham, Earl (ed.). *The Philosophy and Policies of Woodrow Wilson*. Chicago: University of Chicago Press, c. 1958.

Levin, N. Gordon, Jr. *Woodrow Wilson and World Politics: America's Response to War and Revolution*. New York: Oxford University Press, 1970.

Lewinson, Edwin R. *John Purroy Mitchel: The Boy Mayor of New York*. New York: Astra Books, 1965.

Link, Arthur S. *Wilson: Campaigns for Progressivism and Peace, 1916-1917*. Princeton, New Jersey: Princeton University Press, 1965.

————. *Wilson: Confusions and Crises, 1915-1916*. Princeton, New Jersey: Princeton University Press, 1964.

————. *Wilson: The New Freedom*. Princeton, New Jersey: Princeton University Press, 1956.

————. *Wilson: The Road to the White House*. Princeton, New Jersey: Princeton University Press, 1947.

————. *Wilson: The Struggle for Neutrality, 1914-1915*. Princeton, New Jersey: Princeton University Press, 1960.

————. *Woodrow Wilson and the Progressive Era: 1910-1917*. In *The New American Nation Series*. Edited by Henry Steele Commager and Richard B. Morris. New York: Harper and Bros., c. 1954.

Lippmann, Walter. *Men of Destiny*. New York: The Macmillan Co., 1927.

McCloskey, Robert Green. *American Conservatism in the Age of Enterprise, 1865-1910: A Study of William Graham Sumner, Stephen J. Field and Andrew Carnegie*. New York: Harper Torchbooks, 1964.

McKinley, Silas Bent. *Woodrow Wilson: A Biography*. New York: Frederick A. Praeger, c. 1957.

Mason, Alpheus Thomas. *Brandeis: A Free Man's Life*. New York: The Viking Press, 1946.

May,·Henry F. *The End of American Innocence: A Study of the First Years of Our Own Time, 1912-1917.* Chicago: Quadrangle Books, 1964.

Milton, George Fort. *The Use of Presidential Power, 1789-1943.* Boston: Little, Brown and Co., 1945.

Mitgang, Herbert. *The Man Who Rode the Tiger: The Life and Times of Judge Samuel Seabury.* Philadelphia: J. B. Lippincott Co., c. 1963.

Morrison, Joseph L. *Josephus Daniels: The Small-d Democrat.* Chapel Hill: University of North Carolina Press, c. 1966.

Mowry, George E. *The California Progressives.* Chicago: Encounter Paperbacks, 1963.

_____.*The Era of Theodore Roosevelt and the Birth of Modern America, 1900-1912.* In *The New American Nation Series.* Edited by Henry Steele Commager and Richard B. Morris. New York: Harper Torchbooks, 1962.

_____. *Theodore Roosevelt and the Progressive Movement.* New York: Hill and Wang, 1963.

Myers, Gustavus. *The History of Tammany Hall.* 2d ed. revised. New York: Boni and Liveright, 1917.

Myers, Margaret G. *A Financial History of the United States.* New York: Columbia University Press, 1970.

Noble, H. G. S. *The New York Stock Exchange in the Crisis of 1914.* Garden City, New York: The Country Life Press, 1915.

Noyes, Alexander D. *The War Period of American Finance, 1908-1925.* New York: G. P. Putnam's Sons, 1926.

Palmer, James E. *Carter Glass: Unreconstructed Rebel.* Roanoke: The Institute of American Biography, 1938.

Parrini, Carl P. *Heir to Empire; United States Economic Diplomacy, 1916-1923.* Pittsburgh: University of Pittsburgh Press, c. 1969.

Paul, Randolph E. *Taxation in the United States.* Boston: Little, Brown and Co., 1954.

Reed, Harold. *The Development of Federal Reserve Policy.* Boston: Houghton Mifflin Co., 1922.

Richardson, Rupert Norval. *Colonel Edward M. House: The Texas Years, 1858-1912.* ("Hardin-Simmons University Publications in History," edited by Rupert N. Richardson and Escal F. Duke, Vol. I.) Privately printed, c. 1964.

Rippy, J. Fred (ed.). *F. M. Simmons: Statesman of the New South; Memoirs and Addresses.* Durham, North Carolina: Duke University Press, 1936.

Saloutos, Theodore. *Farmer Movements In The South: 1865-1933.* Lincoln: University of Nebraska Press, n.d.

Simkins, Francis Butler. *Pitchfork Ben Tillman: South Carolinian.* Gloucester, Massachusetts: Peter Smith, 1964.

Slosson, Preston William. *The Great Crusade and After, 1914-1928.* Vol. XII of *A History of American Life.* Edited by Arthur M. Schlesinger and

Dixon Ryan Fox. New York: The Macmillan Co., 1962.

Smith, Arthur D. Howden. *Mr. House of Texas.* New York: Funk and Wagnalls Co., 1940.

Smith, Mortimer. *William Jay Gaynor: Mayor of New York.* Chicago: Henry Regnery Co., 1951.

Smith, Rixey, and Beasley, Norman. *Carter Glass: A Biography.* New York: Longmans, Green and Co., 1939.

Spencer, Samuel R. *Booker T. Washington and the Negro's Place in American Life.* In *The Library of American Biography.* Edited by Oscar Handlin. Boston: Little, Brown and Co., c. 1955.

Studenski, Paul, and Krooss, Herman. *Financial History of the United States: Fiscal, Monetary, Banking, and Tariff, including Financial Administration and State and Local Finance.* 1st edition. New York: McGraw-Hill Book Co., 1952.

Swaine, Robert T. *The Cravath Firm and its Predecessors, 1819-1948.* 3 vols. and supplement. New York: Privately printed, 1946, 1948, 1964.

Synon, Mary. *McAdoo, the Man and His Times: A Panorama in Democracy.* Indianapolis: The Bobbs-Merrill Co., 1924.

Taus, Esther Rogoff. *Central Banking Functions of the United States Treasury, 1789-1941.* New York: Russell and Russell, 1967.

Tulchin, Joseph S. *The Aftermath of War: World War I and U.S. Policy Toward Latin America.* New York: New York University Press, 1971.

Van Riper, Paul P. *History of the United States Civil Service.* Evanston, Illinois: Row, Peterson and Co., 1958.

Walworth, Arthur. *Woodrow Wilson.* 2d ed. revised. Baltimore: Penguin Books, 1969.

Weiss, Nancy Joan. *Charles Francis Murphy, 1858-1924: Respectability and Responsibility in Tammany Politics.* Northampton, Massachusetts: Smith College, 1968.

Weyforth, William O. *The Federal Reserve Board: A Study of Federal Reserve Structure and Credit Control.* ("Johns Hopkins University Studies in Historical and Political Science," New Series, No. 19.) Baltimore: The Johns Hopkins Press, 1933.

White, William Allen. *Woodrow Wilson: The Man, His Times, and His Task.* Boston: Houghton Mifflin Co., c. 1924.

Wiebe, Robert H. *Businessmen and Reform: A Study of the Progressive Movement.* Cambridge, Massachusetts: Harvard University Press, 1962.

————. *The Search for Order, 1877-1920.* In *The Making of America* series. Edited by David Donald. New York: Hill and Wang, 1968.

Woodward, C. Vann. *Origins of the New South: 1877-1913.* Vol. IX of *A History of the South.* Edited by William Holmes Stephenson and E. Merton Coulter. Louisiana State University Press, 1951.

————. *Tom Watson: Agrarian Rebel.* New York: Oxford University Press, 1963.

Wreszin, Michael. *Oswald Garrison Villard: Pacifist at War.* Bloomington: Indiana University Press, c. 1965.

Wyllie, Irvin G. *The Self-Made Man in America: The Myth of Rags to Riches.* New York: The Free Press, 1966.

PUBLIC DOCUMENTS

An Appendix to the Report of the United States Section of the International High Commission on the First General Meeting of the Commission, Held at Buenos Aires, April 3-12, 1916. Senate Doc. No. 739. 64th Cong., 2d Sess., 1916.

Carr, Wilbur J., and Crowder, Enoch H. *Report of Hon. Wilbur J. Carr, Director of the Consular Service, and Gen. Enoch H. Crowder, Judge Advocate General of the Army, Upon Uniformity of Customs Regulations, Consular Certificates, and Invoices and Port Charges.* (Pan American Financial Conference, 1915.) Washington: U.S. Government Printing Office, 1915.

Committee Reports and Resolutions Adopted at the First General Meeting, Held in Buenos Aires in April, 1916. Washington: U.S. Government Printing Office, 1917.

Fahey, John H. *Report of John H. Fahey, President of the United States Chamber of Commerce, Upon the Extension of the Means of Arbitration of Commercial Disputes.* (Pan American Financial Conference, 1915.) Washington: U.S. Government Printing Office, 1915.

Fuller, Paul, and Van Dyke, Harry. *Report of Paul Fuller, Esq. and Harry Van Dyke, Esq., on The Conditions Imposed by Latin American Republics upon Foreign Companies doing Business Within their Jurisdictions.* (Pan American Financial Conference, 1915.) Washington: U.S. Government Printing Office, 1915.

Hearings Before the Committee on Foreign Affairs, House of Representatives, Sixty-Fourth Congress, First Session, on H.R. 8235; Statement of Hon. William G. McAdoo, Secretary of the Treasury (January 12, 1916.) Washington: U.S. Government Printing Office, 1916.

Henry, Robert L. *For the Relief of the Cotton Growers: Speeches of Hon. Robert L. Henry of Texas in the House of Representatives, October 16, 20, 21 and 24, 1914.* Washington: U.S. Government Printing Office, 1914.

Inter-American High Commission, Central Executive Council. *Resolution on the Permanent Organization of the Inter-American High Commission, Adopted at the Meeting in Buenos Aires, April 3-12, 1916.* Washington: U.S. Government Printing Office, 1916.

Jones, Grosvenor M. *Government Aid to Merchant Shipping: Study of Subsidies, Subventions, and Other Forms of State Aid in Principal Countries of the World.* Department of Commerce, Special Agents Series No. 119. Washington: U.S. Government Printing Office, 1916.

Latin-American Trade: Report of the Latin-American Trade Committee Appointed by the Secretary of Commerce, Hon. William C. Redfield, Pur-

suant to a Resolution Adopted at the Informal Latin-American Trade Conference Called at Washington, D.C., on September 10, 1914, by the Secretary of State and the Secretary of Commerce. Senate Doc. No. 714. 63rd Cong., 3rd Sess., 1915.

Moore, John Bassett. *Summary of Group Conference Reports.* Washington: U.S. Government Printing Office, 1915.

————. *The Work of the International High Commission; An Address Delivered at the Pan American Financial Conference, Washington, January 19-24, 1920.* Senate Doc. No. 261. 66th Cong., 2d Sess., 1920.

Peters, Andrew J. *Importance of Our South American Trade; Address on the Importance of Our South American Trade, Delivered Before The City Club in Boston, Mass., on November 16, 1916.* Senate Doc. No. 698. 64th Cong., 2d Sess., 1917.

Pound, Roscoe. *Report of Prof. Roscoe Pound Upon Uniformity of Laws Governing the Establishment and Regulation of Corporations and Joint Stock Companies in the American Republics.* Washington: U.S. Government Printing Office, 1915.

Proceedings of the First Pan American Financial Conference, Convened by Authority of the Congress of the United States under the Direction of Hon. William G. McAdoo, Secretary of the Treasury. Washington: U.S. Government Printing Office, 1915.

Report of the General Committee on Transportation and Communication Submitted to the Pan American Financial Conference at the Session of Saturday Afternoon, May 29, 1915. Washington: U.S. Government Printing Office, 1915.

Report of the Latin American Return Visit Committee Appointed by the Secretary of the Treasury of the United States in Compliance with The Resolution of the First Pan American Financial Conference. Washington: U.S. Government Printing Office, 1918.

Simmons, F. M. *Remarks of Hon. F. M. Simmons of North Carolina in the Senate of the United States, July 14, 1913, Presenting Interview of Hon. William G. McAdoo, Secretary of the Treasury, on Financial Conditions.* Washington: U.S. Government Printing Office, 1914.

Transportation Facilities: Summary of the Reports Submitted in Response to a Request of the Secretary of the Treasury on July 19, 1915, by Several Delegations to the First Pan American Financial Conference. Senate Doc. No. 497. 64th Cong., 1st Sess., 1916.

Treasury Decisions Under Customs and Other Laws. Vols. XXIV-XXXII. Washington: U.S. Government Printing Office, January, 1913-June, 1917.

U.S. Auditor for the Treasury Department. *Annual Report of The Auditor for the Treasury Department.* 1913-17.

U.S. Board of Governors of the Federal Reserve System. *Federal Reserve Act (Approved December 23, 1913), As Amended Through November 5, 1966.*

U.S. Comptroller of the Currency. *Annual Report of the Comptroller of the Currency . . . , 1913-17.*

U.S. *Congressional Record.* Vols. LI, LIII.

U.S. Department of Commerce, Bureau of Foreign and Domestic Commerce. *Statements on the Latin American Trade Situation Made by Representatives of Latin American Countries at a Conference held before the Secretary of State and the Secretary of Commerce, Washington, D.C., Thursday, September 10, 1914.* Miscellaneous Series No. 18. Washington: U.S. Government Printing Office, 1914.

U.S. Director of the Bureau of Engraving and Printing. *Annual Report of the Director of the Bureau of Engraving and Printing.* Washington: U.S. Government Printing Office, 1913-17.

U.S. Director of the Bureau of War Risk Insurance. *Report of the Director of the Bureau of War Risk Insurance.* 1916-18.

U.S. Federal Farm Loan Board. *First Annual Report of the Federal Farm Loan Board, Covering the Period from the Organization of the Board Up to November 30, 1917.* House Doc. No. 714. 65th Cong., 2d Sess., 1918.

U.S. Federal Reserve Board. *Annual Report . . . ,* 1914-17.

U.S. Federal Trade Commission. *Report on Cooperation in American Export Trade.* Part I: *Summary and Report.* Washington: U.S. Government Printing Office, 1916.

U.S. House of Representatives. *Government Ownership and Operation of Merchant Vessels in the Foreign Trade of the United States.* Report No. 1149. 63rd Cong., 2d Sess., September 8, 1914.

U.S. House of Representatives, Committee on Foreign Affairs. *Termination of the Treaty of 1832 Between the United States and Russia.* Revised ed. Washington: U.S. Government Printing Office, 1911.

U.S. House of Representatives, Committee on the Merchant Marine and Fisheries. *Creating a Shipping Board, A Naval Auxiliary, and a Merchant Marine.* Hearings on H.R. 10500. 64th Cong., 1st Sess., February 10-March 9, 1916.

_____. *Regulatory Features of Shipping Bill.* Hearings on H.R. 14337. 64th Cong., 1st Sess., April 13-22, 1916.

U.S. House of Representatives, Committee on Reform in the Civil Service. *Segregation of Clerks and Employees in the Civil Service.* 63rd Cong., 2d Sess., 1914.

U.S. Postmaster General, 1913-21 (Burleson). *Report of the Honorable The Postmaster General Upon the Establishment of a Uniform Low Rate of Postage and of Charges for Money Orders and Parcel Post between the American Countries.* (Pan American Financial Conference.)Washington: U.S. Government Printing Office, 1915.

U.S. President, 1909-13 (Taft). *Reorganization of the Customs Service; Message from the President of the United States, Transmitting Plan of Reorganization of the Customs Service and Detailed Estimate of Expenses of the Same.* House Doc. No. 1450. 62d Cong., 3rd Sess., March 4, 1913.

U.S. President, 1913-21 (Wilson). *Address of the President of the United*

*States at the Pan American Financial Conference (Pan American Build-
ing), Washington, D.C., May 24, 1915.* Washington: U.S. Government
Printing Office, 1915.

_____. *Message from the President of the United States Transmitting A
Report of the United States Section of the International High Commission
on the First General Meeting of the Commission, Held at Buenos Aires,
April 3-12, 1916.* House Doc. No. 1788. 64th Cong., 2d Sess., 1916.

U.S. Reserve Bank Organization Committee. *Location of Reserve Districts in
the United States; Letter from the Reserve Bank Organization Committee
Transmitting the Briefs and Arguments Presented to the Organization
Committee of the Federal Reserve Board Relative to the Location of
Reserve Districts in the United States.* Senate Doc. No. 485. 63rd Cong.,
2d Sess., 1914.

U.S. Secretary of Commerce, 1913-19 (Redfield). *Remarks of Hon. William
C. Redfield, Secretary of Commerce, at the Pan American Financial Conference, Washington, D.C., May 24, 1915.* Washington: U.S. Government Printing Office, 1915.

U.S. Secretary of the Treasury, 1913-18 (McAdoo). *An Address Delivered at
the Conference of the International High Commission at Buenos Aires,
Argentina, On April 4, 1916.* Senate Doc. No. 438. 64th Cong., 1st Sess.,
1916.

_____. *Address of the Secretary of the Treasury Delivered at the Opening
Session of the Pan American Financial Conference at the Pan American
Union, Monday, May 24, 1915, at 2:30 P.M.* Washington: U.S. Govern-
ment Printing Office, 1915.

_____. *The Administration and the Shipping Bill; Address Delivered by
Hon. William G. McAdoo, Secretary of the Treasury, Before the Cham-
ber of Commerce of the United States at the Annual Meeting Held in
Washington, D.C., on February 4, 1915.* Senate Doc. No. 950. 63rd
Cong., 3rd Sess., 1915.

_____. *Annual Report of the Secretary of the Treasury on the State of the
Finances for the Fiscal Year[s] Ended June 30, 1913-17.*

_____. *Concluding Address of Secretary McAdoo at the Closing Session of
the Pan American Financial Conference, Saturday Afternoon, May 29,
1915.* Washington: U.S. Government Printing Office, 1915.

_____. *Letter from the Secretary of the Treasury Transmitting Estimates
of Appropriations Required for the Service of the Fiscal Year[s] Ending
June 30, 1913-1918.*

_____. *Letter Written by Hon. William G. McAdoo, Secretary of the
Treasury, to Each Delegation from South and Central America in Rela-
tion to the Future Work of the Conference.* Washington: U.S. Government
Printing Office, 1915.

_____. *A Naval Auxiliary Merchant Marine; Speech of Hon. William G.
McAdoo, Secretary of the Treasury, Delivered Before the Chamber of
Commerce of Indianapolis, Ind., on October 13, 1915.* Senate Doc. No.
4. 64th Cong., 1st Sess., 1915.

_____. *Prosperity and the Future; Speech on the Progress and Prosperity of The United States Under the Present Democratic Administration, Delivered Before the Chamber of Commerce of Raleigh, N.C., on May 31, 1916.* Senate Doc. No. 457. 64th Cong., 1st Sess., 1916.

_____. *The Shipping Bill: Address Delivered by Hon. William G. McAdoo, Secretary of the Treasury, Before the Commercial Club, at Chicago, Ill., on January 9, 1915, Relative to the Merits of the Bill (S.6856) to Authorize the United States, Acting Through a Shipping Board, to Subscribe to the Capital Stock of a Corporation to be Organized Under the Laws of the United States or of a State Thereof or of the District of Columbia, to Purchase, Construct, Equip, Maintain, and Operate Merchant Vessels in the Foreign Trade of the United States and for Other Purposes.* Senate Doc. No. 713. 63rd Cong., 3rd Sess., 1915.

_____. *The Shipping Bill; Letters from the Secretary of the Treasury to Senator Duncan U. Fletcher, Acting Chairman of the Committee on Commerce, Transmitting Certain Proposed Amendments to the Shipping Bills, Together with Letters and Exhibits from the New Orleans Cotton Exchange; Also a Letter from Mr. C. E. Dobson, President of the Chamber of Commerce of Pensacola, Fla., in Regard to the Same Subject.* Senate. 63rd Cong., 3rd Sess., 1914.

_____. *Some International Aspects of Public Education: An Address Delivered at the Annual Convention of the National Education Association, Held in Madison Square Garden, New York City, on July 6, 1916.* Senate Doc. No. 498. 64th Cong., 1st Sess., 1916.

_____. *Subtreasuries and their Relation to the Federal Reserve Banks; Letter from the Secretary of the Treasury Transmitting Report of the Secretary of the Treasury Relative to the United States Subtreasuries and their Relation to the Federal Reserve Banks.* House Doc. No. 1777. 64th Cong., 2d. Sess., December 19, 1916.

_____, and McKellar, Kenneth D. *Remarks of Hon. Kenneth D. McKellar, of Tennessee, In the House of Representatives, Saturday, August 29, 1914, with Remarks of Secretary McAdoo.* Washington: U.S. Government Printing Office, 1914.

_____, and U.S. Secretary of Commerce, 1913-19 (Redfield). *Increased Ocean Transportation Rates.* Senate Doc. 673, Pts. 1-2. 63rd Cong., 3rd Sess., 1914-15.

U.S. Senate, Subcommittee of the Committee on Commerce. *Creating a Shipping Board, a Naval Auxiliary, and Merchant Marine.* Hearings on H.R. 15455. 64th Cong., 1st Sess., 1916.

_____, Subcommittee of the Committee on Privileges and Elections. *Campaign Contributions: Testimony Before a Subcommittee of the Committee on Privileges and Elections, United States Senate, Sixty-Second Congress, Second Session, Pursuant to S. Res. 79 and S. Res. 386.* Washington: U.S. Government Printing Office, 1912.

U.S. Treasury Department. *Combined Statement[s] of the Receipts and Disbursements, Balances, etc., of the United States During the Fiscal Year[s] Ended June 30, 1913-18.* Washington: U.S. Government Printing Office, 1913-19.

288 WILLIAM GIBBS McADOO

———. *Daily Statement of the U.S. Treasury*, 1913-17.

———. *Information Respecting United States Bonds, Paper Currency and Coin, Production of Precious Metals, Etc.* Revised July 1, 1915. Washington: U.S. Government Printing Office, 1915.

———. *Presidential Officers In and Under the Treasury Department (Except Revenue-Cutter Service and Public Health Service).* 1914 edition. Washington: U.S. Government Printing Office, 1914.

———. *Recommendations Made by the Conference of Collectors of Customs, Held at New York, November 3-10, 1913, and Action of the Treasury Department Thereon.* Washington: U.S. Government Printing Office, 1914.

OTHER SOURCES

Actas, Informes, Resoluciones, y Documentación General de la Alta Comisión Internacional de Legislación Uniforme, Reunida en Buenos Aires del 3 al 12 de Abril de 1916, Bajo la Presidencia del Exmo. Señor Ministro de Hacienda de la República Argentina, Doctor Don Francisco J. Oliver. Buenos Aires: 1916.

Broesamle, John J. "William Gibbs McAdoo: Businessman in Politics, 1863-1917." Unpublished Ph.D. dissertation, Columbia University, 1970.

———. "William Gibbs McAdoo: The Making of a Progressive, 1863-1912." Unpublished Master's essay, Columbia University, 1964.

Chamber of Commerce of the United States of America. *Referendum Number Nine: The Up-Building of the Merchant Marine.* July 9, 1915.

Interviews and correspondence with members of the McAdoo family.

McAdoo, William G. "Decent Treatment of the Public by Corporations and Regulation of Monopolies." Speech delivered to the Chamber of Commerce, Boston, Mass., January 20, 1911. Columbia University Library.

———. "The Relations Between Public Service Corporations and the Public." Undated speech read before the Alexander Hamilton Institute, New York City. New York Public Library.

———. "The Subway Problem." Address delivered at Plymouth Church, Brooklyn, January 19, 1911. New York Public Library.

National Democratic Platform. 1912.

Index

294

300

Post Office, Office of the Auditor for, 160

Preparedness, 155-156, 228-229

Progressive Party, 70, 72

Progressivism, 25, 30, 85, 94-95, 107, 121-123, 143, 145, 153, 156, 165. *See also* Conservatism

Public be Pleased policy, 27-30, 48, 239n.4

Public Health Service, 143

Public Service Commission (New Jersey, New York), 21, 28, 37-40

Public Service Corporation, 22-24

Pujo Committee, 149

Pujo "Money Trust" investigation, 96

Quick, Herbert, 187

"Radicals," 108, 110, 112, 122, 125, 171

Railroad Club, 34

Rainey, Henry, 144

Rapid Transit Commissioners, Board of, 22

Recorder of Deeds, office of, 160

Redfield, William C.: appointed Secretary of Commerce, 79; on business depression (1913), 188; and foreign markets, 202-203; and McAdoo, 204, 225; and shipping, 212, 225-226, 228, 230-231

Reed, James A., 122

Republican Party, 7, 9, 16; in 1912 campaign, 49, 55, 70, 72; in Congress, 110, 185, 227-228, 233; and governmental practice, 146-147

Reserve Bank Organization Committee, 118-120, 128, 132

Revenue-Cutter Service, 143

Reynolds, George M., 101, 107-108, 208

Richmond and Danville Railroad, 8

Riggs case, 148-153

Riggs National Bank, 149-153; president of, 149-150

Roosevelt, Franklin D., 71, 86, 88-90, 244n.26, 245n.35

Roosevelt, Theodore: and opening of uptown tunnels, 24; accession to the Presidency, 25; cautions McAdoo regarding Russo-Japanese War, 36; early

relationship with McAdoo, 43; and New Nationalism, 43-44; in 1912 campaign, 49, 55, 65-67, 69, 72, 74; and the race issue, 158-159

Roper, Daniel, 144-145

Rosenthal, Benjamin, 225

Rowe, Leo S., 205, 208, 210

Russia: and treaty of 1832 with U.S., 35

Ryan, Thomas Fortune: and New York public transit, 22-23, 27, 37, 40; and 1912 campaign, 47, 50, 53, 59; and Williams, 80, 251n.29

Saint Louis: opposes early opening of Federal Reserve system, 125

Saulsbury, Willard, 64, 68

Seaboard Air Line, 80, 149

Seabury, Samuel, 91, 245n.35

Seamen's Act, 216-217, 223

Segregation: as an issue in government, 158-165, 252n.47, 253n.53, n.61

Shipping (Ch. XI): pressure mounts for legislation, 155; impact of World War I on, 172, 177-178, 195-196, 213-214, 227-228; and market for Southern cotton, 174; legislation, and U.S. economic expansion, 204-205; as issue at inter-American conferences, 208-211; condition of U.S. merchant marine, 213; rates jump, 213-214, 224. *See also* McAdoo, William Gibbs; Shipping Act; Shipping Board; Ship Purchase bill

Shipping Act: and preparedness, 228-229, 231-233; mounting support for legislation, 229; McAdoo's outline for, 231-233; and issue of socialism versus private enterprise, 231-234, 236; final provisions, 233-234; meaning assessed, 235-236

Shipping Board: origins, 218, 223, 226-227, 230-234; personnel, 91, 234-235

"Shipping Trust," 260n.34

Ship Purchase bill: and issues of socialism, private enterprise, efficiency, 209, 218-221, 223-224, 226-227; origins,

302

centralizer, 114, 165-166,
235-236; reaction to McAdoo's
promotionalism, 114, 121;
appoints Federal Reserve
Board, 120-124, 248n.6, n.8;
and Federal Reserve system,
128; and foreign markets,
129, 200-201, 235-236; and
foreign branching, 129-130;
and redistricting, 133, 250n.44;
and Governorship of Federal
Reserve Board, 134-137; and
marriage of daughter to
McAdoo, 139-140, 250n.3;
relationship with McAdoo,
140-142, 235, 250n.3;
management of Cabinet,
140-142; appoints
McReynolds, Brandeis to
Supreme Court, 142; and
Tariff Commission, 144;
and Vanderlip, 148; and
Riggs case, 152; and taxation
and revenue, 154, 156-157;
and the race issue, 158-165,
252n.47; and class,
agricultural legislation,
168-169; opposes Henry
scheme, 172-173; and
Federal Farm Loan Act, 186;
turns right, 189; in crisis of

1914, 191-192; and Pan
American Financial
Conference, 205-206; and
financing of Latin American
governments, 207; and
shipping crisis, 214-216, 228,
259n.19; and Ship Purchase
bill, 219, 221, 226-228 (*See
also* Ship Purchase bill); and
Shipping Act, 230-231,
233-235; vetoes grade crossing
bill, 241n.20; Latin American
policy, 258n.42. *See also*
New Freedom
Woodward, W. E., vii, 32-33
Woodward, William, 192, 256n.8
Woolley, Robert, 79-80, 160, 164
World War I (Ch. X): impact on
Federal Reserve system, 125,
137; and U.S. trade, 129; and
federal revenue, 153-154;
effect on U.S. agriculture, 172;
and credit, 182-183; and
Federal Farm Loan system,
187; impact on U.S. generally,
189-200. *See also* Latin
America; McAdoo, William
Gibbs; Shipping; South

Zinc Trust, 122